THE
LITERARY
IMAGINATION

THE
LITERARY
IMAGINATION

□ PSYCHOANALYSIS *and*
the GENIUS *of the* WRITER

EDITED WITH AN INTRODUCTION BY

Hendrik M. Ruitenbeek

CHICAGO

Quadrangle Books / *1965* □

To Richard Huett

ACKNOWLEDGMENTS

THANKS are due the following journals and publishers for permission to reprint copyrighted material:

American Imago, for "Heinrich von Kleist—Prussian Junker and Creative Genius" by Fritz Wittels; "André Gide: Rebel and Conformist" by John D. Mitchell; "Walt Whitman: Lover and Comrade" by Paul Lauter; and "Marcel Proust" by Caroline Wijsenbeek.

American Journal of Psychology, for "Psychoanalysis of the Character and Genius of Emily Brontë" by Lucile Dooley; and "A Psychoanalytical Study of Edgar Allan Poe" by Lorine Pruette.

Basic Books, for "Dostoevsky and Parricide" by Sigmund Freud (from *The Collected Papers of Sigmund Freud*).

Hermathena, for "Romain Rolland: The Psychological Basis of Political Belief" by John Cruickshank.

International Journal of Psycho-Analysis, for "Charlotte Brontë: A Study of a Masochistic Character" by Kate Friedlander; "August Strindberg: A Study of the Relationship Between His Creativity and Schizophrenia" by Theodore Lidz; and "Honoré de Balzac—A Disturbed Boy Who Did Not Get Treatment" by E. C. M. Frijling-Schreuder.

International Universities Press, for "The Character of Jean Jacques Rousseau" by Charles Kligerman (from the *Yearbook of Psychoanalysis*, *1952*); "Notes on the Environment of a Genius" by K. R. Eissler (from *Psychoanalytic Study of the Child*); and "Psychoanalytic Comments About the Personality of Goethe" by Edward Hitschmann (from *Great Men: Psychoanalytic Studies*).

Journal of Abnormal and Social Psychology, for "Hölderlin: Greatest of 'Schizophrenics' " by F. L. Wells.

Partisan Review, for "Kafka: Father and Son" by Max Brod.

Southwestern Review, for "Thomas Wolfe: Of Time and Neurosis" by W. M. Frohock.

FOREWORD

The application of psychoanalysis to the study of literary genius has since long been recognized as a most important tool for the interpretation of the lives of great literary writers. Unfortunately there have not been too many psychoanalysts in the last decades who were interested and intrigued enough to write various interpretations of literary lives. Kurt Eissler is one of the notable exceptions and he is represented here with an essay on Goethe entitled "Notes on the Environment of a Genius." Edward Hitschmann is another exception. From the early beginnings of psychoanalysis at the Wednesday evening meetings with Freud in Vienna, he studied the lives of literary people. His contribution is also a study on Goethe. Fritz Wittels was another member of the Wednesday evening group and belonged to Freud's inner circle. His analysis on the bisexuality of Heinrich von Kleist is a masterpiece of psychoanalytic interpretation. The sisters Brontë are the subject of two separate studies, each written by a distinguished female psychoanalyst: Lucile Dooley, who wrote the essay on Emily Brontë, and Kate Friedlander, who wrote the article on Charlotte Brontë. Kafka's relationship to his father has long been a topic for psychoanalytic speculation and interpretation. Max Brod, close friend and associate of Franz Kafka, is represented here with an essay on the father and son. The reader, however, should not fail to read Erich Fromm's interpretation of this relationship in his book *The Forgotten Language*. Marcel Proust and André Gide are no doubt the most important French writers of this century. Caroline Wijsenbeek has written a most insightful and perceptive essay on Proust, while John Mitchell makes interesting observations on the rebellious and conformist sides of Gide's character structure.

That Hölderlin was one of the greatest German poets cannot any more be disputed. Against the background it is extremely significant to read Wells on Hölderlin's schizophrenia. Undoubtedly Marie Bonaparte wrote the definitive psychoanalytic study of Edgar Allan Poe, but this does not diminish what others have said and written about him. Lorine Pruette's essay certainly is a most valuable contribution to the study of the complex character structure of Poe. Walt Whitman's homosexual inclinations have been the subject of studies by both psychoanalytic and literary interpreters. The study by Paul Lauter is one of the most recent and insightful. Thomas Wolfe still remains an enigma in American literature, and the definitive psychoanalytic study on him still has to be written. W. M. Frohock's contribution is a most serious attempt to fill this gap. There certainly could not be a greater difference between the political philosopher of the French revolution, Jean Jacques Rousseau, and the distinguished philosopher and novelist Romain Rolland. Charles Kligerman has contributed an essay on the character structure of Rousseau, while John Cruickshank links Rolland's political beliefs to his psychological structure.

The link between creativity and schizophrenia has always been a most intriguing one and Theodore Lidz, in his paper on Strindberg, presents some exciting new material. The paper on Honoré de Balzac by Frijling-Schreuder is speculative in that we really do not know what would have happened had the young Balzac been treated. But the study gives us some new understanding of Balzac's character. Arthur Jacobson's essay on the relationship between literary genius and manic-depressive insanity was written a long time ago, but it seems still very relevant today. Last but not least there is the classic paper by Sigmund Freud on Dostoevsky and parricide.

CONTENTS

THE
LITERARY
IMAGINATION

▣ INTRODUCTION:

NEUROSIS AND

LITERARY GENIUS

Hendrik M. Ruitenbeek

Are genius, particularly literary genius, and neurosis connected? This question was asked long before the development of psychoanalysis, although, as might be expected, the vocabulary was rather different. The problem was stated quite often during the last third of the nineteenth century and the early years of the twentieth. Max Nordau, for example, wrote about genius as a form of degeneracy. Authors such as André Gide raised the question, too. Gide compared Hugo and Rousseau and wondered whether emotional disturbance was not an essential ingredient in the makeup of many an artist: ". . . the individual who is abnormal refuses to submit to laws already established." The implication is that, by such refusal, the abnormal individual, provided that he be endowed with expressive talent, can both see the flaws in the world and make others sufficiently aware of them to want to change either the flaws or their ways of looking at and apprehending the world.

Divine frenzy was once supposed to possess the poet, and

15

a contemporary poet such as Robert Graves can still write about the White Goddess whose spirit occupies the poet's mind and guides his hand when he is doing his best work. Other poets of our day even practice automatic writing, although they often will say that they let their pencils wander over the page (or their fingers over the typewriter keys) in order to allow their "unconscious" or "subconscious" to take over and so give them greater access to the sources of inspiration.

The use of such terms as "unconscious" indicates how deeply the influence of psychoanalysis has penetrated at least American intellectual circles. The psychotherapist, conversely, is interested in artistic creativity, and not only because he has patients involved in such work. As I have said elsewhere, psychotherapy is itself an art. The therapist today might discuss inspiration in terms of narcissistic acknowledgment of material which has long been in preparation in the poet's unconscious. For Freud and his circle were interested in the problems of literary creativity and their work has done much to elucidate it.

Freud gave modern psychotherapy some of its basic tools: the technique of free association, the interpretation of dreams, and the analysis of everyday conduct. Freud studied such writers as Goethe as well as such artists as Michelangelo and Leonardo, but he acknowledged that Goethe was relatively impenetrable: although Goethe did use his own experience as literary material and did, of course, reveal himself in the process, he told only what, and as much as, he chose to—or so he thought.[1]

Some of Freud's early colleagues were interested in the lives and work of important literary figures and a number of the famous Wednesday evenings at his apartment were spent listening to papers on poets and novelists.[2] Among the contributors to these discussions of literary artists, Freud preferred Edward Hitschmann's work to that of Wilhelm Stekel or Isidor Sadger. On the whole, Freud was not interested in medical inquiries into the morbid conditions that had afflicted certain writers. Such concern with physical pathology, Freud thought, did not illuminate the subject's personality or his work. Useful study, he thought, would concentrate on the manner in which the minds of literary persons had developed, because knowing about that might illuminate the motives which had evoked their work. It would be necessary, too, for the psychoanalytic biographer to deal with such matters as the onset of artistic creativity, the character of a man's technique, and the manner in which he gained access to his own impulses toward literary creation. The relationship between artistic productivity and sexual frustration or abstinence might warrant exploration. The Wednesday group did carry on such inquiry with respect to the German romantic poet, Jean-Paul Richter.[3] Neurotic symptoms, hallucinations, phobias, dreams— all the kinds of material which the patient brings to analytic treatment—are of special interest when the life of a literary artist is being studied. Such material can be gathered directly today, when many artists come to therapy, but the great dead are not so easily accessible. Yet even carefully revised letters and autobiographical material, however misleading they may be in point of objective fact, incorporate much that is revealing to the psychoanalyst. As Marie Bonaparte wrote: "Works of art and literature profoundly reveal their creators' psychology and, as Freud has shown, their construction resembles that of our dreams. The same mechanisms which, in dreams and nightmares, govern the manner in which our strongest, though most carefully concealed desires are elaborated, desires which often are the most repugnant to consciousness, also govern the elaboration of the work of art."

It is possible, therefore, to treat the content of a work of fiction or the imagery which pervades a body of poetry as akin to the dreams and associations which the therapist encounters in his dealings with patients. Of course, psycho-analysts must proceed with cautious respect for the evidence when they turn their professional equipment on a literary work, but wise use of that equipment may yield helpful insights, especially into two categories of problems: the source of creative imagination and the association of literary genius with true psychopathy.

We cannot say absolutely where the literary genius gets either his creative imagination or his power to use it in ways that delight others. We have learned that psychological proc-esses are very similar whether the person is genius or dolt, suffering and mad, or placidly normal. We have all been chil-dren, we all make revealing errors, we all dream, and our dreams employ the same mechanisms of condensation, elabora-tion, dramatization. In our dreams we tend to fulfill our wishes, to achieve some safe gratification of our frustrated and for-bidden desires, sometimes to deal with actual reality-problems. Even scientific questions have been resolved in dreams, after the scientist has been preoccupied with those questions for a long time. Writers have composed poems in dreams and when, like Samuel Taylor Coleridge, they have been wakened, they sometimes have not been able to recapture the mood, the dream, or the poem.

In his study, *Great Men*, Hitschmann stresses the immense importance of the father in the lives of literary geniuses:

I found among my subjects that the father was always the most important person who was decisive for the destiny of the son—not only the main influence but indeed the origin of all biography, of all life, and of all inspiration He is the leader, the authority. It seems as if these creative artists were productive through indenti-fication with the father, who, as the breadwinner, represented achievement through work. We know that the relationship with the father, however, is always ambivalent. The wish to function like the father coexists with the hatred that stems from the oedipal situation, the breaking away from the father, or an unconscious search for a better father, as exemplified in the lives of Eckermann and Boswell. Freud considered the death of the father the most important experience in the life of a man.

If the influence of a presumably present father is thus significant, the psychological effect of the father's absence or inadequacy must be taken into account, too. And no therapist working in contemporary America can ignore the impact on literary genius of a man's relation with the first woman in his life, his mother.

Another way in which we seem to see a link between genius and emotional disturbance is the fear of losing the self. In severe neurosis and in some psychoses, the patient is terrified by threat of his inability to maintain his ties to the real world. The endangered ego may rise to the level where it attempts to recreate aspects of the objective world, if only in fantasies, and so counterbalance the loosening of its own bonds to reality. The creative artist, however, as Ernst Kris describes in his brilliant work, *Psychoanalytic Explorations in Art*, transforms neurotic fear of loss of the self into ability to create other selves; for the artist, loss of hold on everyday existence can result in the creation of new existences, worlds, and people which can be shared with others and which have the unique reality of the work of art.

As Gide's Victor Hugo and our idea of Shakespeare show us the literary genius in "perfect spiritual poise," writers like Kafka and Rimbaud serve as instances of geniuses who were never able to maintain such poise, to place a true value on themselves or their work. Kafka might be taken as almost a scientific "model" of modern man, alone in, and alienated from, the world in which he lives. Kafka sometimes went so far as to find his insomnia responsible for his writing. "Were it not for these terror-ridden sleepless nights," he declared, "I certainly would not have written. By writing, my dark isolation became known to me." And again, as he said to a friend, writing was for him "a form of exorcism."

Unlike Kafka, whose existence moved in external quiet toward his death, Rimbaud led his life in tumult. His poems have inspired generations of poets, and have changed their ideals of poetic imagery and their relationship to language itself. Rimbaud's life has awakened much psychological interest. Typical of this is the work of G. E. Partridge, who says:

> The career of Rimbaud is impressive. Could we but understand him well, we should have much insight into types of mind which we call psychopathic. We might call him a kind of glorified psychopath. Understood, even in part, softened a little by time and distance, he seems lovable. In him there is all the pathos of the psychopath's will-o'-the-wisp life. *Genius* though he was, he never discovered what he really wished to do or why he toiled so mightily to produce apparently so little. The fact that that little is of the quality of high genius is, curiously, almost incidental to the drama of generic human motives we see in the epic, through the symbolism. Rimbaud himself regarded it as somewhat so, and scorned his work as idle play.[4]

If we return to the question raised at the opening of this introduction, we can say that literary genius and the neurotic have this in common: both often are directed by primary-process thinking. The neurotic converts that into suffering; the literary genius possesses the talent which lets him elaborate those processes and his suffering into works of art which others can share. Psychoanalysis can tell us little, if anything, about the source of talent. Psychoanalytic exploration of the lives and works of artists can give a new depth to our appreciation of literature. More significant, perhaps, study of creative geniuses can increase our understanding of creativity in general. It should not be forgotten that, though talent is the good fortune of but a few, creative living is a potentiality for all human beings. Notable artists—poets, philosophers, mystics, sculptors—have described their creative moments in almost identical terms. As Abraham Maslow summarizes these moments of "peak experience" in highly gifted and mature people, he says the person ". . . becomes more whole and unified, more unique . . . alive and spontaneous, more perfectly expressive and uninhibited . . . more effortless and powerful, more daring and courageous . . . more ego-transcending and self-forgetful." [5]

Again, to be gifted is reserved for a few, but we may, perhaps, hope that careful study of those few will help us foster what creativity people may have and rescue others who have some talent, although not the highest, from entangling themselves in the web of neurotic self-destructiveness.

NOTES

1. In 1963, Kurt Eissler published a two-volume study of Goethe which is probably the definitive psychoanalytic discussion of the poet.

2. These meetings began in 1902. The custom of gathering on Wednesday was retained when the intimate circle of pioneers was expanded into the Vienna Psychoanalytic Society. For an interesting record of these early meetings at Freud's, see Herman Nunberg and Ernst Federn, eds., *Minutes of the Vienna Psychoanalytical Society* (New York: International Universities Press, 1962), Vol. I, and Lou Andreas-Salome, *In der Schule bei Freud* (Zurich: Niehans, 1958).

3. Nunberg and Federn, I, 166-75.

4. G. E. Partridge, "Psychopathological Study of Jean-Nicolas-Arthur Rimbaud," *Psychoanalytic Review*, XVII (1930), 421.

5. Abraham Maslow, "Cognition of Being in the Peak Experience," *Journal of Genetic Psychology*, LXXXXIV (1959), 34-66.

HEINRICH VON KLEIST—
PRUSSIAN JUNKER
AND CREATIVE GENIUS

Fritz Wittels

In studying the life and work of Heinrich von Kleist we will not only come to an insight into this great and unlucky man as an individual but, maybe, also to a psychological understanding of Prussian education and its results in the period after Frederick the Great, whose tradition survived for almost two centuries.

Heinrich von Kleist was born and raised on the arid soil of Brandenburg, Prussia's motherland. Kleist was one of the greatest poets and playwrights in the German language. Outside of Germany he is little known, translations cannot re-create the particular flavor of his work. In his own country he was more and more appreciated after his death (1811), his fame reaching a peak during the nationalistic period in Germany after 1870. No other creative genius was deeper rooted in the soil of Prussia, no one better qualified to convey the spirit of his country with its discipline, sense of duty, extremism in obedience, and rebellion.

All his lifetime he was staggering from one failure to the other. He did not see even a single one of his plays performed on the stage. He never could free himself from the doom of self-destruction. He was a clear case of agitated depression, definitely presenting a psychosis in periods of exacerbation. He died, thirty-four years old, a suicide. (His literary critics feel that Heinrich von Kleist would have become Germany's greatest playwright could he have ended a normal span of life. It is, however, futile to make such statements, for the same explosive forces that made him great also destroyed him before his time.)

Von Kleist was a Junker, but his relatives felt that he disgraced them. A Von Kleist should definitely not have been a playwright but an officer sitting on horseback, and commanding soldiers, rigorously. The name of the Von Kleist family can be traced back to medieval times (1175, according to Karl Federn). They gave officers and generals to the Electors of Brandenburg and later to the rulers of Prussia, up to the end of World War II. A general and others of the clan of lower rank were fighting for the Nazis. The famous Field Marshal General Heinrich Ferdinand Emil Kleist, Count of Nollendorf (1762-1823), helped in the liberation of Germany from Napoleonic subjugation.

Some members of the family became prominent in science in the eighteenth century. One of the Kleists discovered the Leyden jar, the device for storing static electricity. Occupation with science, though inferior to military service, was not considered disgraceful. After all, was not war a science? Any scientific research might come in handy in war! It was different with poetry, which was definitely held in contempt. Even before Heinrich, another Von Kleist indulged in poetry. His name was Ewald Christian (1715-1759), but he at least remained a military officer while Heinrich resigned from the army after a few years of service. Ewald Christian was killed a hero in the battle of Kunersdorf on August 12, 1759. Leading his battalion, he attacked a Russian battery. When his right arm was hit, he changed the sword to his left hand and went on until three cannon shells smashed his right leg. He lay unconscious on the battlefield all night, was sacked by the Cossacks, and only on the following day was he transported to Frankfurt an der Oder. There he died and was buried with military honors by the Russian garrison. In the eyes of the family, Ewald Christian was an eccentric who, because of his writing poetry, was skipped several times in military advancement.

Heinrich von Kleist was born in 1777 in Frankfurt an der Oder, a joyless small town in Brandenburg, not to be mistaken for Goethe's native town, Frankfurt am Main, the large city with Western interests. Frankfurt an der Oder was always a center of the Von Kleists. Heinrich's father, a retired major, died when the boy was twelve years old. Heinrich, being the eldest son, had to become a soldier, as a matter of course. He had to join the Potsdam regiment of the guards before he was quite fifteen. There he got his training, but no further schooling. In his earlier years he had been tutored privately and was described as an obedient average student. At sixteen, he participated in the Rhine Campaign of 1793. His letters of that time, written in poor, ungrammatical language, reveal him as a serious boy, full of respect for his superiors, and well-behaved. In the same year—and five years after his father's death—his mother died. He mourned her in unfree, hackneyed phrases.[1] Nothing yet indicated the inspired genius of later years. In 1795, the regiment came home from a rather inglorious campaign, in 1797 Kleist received his commission, and two years later he resigned. We know little of the deeper motivation for this step, a step so unusual for a Von Kleist. From his dry, schoolmasterly, pedantic letters to his fiancée, Wilhelmine von Zenge, we may be sure of one fact: Kleist had not found himself yet.

At the time of his resignation, and long afterward, he remained a typical representative of the Junker spirit—a dry duty-and-service-machine—with the explosive feeling that he could not continue in service.

Why did he resign? We have a letter written to an older friend in which Kleist tried to explain his decision. The letter is of enormous length and boring, as are all of his utterances of those days. In the army—he wrote to his friend—one cannot be both an officer and a human being. That was why he had to quit. As good as this sounds we cannot but consider his motivation a rationalization of deeper instinctive forces. At the time of his resignation, Kleist lived in Berlin and Potsdam and his service, except for a six-week period of maneuvers, was far from strenuous. He was given to studies and to music and he had excellent friends among the officers of the garrison. We mention here two of them, since they will appear further in this short biography: Ernst von Pfuel, who much later, in 1848, became Prussian secretary of war, and Otto von Ruehle, later chief of the general staff.

In order to perceive Kleist's deeper motives, we have to look at the psychology of the Prussian army as organized by the Great Elector in the seventeenth century, filled with compulsive spirit by King Frederick William I, proven a formidable instrument of war by Frederick the Great, and declining after the latter's death (1786). It was in that phase of rapid decline that Kleist entered this "organization of men," spending eight of his formative years in it before he quit.

In other studies, I tried to show the part that obsession, paranoia, and latent homosexuality played in the origin of the Prussian army, with its brittle discipline, its sense of duty and specific honor.

I discussed military, religious, and students' organizations, their bloom and their decay, and also smaller groups of men which not only became hotbeds of overt homosexuality but in addition served a double purpose in cases of latent homosexuality. Double, because the organization prevented the outbreak of the perversion by sublimating the dangerous, undesirable instinct and, on the other hand, turned libido away from woman to its own overheated and therefore sexualized aims. In this way, the community fostered subliminal homosexuality which broke through whenever the original aims weakened.

Quoting myself: "As long as the covenant remains strong in its aims and practices it succeeds in its sublimation. If it is weakened as a result of a clash with inimical social forces, the homosexual drive breaks through—all the more strongly since the specific energy of the drive is continuously fed to grow in the group. In such phases of transition, in the midst of the danger of a breakthrough, the practice of the covenant is usually intensified, which makes it appear more and more morbid until in the end overt homosexuality comes to the fore just the same. History is full of examples of this kind, particularly medieval history. Religious orders of monks and knights before, during, and after the Crusades show these psychological mechanisms, frequently extended over centuries."

Not only history offers examples of men's societies with their double aim; everyday life also is full of such clubs, enthusiastic flag bearers, smaller and larger groups of men which, as a rule, serve well to keep the balance between the components of bisexuality. We may express this in biblical words: Render unto woman the things which are woman's and unto man the things that are man's.

The following will prove that Kleist all through his short life had to run away from his homosexual tendencies; most of the time latent, but occasionally breaking through as overt perversion, he was haunted by them as by the Eumenides. And we reach the conclusion that Kleist resigned from the army because its touch of latent and overt homosexuality was too

27

much for him. We know that Kleist suffered from a slight
anomaly of his penis, most likely a phimosis, the somatic contribution to his compulsive masturbation. He complained about
it in a letter to his friend L. von Brocke, ten years his senior.
That letter does not exist, but we have Von Brocke's reply,
containing words of consolation.[2] Much was written about
Kleist's trip to Würzburg, because he himself wrapped it in
mystery, which is natural enough, and on the other hand he
referred to it in romantic exaggerations quite out of proportion. This gave rise to all kinds of guesswork.

Between Kleist's resignation from the army and that trip to
Würzburg lay one and a half years of studies at the second-
rate university of his home town. He spent there three semes-
ters studying mathematics, philosophy, and physics, according
to the second tradition of his family. Although he was sitting
up with his textbooks every night, he got nowhere and quit
his studies, too. In those days he met Wilhelmine von Zenge.
(Mind you, there was hardly anybody in his company without
a "von.") Wilhelmine was the daughter of a Prussian colonel.
Kleist was soon more or less officially engaged to her. A great
number of Kleist's letters to her were later destroyed by
Wilhelmine and her family. All of the surviving correspondence is strangely dry and boring. The fiery poet of later
years assumes the part of a *petit bourgeois* schoolmaster in his
letters to Wilhelmine.

In 1780, Kleist left Frankfurt an der Oder with its provincial
university. He moved to Berlin, hoping to get a position in
civil service. He was probably pressed by his fiancée's family,
who would not permit a marriage to a man without a regular
income. We know that Kleist's trip to Berlin had another, and
secret, aim: the surgical operation, which was soon performed
in Würzburg. He spoke vaguely of it in a letter to his sister
Ulrike. He hoped, as he put it in that letter, to save by his
journey "happiness, honor, and, maybe, the life of a man."

After the death of his mother, Ulrike von Kleist, three years his senior, was perhaps the only feminine creature whom Heinrich really loved—his mother substitute. Ulrike was a masculine woman who always had to help when her brother fell into a desperate plight, which happened often enough. In his letter he queried: "Why are you not a man?—My God, how deeply I have always wished for that. . . . If you were a man—because a woman can never be my confidante—I would not have to look for a friend so far away! Do not try to find out the aim of my journey; even if you could, do not do it. Think that I can reach my aim only by concealing it from all men. At least for the time being, because some day it will be my pride and my joy to tell it. . . ."

One week after his arrival in Würzburg he wrote to his fiancée that he had been promised certain relief. Of what disease? That he could not say yet. One month later he told Wilhelmine that he was cured now and in a position to marry her. It was a jubilant letter, written on his twenty-third birthday, and it ended with the words: "Let your next goal be to be trained for a mother. My goal is to become a good citizen. Our further goal—which both of us will try to reach and which we can make sure of—is the fulfillment of love. Good night, Wilhelmine, my fiancée, soon my bride, soon mother of my children."

He returned to Berlin, but his jubilant spirit did not prevail. He got the coveted job, but he could not keep it. A few months later he ran away from civil service just as he had from the army. This time he traveled to Paris with his sister. Ulrike disguised herself as a man and in this disguise she lived in Paris for months. Her brother, in contrast, looked amazingly girlish. We have a miniature of Kleist by Krueger which displays these feminine features.

Kleist's always flattering biographers state that this good and true Prussian from the Mark Brandenburg could, as a matter of course, not like the "Babylon on the Seine." We have to add here: the heterosexual Babylon. From Paris, Kleist moved to Switzerland where he decided to become a farmer. He wrote to his fiancée, who patiently waited for him in Frankfurt, to join him in Switzerland as a farmer's wife. When she declined, he abruptly ended that joyless relation (1802). Telling her of his new burning ambition to become a famous writer, he closed his letter with the words: "Dear girl, do not write me any more. I have no other wish than to die soon. H.K."

We realize the contradiction here: burning ambition and death wish. Yet both desires existed in this tortured soul simultaneously. To be sure, marriage was impossible to him.

Kleist's life was a regular museum of defense mechanisms against homosexuality. All of his reaction formations either were destined to break down or did not succeed sufficiently to redeem him for any length of time. His resignation from the army shows the runaway complex, which psychoanalysts frequently observe in their patients.[3]

Kleist ran away not only from the army, but also from his scientific studies, from civil service, from his fiancée, from Germany, from Paris, from Switzerland, from anyone and everywhere. With this trend was coupled an obsessional desire to withdraw, to be left alone: a hermit complex. The hermit is the logical sequence of the quitter. Withdrawal from the social danger of overt homosexuality is followed by the flight into solitude. We know many examples of this form of narcissism in psychiatric practice as well as in universal history. This defense mechanism cannot last, because the same forces that drive a man into solitude drive him out of it after a relatively short time. Temptation follows the hermit into the desert.

Kleist met a number of literary men in Switzerland, who accepted him as their equal. Then and there, his burning ambition to be a great writer was born. Later he was not only to be their equal, but to develop outstanding genius. This gift of the gods could have saved him had he been able to keep his sublimation alive. He could not—for reasons we shall discuss later.

We wish to repeat here what Freud often emphasized in his writings (on Leonardo da Vinci, Dostoevsky, etc.): Psychoanalysis is not in a position to solve the mystery of artistic creativeness. We can tell why a certain author must choose his particular material and work it out his particular way. Dostoevsky had to describe parricide and glorify a certain type of woman. In the case of Leonardo it was the "Leonardesque" smile and bisexual motifs. In the case of the Prussian militarist, Heinrich von Kleist, it was *Schrecklichkeit* and supermasculinity. Psychoanalysis cannot tell, however, what makes an author great and creative. In our treatises on creators we do not even try to tackle this problem.

As a rule, writers show their talent early. We do not know why it unfolded so late in Kleist's life, and we refrain from guessing. Sudden eruption of artistic qualities in people who did not betray them before, although it is the exception, could be observed in some of our great authors, e.g. in Samuel Clemens (Mark Twain). In the case of Kleist, recognition by a group of congenial men became the catalytic agent.

We have a number of Kleist's letters to and about friends in which he displayed enthusiasm and warmth that impress the reader nowadays as homosexual. However, we are told that the style of letter writing in his era was different from ours and that we have no right to suspect phrases like the following as being of homosexual nature:

(January, 1801) "Sometimes, at night, when I fell asleep at his breast, he held me without falling asleep himself." Or, in a letter to Henry Lohse (December, 1801): "And you think that I do not love you? Oh, how will you ever be able to convince any man that I do not love you? . . . And yet you could desert me? So soon? So easily? . . . It is so hard for me

31

to say the last word—we were so good, oh so good, to each other in Paris—are you not too unspeakably sad? I say, do you not wish to put your arms around me once more? Do not think at all, ask your first impulse and obey it—and should it be really the last word—my God, then I say good-bye to you and to all joys! Goodbye, goodbye. Heinrich Kleist."

All this is supposed to be just eighteenth century emotional style. What a difference, however, between this outburst and the hackneyed decrees which the same man sent to his fiancée at about the same time.

At least one letter, discovered only some time ago, with all allowances deducted, cannot be considered other than a homosexual love letter. It is addressed to Ernst von Pfuel: . . . "How did we fall into each other's arms a year ago in Dresden? . . . The fault is all mine. I have involved you, oh I cannot explain it to you the way I feel it. . . . We will never again embrace each other that way. . . . You restored the age of the Greek in my heart, I could have slept with you, my dear boy; my soul embraced you! Often have I watched your lovely body with truly *girlish* feelings when you took a swim before my eyes in the lake at Thun. It could really serve as a model to an artist. . . . Your small, curly-haired head over a massive neck, two broad shoulders, an athletic body, in its totality a flawless picture of strength as though you were formed in the image of the most beautiful young bull who ever had to bleed for Zeus. Lycurgus' entire legislation and his concept of the youth's love has become clear to me by the emotions you woke in me. Come to me! Go with me to Anspach and let us enjoy our sweet friendship. . . . I will never marry, be you my wife, my children and grandchildren! . . . I would like to say more to you, but it is not fit for a letter. . . . Heinrich von Kleist, Berlin, January 7, 1805."

This letter calls to mind Oscar Wilde's letters to his boy friend. The same exalted and "knowing" style. It is not necessarily the letter of a man indulging in the sexual practice of homosexuality, but undoubtedly of a homosexual who fought his own feminine component most of his life. Kleist lived in a continuously repeated homosexual panic.

In contradistinction to his femininity, Kleist grew into virility by way of his writings. His features betray him as feminine; his writings shout: "I am a man, a heartless man." The drama, with its sharp ascent to its climax and relentless descent to its end, is the most masculine art anyhow. As mentioned above, Kleist would have become the greatest German playwright without doubt, had it been given him to survive. In his writing, he is ruthless and harsh; his characters are blocks of granite, and this not only in his stage plays but also in his short stories, which in terms of atrocities approach Nazi cruelty— except that Kleist did not commit them, he only recorded them. It was once said that Shakespeare would have become a horrible criminal had he not been given the ability to objectivate his cruel instincts in the form of gruesome characters in his plays. The same is true of Kleist, who belonged to a nation which has shown the world more than once that it can do both: on the one hand kill and torture, on the other sublimate cruel tendencies into creations of art, sometimes of the highest order (German music!).

In Kleist's stories, people are buried alive, burned, quartered, and broken on the wheel. Children's skulls are smashed against the skulls of their own mothers, the inhabitants of large islands are wiped out, earthquakes swallow towns completely. This unhappy man found a way of his own to free himself of humane feelings which he considered a weakness—his feminine component. As a playwright as well as a narrator he possesses enormous force; he carries you along with the violence of his actions and words in a pace that takes your breath away. One cannot help feeling that something is wrong with this master of horrors; he is driven by an infernal power, by unspeakable, morbid suffering, something close to insanity, often trespassing the borderline.

Kleist's tragedy, *Penthesilea*, although more than long enough for one theater evening, rushes from start to finish without any subdivision into acts. It is a masterpiece of composition and characterization, and replete with beautiful verses —yet it is the work of an insane genius.

Penthesilea is the queen of the Amazons, who derive their name from their custom of mutilating their bosoms in order to be better able to set a bow against their chests. At their festival of the roses, they give themselves lovingly to men— but only after having first defeated these men in bloody battle and forced them into bed as prisoners. Kleist's Amazons are supposed to be quite feminine, notwithstanding the absence of a bosom and the custom of accepting defeated men only. Penthesilea even says she would prefer to be dirt to being an unattractive woman. She sees the Greek hero, Achilles, and falls in love with him. According to the law of her country, she has to "embrace him with iron" first. This is not impossible, in spite of Achilles' striking superiority, because she can take him on with bloodhounds and elephants. Achilles, however, is not defeated, at least not by her first assault. He, too, falls in love, and in order to spare her feelings he makes her believe that he has been vanquished by her. In the eyes of her pagan mother superior, Penthesilea is a renegade anyway, because she has singled out and fallen in love with Achilles instead of accepting anybody whom she has first prostrated in battle. To an Amazon, one man is no different from another.

Achilles, on learning from Penthesilea that all Amazons have their right breast amputated, exclaims:

> Could the terrific rumor yet be true?
> And all these blooming figures
> Surrounding thee, the flowers of their sex,
> Perfect, each one of them, as if an altar

> To kneel in love before it and in worship,
> They all are robbed, inhuman, sinful?
> PENTHESILEA: Did you not know that?
> ACHILLES (*pressing his face against her breast*): Oh Queen!
> The seat of all young and lovely feeling
> Because of a mania, barbarian—
> PENTHESILEA: Be reassured,
> They all take refuge in this left one,
> Where they dwell closer to the heart.
> I hope you will not miss the other.

It is very difficult to remain serious about this love scene, all too close to a parody on the mamma complex (Edmund Bergler and Ludwig Eidelberg).

Achilles' delicate ruse is betrayed and Penthesilea learns that she has not defeated him but, on the contrary, he has defeated her. No sooner has she discovered his romantic deception than she changes into a monster. The man loves her and waits for her unarmed, not expecting hostilities, but she attacks him and hunts him to death with her dogs and arrows. With sadistic voluptuousness—a super-Salome—she assaults her murdered lover with her teeth and, with her dogs' help, tears the corpse to pieces. His blood drips from the corners of her mouth.

It was often said that Penthesilea, who desires to surrender to man and then despises surrender, who loves man and then hates him, was Kleist himself. Penthesilea expresses his girlish instincts and his masculine protest against them. Undoubtedly, his masculine sister Ulrike played a more or less unconscious part in the conception.

Kleist sent his tragedy to Goethe (1808), who was then about sixty and enthroned in Weimar as the recognized prince of Germany's poets. He had grown old in reverence of proportion, ancient Greek ideals, and rejected the play and its author with a kind of horror. He said he was sorry that an otherwise remarkable talent could go astray so far.

35

Shortly after *Penthesilea*, Kleist wrote his fairy-tale play
Käthchen of Heilbronn, Penthesilea's antipode. He said himself
that the two plays belong together like plus and minus. Penthesilea is bloody protest against the man she loves, Käthchen is
all devotion and subservience. Finally, she gets her man just
the same, having chosen the better way to his subjugation.
The fifteen-year-old Käthchen who, as we eventually hear, is
the illegitimate daughter of the emperor, follows her knight
Friedrich Wetter Graf von Strahl (Frederick Thunderstorm
Count of the Flash) like a dog in spite of all the terror he has
in store for her. She sleeps on straw in his stables. He does not
want to have anything to do with her, but he cannot get rid
of her, either with dogs or with the whip. She is all humility,
but in her somnambulistic state she knows that he will marry
her within a year's span.

In spite of these extremes, we do not get the impression of
perversion here. Kleist approaches the peak of his art, his
salvation—it is time, because he is only a few years from his
death. Käthchen is filled with the spirit of Grimm's fairy tales
in the best sense: natural fragrancy, humbleness, hope, and
happy ending. The play is a medieval saga. Cherubs protect the
girl, innocence is finally exalted, intriguing ugliness and falsehood are unmasked. We feel Kleist's love for Germany; no
atrocities in this play, if we forget the count's threats with
dog and whip. The count is rather a good fellow who does not
seem to relish the girl's constant answers: "Yes, my sublime
lord." "No, my worshipped master!" "Gracious Sir!"

We do not know whether Goethe saw this play before
Kleist's death. Most likely it would not have changed his judgment. Käthchen is pining away, a case of hysteria without any
personality aside from her masochistic eroticism. Even Goethe's
Gretchen was a much stronger person. Faust had to conquer
the resisting maiden. At the conclusion of Kleist's play, our

masochistic Käthchen eats up her man, but figuratively, unlike sadistic Penthesilea; no blood is shed and nobody dies.

The Count von Strahl is visibly afraid of her, following him like his shadow. Once she jumps out of an upper window and breaks both her legs while he is happening to pass by. Another time he shouts: "Kick her out, I do not want to have anything to do with her!" It is all in vain; she is his inescapable fate.

Käthchen remains consistent to the very end. Shortly before the wedding, the count apologizes for all the injuries he inflicted upon her and he weeps. Replies Käthchen, with anxiety:

> Heavens! What is the matter? What moves you so?
> What have you inflicted upon me?
>   I know nothing of it. . . .

Kleist knew it: You cannot get rid of women. Not of actual women without, not of one's own femininity within. He was afraid of both of them and described them as two extremes (Penthesilea and Käthchen) who hardly exist in reality. Käthchen, in all her sweetness and poetic glorification, cannot be a man's comrade as can a normal woman.

Not more than eight years were granted to Kleist, the writer, between his first literary attempts and his death. In this short span of time he created his classics, plays and stories, all of them born under terrific pain—his sublimation.

Under sublimation we understand (1) desexualization of an undesired instinct, plus (2) continuous drain of the instinct by action acceptable to the ego of the sublimating individual, and (3) success with the contemporary group in and for which the individual lives.

Kleist met with very little recognition, either in terms of royalties or of praise. Few creative spirits are strong enough to benefit from their production even without recognition.

They rid themselves of their vexing sense of incompleteness by the completeness of their work. Kleist with his feminine sensitivity was not one of those, except very temporarily toward the end of his life, when he became able to see and feel the plight of his countrymen.

He suffered with Germany, at that time subjugated by Napoleon, and helped kindle the spirit of liberation. After the two plays described, he wrote two patriotic plays. One of them (*Die Hermannsschlacht*), an allegory on Napoleon's conquest of Germany and the coming fight for liberation, sings of the defeat of the Roman general, Quintilius Varus, in the forest of Teutoburg, A.D. 9. Here, too, we happen upon Kleistian atrocities. Thusnelda, Hermann's wife, has the Roman Ventidius dismembered and disemboweled by a hungry she-bear, because he had cheated her in love. She learned that Ventidius intended to strip her of her golden hair in order to send it to his empress Livia in Rome. He even felt like breaking out her teeth for the repair of the empress' bad denture. With Kleist, things are never quite without a streak of insanity.

His last play, by far his best and one of the best ever written in the German tongue, is a patriotic drama, glorifying Prussian army discipline and the strictest fulfillment of the soldier's duty in the service of his sovereign. By that time, Kleist had in his active life returned to his origin and had applied successfully for rehabilitation as a commissioned officer in his king's army. He united two forms of sublimation: to be again the active officer and to glorify the Prussian officer on the stage.

The play, *Prince of Homburg*, was not shown in the author's lifetime, and later when it was performed it could not have the applause of his Junker class. These machine-men had no sense for the lofty poetry of duty and heroism, the way Kleist saw it. Any individual enthusiasm was suspicious and against their principles. The prince of this play is sentenced to die by Friedrich, the Great Elector, his uncle, because of disobeying an order. The prince wins the battle by his disobedience, but the Elector, as a matter of principle, considers discipline more important than a battle won. Prussian military glory in quintessence. Like the older Junius Brutus, whose son had to die for a similar offense, Friedrich had his nephew arrested and court-martialed. The playwright, understanding that heroic valor can be coupled with heroic fear, shows us the prince facing death with fear, expressing it in frantic words. This was more than Prussian officers could take. The author was not one of them, although he was a Von Kleist. A Junker, the perfect automaton of militarism, is never afraid to die, and if he is, he does not admit it. The prince's heroic march from fear to lofty acceptance of his fate in the name of Brandenburg's grandeur was not palatable to Brandenburg's machinery. Dostoevsky, and before him Stendhal—in his novel *The Red and the Black*— could display emotions of this kind, but Kleist was once more rejected by his caste just when he felt ready to rejoin it.

Soon after, Kleist was dead. He happened to meet Henriette Vogel, a very sick woman, the wife of an accountant. She was not young, not attractive, her face was disfigured by pock-marks. Her disease was supposed to be cancer, she had to expect painful ailment, she was longing for death but lacked the courage for lonesome suicide. Kleist, who had been longing for death all his life almost uninterruptedly, promised her on a day of exaltation that he would kill her and himself whenever she would ask it. The reverse is also possible. Maybe he made her promise him that she would depart with him whenever he asked her. Anyway, Kleist fell vehemently in love with Henriette. Here he saw the solution: one cannot live, but one can die with a woman! All secret guilt, all anxiety, all tension vanished; he felt happy as never before in his life. All his friends unanimously bear witness that never was there a regular affair with Henriette. Yet, outbursts such as the following over a year before their joint death show the flames of passion:

39

TO ADOLFINE HENRIETTE VOGEL

Berlin, after Michaelmas, 1810

My Jettchen, my heart, my darling, my little pigeon, my life, my dear, sweet life, light of my life, my everything, my goods and chattels, my castle, my soil, meadows and vineyards, oh sun of my life, sun, moon and stars, heaven and earth, my past, my future, my bride, my girl, my dear friend, my love, my heart's blood, my entrails, apple of my eye, oh you dearest, how am I to call you? My golden child, my pearl, my gem, my crown, my queen and empress. Sweet darling of my heart, highest, most cherished, my everything and anything, my wife, my wedding, christening of my children, my tragedy, my immortality. *Oh you are my better alter ego*, my virtues, my merits, my hope, remission of my sins, my future and salvation, daughter of heaven, God's own child, my pleader and defender, guardian angel, my cherub and seraph— I love you so! . . . [*My translation. F. W.*]

The letter of a maniac! Evidently, Kleist was in the midst of one of his numerous nervous calamities. This time he did not come out of it, but embraced the rapture of anticipated death. Kleist's soul, after the pressure of a lifetime, is at long last freed of ever-burdening guilt and anxiety. He responds with the exuberance of the letter quoted above.

"November 20th, 1811, at two o'clock P.M., the couple arrived at an inn at Wannsee near Potsdam. The landlord reported that they walked around the lake, ate and drank, chatted and laughed together. Light was on in their room all night and the valet saw them walk to and fro all the time. The twenty-first noon they sent a messenger with letters to Berlin. When they could be reasonably sure that the letters had reached their destination, they ordered coffee, rum, a table and chairs to be brought to a hill, about thirty feet from the lake. When the waitress returned to the inn, she heard the shots. Henriette lay in a pit; Kleist had shot her through the left breast and, kneeling in front of her, shot himself in the brain through his mouth. . . ."

Much has been written about this double-death, murder and suicide.[4] Some of the explanations speak of Kleist's economic plight, actually just then hardly bothering him. Others exalted Henriette Vogel, with whom he died, to Dante's Beatrice, a *unio mystica*. What does such a union mean? We may confirm his friend Ernst von Pfuel's sad epitaph that Kleist loved death more than life. But why? Some people are so discontented with part of their person that they decide to free themselves of this part at all cost. They wish to kill the unwanted component. The idea is to continue living with the other part. However, when they shoot at themselves, they naturally perish, the two parts being inseparable from one another, psychically as well as bodily. Caught in a tragic mistake close to insanity they kill themselves.

Ernest Jones emphasizes the underlying wish to return to mother; mother means birth, and birth equals death. From dust we come, to dust we go. We add here another approach which explains suicide—solitary suicide as well as "dying together" in terms of bisexuality, understanding them as an intrusion of the primary function against the inexorable fact that one cannot kill one component and survive with the other. The primary function, immortal as a god, does ask: Why not? And the secondary function is silenced—its objections are overruled.

When Kleist met Henriette, he was able to project his feminine part into the sick woman and kill it in this shape. Naturally, he had to go with her. The body of the dead woman next to his own spoke out, saying to her macabre lover: Here lies the sex that made you suffer, and you lie with it.

Let us refer once more to Kleist's love letter to Henriette. In spite of his Titanic attempt to prove his love, he cannot reach the level of genuine "genitality." All his exuberance cannot conceal the absence of normal heterosexual feelings. His fear of his own femininity killed him. His life was dominated by homosexual panic.

The term homosexual panic came up during the First World War, when paroxysmal fright was observed in soldiers and could be recognized as originating in latent homosexuality, stirred up by constantly living with men only. Ferenczi divided the concept of homosexuality into active and passive inversion. Panic arises from the passive form, the fear of being overwhelmed, raped, emasculated. This was Kleist's case. The struggle against latent homosexuality of this kind, as we know only too well, may lead to diabolic (paranoiac) destruction.

With Heinrich von Kleist, the greatest son of the race of the Von Kleists, the destruction took place in fiction. Other members of his family had been producing "frightfulness" in active life. Their "degenerate" offspring died, unmourned by them, his death hardly deplored even by his friends.

1954

NOTES

1. He never mentioned his father. We know nothing of his Oedipus conflict except what can be deduced from his later fiction and plays.

2. I. Sadger, in a monograph on Kleist (Wiesbaden, 1910), expressed the opinion that Kleist suffered from compulsive masturbation and consequent compunctions. Around 1910 even Sadger, who was one of the first psychoanalytic explorers of homosexuality, did not know yet of the explosive power of latent homosexuality as first described in 1913 in Freud's classic on the "Schreber Case."

3. A successful businessman had to retire, because his surroundings and particularly one of his partners became obnoxious to him. That partner had a huge frame, an excellent set of teeth which he bared broadly with every grin and laugh. In such moments, my patient was afraid of being grabbed by the man, lifted up and sat down on the desk like a little child. Yet the patient was that man's superior. The patient always received another shock when the errand boy, a small blond fellow, entered his room with a message. It was easy to read from the patient's dreams that he was living in homosexual panic, but by no means was it easy to make the man see his complex with equanimity.

4. Ernest Jones, "On Dying Together, with Special Reference to Heinrich von Kleist's Suicide," in *Essays on Applied Psychoanalysis* (International Psychoanalytic Library, V, 1911 and 1923).

PSYCHOANALYSIS OF THE CHARACTER AND GENIUS OF EMILY BRONTË

Lucile Dooley

It is probable that no English writer except Shakespeare has had so many books, essays, and articles written about him as have the Brontë sisters. Literally dozens of volumes and hundreds of magazine and newspaper articles have appeared since the day in 1847 when *Jane Eyre*, written by Charlotte Brontë, was published in London; and the interest is still growing in spite of the fact that comparatively a small portion of the reading public now reads any of the Brontë books. Those who do take them up and find them congenial and interesting discover a growing fascination. They have the perennial charm of the true work of genius. The reader finds something new at each rereading. It is not, however, the excellence of the books themselves, in which, indeed, many literary faults can be found, but even more the challenging and enigmatical character of the writers which engages this interest. Attempts have

43

been made to explain how such unusual genius could have flowered in such bleak and unfavorable surroundings. This enigma alone makes a study of the family seem worthwhile to a psychoanalyst, for it is as much the psychoanalyst's business to account for psychological phenomena as it is to change pathological mental conditions.

The fact that an obscure Yorkshire parson and his three daughters and one son who, while they lived, were scarcely known in the outside world, have enlisted all this interest, indicates that there must be something in these lives or in the artistic creation that proceeded from them that makes a universal appeal. The growing volume of literature on this subject shows also that those who are interested feel that the ultimately satisfying word has not been said. Perhaps it will never be said, but at least there ought to be an attempt to apply the principles of psychoanalysis to an explanation of these extraordinarily simple lives and unusual types of genius.

The Brontë family presents a unique example of the effect of an almost closed family circle upon the development of character. If the psychoanalyst's contention is true, that family influence and experiences of early childhood are by far the most important determining factors of personality, then we have here almost a "pure culture" as no family of ambition and education could have been more isolated from other influences . . . at least, influences of human contact. It is my general thesis that this peculiar isolation, with its intensifying of family relations and with the conservation of the emotions of infancy, is the explanation of much that is extraordinary in the character and genius of these writers. That it creates the genius, of course, I cannot say. I do not believe that anyone has ever sufficiently accounted for genius. Through psychoanalysis, we have sometimes been able to account for the direction which the genius took and for the content of its artistic creation.

In the case of the Brontë family, we have six rather unusual

children, two of whom are of undoubted genius, one who died too young for judgment, but whose precocity seemed to give promise of genius, two who were talented enough to attract attention in any ordinary family but were overshadowed in this family by the more brilliant sisters, and a father who certainly showed no genius, and who still, considering his humble beginnings, made an unusual advance in life.

Nothing of what we know of the ancestry of the Brontës in any way accounts for this burst of ability in one generation. Patrick Brontë, the father, came from Irish peasant stock. The name was spelled in Ireland variously—Prunty, Brunty, Branty, and in still other forms, as often happened in the eighteenth century with illiterate people. Possessed of ambition and some measure of ability, he succeeded in getting an education far above his ten brothers and sisters and at the age of twenty-four left Ireland and entered St. Johns College at Cambridge, England, where he studied for the church. He received his degree four years later and became a curate. He wrote an essay called *The Cottage in the Wood* and some volumes of poems, *Cottage Poems, The Rural Minstrel*, and others, which were in no way remarkable, but they achieved publication. He married in 1812 Maria Branwell, a native of Cornwall and a woman apparently of character and intelligence, but without any evidence of literary talent. To them six children were born in quick succession, Maria, born in 1813, died in 1825; Elizabeth, born in 1814, died in 1825; Charlotte, the Brontë who has won widest fame, born in 1816, died in 1855; Patrick Branwell Brontë, the only boy, born in 1817, died in 1848; Emily, considered by most critics the most remarkable genius of the family, born in 1818, died in 1848; Anne, born in 1820, died in 1849. The mother died in 1821 when her youngest child was about a year old. Five of her children are said to have died of tuberculosis. The mother is said to have had tuberculosis but died of cancer. The father lived to be eighty-four years old, dying in 1861, having outlived all his family.

46

Perhaps this tragic succession of early deaths had some part in the remarkable appeal that the family makes to the English imagination.

Brontë was a curate at Hartshead in Yorkshire, when he was married and where his first two children were born. He then moved to Thornton, where the next four children were born, and just after the birth of the last one was given the charge of Haworth, where he remained to the end of his life, and where his children spent the greater part of their lives. Many descriptions of Haworth have been published, not one of which gives a cheerful picture. It is a small manufacturing and mining town, in the heart of the Yorkshire moors, four miles from a branch railway station, and at the time the Brontës lived there, had no regular coach road or daily communication with the outside world. The houses are built of the native gray stone; the streets are narrow, the whole place gloomy and cheerless. The parsonage was next to the church and surrounded on two sides by a churchyard crowded with graves.

The children who survived until adulthood and whom we are studying remember little or nothing of their mother. Varying accounts have been given of the characteristics of the father. Mrs. Gaskell, the first biographer, trusting too much to the tales of an uneducated and unreliable servant who was not with the family long, emphasized his violent temper and his excitability. Others who knew him better deny these things, and while they admit that he was a recluse, preferring to spend most of his time in solitude, and while he was stern in his ideas of discipline they insist that he was a kindly father, taking great interest in his children's welfare and devoting some part of every day to their education. They shared his reading and he discussed politics with Maria, the older one who died at twelve, as if she had been a grown-up person.

In later years it was certainly the opinion of friends of Charlotte Brontë that he was very selfish with her, making her feel that it was her duty to remain always with him, and being very much opposed to the idea of her marrying. She exercised her self-denial in thus living in this lonely spot with him and remaining forever out of the world which she could so easily have entered.

John Stewart Smith, visiting Brontë after fame had come to his daughter, said that Brontë would evidently have liked to stop his children's literary activities. In his account of a visit to father and daughter at Haworth, Smith writes:

And then he talked about Emily and the other sister, and told me how he considered Emily the genius of the family, how he never fancied Charlotte capable of writing anything, and how he could scarcely realize it, and as he did so, he ever and anon fell into a reverie again, and muttered the old refrain: "And I knew nothing about it, positively nothing. Strange! Perhaps I might have stopped it if I had. But I knew nothing—nothing."

Madame Duclaux says in her biography of Emily Brontë:

He had a vivacious impressible manner which effectually matched a certain selfishness and rigor of temperament which became plain in after years. He seemed a generous, quick, impulsive lad . . .

In his strange nature, violence and coldness were equally genuine, both being the means to gratify some personal ambition, desire, or indolence. It is not an uncommon Irish type; self-important, upright, honorable, yet with a bent towards subtlety; abstemious in habit, but with freaks of violent self-indulgence; courteous and impulsive toward strangers, though cold to members of the household; naturally violent and often assuming violence as an instrument of authority; selfish and dutiful; passionate, and devoid of intense affection.

Reading the various memoirs, one cannot but conclude that his was a very repressed nature, that he held himself in strict discipline, that sometimes the inner force broke out into violent storms, and that his influence could never have been sunny or genial for his children. Moreover, while he was in the house with them, he kept himself in his study alone most of the time and they were never free to approach him. The account of servants and friends is that the children were very much alone, their mother being too ill for a year before her death to see them. The older ones took care of the younger ones. They all kept very quiet and had to be very good— there could be no outbreaks of childish glee, no romping of children's games in the parsonage. When in the house they sat and played in a tiny second-story room, significantly called the "Children's Study," where at least for a time all six of them slept. Here they read, told each other stories in low tones, and as soon as they were able to write, began to write little magazines and books of their own. They used to take long walks over the moor, all six holding hands, the little ones toddling along by the older ones, and only out-of-doors on the moor were they free to run and shout. After their mother's death the children saw more of their father, who read with them sometimes in the evening. They had no children's books and as they read *Blackwood's Magazine* and the leading newspapers of the day, they were at a very tender age quite conversant with national politics, with the doings of Parliament, and with the leading literary productions and authors of the time. Their father constantly wrote poetry himself and they very naturally took up the idea of producing literature on their own account. At thirteen years of age Charlotte compiled a list of the books she had written and found they made "twenty-two volumes in all." The others were almost as productive.

The two older girls were sent to a boarding school for poor clergymen's daughters at Cowan Bridge in 1824, when they were eleven and ten years old. Three months later the next two girls, Charlotte and Emily, were placed in the same school, Emily being at that time six years old. Charlotte has given a very unflattering portrait of this school in her *Jane Eyre*. Whether this school was extremely unhealthy or not, it was not a good place for the delicate little Brontës. Maria, the oldest child, died of what was said to be tuberculosis ten months after entering the school and her sister Elizabeth died five weeks later of the same disease. It was doubtless the suffering of the oldest sister—suffering too little appreciated or considered by the busy and somewhat rigid teachers of the school who never relaxed discipline because a child was ill—that made the deep and unfortunate impression of severity and cruelty on Charlotte's mind. How it affected Emily we have no means of knowing, but she could not have been unaware of it.

The loss of the oldest sister was to the remaining children like the loss of a second mother, and they never forgot her nor ceased to talk about her. Charlotte, aged nine, now took the place of the oldest child and little mother to the others; also of companion to her father. She became to him somewhat the same sort of a companion that Maria had been except that he never saw in her the brilliance of intelligence that he had seen in his oldest daughter and never expected more of her than domestic attainment and daughterly devotion. That he expected far too much of the latter quality is clearly apparent.

Charlotte and Emily spent another term at Cowan Bridge School after the death of their sisters, and then did not go away to school until they were fifteen and fourteen years old, when they went to a very much more congenial school, kept by the Misses Wooler, at Roehead. Here Charlotte made her lifelong friends, Ellen Nussey and Mary Taylor, to whose preservation of her correspondence we owe much of our biographical data. Emily, apparently, made no friends, was piteously homesick and could remain only three months at the school. Both girls were preparing themselves to be governesses as this seemed the only probable way of earning a living. Charlotte had two situations as governess in private families, and was also teacher in the school at Roehead where she had been a pupil for a time. Emily taught at a large girl's school

50

at Halifax for six months; then had to give this up as she had given up when a pupil at Roehead because she could not stand life away from home. The work was far too hard, from six in the morning to eleven at night.

After several years spent at home, in which they continued to write assiduously, did a great deal of housework, needle-work, drawing and painting, and, of course, omnivorous read-ing, they decided that in order to be successful as teachers and at the same time fulfill the demands of their father and brother upon them, they must open a school at home. For this they would need further education in foreign languages. So it was determined that Charlotte and Emily should go to a school at Brussels in order to learn French, German, and music. Ac-cordingly, in February, 1842, the step was taken which had a most profound influence on Charlotte's life, but which prob-ably had very little influence on Emily, who, like a granite boulder on her own beloved moors, was only very slightly affected by any of the external events passing around her.

Charlotte enjoyed the experience at Brussels very much. Emily. suffered from the malady of homesickness as much as ever, but determined to endure it for the sake of the object to be gained. The head of the school, Professor Héger, was evi-dently a brilliant scholar, a proficient teacher, and a kindly and sympathetic though temperamental man. Charlotte fell in love with him and it was this affair, added to her deep father attachment, that determined much of her literary production. Her love was largely unconscious, as far as her perception of its true nature was concerned, but it wakened and kindled the emotional fire that marks the chief claim to distinction in her work. While she had written much and so had practiced, she never attempted to publish anything until after this. And while many of the little manuscripts which she wrote before this, her twenty-sixth year, have been preserved by the Brontë votaries, they have only the significance that attaches to the juvenilia of any writer. In her artistic creation, it is the struggle with the powerful emotions generated by this conflict that gave her insight into the inner emotional life of a fairly universal type of woman. In each of her stories is found a more or less sophisticated version of the family romance as played out between father imago, embodied in an older lover, and a daughter-heroine, a young and friendless girl.

The effect of this experience on Emily is very difficult to trace. Emily made a special study of German, while Charlotte concentrated on the French. Some writers, including Mrs. Humphrey Ward, have attempted to trace the wildness and romanticism of Emily's *Wuthering Heights*, her one novel, to the influence of German literature, especially to Hoffman, which she must have read. It is possible that she received some suggestions but it is just as likely that the life in the wilds of Yorkshire and her own imagination, working over the secret annals of the solitary families living near her, could have produced precisely the same material without any German influence whatever. Others have thought she showed the influence of Goethe.

It is interesting to note before we dismiss the Brussels era from the Brontë history entirely—an era which represented their only departure from England, and almost their only departure from Yorkshire—that their teacher, Professor Héger, agreed with their father in seeing in Emily the greater genius of the two. This was in spite of the fact that she frequently rebelled and could not acquiesce in some of his methods of teaching, or in the tasks that he gave her, whereas Charlotte was his docile and devoted pupil.

Emily did not like the atmosphere of Brussels. As Charlotte said, her upright Protestant nature rebelled against the "gentle Jesuitry of the school." She was glad when the death of the aunt, who had lived with them after they returned from their first school, recalled her to England. In passing, their aunt,

Miss Branwell, had no perceptible influence on the girls' character. Therefore she has not been mentioned. She kept house and taught them sewing, but had no sympathy with any of them except the youngest who was almost a baby when she came and who was always most gentle and docile. After her death Emily remained at home taking care of the house, while Charlotte remained at Brussels for another year to complete her studies in French and literature.

About this time the influence of the brother, Branwell Brontë, became important in the lives of all three of the sisters, most especially in those of Emily and the youngest one, Anne. We cannot explain the character of any one of them without sketching his character. Patrick Branwell Brontë was a year older than Emily and as the only boy had always been treated as *the* important member of the family. He was educated at home because his father felt that he could give him more instruction than he could get in any school within his means, while to get him sent away to a semi-charitable institution such as the one at Cowan Bridge which his daughters had attended, was not feasible. He was the special pet of his aunt, and could not be expected to be anything but spoiled. His sisters were taught to wait on him and defer to him. It was taken for granted by the whole family, in the early years, that Branwell would be the genius, the one on whom most effort was to be concentrated. He joined with his sisters in their literary attempts and wrote with them a number of novelettes, essays, and chronicles as well as poems. The whole family had a strong urge toward drawing and painting, and they thought that Branwell was really talented in this line. He accordingly had some instruction in art. Mr. Brontë employed a drawing teacher for all the children when Charlotte was about sixteen, and Branwell fifteen. After that Branwell was allowed to study with a portrait painter in a nearby city.

Branwell expressed no doubts of his own power, and even

when his life came to an utterly miserable end, from self-indulgence and dissipation, he still boasted of what he could do and had done. It is probable that he had a fair amount of talent, as much perhaps as his little sister Anne, who left behind her two mediocre novels (which would have been forgotten by now had it not been for the fame of her sisters) and some religious poetry.

Had there been strength of character to sustain Branwell's talent, it might have been that he could have made a name for himself, having much more encouragement than his sisters. The fact was that he was utterly spoiled by lack of discipline, by self-indulgence, over-praise, and conceit, working on a mind that subconsciously knew itself unequal to his world's expectations. Living in a small village, associating almost of necessity with those beneath him, socially and culturally, precocious, and looked up to by his associates, there was nothing really to bring out his talent or to develop his character and everything to undermine it and destroy it. He was a ready, voluble talker, like his sisters a great reader, and he could be very entertaining to people of mediocre attainments. The parsonage was just across the churchyard from the village tavern where commercial travelers put up. It became the custom, when Branwell was a boy of fourteen or fifteen, for the innkeeper to send for him to pass the evening when visitors were at the inn. "Do you want someone to help you with your bottle?" the landlord would say to the visitor. "If you do, I will send for Patrick." While the messenger went to call him the landlord entertained the guests with wonderful accounts of the boy whose precocious cleverness and great conversational powers were the pride of the village. In this way, Branwell very early contracted a taste for alcohol which his poor constitution could not bear.

There is no doubt that the relation between him and his

father made life difficult for him, as he was his father's pride and special care; and his father was at once very strict with him in some things and over-indulgent in others. He became addicted to opium and his mind and character gradually deteriorated. The last three years of his life he was evidently insane, his letters and various sayings quoted by others being typical of the drug addict. He made his sisters' life a burden. What with his drunkenness and his opium-eating, his wild behavior and one or two disgraceful affairs, one in money and the other in an imaginary love affair with his employer's wife, they found themselves forced to avoid other company. For a long time Charlotte's school friends had visited her and she had returned visits, but she could never have them come when Branwell was in this deplorable condition. The cherished plan for opening a school had to be given up because there was no capital to purchase quarters other than Haworth, and if there had been, no one of the girls could have thought it right to leave their father alone with this lunatic son. Through months and even years when Branwell had to be watched over and nursed through drunken stupors and opium dreams, Emily Brontë shared with her father the chief burden. She had been deeply attached to Branwell, and although she was disgusted with him, she still had more patience and toleration for him than had the other sisters. She waited up at night for him to come reeling home, and helped him to bed. She rescued him from the bed to which he had, in drunken madness, set fire one night, carried him out in her arms and then hastened back with two pails of water to extinguish the fire while the other two girls stood petrified with fright.

It has been thought that something, if not much, of the brutality and horror which informed her remarkable novel *Wuthering Heights* was derived from her contact with this pitiable brother. A poem she wrote might have expressed her feeling for him. It was thought that his death had inspired it until later research showed that it had been written much earlier:

> Well, some may hate, and some may scorn,
> And some may quite forget thy name;
> But my sad heart must ever mourn
> Thy ruined hopes, thy blighted fame!
> 'Twas thus I thought, an hour ago,
> Even weeping o'er that wretch's woe;
> One word turned back my gushing tears
> And lit my altered eye with sneers.
> Then "Bless the friendly dust," I said,
> "That hides thy unlamented head!
> Vain as thou wert, and weak as vain,
> The slave of Falsehood, Pride, and Pain—
> My heart has nought akin to thine;
> Thy soul is powerless over mine."
> But these were thoughts that vanished too;
> Unwise, unholy, and untrue;
> Do I despise the timid deer,
> Because his limbs are fleet with fear?
> Or, would I mock the wolf's death-howl,
> Because his form is gaunt and foul?
> Or, hear with joy the leveret's cry,
> Because it cannot bravely die?
> No! Then above his memory
> Let Pity's heart as tender be;
> Say, "Earth, lie gently on that breast,
> And, kind Heaven, grant that spirit rest."

The house with Branwell was indeed like a mental hospital. Often the father was up all night with the raving boy who would come forth in the morning saying, "Well, the old man and I have had a sad night of it. I wonder that I did not kill him." He frequently threatened his father's life.

Branwell tried not only to make a place for himself in the arts, actually starting up for himself in Leeds as a portrait painter, but at the very time his sisters were planning (without his knowledge) to publish their works, he was sending his poems and stories to leading writers and publishers of the day. None of them were accepted, and few critics can find anything worth accepting in them.

Branwell died in September, 1848, aged thirty-one, and Emily died the following December. She became seriously ill the very day of his burial. She fought against her illness, would not acknowledge it, would not keep her bed, would not see a doctor. There is something terrible and impressive in those last months of hers, during which her sisters watched her faltering and failing step and her impeded breathing, her terrible attacks of coughing, without daring to offer sympathy or help. On the day of her death, she arose as usual and came down to the parlor. Here the servant found her sitting by the fire, where she had been trying to comb her long hair, and the comb lying under the grate. "Tabby," she said, "my comb's fallen down there and I was too weak to pick it up." A little later, after a paroxysm of coughing, she said, "If you will send for a doctor, I will see him now." But an hour or two later she was dead.

This picture of her death gives one side of her character as well as anything we could say of her. On the other hand, a calm serenity gave an impression of seasons of joy—or better, perhaps, of exaltation. Charlotte says, "She was torn—conscious, panting, reluctant—from a happy life." Charlotte was a romancer and saw much in life in terms of what she wished to see. She adored Emily without understanding her and tried to manage her, with success when Emily did not care much about the point at issue. Emily's misery and Emily's happiness were both kept as much as possible in her own breast.

On the day that Emily died, the youngest sister, Anne, became ill, showing symptoms of tuberculosis. A few months later she was dead. This left the father and Charlotte the sole survivors of the family of eight. Charlotte's literary fame grew.

She was sought out by other writers of her time and thereafter
had some contact with the literary world though she still continued to pass the greater part of her time with her father,
keeping the house, putting her domestic duties first, and writing only in her intervals of leisure. She produced two more
novels. In her thirty-eighth year, she married her father's
curate, Mr. A. B. Nicholls. Eight months after her marriage
she died from a disorder incident to pregnancy. She survived
her sisters by six years. Her father lived six years longer, and
died in his eighty-fifth year. That was in 1861. Before his
death, *The Life of Charlotte Brontë*, by Mrs. E. C. Gaskell,
was published and from that time on few years have passed
without the publication of some writing on this family.

The facts of Emily's life are few and we have covered practically all of them. Left motherless in her third year, cared
for by older sisters and servants until the coming of the unsym-
pathetic aunt, partly educated by a father whose character we
have discovered was unstable, stern, passionate, and aloof; passionately loved by her sister Charlotte and loving her younger
sister Anne, who was in few things her rival and who followed
her lead with docility; living almost her whole life on the
Yorkshire moors which seemed more to her than any human
beings; expressing herself through many secretly written poems
and a unique novel; closing her mind to human influences from
without; getting very little from her brief sojourns away from
home; she died in her thirtieth year. There has scarcely been
a less eventful life in the annals of literature. The family
tragedies were all she knew of life, and yet her writings show
the deepest acquaintance with the tragic and deep experiences
of humanity. As Maeterlinck has said of her in his *Wisdom
and Destiny:*

Not a single event ever paused as it passed her threshold yet did
every event she could claim take place in her heart, with incom-
parable force and beauty, with matchless precision and detail. We

say that nothing ever happened; but did not all things really happen to her much more directly and tangibly than to most of us, seeing that everything that took place about her, everything that she saw or heard was transformed within her into thoughts and feelings, into indulgent love, admiration, adoration of life?

And again Maeterlinck:

Of her happiness none can doubt. Not in the soul of the best of all those whose happiness has lasted longest, been the most active, diversified, perfect, could more imperishable harvest be found than in the soul Emily Brontë lays bare. If to her there came nothing of all that passes in love, sorrow, passion or anguish, still did she possess all that abides when emotion has faded away.

And May Sinclair gives us a striking statement of the enigma of her character:

Strangers received from her an impression of a creature utterly removed from them; a remoteness scarcely human, hard to reconcile with her known tenderness for every living thing. She seems to have had passionate repugnance to alien and external contacts and to have felt no more than an almost reluctant liking for the friend of the family, the charming Ellen Nussey. Indeed, she regarded Charlotte's friend with the large and virile tolerance that refused to be charmed.

And yet in the depths of her virginal nature there was something fiercely tender and maternal. There can be no doubt that she cared for Charlotte, who called her "Mine own bonnie love . . ." [1]

Speaking of her death day, Charlotte says:

Yet, while physically she perished, mentally she grew stronger than we had yet known her. Day by day, when I saw with what a front she met suffering, I looked on her with an anguish of wonder and love. I have seen nothing like it; but indeed I have never seen her parallel in anything. Stronger than a man, simpler than a child, her nature stood alone. The awful point was, that while full of ruth for others she had no pity on herself; the spirit was inexorable to the flesh; from the trembling hand, the unnerved limbs, the faded eyes, the same service was exacted as in health. . . . [2]

It has been fairly easy to reconstruct Charlotte's character and the springs of it, to read her own inner life in her novels. For the understanding of Emily, our material is much less open and plain. She has put nothing of her personal life into her work. We cannot guess her small personal likes or dislikes as we can those of Charlotte and Anne. She never speaks in the first person, she is as objective as Shakespeare himself. We can only infer certain things; inference is dangerous but it is fascinating.

Through her poems, especially those unpublished until after her death, runs the theme of an unfortunate lost and abandoned child; a child whose father was not acknowledged or whose father was a traitor, disgraced in exile; a child who had no hope of happiness or recognition. Such a child reappears in the hero of *Wuthering Heights*, Heathcliff. From this conception of hers more than anything else that has been left us, we may guess the dominant trends in her life; this and her passionate love of nature. We can see her powerful, unyielding, and self-contained character. We can guess at the fires which smouldered beneath and at the elements which kindled this fire. Matthew Arnold describes her in his poem, "Haworth Churchyard":

> . . . and she
> (How shall I sing her?) whose soul
> Knew no fellow for might,
> Passion, vehemence, grief,
> Daring, since Byron died,
> That world-famed son of fire—she, who sank
> Baffled, unknown, self-consumed;
> Whose too bold dying song
> Stirr'd, like a clarion-blast, my soul.

These poems, containing the story of the doomed child, were mostly unpublished until after her death and were never meant by her for publication. (The seventeen poems published during her life, in fact, were surrendered only after days of persuasion by Charlotte, who accidentally discovered the note-book containing them. Emily evidently regarded her poems as a personal and private matter, and never evidenced by word or sign that she cared at all what anyone thought of them.) These unpublished poems evidently were an incidental part of a series of writings carried on as a game by Emily and Anne, called the Gondal Chronicles, written apparently just for their amusement, and kept secret from everyone else, about an imaginary Gondaland and certain great heroes and great wars of this land. Their diaries contained references to the chronicles, most of which were destroyed after their deaths. Poems are identified as belonging to these chronicles by proper names recurring in them and in the fragments preserved. *Zamorna* was a sort of Achilles, the man of sin, the son of war and love, the child unblessed of heaven, abandoned by its mother, cradled in the heather and rocked by the winter storm, the doomed child grown to its doom, like Heathcliff.

Two poems express Emily's idea of the doomed child:

I

Heavy hangs the rain-drop
  From the burdened spray;
Heavy broods the damp mist
  On uplands far away.

Heavy looms the dull sky,
  Heavy rolls the sea;
And heavy throbs the young heart
  Beneath that lonely tree.

Never has a blue streak
  Cleft the clouds since morn;
Never has his grim fate
  Smiled since he was born.

Frowning on the infant,
  Shadowing childhood's joy,
Guardian-angel knows not
  That melancholy boy.

61

Day is passing swiftly
  Its sad and sombre prime;
Boyhood sad is merging
  In sadder manhood's time:

All the flowers are praying
  For sun, before they close,
And he prays too—unconscious
  That sunless human rose.

Blossom—that the west wind
  Has never wooed to blow
Scentless are the petals,
  Thy dew is cold as snow!

Soul—where kindred kindness,
  No early promise woke;
Barren is thy beauty,
  As weed upon a rock.

Wither—soul and blossom!
  You both were vainly given:
Earth reserves no blessing
  For the unblest of heaven!

II

I am the only being whose doom
  No tongue would ask, no eye would mourn;
I've never caused a thought of gloom,
  A smile of joy, since I was born.

In secret pleasure, secret tears,
  This changeful life has slipped away,
As friendless after eighteen years,
  As lone as on my natal day.

There have been times I cannot hide
  There have been times when this was drear,
When my sad soul forgot its pride
  And longed for one to love me here.

But those were in the early glow
  Of feelings that subdued by care,
And they have died so long ago,
  I hardly now believe they were.

First melted off the hope of youth,
  Then fancy's rainbow fast withdrew:
And then experience told me truth
  In mortal bosoms never grew.

'Twas grief enough to think mankind
  All hollow, servile, insincere;
But worse to trust to my own mind
  And find the same Corruption there.

The child was the unacknowledged child of a traitor. He carried away and married the daughter of his archenemy. Heathcliff presents a variation of this theme. A gentleman farmer, Earnshaw, brings a swarthy foundling from Liverpool to Wuthering Heights, a lonely Yorkshire farm, to share the home with his two children, Hindley and Catherine. Catherine and Heathcliff grow up loving each other. The father dies. As May Sinclair wrote:

Hindley Earnshaw is brutal to the foundling, Heathcliff, and degrades him as a farm laborer. Heathcliff when his hour comes pays him back his wrong with the interest due. He is brutal beyond brutality to Hindley Earnshaw, and he degrades Hareton, Hindley's son, as he himself was degraded; but he is not brutal to him. The frustrated passion of Catherine Earnshaw for Heathcliff, and of Heathcliff for Catherine hardly knows itself from hate: They pay each other back, torture for torture, and pang for hopeless pang. When Catherine marries Edgar Linton, Heathcliff marries Isabella, Edgar's sister, in order that he may torture to perfection Catherine and Edgar and Isabella. His justice is more than poetic. The love of Catherine Earnshaw was all that he possessed. He knows that he has lost it through the degradation that he owes to Hindley Earnshaw. It is because Earnshaw and Linton between them have robbed him of all, that, when his hour comes, he pays himself back by robbing the Lintons and the Earnshaws of all that they possess, their Thrushcross Grange and Wuthering Heights. He loathes above all loathly creatures, Linton, his one son by Isabella. The whiteblooded thing is so sickly that he can hardly keep it alive. But with an unearthly cruelty he cherishes it, he nourishes this spawn till he can marry it on its death-bed to the younger Catherine, the child of Catherine Earnshaw and of Edgar

Linton. This supreme deed accomplished, he lets the creature die, so that Thrushcross Grange may fall into his hands. Judged by his bare deeds Heathcliff seems a monster of evil, a devil without any fiery internal splendor: a mean and sordid devil.

His love for Catherine never fades. When she dies in child-birth he implores her to haunt him and sixteen years later he believes that she does haunt him. He is tortured and delighted by her elusive presence. He abstains from food or sleep and dies in a strange ecstasy, seeing her in his arms. Nothing more uncanny, scarcely anything more moving, is found in English fiction.

What can we read of Emily's mind in this theme? That she loved solitude we know, but though silent she was cheerful; she was liked by the villagers, beloved by her family. She never had nervous tremors and phobias like Charlotte nor religious melancholy and despondency like Anne. Nor did she need the refuge of drugs like Branwell. She never complained aloud of loneliness or friendlessness. The fragments of her diaries show an active spirit, viewing the past with satisfaction, looking toward the future. She looked death in the face and was not afraid. She showed this in her memorable poem beginning "No coward soul is mine," the poem referred to by Matthew Arnold in his stanza quoted above.

Yet, as Maeterlinck says, to write of passion and the deep springs of life as she wrote she must have known them.

My guess—it is no more—is that the early loss of her mother and then of the elder sister gave her a tragic sense of deprivation heightened by experiences of coldness and severity from her father. There is a parallel to this in Freud's study of Leonardo da Vinci and Abraham's of the artist Segantini. In Leonardo da Vinci and in Segantini there was reproach for the mother who deserted her child so early, together with a deep attachment that showed itself in preoccupation with the mother-theme in painting the theme of mother and nature. Emily has little to say of motherhood but much of nature, her adopted mother. She seemed to feel herself a very child of earth and others said of her that she was akin to the Titans.

Her surviving sisters were two years older and one year younger than herself, and she must have recognized her own mental superiority to both. The feminine maternal influence was lacking, therefore. She could not consciously remember her mother, and she was but six when the eldest sister died.

The introjection of the mother was certainly much altered here. All the influences that help most to make ties of affection and sociability and that cultivate the more positive emotions were attenuated if not absent. The brief possession of mother-love followed by early loss left a sharp, unchanged, unsoftened, unassimilated body of childish feeling and mental processes that can hardly be called thoughts. The dream-like quality of much of her writing, together with her vivid and forceful description, indicated the existence of such an unconscious mind near the surface where it could be used. Two of her dominant traits—those referred to by those who knew her as the leading traits of her character—her love of her native heath, and her love of solitude and of liberty, grew out of this loss and the feeling of being unloved. Nature became her mother as nature is the mother in our dreams and myths. She was thrown on herself and she made herself and Mother Nature sufficient. She disowned the cruel human parents. The lonely existence imposed by circumstances she deliberately made more solitary in order to prove her self-dependence and to claim her absolute liberty. Her poem of "The Old Stoic" voices this desire:

> Riches I hold in light esteem,
>   And love I laugh to scorn;
> And lust of fame was but a dream,
>   That vanished with the morn:
>
> And if I pray, the only prayer
>   That moves my lips for me
> Is, "Leave the heart that now I bear,
>   And give me liberty!"

> Yes, as my swift days near their goal,
>   'Tis all that I implore;
> In life and death a chainless soul,
>   With courage to endure.

She would have no other abiding place than that given her by fate. This is shown in the dream she imputes to Catherine, heroine of *Wuthering Heights:*

"Nelly, do you never dream queer dreams?" said Catherine, suddenly, after some minutes' reflection.

"Yes, now and then," I answered.

"And so do I. I've dreamt in my life dreams that have stayed with me ever after and changed my ideas: they've gone through and through me like wine through water, and altered the color of my mind. And this one; I'm going to tell it—but take care not to smile at any part of it."

Nelly refuses to hear her dream but after some arguing she tells it. She dreamed she died and went to heaven and—

"This is nothing," cried she; "I was only going to say that Heaven did not seem to be my home; and I broke my heart with weeping to come back to earth; and that the angels were so angry that they flung me out into the middle of the heath on the top of Wuthering Heights, where I woke sobbing for joy. That will do to explain my secret, as well as the other. I've no more business to marry Edgar Linton than I have to be in heaven and if the wicked man in there hadn't brought Heathcliff so low, I shouldn't have thought of it."

The intense love Emily had for the moors inspired some of her loveliest verses, the exquisite description from *Wuthering Heights,* and even perhaps a part of the spirit of that rugged, imaginative yet strongly realistic story. Charlotte said of her: "My sister Emily loved the moors. Flowers brighter than the rose bloomed in the blackest of the heath for her; out of a sullen hollow in a livid hill-side her mind could make an Eden. She found in the bleak solitude many and dear delights; and not the least and best loved was liberty."

There was something, too, in the vast rolling hills, with

their sparse vegetation and absence of animal life, that almost irresistibly suggests the dominance of a stern and immovable fate. The influence of the country in which she lived might be compared to the influence of the heath in Hardy's novels; for instance, in the *Return of the Native*, where one feels that the real mover of the story and the fate which seems to drive the characters on to their destiny is the heath itself.

So, in *Wuthering Heights*, Heathcliff and Catherine as well as some of the minor characters are native products of the moors themselves. Catherine's moods are the changing moods of the moor in storm and wind, sunshine and beating rain. Stories and poems, too, are native to the land, not so much because they copy faithfully any inhabitant of the country as because they express the nature and spirit of the country itself. Nothing could have produced this closely knit relationship of soul to earth except a strongly felt bond like unto the bond of child to parent, a bond that is felt entirely in the unconscious, and never consciously analyzed and put in its place.

Her love of liberty which again has been so emphasized and which her own poems have expressed over and over did not come so much as her critics have imagined from her love of the moors but rather from her rebellion against the father. The two traits—love of nature and love of liberty—are coordinates rather than cause and effect. She was too clear-sighted and too independent, too free from either fear or convention, not to pass judgment on those about her, whether society placed them above or below her. Just as she never hesitated to resist the authority of her Brussels professor—somewhat to his astonishment—so she did not fail to see clearly the faults and shortcomings of her authoritative father and her spoiled brother. There was a necessity to free herself from the domination of these false gods, and this necessity led her to insist upon her liberty.

Father and brother meant much to her but they gave no

high ideal of manhood to revere. She could not bow in subjection, as Charlotte did, to such as these. She felt the compulsion of the awe the small child feels for the shadowy,
powerful parent, but she rebelled and renounced allegiance.
So she became herself the traitor unloved, unblessed, that she
pictures in her poems. She orphaned herself. You may, if you
choose, draw a parallel between this and some of the manifestations of the castration complex, as the latter is typical of
the conflict arising from the loss of the darling object.

Furnishing a parallel to the doomed child and the traitor
idea, I had a patient in whose free associations the words
regicide and *renegade* frequently occurred (without her understanding their significance), for some time. Finally began to
come out that which she held back longest, through loyalty—
namely, the fact that she had early ceased to respect her father
because he was weak in character though able, financially successful, kindly and loved. She was therefore a traitor, a renegade, and a regicide (king killer) for thus repudiating him. This
analysis has helped me to understand a little more of Emily
Brontë whose character had long been an enigma. She had
here in her unconscious soul a conflict that brought much
knowledge, its source unguessed, of feeling and passion.

The patient referred to had felt deeply her father's desertion
of her. He made a pet of her in babyhood but withdrew
all demonstrations of affection soon because he submitted himself to his wife who was insanely jealous of her only daughter.
His weakness in this submission inspired the daughter's contempt, and at the same time made her doubt her own worth.
This case is, of course, not parallel to Emily Brontë's but
some of the psychology in it illustrates what may be found
in Emily's childhood. Emily's father respected her genius, by
his own testimony, yet apparently he never showed her much
attention. First Maria, and then Charlotte, were his chosen
companions. Branwell received his chief care. Emily discloses

no memory of their mother, but Charlotte records that her only memory of her was of seeing her playing with Branwell in the parlor in the evenings. The aunt who lived with them was fondest of Branwell and Anne. Emily very probably felt herself left out and unloved by anyone. It does not take a long and consistent course of slights to make a child feel this. A few instances of neglect loom large in memory, completely blotting from thought many and continuous quiet instances of love. Those who have observed families of children closely as well as those who have analyzed the childhood jealousies of their patients have seen this. The little Emily was an unloved, perhaps an unwanted, child—in her own imagination. If so, then she must be an unattractive child, one who had nothing to win love—for so she must have reasoned in typical child fashion. She never in later years developed any coquetry or made the slightest attempt to render herself physically attractive. She made no effort to win any regard. People who act so are either satisfied with the regard they have won or else they think their cause hopeless and in pride refuse to make an effort. Emily does not belong to the former class.

We know too little of the actual incidents of the Brontës' early life to say what actual rebuffs may have led to the despair expressed in "The Doomed Child" theme. Charlotte's *Jane Eyre* abounds in incidents of cruelty and unfeeling harshness in the treatment of children, and Emily's *Wuthering Heights* is worse. What experience had the sisters that stimulated their imagination thus? An unjust punishment, convincing her that she was unloved, might have come to Emily's share more than once. All the dark thoughts that arose at such a time were revived and reapplied through her fruitless adolescence and found expression in the hero of the secret Gondal Chronicles and in Heathcliff. These creatures were the gloomy self-condemned other self of Emily.

That she embodied this self in a masculine creature is the

outcome of her desire, felt in childhood and later repudiated as we shall see, to be a boy. No girl-child in the Brontë family could fail to see the advantages accruing to masculinity. At the same time the anger and contempt inspired by the father and brother led to the suppression of all active envy and the feminism expressed in the novels of the two older sisters.

But where save from these two and her dual self, was she to get knowledge of heterosexual love? Maeterlinck, in his chapter on Emily Brontë in *Wisdom and Destiny*, has this to say:

Love never came to her; there fell never once on her ear the lover's magical footfall; and, for all that, this virgin . . . has known love, has spoken of love, has penetrated its most impenetrable secrets to such a degree, that those who have loved the most deeply must sometimes uneasily wonder what name they should give to the passion they feel, when she pours forth the words, exaltation and mystery of love beside which all else seems pallid and casual. Where, if not in her heart, has she heard the matchless words of the girl, who speaks to her nurse of the man who is hated and harassed by all, but whom she wholly adores? "My great miseries in this world have been Heathcliff's miseries, and I watched and felt each from the beginning; my great thought in living is himself. If all else perished, and *he* remained, *I* should still continue to be; and if all else remained, and he were annihilated, the universe would turn to a mighty stranger; I should not seem a part of it. My love for Linton is like the foliage in the woods: time will change it, I'm well aware, as winter changes the trees. My love for Heathcliff resembles the eternal rocks beneath—a source of little visible delight, but necessary. Nelly, I *am* Heathcliff! He's always in my mind: not as a pleasure any more than I am. a pleasure to myself, but as my being. . . ."

She has but little acquaintance with the external realities of love, and these she handles so innocently at times as almost to provoke a smile; but where can she have acquired her knowledge of those inner realities, that are interwoven with all that is most unexpected, most impossible, and most eternally true? We feel she must have lived for thirty years beneath burning chains of burning kisses to learn what she has learned; to dare so confidently set forth, with such minuteness, such unerring certainty, the delirium of those two predestined lovers of *Wuthering Heights*; to mark the self-conflicting movement of the tenderness that would make suffer and the cruelty that would make glad, the felicity that prayed for death and the despair that clung to life; the repulsion that desired, the desire drunk with repulsion—love surcharged with hatred, hatred staggering beneath its load of love. . . .

And yet it is known to us—for in this poor life of hers all lies open—that she neither loved nor was loved.

The identification of the personalities of the lovers, Heathcliff and Catherine, is given again in this passage from *Wuthering Heights:*

"It would degrade me to marry Heathcliff now, so he shall never know how I love him; and that, not because he's handsome, Nelly, but because he's more myself than I am. Whatever our souls are made of his and mine are the same; and Linton's is as different as a moonbeam from lightning, or frost from fire."

Mrs. Humphrey Ward says, concerning Emily's sources of information about men:

Emily knew less of men personally than Charlotte. But she had no illusions about them, and Charlotte had many. Emily is the true creator, using the most limited material in the puissant, detached impersonal way that belongs only to the highest gifts—the way of Shakespeare. Charlotte is often parochial, womanish, and morbid in her imagination of men and their relation to women; Emily who has known two men only, her father and brother, and derives all other knowledge of the sex from books, from Tabby's talk in the kitchen, from the forms and features she passes in the village street, or on the moors—Emily can create a Heathcliff, a Hareton Earnshaw, a Joseph, an Edgar Linton with equal force, passion, and indifference. All of them up to a certain point, owing to the fact that she knew nothing of certain ground truths of life, are equally false; but beyond that point all have the same magnificent, careless truth of imagination. She never bowed before her creatures, in a sort of personal subjection to them, as Charlotte did.[3]

71

It is true that she had a wide reading of eighteenth century literature, so much freer and franker than the Victorian era was allowed to be, but not out of books does one get such vital and accurate and true penetration of the movements of the psyche as she gives us in *Wuthering Heights*. Charlotte's explanation was that Emily, while she had almost no actual contact with her neighbors, knew the secret histories of many of the old families living within twenty-five miles of them and used in her novel the tales of love and greed and vengeance she heard the servants retail. Charlotte said, and rightly, that though Emily rarely exchanged a word with these people she knew them and their country so thoroughly through these stories and through her deep and intimate sympathy with them, that she could not fail to represent them truly. All this is true—Emily gleaned knowledge from books and from the countryside, but the inner knowledge of passion comes only through the interpretation of what one sees and hears by that which one has felt within himself. The artistic genius is he who can transmute his own experience into forms of expression that serve to convey universal experience, and can understand and render universal experience, in turn, by means of his own experience. This faculty Emily Brontë had in even greater degree than Charlotte. Of both women G. K. Chesterton said:

Upon the whole, therefore, I think it may justifiably be said that the dark wild youth of the Brontës, in their dark wild home, has been somewhat exaggerated as a necessary factor in their work and their conception. The emotions with which they dealt were universal emotions of *the morning of existence*, the springtide joy and the springtide terror. Every one of us as a boy or girl has had some midnight dream of nameless obstacle and unutterable menace in which there was, under whatever imbecile forms, all the deadly stress and panic of Wuthering Heights. Every one of us has had a daydream of our own potential destiny not one atom more reasonable than Jane Eyre.

Emily knew but two men, indeed, but she knew them with an intimacy and intensity, and an emotional interest combined with a detachment and judgment that enabled her to use their complex and ill-balanced characters as a basis for all the men she drew. Not so much added to their known images as filling their lifeless molds with an inner life was the personality that she felt and perceived most clearly of all—her own emotion-torn self. The real core of her characters is still Emily. For Charlotte the childhood conception of fatherly love was the ideal on which her romances were constructed, because Charlotte knew herself the well-beloved of her father. For Emily the shape assumed by the Family Romance was that of frustration, hideous conflicts, despair, death, because she felt herself the unloved.

She knew practically nothing of the physical side of love; she knew a great deal of the psychological side because the psychological basis of adult love is contained in the ardent and wild passion of the Family Romance of childhood. And this early romance remained unchanged, unvitiated by the normal series of transferences and the normal integrations at higher levels of sexual development. Elemental feelings that usually remain buried or express themselves indirectly are very frankly given vent by her—calling forth the accusation from her Early Victorian world of brutality and coarseness in her novel.

The masculine traits of Emily Brontë have come in for a good deal of attention. How far they were native and how far, consciously and unconsciously, cultivated, it is difficult to determine. There was little of the masculine in her physical appearance and little in her tasks and occupations, which were largely domestic, but there was that direct and objective quality of mind which is called masculine, that impatience of detail and independence of the personal, which were, in her time, at least, considered foreign to the feminine temperament.

She herself, as Charlotte tells us, was quite intolerant, however, of the prevalent notion that certain qualities were the peculiar and exclusive attributes of men, and others of women. When some readers of *Wuthering Heights* thought the character of Edgar Linton showed a gentleness, a patient kindness and constancy that were too feminine, Emily repudiated such an opinion with scorn. Men could be tender and constant, women could be hardy and daring; sex is irrelevant to moral qualities; such was her more modernistic view. She, like Charlotte, thought that women should work, and that occupations should be open to them as freely as to men. They perceived that women's inferior position was an artificial creation of society and Emily apparently never showed any particular deference to the lords of that creation. She graciously served father and brother in conscious superiority. Possibly this was a compensation for a feeling of female inferiority impressed on her in early childhood and later repressed, as some have suggested.

It has been shown, however, in psychoanalysis of many cases, that boyish traits have been carefully nurtured—till at last they became second nature—by little girls as a reaction to their rejection by the father. If they cannot be the beloved mate and companion their infantile wishes portray, they seek to propitiate and please by imitating and competing with the all-powerful man. Girls are not wanted, so they will be boys. This has been found true of living patients under analysis; it may have been true of Emily Brontë when she felt, somewhere in early childhood, that she had lost her father's love. This sense of rejection—the sense of frustration of love impulses—has proved much more powerful in generating masculine strivings than a mere sense of inferiority derived from seeing the obvious physical, sexual, and social advantages of men. It seems more in keeping with the other facts of Emily's personality.

That the keynote of her personality was compensation for

many privations one cannot doubt, nor can one doubt that much of her compensating activity was unconscious. Primordial feeling is found fresh and unvitiated in her novel and her poems. Chesterton has spoken of the powerful effect of *Wuthering Heights* on the emotions, and has called the book the expression of the "springtide joy and the springtide terror." This characterization is profoundly true. Nothing ever came into Emily's life to add to or to modify the simple, strong primordial emotional attachments and repulsions of early life. When she gives herself to self-expression in writing, these emotions come out with the force and power of an icebound torrent suddenly released. The ego is scarcely present. The unchanged unconscious self speaks with as much freedom, almost, as it speaks in the psychotic. *Wuthering Heights* expresses that which is deepest, most terrible, and most beautiful in human life. The passions in it are as universal as those of Greek tragedy.

Some of the most discerning critics of the time saw this depth in it, but to most it was coarse and brutal. Dante Rosetti said of it, "The best novel I have read for an age, except 'Sidonia.' But it is a fiend of a book; the action is laid in Hell, only it seems the places and people have English names there." Such glimpses of hell come to mortals when some of the background of the buried unconscious emerges into the light of day.

Yet this novel whose scene is laid in hell ends in a note of peace. Heathcliff's death is the climax of the story—a death that unites him with his lost Catherine. The country people claim he "walks": a little shepherd boy is found weeping because he sees "Heathcliff and a woman" under the hill and he does not dare pass them. In the closing paragraph the narrator of the story after comforting the little shepherd visits the churchyard where Catherine, Edgar Linton (her husband), and Heathcliff (her lover) are buried, and he is made to say,

75

"I lingered around them, under that benign sky; watched the moths fluttering among the heath and harebells, listened to the soft wind breathing through the grass, and wondered how any-one could ever imagine unquiet slumbers for the sleepers in that quiet earth."

The tragic struggle and stress of the story, ending in the peace of death, shows Emily Brontë's conception of her own life. Out of privation, rebellion, struggle, she brought the peace that comes from shutting out from her world all the elements that challenged her self-mastery and threatened to bring uneasy realization of her weaknesses; and self-contained, she lived to rule supreme in her inner world. She made life so narrow in its external dimensions that no adverse winds could shake her out of her calm. No other human being had power over her. No other Brontë had this peace of hers, not Charlotte with her nervous terrors and headaches, not Anne, with her trembling despondency, not raving, blubbering Bran-well, nor the proud, selfish old father. Emily overcame every conflict she could, sublimated almost every passion, and ignored or fled from those that were too powerful for her. She could admit no superior; to do so would destroy her peace.

She formed her own religion, leaving out the submission of the orthodox Christian. Having made her own world, in which she could live undisturbed, she then made her God, recogniz-ing Him in the spirit within. That "too bold dying song" to which Matthew Arnold refers in his lines on Emily Brontë contained in his poem "Haworth Churchyard" gives us her conception of her relation to divinity. Not unorthodox, but carrying the challenge of her soul to the infinite and proclaim-ing that *she* need not bow or tremble:

No coward soul is mine,
   No trembler in the world's storm-troubled sphere.
I see Heaven's glories shine,
   And faith shines equal, arming me from fear.

76

O God within my breast,
  Almighty, ever-present Deity!
Life that in me has rest,
  As I—undying Life—have power in thee!

Though earth and man were gone,
  And suns and universes ceased to be,
And Thou were left alone,
  Every existence would exist in Thee.

There is not room for Death,
  Nor atom that his might could render void:
Thou—Thou art Being and Breath
  And what Thou art may never be destroyed.

She is one with her God. The father has been vanquished, overcome, appropriated, united with her.

What conclusion, then, can we draw as to the springs of the character and genius of Emily Brontë? To me it seems that it is the very isolation, the very barrenness of her life that accounts for a part of her power. There was no deadening influence of mass education, and there was no contact with the ironclad rules of conventional society. There was no demand for conformity to other people's views and thoughts. All of us who have had contact with young children have been surprised and delighted sometimes at the freshness and originality of the childish imaginative productions. Fond parents are perhaps not unjustified when they see budding geniuses although their hopes are never fulfilled. If we observe, we may see what irresistible pleasure most adults take in suppressing the sprouting of different ideas in the young and how much spontaneous resentment is aroused in adults toward any young person that dares to be original in their presence.

Charlotte Brontë gave a perfect and beautifully satirical embodiment of this adult spirit in the character of Mrs. York in *Shirley*. The Brontës probably met this spirit in their puritanical withered and prudent aunt, Miss Branwell, who kept house for them; and in their brief experience at school away from home. But fortunately these influences were too few and far between to have the totally blighting effect on them that they have on most. It is to be noted that Emily Brontë was the least of all subjected to influences outside her home.

That isolation and exclusive and concentrated family life alone could produce such a literary genius, of course, no one would seriously claim. The Brontës had in their childhood constant incentive to literary labor. They had little to do except to read and their father spent much of his time in writing verses and essays. This combination of a literary tradition and environment with complete seclusion from all vitiating influences, taken with the interaction of passionate, spirited, and emotional natures upon each other is perhaps what is needed to explain this family of genius. It has been the wonder of the literary world that such remarkable work came out of such rude and unpromising surroundings; by the psychoanalytical theory the surroundings are favorable rather than otherwise and the wonder would be if such genius should flower in just this way in conventional and populous surroundings. If, for instance, the Brontës had been born in a London suburb, had lived the usual community and neighborhood life in such a place, had received the usual education given to girls, had had the usual social distractions, would they have written such books as *Jane Eyre, Villette*, and *Wuthering Heights*? I do not think anyone could answer "yes."

Emily Brontë sought freedom, emancipation from wild conflict and dependence, in sublimation through physical and mental work. She sought substitutes for sustaining human love in nature. By confining her life within very narrow social limits she made her inner freedom effectual and attained a calm and poised carriage that effectually hid, even from herself, the raging conflicts underneath. She did for herself what is done for the inmates of sanitariums in simplifying her environment. She refused to be moved by praise or censure and would have preferred to avoid both by keeping her productions to herself, or by showing them only to her faithful little sister Anne. She was genuinely provoked to anger when Charlotte discovered her poems. Having given up hope of approval in early childhood, she put behind her the childish desire for it, and held proudly aloof.

Yet to those who knew her this isolation was not repellent. The villagers who came into her kitchen loved her; she was the best loved of the family by sisters and brother. This love and the happy companionship of the sisters and brother in their youth furnished the imagination for the brighter and softer parts of her work and inspired the passionate love of her home. There were two sides of her nature, separated and opposed: the brighter, less suppressed self that lived in everyday companionship with her family and the darker, despairing, rebellious one that grew from the bitter grief of a child who fancied herself unloved. This darker one spoke audibly only in her writings. The two selves furnished the contrasts in character for her novel. So in all things she is self-contained, self-circumscribed, and all her power is poured into the one outlet, her writing.

She professed to be "content and undesponding" as she states in one of the little letters she and Anne exchanged to be opened on future birthdays (July 30, 1845, was the date of this one). Perhaps she was. Her life flowed tranquilly under her own control. We know her conflict from her writing and from her seclusion, from her inability to live away from home or to meet the more complex life situations. Out of the conflict itself she developed the power that has given her a lasting fame.

1928

NOTES

1. May Sinclair. *The Three Brontës*. Hutchinson & Co., London, 1912.

2. Emily Brontë. *Wuthering Heights*. Thornfield Edition; introduction by Mrs. Humphrey Ward. Harper & Bro., N. Y., 1900, p. xxiii.

3. Charlotte Brontë. *Shirley*. Thornfield Edition, introduction by Mrs. Humphrey Ward. Harper & Bro., N. Y. & London, 1900, p. xxi.

◫ KAFKA:

FATHER AND SON

Max Brod

All his life Franz Kafka stood in the shadow of his father's powerful personality. Hermann Kafka was physically impressive: tall, broad-shouldered. His long life had been filled with hard work, rewarded by considerable success in business, burdened by much sickness. He left behind him a large family of children and grandchildren in whom he took a patriarchal pleasure. And after the wholesale house on the Altstädter Ring had been sold, his estate still included a four-story apartment house in the center of Prague. By his own labors and sacrifices he had built up an extensive family and kept it going. This achievement, taking hold of his son's imagination, left its mark on all his work.

In November, 1919 Kafka wrote a lengthy and detailed *Letter to My Father*. More than a hundred pages long, the letter was, as I gathered from conversations with Franz, really intended to be given to his father (through his mother); and Franz believed at the time that in this way he could clarify the painfully deadlocked relation between them. Had the letter been delivered, the effect would in all probability have been the opposite of what Franz intended; it could scarcely have helped the father to understand the son. But in any case Frau Kafka did not deliver it: with a gentle word or two she returned it to Franz. And after that we spoke no more of the matter.

"Dear Father," it begins. "You once asked me why I claimed to be afraid of you. As usual I could find no answer, partly because I *was* afraid of you, partly because my fear was too complex to talk about." There follows a detailed analysis of the relationship between this strange father and this strange child, together with a study of his own character, that amounts to a short autobiography. Here and there the perspective appears to me distorted; facts are found in combination with unwarranted assumptions; from seemingly trivial perceptions there emerges an edifice of almost unfathomable complexity; and in the end the whole structure explicitly turns on its own axis, seems at once to refute itself and yet to remain valid. In conclusion Kafka makes the father himself speak, as if in reply:

"While I openly and sincerely attribute the sole blame to you, you try to outdo yourself in 'cleverness' and 'tenderness' by acquitting me of all blame. Of course your success in this is purely illusory (you do not want more) and, despite your phrases about 'being' and 'nature,' 'contradiction' and 'help-lessness,' it can be read between the lines that I was the real aggressor, while you acted purely in self-defense. You really should be satisfied with the results of your disingenuousness, for you have succeeded in proving three things: first that you are innocent, second that I am guilty, and third that out of pure magnanimity you are prepared, not only to pardon me, but what is at once more and less, to prove, and yourself to believe, that I, contrary of course to the actual truth of the matter, am also innocent. That might have been enough for you, but you go still further. You make up your mind to live entirely at my expense. I admit that we fight one another, but there are two kinds of combat. The chivalrous sort, in which two independent opponents measure their strength, in which each exists for himself, loses for himself, and wins for himself. And the sort waged by an insect, which not only stings, but also sucks blood to preserve its own life. That is in the character of the true professional sodier, which is what you are. You are unfit for life; but to make things comfortable and easy for yourself and to spare yourself any self-reproach, you prove that I have robbed you of all your fitness for life and put it in my pocket." (These remarks cast considerable light on the genesis of Franz Kafka's "insect story," *Metamorphosis*, and also on *The Judgment*.)

The central theme of the whole letter can be summed up in the following formula: the son's weakness as compared to the father's arrogant strength. Yet, Kafka was aware that the contradictions were not as sharp and simple as the letter makes out. This awareness, inevitable in a work of Kafka's, runs through the entire text, becoming most pronounced in the concluding words, which are the most conciliatory in the entire piece:

"Living facts cannot of course fit together like the demonstrations in my letter; life is more than a Chinese puzzle; but with the correction resulting from this fact—a correction which I cannot and have no wish to execute in detail—I believe that something very close to the truth will have been achieved. This should have a soothing effect on the two of us and make both life and death easier."

With this reservation, the contradiction between the two characters is sharply delineated. The letter stresses the difference in the heredity of the two families from which Franz Kafka sprang: the shy, eccentric Löwys on his mother's side, and the strong, realistic Kafkas. "Compare the two of us: I, to oversimplify, a Löwy with something of the Kafka at the base, which however does not express itself in the Kafka will to life, business, conquest. . . . You, on the other hand, a real Kafka, as to strength, health, appetite, loudness of voice, eloquence, self-reliance, endurance, presence of mind, knowledge of people, a certain *largesse*, and, of course, all the faults and weaknesses belonging to your very virtues; weaknesses that are brought out by your changing moods and sometimes by your temper." To this compare the qualities which Franz (in another work) describes as his heritage from his mother's family: "sensitivity, sense of justice, restlessness."

Toward the end of the letter, Kafka, in speaking of his vain attempt to get married, again paints an animated portrait of his father. "The most important obstacle to my marriage," he writes, "is the ineradicable conviction that the support and conduct of a family require everything that I have recognized in you, the good and the bad together, as you organically combine them: strength and arrogance; health and a certain immoderation; eloquence and unwillingness to listen; self-confidence and contempt for the abilities of others; power over men and an inclination to tyranny; knowledge of people and mistrust toward most. Not to mention such unmixed virtues as diligence, endurance, presence of mind, fearlessness. Such are your qualities—mine by comparison seem next to nothing. Could I, thus equipped, venture into wedlock, when I saw that even you had to struggle hard in your marriage and were positively deficient in your relations with your children? Of course I did not ask myself this question so explicitly; otherwise my common sense would have shown me men quite different from you (Uncle R., for instance), who had married and at least not collapsed under the strain—a considerable accomplishment, that would have been plenty for me. But I did not ask this question, I *experienced* it from childhood on. I examined myself not only in reference to marriage, but in my relation to every trifling matter. Everywhere you convinced me of my incapacity, both by your example and by your training (as I have attempted to describe it). And what was true in connection with trifles could not help but apply to the greatest step of all: marriage."

Here it seems impossible to deny the applicability to Kafka's case of Freud's theories of the subconscious. And yet this interpretation seems too facile. For one thing Franz Kafka himself was thoroughly familiar with these theories and never regarded them as anything more than a very approximate, rough picture of things. He found that they did not do justice to details or, what is more, to the essence of the conflict. In the following pages I shall attempt a different interpretation of the facts, by adducing the example of Kleist. For the present, however, it must be admitted that Kafka himself, in stating that he had not explicitly, or "in ordinary thinking," formulated his attitude toward his father's superiority, but had "experienced it from childhood on," seems to confirm the psychoanalytical point of view. So do his remarks on his father's "methods of training"—amplified in numerous diary entries dealing with his "miscarried education"; and his letters on pedagogy, based on Swift's thesis that "children should be brought up outside of the family, not by their parents."

The greater part of the letter, in fact, is devoted to his father's type of "training." "I was a timid child," says Kafka. "However, I was assuredly headstrong, as children are; it is true that my mother spoiled me, but I cannot believe that I was more intractable than the average. I can't help thinking that a friendly word, a guiding hand, a gentle glance would have obtained any results desired. At bottom you are a kindly, soft-hearted person (the following does not contradict this; I am speaking only of the outward form in which you affected the child); but it is not every child who has the endurance and the courage to keep on searching until he finds kindness.

In your dealings with a child, you could not help but be your own violent, noisy, hot-tempered self; as a matter of fact you thought your methods calculated to produce a strong, courageous boy."

His father's unfavorable judgments regarding Franz's recreations, his friends, his whole manner of being and acting, were an intolerable burden to him; they caused him to despise himself. Yet the father did not always adhere to his own judgments and rules, and this very lack of logic seemed to the son in retrospect a sign of his untrammeled vitality, his integrity of will. "By your own unaided strength you had worked yourself up so high that you had unlimited confidence in your opinions . . . in your easy chair you ruled the world. Your opinion was correct, and every other was crazy, hysterical, *meshugge,* abnormal. Your self-confidence was so great that you could be inconsistent without ceasing to be right. Sometimes you had no opinion at all in a certain matter, and then all opinions that were possible on the subject had without exception to be wrong. For instance, you might curse at the Czechs, then at the Germans, then at the Jews, not for any particular qualities but for everything at once, and in the end there was no one left but you. For me you became imbued with the mysterious something that is proper to all tyrants whose right is based not on thought, but on their own person."

Here we might recall the prominent rôle played in Kafka's works not only by the concept of human dignity or democracy, but also by the principle of authority (see *The Trial, The Castle,* and all the stories and fragments that make up *The Great Wall of China*).

Why did Kafka need his father? Or, more correctly, why was he unable to free himself from his father despite his critical attitude toward him; why did he not, like so many children, build a protective wall between himself and his parent? Or rather, since he actually did create such a barrier and in later years almost ceased to speak to his father: why did he suffer so deeply from the coldness between them? Must he not have known that between characters so diverse as himself and his father an intimate relationship was simply impossible? Franz in any case was able to understand his father; he was more than fair in his loving admiration of him—but the father by his very nature, and of course without any blame, as the letter repeatedly emphasizes, was hopelessly closed to any understanding of his son's peculiar character. Even in my friend's lifetime, when I had no knowledge of his diaries, I realized how deeply this wounded him, but it was vainly that I tried to convince him how foolish he was in overestimating his father and belittling himself. The swarm of arguments on which Kafka based his case (when he did not, as frequently happened, prefer to say nothing) actually did succeed in shaking me for the moment.

The life and death of all his own aims and desires—says Kafka in the letter—depended on his father's judgment (see *The Judgment*). He writes: "My courage, decision, confidence, joy in a thing did not endure if you were opposed to it, or if your opposition could even be surmised; and I surmised it in almost everything I did. . . . In your presence I developed a halting, stuttering speech—you are an excellent speaker as long as you are speaking of the things that interest you—but even my halting speech was too much for you, and ultimately I stopped talking altogether, at first for spite, and then because I could neither talk nor think in your presence. And since you were my actual teacher, this affected everything in my life." Here we encounter an interesting parallel: Kleist is also said to have stuttered. Kafka's stuttering, indeed, can only be applied to his relations with his father; otherwise, whenever he opened his mouth at all, he spoke freely, easily, elegantly, often humorously, with a charming, overflowing fantasy and disarming naturalness.

87

According to the letter, the results of his "training" (and here Kafka offers his own commentary to the final words of *The Trial*) was as follows: "I had lost my self-confidence in your presence, and exchanged for it a boundless consciousness of guilt. It was this sense of guilt that I had in mind when I aptly wrote of a certain person: 'He is afraid that his shame will survive him.'" Kafka then construes his further life as a series of attempts to break away from his father, to attain to regions removed from his father's influence. It is remarkable that Kafka, who in his judgment of literary works absolutely rejects all lifeless, abstract "constructions," should in this case himself employ "constructions" which, along with correct elements, contain many half-truths and distortions. Thus, for example, he attempts to classify his entire literary work under the general heading of "attempt at flight from his father," as if his love of artistry, his creative pleasure had no existence of their own. Those who knew him were, of course, far from accepting the simple picture of a man tortured by a father complex. They saw in him a man inspired by form, creative will and ability, thirst for knowledge, a love of life and humanity. A component, though no more than a component, was that aspect of his literary work which the letter so movingly describes: "You were the subject of my books," he writes. "In them I poured out the sorrows that I could not pour out on your breast. My writing has been purposely drawn-out parting from you. But though this parting was forced by you, its direction was determined by me."

In the letter Kafka views other aspects of his life as an attempted flight: family, friendship, Judaism, profession, and ultimately his two attempts to marry: "My self-evaluation depended far more on you than on anything else—more even than on outward success. . . . Where I lived I was despised, ill-judged, defeated, and though I exerted myself to the utmost to escape, I did not succeed, for with rare exceptions that was beyond my powers."

His remarks on Judaism as a flight from his father's power may here be mentioned, because they cast an important light on his childhood and also on his later religious development. "I found just as little salvation in Judaism. Here, other things being equal, a salvation was conceivable. Even more likely was the possibility that we should find one another in Judaism or use it as a starting point for further relations. But what sort of Judaism was it that I received from you? In the course of time I have had some three different attitudes toward it.

"As a child I emulated you in reproaching myself for not going to temple often enough, for not fasting, etc. I thought that I was doing an injustice, not to myself but to you, and the consciousness of guilt, which always lurked in readiness, ran through me.

"Later, as a young man, I failed to understand how you, with your pretense of Judaism, could reproach me for not exerting myself (if only for piety, as you put it) in the service of a similar sham. The whole thing, as far as I could see, was a delusion, a joke, not even a joke. Four days in the year you went to temple. When you were there, you were certainly more indifferent than anything else; you patiently ran through the prayers as if they had been a mere formality, and occasionally startled me by your ability to find the place in the prayer book. For the rest, I was permitted—and that was the main thing—to run around wherever I liked. And so I yawned and dozed through many hours there (I think that since then I have never been so bored, except in dancing school) and tried to get as much pleasure as possible out of the few little novelties that occurred, such as when the Ark of the Covenant was opened. This always reminded me of the little box that opened at the shooting galleries when you hit a bullseye, except that in the shooting gallery it was something interesting that came out, while here it was always the same old headless dolls. What is more, I was very much afraid there too, not only, as was natural, because of all the people, but also because you once mentioned in passing that I might be called up to the Torah. This possibility kept me trembling for years. Otherwise I was never seriously disturbed in my boredom, except perhaps by my *bar mitzvah*, which, like a meaningless examination, required only a certain amount of memorizing. And then again my attention was attracted by little insignificant events, as when you were called to the Torah and cut a good figure in this function, which I regarded as purely social; or when in the memorial service you remained in the temple while I was sent away. I did not understand this last occurrence, and for a long time it aroused in me the almost unconscious feeling that something disreputable was going on.

"That was the temple. At home your religion was if possible even more wretched. It was restricted to Passover, which became more and more of a slapstick comedy, though, to be sure, the influence of your growing children had a good deal to do with that. (Why did you have to give in to this influence? Because you were the cause of it.) This was the faith that was handed down to me. Unless I include your pointing out to me 'the sons of F., the millionaire,' who on the principal holidays came to temple with their father. It seemed to me that the best thing to do with such a heritage was to get rid of it as quickly as possible, and this riddance seemed to me the height of piety.

"Later I adopted still a different attitude. I came to understand how you could believe that here too I was maliciously betraying you. You had really brought a certain Judaism with you from your little ghetto-like village community. It was not much, and what there was of it dwindled in the city and the army: yet the impressions and memories of youth did constitute a sort of Jewish life. The fact is that you did not have much need for that sort of sustenance, since you came of a powerful stock and were impervious to religious forces when they were not closely bound up with social considerations. Basically the faith which supported your life was your belief in the unquestionable correctness of the opinions of a certain Jewish social class; since these were your own opinions, your faith was your belief in yourself. This was enough Judaism for you, but for handing down to a child, it was too little; in the transmission it disintegrated entirely. All that remained were a few untransmittable childhood impressions and your much feared person. It was impossible to persuade a child, whose very fright had made him a sharp observer, that the meaningless forms you went through in the name of Judaism, with an indifference suiting their insignificance, could have any higher meaning. For you they held meaning as little memories of former times, and that was why you wanted to pass them on to me; but since even for yourself they had no independent value, you were able to do this only by arguments and threats. This method was, of course, unsuccessful, and since you did not understand your weak position, you became furious at me for my apparent recalcitrance.

"All this is no isolated phenomenon; the same was true of a large part of this transitional generation of Jews, who emigrated from the country, where a relative piety still prevailed, to the city. It was more or less inevitable, but it added one more asperity to our already difficult relationship. I am quite willing for you to believe—as I do—that you are guiltless in this respect; but you should explain your guiltlessness by your character and the nature of the times, not by outward circumstances. You should not say you had too much work and worry to permit you to occupy yourself with such matters. For in this way you turn your indubitable guiltlessness into an unjust reproach to others—a reproach that is very easily countered. For we are here concerned not with any instruction that you should have given your children, but with an exemplary life; if your Jewishness had been stronger, your example would also have been more cogent; this is self-evident and again no reproach, but only a defense against *your* reproaches.

"I have received a certain tardy confirmation of this estimate of your Judaism through your conduct in the last few years, when it seemed to you that I was busying myself more with Jewish matters. You have always been prejudiced in advance against my occupations, and even more so against my enthusiasms. Here you showed the same distaste; yet in this case you might have been expected to make a slight exception, for this was Jewishness of your Jewishness and hence offered the possibility of a new relationship between us. I do not deny that if you had taken any interest in these matters, they might have aroused my suspicions by that very fact; I do not claim to be any better than you in this respect. But the matter never came to a test. Through me Jewishness became repulsive to you, Jewish books unreadable. They 'disgusted you.' This may have been because you insisted that the Judaism you taught me during my childhood was the only true sort and that beyond that there was nothing. But it is hardly thinkable that you should have insisted on this point. In this case your 'disgust' (let us forget for the moment that it was immediately directed not against things Jewish but against my person) could only signify that you unconsciously recognized the weakness of your Jewishness and of my Jewish training, but, not wishing to be reminded of this, replied to all reminders with open hatred. Anyway, the negative importance you attached to my new Jewishness was much exaggerated; in the first place it bore your curse within itself, and moreover, since this sort of development depends largely on the nature of one's relation to one's fellow men, it was in my case doomed to failure."

Compared to Kafka's father, his mother, seen "in the kaleidoscope of childhood," seems "a paragon of reason." Her son indeed deplores her lack of independence toward his father, but also understands it. He understands her love for her husband and realizes that opposition to his will would have been impossible. Yet he resented the fact that his parents formed a sort of unit, a common front against their son, which his mother dared abandon only in secret. This resentment has left a profound trace in Kafka's work. See *Das Ehepaar* ("The Married Couple"), which from this point of view is one of Kafka's most revealing works.

The Kafka household in many ways resembled the Prousts' (see Léon Pierre-Quint: *Marcel Proust, sa vie, son oeuvre:* "His father left home early in the morning and rarely saw his son." His mother, by contrast, "was gentle and kind . . . she watched over him with the utmost care, excusing in advance his fantasies and the careless habits in which he indulged.") If we study the common elements in the relations of Proust and Kafka to their parents we may perhaps begin to understand the similarity in outlook and style of two writers who, though they lived at the same time, never heard of one another. Their special precision in description, their love of detail, their meticulousness; the obsession of both with the family circle, a certain similarity in their racial make-up (Proust's mother was a Jewess) and even in their outward lives—all this encourages comparison, though of course the difference between Proust's cosmopolitan environment and Kafka's bourgeois Prague led to important divergences in their work.

In dealing with cases such as Proust, Kleist, and Kafka who, as long as they lived, never tore themselves away from the domination of family and family tradition, psychoanalysis sets up its theory of subconscious erotic attachment to the mother and subconscious hatred for the father. But there is also a simpler explanation for this attachment to the infantile (though it

93

does not entirely exclude the psychoanalytical). This explanation is that the parents are the first problem confronting the
child, the first resistance he has to deal with; his conflict with
them is the model of all his life struggles to come.

The seriousness and intensity with which this first conflict
(with parents and family) may be felt is shown by the career
of a typically infantile poet: Heinrich von Kleist. All his life
Kleist was haunted by the thought: what will my family (the
extended family circle) say to my omissions and commissions?
Will they trust me? There was bound to be an unbridgeable
gulf between Kleist's old Prussian family, which saw fame
exclusively in the spheres of warfare and government, and
the delicate, emotional, erratic poet. Kleist was literally terror-
ized by the most elevated ethical principles. He knew that in
the eyes of his family his verses and dramas were not much
better than a base and contemptible debauch. Kafka read
Kleist's letters with especial sympathy, underlined passages telling how Kleist's family regarded the poet as "an utterly useless member of human society, unworthy of further consideration." With silent irony Kafka noted in the margin that on
Kleist's hundredth birthday the family had laid a wreath on
the poet's grave with the words: "To the best of our race."

It has often been noted that Franz Kafka's works, especially
in their prose style, show a considerable resemblance to Kleist.[1]
This resemblance cannot be attributed to mere influence. To
my knowledge, no one has yet pointed out the similarity in
their basic attitude. This attitude is, in the truest sense of
the word, "incarnate" in both men. Even their portraits show
a resemblance, at least in the boyishness and purity of their
features. In Kafka's work the central theme is again responsibility toward the family. This is the key to stories such as
Metamorphosis, The Judgment, Der Heizer ("The Stoker")
and many details in other works. Also a special way of using
symbols that are utterly realistic is common to both writers.

94

It is not really so far from Kleist's virgin who, before the eyes of her aristocratic family, is transformed into a pregnant and dishonored woman, to the young man who in the bosom of his family is mysteriously transformed into a contemptible insect. (*Metamorphosis.*)

In both writers there is the same attachment to family and childhood experiences. In both there is the unconscious survival of an austere tradition (in Kleist's case a Prussian tradition refreshed by Kantianism, in Kafka's the Jewish ethics of justice, reawakened by later Jewish studies). In connection with the childlike appearance of Kleist, I might mention one of Kafka's utterances to me: "I shall never experience the age of manhood," he said. "From a child I shall grow directly into a white-haired old man." He often pointed out, even in his diaries, that people thought him very young.

In both men we find an occasional distrust toward the sexual function. Finally, both made excessive demands on themselves, as if they owed it to their family to prove that they were not good-for-nothings. This explains the dislike for every kind of "dependence," that tormented Kafka even in the hungry Berlin winter of 1923 (the last year of his life), when he received packages of food from his parents in Prague.

Finally, Kafka's highest ideal is nowhere better expressed than in Kleist's longing words: "To cultivate a field, to plant a tree, to beget a child." Yet the careers of both men were far removed from the coveted peasant simplicity. The analogy can even be pursued in studying their literary form, though of course we must bear in mind that Kafka consciously learned from Kleist's style. Both writers are remarkable for a sort of fantastic invention that seems to spring from the child's inclination to enchant everything he plays with. These two men actually did know "the way back"—and often traveled it. Their crystal-clear style, their realistic treatment of detail are a compensation, a defense against their childlike dreams.

For both of them describe with the clearest, simplest, most definite words they can possibly find, the most secret, dark, and unresolvable things.

1938

NOTES

1. It is Kleist's long short story, "Michael Kohlhaas" which most directly influenced Kafka, both in his prose style and his treatment of the problem of justice.

AUGUST STRINDBERG: A STUDY OF THE RELATIONSHIP BETWEEN HIS CREATIVITY AND SCHIZOPHRENIA

Theodore Lidz

Some fifty years ago—on 15 May, 1912—an extraordinary procession took place in Stockholm as the populace in tens of thousands silently trudged behind a hearse. This was not the funeral of a king or military hero, but of an isolated man who had long shielded himself from the gaze of his fellow man; one who felt himself an outcast, whose very name had aroused violent antagonism, and who, indeed, had been a target for censure and contumely. Sweden had suffered the loss of August Strindberg, its greatest son, whom it had come to honor and love despite his attacks, his perverse spirit, and his insanity. It seems fitting that at this first meeting of the Psycho-Analytical Association in this city of his birth and death we pay tribute to this man who, even before Freud, sought to probe the deepest depths of the unconscious, recognized and studied the oedipal complex, and left behind a legacy of self-revelation in autobiographies and plays that provides a unique source of information concerning the nature of schizophrenia and the integrative and disintegrative forces playing upon the ego.

I have long been interested in Strindberg as one of the elect dramatists who produced tragedies of timeless interest, but also because he merits study as one who ascended from the Inferno of flagrant schizophrenia with the help of self-scrutiny, catharsis, and the power to create and re-create himself and his world on the stage, to restitute sufficiently to write his series of "dream plays" that provided the model for the contemporary existentialist theater.

We are not intruding into the privacy of a dead and defenseless genius. Strindberg was a scientist as well as an author, ever challenging prescribed truths. As he felt himself slipping into an unreal world, perplexed whether he saw with unwonted clarity or through a screen of paranoid delusion, he started his task of writing the eight volumes of his self-analysis: "I determined to examine my life . . . to make use of all of the resources of psychology . . . to probe the deepest depths . . . I appeal to the reader for a verdict after a careful study of my confession. Perhaps he will find in it elements of the psychology of love, some light on the pathology of the soul, or even some fragment of the philosophy of crime." There can be no verdict, but I shall seek to further the understanding of this tormented soul, and thereby of ourselves and everyman.

Strindberg had certain characteristics often found in dramatists. He lacked a well-integrated ego, and sought an identity in the characters he created from his poorly integrated part identifications. A strong bisexuality permitted an empathy and identification with his female characters. Immobilized from self-realization by deep guilt and by profound ambivalences,

and disillusioned with his parental objects, he early found refuge in a world of his own creation. Envious of the natural creativity of women, he sought compensation in creating persons through his pregnant brain. His greatness, however, derives from his ability to portray the fundamentals of human existence; to become involved with the timeless questions of humanity that preoccupied the Greek tragedians and Shakespeare. Freud wrote: "The hero of the tragedy must suffer . . . to bear the burden of tragic guilt . . . (that) lay in rebellion against some divine or human authority." In Strindberg's plays the characters suffer for their rebelliousness [1] and presumptuousness, but also because they are caught unwittingly in primal conflicts. As all his plays, aside from his historical dramas, are essentially autobiographical, to understand their origins we must understand his own conflicts. His tragedies are all variants of the tragedy of August Strindberg. He was caught up in and preoccupied with the essential problems of human destiny, impelled towards infractions of the basic taboos for which heroes were punished according to age-old myths. He is tormented as Prometheus for defying the gods by freeing mankind; he is punished as Uranos for eating his children lest he be eaten; he not only suffers from parricidal guilt but like Orestes is pursued by the Furies for his matricidal impulses; he is, like Oedipus, driven into exile because of incest; he is caught in the struggle for power between men and women, but like Hercules with Queen Omphale enjoys being enslaved and made to play the woman's role. Such are the guilts and torments Strindberg experienced and for which he provides expiation for the audiences of his plays, experienced with the ego-shattering intensity of schizophrenia rather than simply as creations of his art.

How did Strindberg become enmeshed in these primitive conflicts; and how could he experience them and still retain the mature creativity of genius? These conflicts, indeed, are the essential problems of human tragedy and therefore also of insanity. Strindberg, like Shakespeare before him, portrayed insanity as the ultimate of tragic conflict. In seeking to understand, I shall focus primarily upon the strange circumstances of his first marriage that demolished the tenuous ego defenses that covered the insecurities resulting from a deprived and troubled childhood. To discuss Strindberg's psychosis and his creativity in such simplified terms is particularly onerous, for Strindberg, like Freud, emphasized the overdetermination of human events; but I can here only seek to convey the essence of his basic conflicts.

As Strindberg's schizophrenic development suggests, he experienced grave emotional deprivation and insecurity during his earliest years and came to distrust profoundly the parents whose love and approbation he craved. Strindberg portrays the origins of his timidity, enduring anxiety, disillusion, and feelings of incompletion as an individual in his autobiographical *The Son of a Servant*, which vies with Samuel Butler's *The Way of All Flesh* in its devastating scrutiny of the destructive influences of pious, self-righteous, and unempathic parents who created a family in which the child has no rights and feels betrayed by the mother he wishes to adore. An unwanted child soon displaced by younger sisters, Strindberg felt deprived of a will by being born against his parents' will. Placed between three sons and three daughters, he resembled a girl as much as a boy. Born at the lowest ebb of the family fortunes, when his bourgeois father was in disgrace because he had gone bankrupt and had then married the former servant girl who had been his mistress, Strindberg assimilated his father's shame and fears. Above all, he felt that he had been cut off from maternal nurturance before he had established his own roots. He wrote of himself, "He had come too early and incomplete into the world. What held him so closely bound to his mother? . . . He never became himself, was never liberated,

101

never a complete individuality. He remained, as it were, a mistletoe, which could not live except upon a tree. . . . He seemed to have been born frightened and lived in a continual fear of life and men." When his mother died during his early adolescence, he could no longer seek to complete the unfinished task of establishing a meaningful relationship with her. The children's nurse who soon became his stepmother had little time for Strindberg.

Strindberg had become embittered about his family. "Family," he wrote in retrospect, "thou art the home of all social evil, a charitable institution for comfortable women, an anchorage for fathers, and a hell for children." In the pietist home, he was taught a strict adherence to truth, but learned that truth was a convenience for parents, and justice was arbitrary, applied without understanding. God, like his father, punished for sins of innocence.[2] He would pursue truth throughout his life, challenging the fraudulent in conventions, and fall into disillusionment.

However, there were better times and relatively good years as the family circumstances improved. He became a good scholar, gratifying his father who directed him to become the student of the family. When he left home for the university, "he had not yet found what role he was to play, nor his position in life. . . . He had not yet determined which of his impulses must be restrained, and how much of his 'ego' must be sacrificed for the society into which he was preparing to enter." Still, he had a strength—a strength derived from the conviction that the "truth" he had been taught was false or fraudulent. It was a negative directive of iconoclasm, but behind the rebelliousness lay the search for the person or creed he could trust, and upon which he could build.

His father had sent him to the university, but did not provide support. Strindberg's preconceptions of university life soon faded amidst his grinding poverty and his disillusion in his teachers. He turned to a great variety of ventures seeking to find himself; but his idols had feet of clay; and he was a master at defeating himself. Not until later in life would he realize that because of his "hubris," his insolent defiance of authority, he had to punish himself mercilessly and through attacking authority defeat himself. Freud, like the Greeks before him, recognized that "hubris" was the prologue to tragedy.

The young Strindberg, a man of many talents but no identity, was unable to find his role in life. He taught school; prepared to study medicine; ran off to become an actor; turned playwright with reasonable success for a twenty-year-old; became an artist; a linguist; a telegrapher. He held several jobs as a newspaperman, but always lost them because of his tirades against the established order. He passed through one major crisis. When he became involved in marine insurance, which had been his father's business, by editing a trade journal, he, too, went bankrupt and felt disgraced. Then, in his first serious affair, when the woman with whom he lived for a few days left him for another man he went into a frenzy, dashing headlong through the woods, trampling upon nature and beating upon trees which he envisioned as his enemies. He now recognized that all his relationships with women were disturbed because he was seeking his mother in them, and "the desire for his mother was incest of the soul." However, he recovered his equilibrium and when his future seemed bleak, he gained a post in the Royal Library, a position of prestige, a modest but secure income, and the opportunity for scholarly work that brought international recognition. The period of *Sturm und Drang* appeared to be over; the position provided a role and an identity, and a place in which he could use his talents. But then, at the age of 26, a door opened and he met the Wrangels and was face to face with his fate.

The net was woven from the unfinished strands of Strindberg's childhood: from his longing for a mother he could adore, a father he could admire, and for parents who cherished him; from the discomfort of being the son of an impoverished gentleman married to a servant; from the physical and emotional bleakness of his childhood; from his need to dichotomize women into virgins and prostitutes to avoid the incestuous; from his unrecognized homosexual attractions; from his desire to find completion through blending with a woman.

Strindberg was taken by a woman friend to the home of the Baron and Baroness Wrangel, who were intensely interested in the theater and wished to meet him. He found himself at the house in which he had lived as a youth, where his mother had died, and his father had remarried. He wrote that he half expected to hear his parents scold him when the door opened. Instead of his dowdy mother and his misanthropic father, he was greeted by his dream princess and a handsome captain of the guards, the epitome of masculine nobility. Strindberg did not see Siri Von Essen, the Baroness Wrangel, but the Virgin Mother. "The instinct of worship awoke. The void which had been filled by religion ached no longer; the yearning to adore had reappeared in a new form. God was deposed, but his place was taken by a woman . . . a woman who was both virgin and mother. . . . I worshipped her . . . without her husband my longing to worship could not have been satisfied . . . married to me she could no longer be the wife of this particular man, the mother of this particular child, the mistress of this particular home; . . . was it because of the melancholy recollections which the house had awakened in me?"

The Wrangels were strongly attracted to Strindberg and an intimate friendship immediately developed. Strindberg had found the idealized parental figures—a love object and a figure with whom to identify and whose admiration he sought. The three became inseparable, and when Strindberg followed his premonitions and sought distance, the Wrangels both sought him out and insisted he return. They needed him to bring balance to their marriage. Strindberg's idealization of the Wrangels did not last long. When Siri was in Finland visiting her family, the baron confided that Siri was frigid; this only enhanced Strindberg's image of her, but he was disturbed that the baron, with Siri's consent, was having an affair with her cousin. It soon became apparent that Siri reciprocated Strindberg's love. He sought to flee to Paris, but felt himself going insane without her. He soon found himself in a situation that he could not let himself understand. The Wrangels wished him to become a member of their household. He could have a liaison with Siri while the baron continued his affair with her cousin. The situation makes good sense to an analyst, if not to Strindberg, for Siri admitted having a strong physical attraction for her cousin, and the baron was clearly attracted to Strindberg.

Strindberg could no longer remain the favored child who could worship his parents. "The statue of the Madonna had fallen; woman had shown herself behind the beautiful image, woman treacherous, faithless, with sharp claws!" He sought to save his image of Siri by removing her from the sordid marriage. Identifying with the idealized Siri, he considered the baron's infidelity unbearable to her. He sought to shield himself from the eroticism he felt flow from her into him. Despite his passion, he did not wish to possess her sexually, but his pride and insecure masculinity intervened. He felt that the baron held him in contempt as an asexual child in permitting and even pushing him to be alone with Siri. When, in addition, he believed Siri mocked him as a "Joseph" who refused her seductions, he felt forced to prove his masculinity.

Now he had committed the incest: he had violated the mother-goddess. He was one with Oedipus; with the countless ancient figures real and mythical who paid the penalty of death or castration after serving the sexual needs of the god-

105

dess-queen for a year. The benevolent baron must be turned into the avenging father. Siri was transformed, at times, into the mother who enveloped him and with whom he sought to fuse himself and regain an infantile bliss; at times into a vampire who lived by robbing him of his strength; at times into the faithless, painted harlot. He could not live without her; when separated he "was like an embryo prematurely detached from the umbilical cord." He could not live with her sexually without overwhelming guilt. Still, Siri could not remain with the baron and he persuaded them to divorce.

He did not intend to marry Siri, but simply to free her from the unhappy marriage and lead her to fulfill her dreams of becoming an actress. He could not stand the actress he created who appeared more interested in success and adulation than in him or her child. He found refuge in Paris, but Siri was already pregnant. The ensuing marriage lasted for about fifteen years; years with brief periods of bliss when Siri was an adored mother, and increasingly long and intense periods of bitter hatred, contempt, and physical loathing of her even while he loved. He felt that his wife, any woman, could only love the little boy she mothered, but when "the mother became mistress—horrible!" "The mother is a friend, the woman an enemy, and sexual love is conflict."

I cannot attempt to depict these years of increasing delusion —of intense jealousy, of conviction that Siri was promiscuous, that she was poisoning him, driving him insane to hide her guilt and be rid of him; that his children were not his own.[4] These were years of wandering as an outcast, unable to accept his growing fame; of increasing rebelliousness that brought formal charges and a court trial for blasphemy.[5] It is, I believe, important to note that his jealousies of Siri focused more upon her attachments to women than to men. While he could not tolerate any indication that Siri had other interests, any evidence of interest in women drove him into an insane frenzy.

It contained elements of the jealousy of his sisters; but it also involved his feminine identification and his desire for fusion with a woman, including the unconscious wish to experience woman's love as a woman. There seems to be clear evidence that Siri had strong homosexual trends which had something to do with her love for Strindberg; and that Strindberg, who was violently jealous of masculine women, was also attracted to them.[6]

Strindberg, having once given in to his longing for reunion with a mother and to gain an identity through a woman, could never again maintain his own ego and defend it against intrusion. His ego boundaries evaporated. He could storm about Siri devouring him, but he wished to be devoured and also to incorporate her. He was in a perpetual struggle to retain his integrity. "When I realized that I had lost my integrity (by being dominated by a woman) I wanted to blot out my humiliation by some heroic action—some feat, some discovery —even by committing hari-kiri." He left her many times, but as soon as he was alone, the image of the pure and mothering Siri haunted him and his longing for her became desperate.

As the marriage was coming to an end Strindberg lived in a world of delusional jealousy; frantic over his inability ever to know if his children were his own, prying and spying, even considering that his first child had not died but Siri had secreted her away to hide her guilt—for the baron must have been the father. Yet at the height of this paranoid passion Strindberg could write *The Father*, one of his greatest plays, which is but a fictionalized version of his own life situation. While unable to differentiate reality from delusion in his own life, in the play he could attain perspective; he could identify with and understand Laura, the wife, who was destroying her husband; even more clearly see how the Captain was destroying himself caught in the net of his delusions; portray the dilemma of the friends who sought to help, but whom the Captain believed sought to betray him; empathize with the daughter who could not let herself be devoured by the father who feared that she would devour him; affectionately portray the old nurse who loved the Captain and yet found it her duty to entice him into a straitjacket. In the play he expressed the Captain's wish to be completed through a woman and to let his wife dominate him, and the suffering he experienced because of his incestuous guilt and lack of masculinity; and finally, he portrayed the broken Captain finding bliss in dying with his head on his nurse's breast.

In the play, Strindberg could express the insights he could not utilize in life. If he is bitter and condemnatory to his wife, he is as merciless towards himself. There is a split between the artist and the man. The man could not transcend the early childhood problems. The artist, as the analyst, could view the human tragedy in perspective. The play sought resolution of his conflict and suffering through catharsis and ego control, but his unconscious gained the upper hand. He had intended to write about how Laura was unwittingly but relentlessly carried along by the circumstances and the inherent incompatibility of man and woman to destroy her husband, but the portrayal of Laura escaped from his ego control and she was involuntarily turned into a plotting and malicious woman—resembling his delusional ideas of Siri. "I don't know," he wrote to a friend, "if *The Father* is an invention or if my life has been so, but I feel at any moment, not far off, this will be revealed to me and that I shall crash either into insanity from the agony of conscience or into suicide. Through inventing so much my life has become a shadow life." Not until many years of suffering and self-searching had passed would he grasp more clearly and profoundly the self-punitive aspects of paranoid delusions. Yet, as if he were guilty about portraying only the tragedy of the male, he almost immediately wrote *Miss Julie,* the tragedy of a woman deprived of her femininity and her will by being raised by her mother to despise men and take vengeance upon them.

Indeed, it was not long until Strindberg crashed into full-blown insanity. The loss of Siri Von Essen whom he drove away by his delusional jealousy left him bereft of his single important object relationship and his attempt at restitution through a second marriage was foredoomed: he believed no woman could forgive his brutal exposure of Siri in *The Confession of a Fool*.[7] Guilt-laden over his vengeful behavior, and expecting retribution from all women and from God for his incestuous and rebellious defiance of paternal authority, he sought to regain self-esteem through the pursuit of science. He was tormented and enraged because Siri and his children were now being cared for by a masculinized woman who had displaced him. He could not tolerate the success and acclaim he had sought, and just when *The Father* was hailed as the masterpiece of a genius, he withdrew from the world to try to transmute metals into gold in the loneliness of a dingy Paris hotel room.[8] Thus isolated, he soon lived in torment and terror: threatened by rays from electrical machines; hearing his neighbors plotting against him; convinced that a former friend had come to Paris to kill him, etc. He was guided by his interpretations of trivia—a number on a scrap of paper found in the street, a sign in a shop window, the flight of a bird, the look of a passer-by. When he became ill through self-neglect, friends arranged for his hospitalization, but he soon returned to his alchemy. When he went to live with a psychiatrist friend in Sweden, he fled the house in the middle of the night believing the doctor was killing him with electrical rays. For years he existed in an inferno of delusions and hallucinations but constantly sought the reasons for his persecution. I cannot here discuss these years and the insights he achieved. The factors that eventually led to his renewed productivity are complex, a compound of unusual insight and restitutive delusion.[9]

In essence, he achieved a reasonable respite from torment by renunciation: renunciation of companionship because all human contacts threatened to invade his tenuous ego boundaries and upset the identity he guarded; renunciation of reward that would rearouse fears of retribution; renunciation of his aggressive doubting that brought hallucinated punishments; and renunciation of libidinal gratification. He became passive, following the direction and limitation imposed by the hallucinated punitive superego forces—extrajected introjects to which his ego became subservient. Thus restricted, his unconscious creativity came to the fore, and plays were created in a dream world, sometimes built upon dreams and sometimes composed unconsciously in something resembling a trance state. Living a constricted life, he gained gratification and expressed various identities in the fantasy world of the stage.[10]

The "dream plays" even as dreams could condense the timeless, the contradictory, the unresolvable ambivalences, and the multiplicity of interrelated primitive conflicts with which he had become preoccupied. Only through these symbolic dream plays could the complexity of the tragedy of Strindberg's life be expressed other than through psychosis.

The focus of this study has been limited to relating the circumstances of Strindberg's first marriage to both his schizophrenic development and to his genius—his capacities to create tragedies which are concerned with fundamental problems of human existence, the topics of the basic myths and classic drama; and which are replete with new insights concerning these issues. The marriage reawakened the unresolved and intense preoedipal and oedipal conflicts concerning longing for reunion with the mother, distrust of the parental objects, the rebelliousness against the authority of the father, the castration fears, and the insecurities over his sexual identity with its envy of the prerogatives of women. The tenuous defenses against these childhood strivings were demolished when the oedipal

110

situation was recreated through his relationship with the Baron and Baroness Wrangel. He had been attracted to a relationship in which he could rectify his unfortunate childhood through finding a Virgin Mother whom he could deify and a father figure whom he could adulate and both of whom cherished him. However, the erotic components of these relationships could not remain sublimated, particularly as the other parties were not sharing his childhood fantasy. The situation became catastrophic to Strindberg when his oedipal fantasies turned into an incestuous reality. He then not only suffered from primal guilt and fears of paternal retribution but also other profound consequences. Experiencing victory over the acquiescent father figure increased his megalomanic narcissism. Achieving reunion with his mother through the marriage to Siri Wrangel, he lost his own identity and was caught in the symbiotic unification which he could never again relinquish—even as a child who achieves the desired incestuous union becomes fixated and cannot seek completion as an independent individual.

The encounter with the Wrangels fitted uniquely into Strindberg's strange and complex life to open the door for the living out of unrequited childhood needs and fantasies. Thereafter, repression and his defenses against the return of the repressed failed. Strindberg and the characters he created paid the penalties for infractions of basic taboos; and the audiences who could tolerate his plays experienced catharsis for their unconscious fantasies.

1963

111

NOTES

1. "The sense of guilt and rebelliousness never became extinct . . . whatever reconciliation was effected between these opposing mental forces sooner or later broke down" (Freud). This statement concerning the guilt of sons is particularly pertinent to Strindberg who throughout his "Inferno" period was caught between these forces, and eventually gained some peace by becoming alert to hallucinations that indicated to him that he was being punished for rebelliousness, and would then alter his thinking and activities. He reluctantly gave up his alchemy because the impiety of transmuting elements required punishment.

2. An episode, whether real or a "cover memory," profoundly influenced his development, and variants of it recur in his plays. In a classic "double-bind," the preschool child was accused of drinking his aunt's wine. When he denied it, his father said: "You also lie and will get a beating." His mother urged him to ask his father's forgiveness. Later, his mother hears him tell the nursemaid that he has done nothing, and tells his father that August is still lying and he receives another beating. From then on, he writes, he experienced constant anxiety, not daring to confide in anyone. From such circumstances, he believed that he developed an abiding sense of guilt and a distrust of authority. The episode is of particular interest because Samuel Butler, another iconoclast who challenged conventional values, narrates an almost identical experience in *The Way of All Flesh* that crystallized his distrust of his parents and their religious value system.

3. "Was she really an embodiment of the Virgin Mother, such as I had already dimly divined?"

4. The unbearable delusional uncertainty concerning the paternity of his children not only furnishes the theme for *The Father*, but had grown into Strindberg's all-encompassing preoccupation.

5. Strindberg was terrified, fearing a two-year jail sentence would certainly drive him insane—but he returned to Sweden to stand trial and unexpectedly was received as a hero—a martyr to the cause of freedom. Despite the triumph, it was a shattering experience that increased his persecutory ideas that women were in league against him.

6. Strindberg was originally attracted to Marie David, whom he came to consider as a homosexual seducer of Siri, and the woman with whom Siri lived after the divorce. It is of interest that the only man who figured prominently in his persecutory delusions during his overt schizophrenic period was a Polish author who had adored and almost worshipped Strindberg and who married a woman with whom Strindberg had a brief affair between his first and second marriages. Strindberg was

then in a position of a father displaced sexually by a son. He projected his guilt toward the baron onto the Pole. He would be killed by the son—as Kronos killed Uranos.

7. Strindberg admitted to the malicious pleasure he gained from being able to pay Siri her alimony from the proceeds from *The Confession of a Fool*—that exposed her, or his delusional ideas of her, to the public— but before long he found the book one of his major sins.

8. The anal characteristics of his efforts to manufacture gold amidst stench and fumes in his room, as well as his fears of attack and his pervasive ambivalence, are apparent. However, his strong *will* may also be related to his anal fixation and regression. His alchemy came to be recognized as the essence of rebelliousness against God—an attempt to alter nature—and to disprove basic tenets of the great scientists. He believed Pasteur died because one of his treatises had been published on that day; and that one of his astronomical publications was responsible for the death of several prominent astronomers.

9. A significant step toward restitution appears after he found that Swedenborg had experienced almost identical delusions and hallucinations. He was reassured that he was not insane, but like the earlier Swedish genius was being punished in this earthly Hell in preparation for a future life. He remained a follower of Swedenborg for the remainder of his life, sharing his strange concepts. He gained a compassion for his fellow sufferers that pervades his late plays.

10. His life contained realistic satisfactions as well. His third marriage to Harriet Bosse (1901-1904) brought him much happiness despite the separations and the divorce after only three years. They remained devoted friends until Miss Bosse remarried in 1908. Strindberg clearly loved her and their daughter until his death. The relationship endured because his wife refused to tolerate his defamations and suspicions of her; and she knew that she could not sacrifice her individuality and freedom of movement to his eccentric and incomprehensible needs. She respected and adulated Strindberg, but realized she must retain her own self-respect. Separated she remained an ideal and source of inspiration for Strindberg. It is of interest that although she considered him to be moody, eccentric, shy, and pathologically suspicious and jealous, she did not consider him mentally ill. "This depends upon what is meant by mental illness," she wrote. "If a person during life's trials should become highly sensitive, shy and suspicious, this need not come under the heading of what is commonly called mental illness." Strindberg's letters to her and the *Blue Book* written during these years show that he was often motivated by projected controls and continued to believe in telepathy, *Doppelgänger*, and the success of his alchemy; and found guidance through interpreting trivial occurrences; but he remained integrated and highly creative.

PSYCHOANALYTIC COMMENTS ABOUT THE PERSONALITY OF GOETHE

Edward Hitschmann

In contrast to some authors, especially to Theilhaber—though he does not belong to the psychoanalytic school—I think I should at once define my point of view. I refuse to adopt an attitude of professional superiority and to explain how Goethe could have been different, or how he could have behaved differently. On the contrary, in profound admiration of Goethe's genius we must admit that we owe his existence, his work, and his personality to an optimal set of circumstances. "Goethe," says Brandes, "guarded his self-development with an instinct that was wisdom."

Despite the deep grief it has brought us, this twentieth century is a wonderful age with its new spirit, its striving for truth, and its love for facts; these trends are especially manifest in psychology. Psychoanalysis is both a natural science and a method for experimental research. Goethe, towering spirit and universal talent that he was, would have accepted psychoanalysis without prejudice. Did he not remark: "The most harmful prejudice is the banning of any form of scientific investigation"?

This essay, of course, cannot do justice to the whole personality of Goethe; it can only discuss certain aspects and the problems they raise. It intends to appraise the importance of Goethe's father, to solve the riddles of Goethe's love life, and to say something about the poet's inner development.

There is no need to speak about Goethe's mother. Her forthright, cheerful nature, her soul, receptive to everything beautiful and good, her delightful letters—all this is well known to every educated person. I only want to quote one observation of Freud about the mother-son relationship: ". . . he who has been the undisputed darling of the mother retains throughout life that victorious feeling, the confidence in ultimate success which not seldom brings actual success with it."

From its beginnings, psychoanalysis has emphasized the decisive importance of the father for the fate of the individual. Strangely enough, Goethe's biographers have by-passed his father—as Rudolph Glaser stresses—"because of a peculiar prejudice." The poet himself has not always done the figure of his father complete justice; and it was Merck's judgment in particular that put the aging, ailing man, grown taciturn through deep disappointment, in the wrong light.

Besides many contemporary reports, Glaser drew from a hitherto concealed source, namely, Kaspar Goethe's own account of his Italian journey which had Vienna as its point of preparation and departure. This diary dates from his thirtieth year, but he was busy with its elaboration and completion till he was fifty-eight so that his children were brought into intimate contact with it.

From this diary Goethe's father emerges as an enlightened man of the world with high moral principles, open-minded, intent on self-education, widely interested in art, natural sciènce, history, theater, etc. With amazement we gain the conviction that the far greater individual, the genius that was his son, was, after all foreshadowed in the personality of his father. The elder Goethe was already ahead of his time; he had an inquiring mind, was full of ideas, collected specimens for his natural science cabinet, and brought home samples of marble, just as his son was to do later on. The father was especially interested in inscriptions and showed some skill in poetic translations from ancient languages.

If we realize that the Italian journey was the climax of the father's life and that he cherished its memories to the end of his days—only then can we understand that the same goal hovered before his son's eyes for many years, until he finally reached it. And, strangely enough, Italy meant for the father too—an adventure of love. The diary mentions a love affair this solemn gentleman experienced in Milan, and a collection of love letters, written in the style of the period, gives us more details. It did not go beyond words and outbursts of emotion. Kasper Goethe, the "habitual moralist," was too easily intimidated; his infatuation was, as he stressed several times, a "pure one"; he withdrew, not unlike his famous son who so often was to take flight in later years. He begs forgiveness for "the weakness he has shown in love."

Though Goethe the son often felt oppressed by his father's persistent pedantry and unbending sternness, and sometimes even rebelled against it, "the relationship between father and son was confident and friendly, while due respect was shown." The son felt the gentle soul behind the stern exterior. For the father Goethe collected Wolfgang's early verses, had them bound, and presented them to him, and the father encouraged him. The father preserved the son's first drawings, recognized his talents, urged perseverance, and occasionally criticized the neglect of these talents. The father's schedule of studies could not have been more comprehensive. There was scarcely a field of knowledge that he ignored. When the poet puts his father's inheritance into the words "life's serious conduct"—originally it was "serious features"—we know now how all inclusive this is: it implies character, the ideal of education and culture, the aim of universality. The father's upbringing pointed the way to that recording of experience which the son's genius made so peculiarly his own that he could call his literary work a "great confession."

Goethe's so characteristic propensity for self-education was the consequence of an inner voice, the echo of his father.

If we see his father's influence in this light, we must trace back to this same source the restraining force which again and again recalled Goethe from his amorous wanderings and his restlessness to his own true self and his nobler ideals. "The earnestness with which I looked at myself and the world from an early age was revealed in my behavior . . . ," wrote Goethe in *Dichtung und Wahrheit*.

Many other resemblances could be pointed out: father and son shared the predilection for collecting. The father collected maps, old firearms, Venetian glass, cups and goblets, ivory, bronzes, specimens of natural history, and Frankfurtiana. Anybody who has visited the Goethehaus in Frankfurt will remember the pedantic tidiness with which his collections were arranged. He was especially fond of studying and showing his copperplate engravings. "I have to own things," said Goethe, "to be able to evaluate them properly. Only when I own a thing can I judge it calmly and objectively, free of the illusions that are generated by desire. That is why I love possession, not for the sake of the thing possessed, but for the sense of comprehension it gives me which makes me happier and more serene." [1]

The didactic element took early and permanent hold of Goethe's nature. He shed no tears at the death of his little brother Hermann Jakob. When his mother asked the defiant lad whether he had not loved his brother, he ran into his room and, from under the bed, pulled out a pile of paper, all filled with lessons and stories. He told her he had done all that to instruct his brother. (According to Bettina Brentano's report, this story was told by Frau Rath.) Wolfgang was ten years old at the time! Schoolmasterly, quite in his father's vein, was his attitude toward his sister Cornelia; and toward Maddalena Ricci in Rome. Before he fell in love with her, he taught her English! All his life Goethe remained eager to teach and be taught. Even toward Eckermann and Soret his attitude was didactic. The poet himself once said that his father had bequeathed upon him "didactic loquacity." *Wilhelm Meisters Lehrjahre* treats of the education of an individual; the *Wanderjahre* of the education of man as citizen in an ideal state.

To be sure, Kaspar Goethe was successful as a pedagogue with his son only. His daughter suffered too much from his severity and pedantry; presumably she missed the father's affection, while the son enjoyed at least the mother's tenderness in abundance besides getting more recognition from the father. Goethe's identification with his father also becomes obvious through his predilection to play the role of father, as Wilhelm Meister toward Mignon. Goethe had the desire to attract younger people who needed assistance, to help them and to teach them. Eckermann considered his relationship to Goethe that of pupil to master, son to father. Goethe was full of paternal feelings toward Fritz, the son of Frau Von Stein. All the greater was the tragedy of Goethe's old age, to see his own son unhappy and a failure.

When we see how contradictory Goethe's personality was despite everything, how full of strife and suffering his life was, we must recognize that the one force which fought in him was the influence of his father's seriousness and severity.

Two souls, alas, dwell in my heart . . .
One, in crude sensuality, cleaves
To the earth with clinging organs.
The other yearns to soar aloft
To the purer air and the broader view.

Faust

Goethe's preference for friendship with men of high intelligence and culture is evident all through his life. At first he is the younger one, the pupil, so that Behrisch, Herder, Lavater, Merck, and others who befriended and stimulated him must be regarded as successors of his father, continuing and complementing his education.

The unconscious influence of father on son can often be seen quite plainly in the realm of belief in God. In general, the relation to a personal God receives its basic coloring from the relation to the father. I was able to demonstrate, in the instance of another poet (Dauthendey), that he exchanged his deism—quite involuntarily—for pantheism at the very moment he broke with his father and turned away from him. Goethe's towering personality that encompassed all humanity could never be understood in such a simple way. A harmonizing tendency moderates every characteristic, every one-sidedness. And yet, even with Goethe the impression remains that his faith was influenced partly by the strong father personality, overwhelmingly experienced in childhood, partly by his own conquest of the father, against whom a strong rivalry was often manifest. This influence also comes to light in his poetic outpourings.

Could I but be replete
With Thee, Eternal One—
Alas, this deep torment
How it endures on earth.

These verses reveal a wholly feminine passive feeling and humble longing. The poem *Ganymed* is a glorification of

120

becoming one with the universe; the poem *Prometheus*—open revolt, rebellion against Titans. Most characteristic seems to me Goethe's reply to his friend Jakobi, when the latter persisted in his efforts to convert him to one faith:

> For my part, if I consider the manifold tendencies of my nature, I cannot be satisfied with one single mode of thought. As a poet and an artist, I am a polytheist; as a natural scientist, I am a pantheist. I am as decidedly one as I am the other. And if I need a God for my own person, as a moral being, this, too, has been taken care of. The celestial and terrestrial matters are so vast a realm that only the organs of all beings together are able to grasp it.

In comparison with the father's Protestantism, we find a turning away, a less deistic faith, a more diffuse and impersonal pantheistic religion of nature, a sort of victory over the paternal. Nevertheless, all his life Goethe remained religious in a wider sense of the word. The father had been tolerant toward his son. The son says of him proudly: "Though more old-fashioned in his religion, he did not take offense at my views and speculations."

This brings to mind the highly original altar the boy once erected, rather pagan, put together from products of nature for a God of nature, to offer sacrificial fires. "The God who was closely connected with nature. . . . He seemed to him the real God. . . . The boy could not bestow a definite shape on this deity. . . ." (*Dichtung und Wahrheit*)

Perhaps we may trace the uncertainty, the conflict, and the withdrawal of a personal God to the ambivalent relationship with his father. Perhaps a certain longing for the mother was interwoven with the feeling for nature. These relationships are complicated by the fact that to Goethe nature represented something divine: the religious feeling flowed together with the feeling for nature. It was for him a "pure, deep, innate, and familiar perception to see God in nature and nature in God." Faust's confession of faith is that of a pantheist, too.

Goethe was, of course, particularly conversant with both these words, nature and God; and in both the content kept changing. "Neither the philosopher nor the theologian is able to arrive at a satisfactory idea about Goethe's God and Goethe's nature." (Chamberlain)

In summing up, I may repeat that we rate the effect of the father's influence on the development of Goethe's character extremely high; higher even, we might say, than Goethe himself rated it. For this influence, as we understand it, was largely unconscious for the son. Here a slight theoretical digression may be permitted, to indicate how we conceive of this paternal influence, and to clarify the psychic mechanism.

Taking neuroses as the point of departure, psychoanalysis in its beginnings was primarily concerned with the repression from consciousness of unacceptable impulses. Later on it directed its attention to the moral and aesthetic tendencies and their origins which furnished the impulse for repression. Prominent here is a process we call "identification," which plays an essential role. At a certain stage of development the boy identifies himself with his father, sets himself on equal terms with the father, incorporates him into his personality, and makes the father's ideals his own. This is an unconscious process. It goes without saying that an analogous influence is exerted by the mother.

The ego of the child changes according to these identifications. The child shapes for itself an ego ideal which it follows in the future and strives to achieve. Teachers, older friends, and other persons who inspire respect continue this role of the father. Their commands and prohibitions, like those of the father, now exercise, by means of the conscience, a censorship of morals and taste. The voices of these authorities have become an inner voice, the voice of conscience. The discord between the claims of conscience and the actual achievements is experienced as a feeling of guilt. Our early identifications form our character.

Identification is not imitation, voluntary imitation, but an unconscious, compulsory process. It is especially the less loved parent, the parent who is feared, who has a strong influence.

In his later years, Goethe's father may be regarded as an eccentric. His choleric temperament, his touchiness and quarrelsomeness isolated him, his strictness and pedantry at times estranged his children. In his old age he became silent, dull and petty. But his cultural ideal, his restless striving for continuous development and enrichment of the personality, his methodical instruction, his guidance in evaluating and recording experiences, all this had set a pattern. In his son his severity and seriousness resulted in moral strictness toward himself and a tendency to guilt feelings. According to the son, though, Kaspar Goethe's achievements were not due to innate endowments but "to incredible industry, perseverance, and repetition." Nevertheless, Kaspar Goethe would seem to have been the trunk of the tree which, in his son, branched out and blossomed under the rays of genius.

The parents were so different in age and in their attitudes toward life that many a discordance, many a conflict in the son's heart may be explained by it. One biographer says of Goethe: In character, in imagination, in ethics, everywhere Goethe perceives paradoxes that arrest his attention. Thus the opposing extremes in his origins contributed to corresponding contradictions in his temperament and thereby influenced the outcome of many of the situations in Goethe's life.

We shall also find a peculiar discordance in his love life, the riddles of which we now propose to solve.

Goethe's rich and varied love life exhibits such peculiarities and puzzles that it has been exhaustively discussed in literature, notably by Wilhelm Bode. Otto Rank devoted a chapter of his book, *The Incest Motive in Poetry and Legend*, to Goethe's love for his sister. Brunold Springer, in his monograph The Key to Goethe's Love Life, has adopted a similar point of view. The fundamental importance of Otto Rank's work must be stressed: it reveals the two most important complexes in Goethe's psychic life and poetic creativity—the revolt against his father, and the love for his sister. Proof is given by the evidence of motives and choice of subjects, but that would lead us too far afield.

Freud himself, in "A Childhood Recollection from *Dichtung und Wahrheit*," emphasized the fraternal jealousy of the child Goethe. I have taken up the problem of the two contrasting types of womanhood, as represented by Frau Von Stein and Christiane Vulpius, and have taken into consideration the change that occurred in Goethe during his stay in Rome, exemplified by the *Römische Elegien*.

Goethe loved often and at every stage of his life; he has given us the most beautiful love poems and letters. Again and again he was capable of the ecstasy of love; he himself attributed recurring puberty to men of genius. Moebius has estimated a periodicity of seven years for Goethe, and Kretschmer, too, believes that various love phases can be explained in this way.

At the age of seventy-three Goethe once complained: "I feel poorly, for I am not in love with anyone, and no one is in love with me." And a year later, through Herzog Karl August, he asked for the hand of the nineteen-year-old Ulrike Levetzov in marriage. The fruits of this hopeless love were the *Marienbader Elegien*, one of the most stirring and most perfect of Goethe's poems.

Goethe never was a saint and especially in the early Weimar years there may very well have been fleeting debauches with girls of the lowest classes. But with girls of a higher social stratum, with Käthchen, Lotte, Friederike, and Lili, the relationship follows a peculiarly typical course: a violent, stormy infatuation, then a period of irresolution and inner torment, and finally flight from the beloved, usually followed by self-reproaches.

According to Bode, Goethe was very reserved. We know of no permanent liaison prior to his Italian journey. Up to that time his psychic life often suggests that of a man who misses sexual satisfaction. Compared to contemporary writers he was especially reserved in his expression, never reveling in erotic descriptions. He had the inclination as well as the capacity to suppress his instinct; he suppressed it to a remarkable degree in the eleven years of his relationship with Frau Von Stein. All the more sensational, of course, was the publication of his *Römische Elegien* with its more than frank description of Southern passion.

After these allusions you must permit me to talk about Goethe's development since childhood in some detail; for the affective impressions of our childhood have an intense after-effect on our whole life.

The mother, so much younger, gayer, and livelier, drew the son to her; the serious, strict, and pedantic father became an object of rebellion, aversion, anxiety, and guilt feeling. There is a scene in *Dichtung und Wahrheit,* in which the children, kept from falling asleep by anxiety, are seeking out the servants; they are frightened back by the father who is difficult to recognize because he wears his dressing gown inside out. For many years little Wolfgang suffered from anxiety dreams. He had a bell of his own to calm him.

Thus the father became the representative of intimidations and prohibitions. The difference in temperament between father and mother had its share in fostering the "oedipal situa-

125

tion" which is natural in the early years. The psychoanalyst considers it most likely that the boy was harried by something like castration fears.

The great love he felt for his mother helps to explain his jealousy of the brother. This is how Freud explains the naughtiness with which Wolfgang one day threw a great deal of crockery out of the window, egged on by the Ochsenstein brothers, who lived across the street. Supported by analogous cases from his analytic practice, Freud conjectures that it was not mere chance that this behavior coincided with the mother's going to the christening of a newborn son. The poet's love for his sister Cornelia was complete and unconcealed; it decisively influenced not only the choice and treatment of many poetic themes, but his actual love life. "Even when she lay in the cradle he loved her tenderly, brought everything to her, and wanted to feed her by himself." (Witkowski)

In Charlotte Von Stein we also see an image, a reflection of the sister, and in his love for her, probably the deepest love of Goethe's life, a continuation of the attachment to his sister. It is by no means self-evident that the radiant, brilliant young poet was captivated for so long by this ailing woman, seven years his senior, who was neither magnanimous nor particularly understanding. Numerous utterances of Goethe prove that he suspected she awakened in him the image of his sister. He described his relation to her as the purest, finest, and truest he had ever experienced for any woman except his sister. "If only my sister had a brother, as I have a sister in you," he said elsewhere. In one poem Goethe said to Frau Von Stein: "Ah, in another existence, you have been my sister or my wife." And in a letter about her he wrote: "She has gradually inherited the place of mother, sister, and mistress, and a bond has been formed like the bonds of nature."

The superlative feelings, the perfection of his love, the asser-

tion that he found everything in her, show plainly an idealization and fantasy glorification with unconscious motives.

Goethe sacrificed almost twelve of his most fervent years
to this woman who proved herself only to a small degree
worthy of this touching devotion. In answer to the oft-repeated
question as to the limits of this compelling attachment, it must
be said that this prudish woman clearly never granted the
ultimate. Every possible gradation of partial and inhibited, hasty
and unhealthy relief exists in such relationships; but complete
and uninhibited gratification Goethe never found with her.

This first decade in Weimar, full of varied official activities,
was by no means productive and did not advance the development of the great poet. Only outlines and fragments mark this
period. Nothing was completed except lyric poetry. Rightly it
is Frau Von Stein who is considered the work of this period—
Frau Von Stein who was so highly exalted through infantile
reminiscence and unsatisfied desire. In the earlier Weimar years
new plans still appear, such as *Iphigenie, Tasso, Wilhelm Meister*; but from 1780 until the flight to Italy the well of inspiration had gone dry.

The deep happiness of love which those years brought is
evident in the letters to Frau Von Stein; they mirror love's
every facet and are a treasure of German letters.

But toward the end of this period despair seized the poet.
"Rather death than the life of the past years," he wrote to Frau
Von Stein. And later to the duke: "It was the main purpose of
my journey (to Italy) to cure myself of the physical and moral
ills which tormented me in Germany and rendered me useless
in the end." Goethe later called this period "years of illness."
Of course there were many other reasons for this weakening
of his creative powers, such as his absorption in official duties.
But it cannot be regarded as natural that in the prime of his
manhood Goethe languished. Goethe started on his flight to

127

Italy without even telling Frau Von Stein. It was both flight and longing. A healthy instinct tore him free, the narcissism of the creative artist asserted itself once more. In a work entitled "On the Psychoanalysis of Travel," Winterstein made special reference to the interconnection between the urge to travel and eroticism, and he mentioned a significant symptomatic action of Goethe's: a few days before his flight he lost off his finger the ring which Frau Von Stein had given him.

Flight from the beloved was always characteristic of Goethe's love life. Thus he fled from Käthchen, from Friederike, from Lili and Lotte, from Marianne Von Willemer and others. The most obvious motive each time was of course the flight of the creative artist from disturbing obligation. Did not Goethe himself advise the creative person to be "highly egotistic"? Our poet was concerned with his own growth and that of his work like no other. Yet more searching investigations, such as the one Reik has published, dealing with Goethe's flight from Friederike, have more to say and trace the succession of motives back to childhood events.

We stressed the tender attachment to the mother and the secondary one to the sister, the father as the source of prohibition and punishment, and the anxiety in the evening and in dreams. More needed details can be found only in other childhood observations. Here may lie the origin of the guilt feelings, the fear of consequences of forbidden actions, as well as the later fear of permanent ties. Again and again it comes to flight and abandonment. "And yet to seize hold is the most natural impulse in man. Do not children seize hold?" (*Werthers Leiden*) To be sure, what follows after the flight is the creative realization of the experience.

Added to this is Goethe's sense of purity. Goethe had a peculiar fondness for the word "purity." He said, for example: "The observation of nature needs a certain calm inner purity." Once, when he was to see some criminals, he suffered inner torments and wrote: "I flee from what is impure." He quickly put aside *Der Arme Heinrich*, because the description of disease in this morbid work "had such a powerful effect upon him that he feels contaminated by the mere contact with such a book." Kaspar Goethe's travel diary warns of the dangers of venereal disease. So do Goethe's letters to the duke, and his *Römische Elegien.*

"May the idea of purity, which extends to the bite of food I put into my mouth, grow ever more shining within me!" he wrote elsewhere. Goethe had an insurmountable aversion against everything that was ugly, disgusting, or diseased. When the duke wanted to show him a human malformation, Goethe, the scientist, begged off: "His aversion against everything pathological seems to grow stronger with the years."

When his daughter-in-law fell from a horse and her face was disfigured, he did not want to see her before she had recovered: "He finds himself violently affected by defects and deformities." This also explains why Goethe finds caricatures repugnant.

We may recall the following verses:

> In our bosom's purity an effort surges
> Freely to give our self in gratitude
> To the higher, the purer, the unknown.

In old age, reason could let his microcosm—the goal of his longings—"revolve around a pure center. . . ."

To a certain extent physical and moral purity run parallel; their appraisal has one of its origins in the instincts, as has been previously stated.

Particularly characteristic for the flight from the beloved was the strong guilt feeling that pursued the fugitive. In *Faust,* where the crime against the girl is actually committed, it is committed with the help of the devil.

Stendhal—out of a different world—mockingly expressed

his amazement "that Faust compacts with the devil to do what every one of us has done in his youth: to seduce a milliner." Goethe depicted the struggle between instinctual desires and the power of the inner conscience, just as once his own instincts had to struggle with external prohibitions. Years later, after Lotte Buff had been married to Kestner, Goethe was awakened by anxiety dreams which portrayed his guilt feelings, his need for punishment, and his father (symbolized by the duke). He wrote:

The other day I felt great anxiety in a dream about Lotte. The danger was pressing, there was no hope of success for any of my schemes. We were watched; everything depended on my speaking to the duke. I stood by the window and thought of jumping down. It was two stories high: "You will just break a leg," I thought, "then you might just as well surrender."

So we see that despite the tendency to fall passionately in love, Goethe as a young man showed self-restraint and a sense of purity. Moral inhibitions, guilt feelings, and the fear of disease were at work, but there undoubtedly also was the self-protection of the creative artist who puts imagination above reality and says: "Happiness is ever greater far from the beloved," or: "If I love you, what concern is that of yours?"

Love does not exist for its own sake. Every love affair— from *Werther* to the *Marienbader Elegien*—led to creative work which offered freedom from conflict and psychic distress. In creative work the release from the love object is completed and, as it were, celebrated. And yet, it remains unlikely that a nature as strong as Goethe's should not long to taste fully of life and love.

We now turn to the second half of his life, separated from the first by the Italian journey. Our attention is drawn to a poetic work which is based on the records of this journey, even though it was completed in Weimar, the *Römische Elegien*.

Although Goethe finished this work in the peacefully happy time with Christiane Vulpius and refers to her in it, there can be no doubt that its theme is his happiness of love in Rome. It sets a memorial to Faustina Antonii, née di Giovanni, the young widow whose actual existence can no longer be doubted since A. Carlotta has provided documentary proof. When Goethe met her she was already a mother, and stood under the guardianship of her uncle. Goethe spent nights with her that were replete with unrestrained enjoyment of love. "She takes delight in him, the free and vigorous stranger," Goethe wrote. "She shares the fire that is enkindled in his bosom." Eros had bestowed upon her the supreme gift "to awaken joy that slowly burned itself out as to ashes." For the first time he could give himself to sexual fulfillment without fear of infection. Plainly enough he says in the eighteenth elegy: "It is wholly abominable to fear serpents on love's path, and poison under the roses of pleasure, when at the fairest moment of the joy of surrender, worry is whispering close to your ear."

This fear of disease was unnecessary with Faustina. "That is why Faustina is my happiness. She likes to share my bed and keeps faith with the faithful." And he continued: "What bliss! We exchange carefree kisses, breath and life we imbibe and infuse, full of trust." In another, incomplete poem which was withheld from publication, fear of disease appears as the greatest killer of joy; and mention is made of mercury as a remedy. To quote further:

> But we do not kiss all the time, there is sensible talk.
> When sleep overtakes her, I lie awake and reflect.
> Many a time in her arms I have written verses.
> The hexameter's measure softly my fingers count
> Tapping her back. She breathes in delightful slumber,
> And her breathing thrills me to my innermost heart.

When a man of forty in his elegiac recollection of Rome speaks with such enthusiasm about his enjoyment of love free from restrictions and free from the fear of infection, we have the right to assume that he had never before known such uninhibited passion. The elegies still contain words enough that have to ban guilt feelings: he states that he works during the day, at least: "though I am only half instructed, I am doubly blessed."

Only since he had seen and felt his beloved naked, does he fully understand marble. "When sleep overtakes her, I lie awake and reflect"—should this indicate that erotic gratification is after all something for which he has (or once had) to find an excuse? This would fit the introduction of Alexander, Caesar, Heinrich, and Frederick the Great—obviously father images—as men who would gladly give him half of their glory:

> Could I grant to each one this bed for a night.
> But Orcus holds them in his stern powers, poor creatures.

A slight satisfaction over the death of these fathers can be detected; a sort of victory for the rival son. Many a sternly ruled son cannot find free enjoyment of love until the death of his father.

The father rivalry shows through these ironic lines, but it finds its full satisfaction in deceiving the uncle guardian, "whom the dearest so often deceives, to possess me." No wonder that the lover once imagines to see the dreaded uncle in a scarecrow and flees:

> Now the old man's wish is fulfilled; the loose bird
> He scared off today, that robs both his garden and niece.

But the complete possession of a woman finally banishes any rivalry:

> Grant me, O Quirites, my happiness, and may each
> Be granted by God the first and the last of the world's
>   blessings.

Paternal injunctions are most easily overcome away from

home; in the outside world there need be no fear of censorship.

It was apparently then, in Italy that Goethe encountered, for the first time, full gratification, without any feeling of anxiety or reproach; and it seems self-evident that upon his return to Weimar he seized the first opportunity to attract a suitable love object. The dictum, "Between sensual pleasure and peace of mind a man has only an uneasy choice," was presumably resolved. At first he was disappointed and gloomy. But a few weeks after his arrival he was accosted by a simple girl who made artificial flowers in a factory. She interceded for her brother who wanted Goethe's help in securing a position. She soon became his mistress and lived with him, despite the malicious small town gossip. She bore him a son, and, later, several other children who did not survive. He gave her his affectionate love and respect and regarded her as his wife. The actual wedding did not take place until eighteen years later. With her in mind he wrote these verses during his second Italian journey:

> Long did I seek for a wife, but I found only harlots.
> At last I caught you, harlot, and in you found a wife.

As soon as Goethe had gained full sexual freedom he was capable of marriage, though only with a love object of a lower social class. His attachment to higher love objects, such as his mother and sister, still influenced him. His marriage began as a purely erotic relationship which had to prove itself before he could permit the development of that higher affection which transformed this liaison with the simple girl into a quite happy marriage.

If we now look at the change the first Italian journey wrought in Goethe, we see the word "rebirth" leap out from his letters more than a dozen times, even in the first ones to his mother, then to the duke, to Frau Von Stein, and to his friends: "I am a new man, a different man, reborn." Of course,

133

not only the wrenching away from Frau Von Stein worked this transformation but the finally realized fulfillment of the wish to experience Italy, like his father, and to taste freedom. We know how much a visit to Italy means to every cultured German. What must it have been for Goethe!

The change in Goethe's love life has to be taken into consideration if we want to explain this continuous stream of *joi de vivre:* "In Rome I have found myself for the first time, for the first time in harmony with myself I became happy and reasonable." And in *Four Seasons* he wrote:

> Know'st thou the glorious effect of love
> that is satisfied at last?
> It binds together bodies in beauty, as it
> sets free the souls.

There was an upsurge of creative powers. *Egmont* and *Iphigenie* were completed in Rome, *Erwin* and *Claudine* were completely recast. The Roman elegies were sketched out and later written for Christiane. Many of the Venetian epigrams were meant for her. She hovered behind *Alexis und Dora.* Considerable progress was made with *Tasso,* to be finished later at Christiane's side. After an interval of twelve years, *Faust* was again taken up.

Not only the poet Goethe went to Italy, but also the art critic and scientist; and here too we see that great strides have been made since the early beginnings: Goethe outlined the *Farbenlehre* ("Theory of Color") and wrote his essay on *Die Metamorphose der Pflanze* ("The Metamorphosis of Plants"). And he decided to take on the management of the theater in Weimar.

Then there is another striking fact. Upon his return from Italy Goethe was cool toward all social and political movements of the idealists, the patriots, and the religiously inclined. (Bode) In support of our theory about this disenchantment, let me cite a case that was reported by Oskar Pfister: he tells about a man who pursued his philanthropic ventures only as long as he exercised restraint in his sexual satisfaction. As soon as he gave rein to his sexual functions, he lived for his more immediate interests.

One more point on psychosexual parallelism: Goethe, who had hitherto composed only single poems, occasional poems, now with the elegies wrote his first cycle; a great number of these was to follow. Gundolf draws attention to another fact: "Erotic mysticism no longer interested him. . . . Now, when he loved, he no longer wanted spiritual exaltation, but immediate, pagan, and physical gratification."

Goethe now used the word "infinite" less, and the word "clarity" more. He grew from genius to sage and self-contained Olympian.

Goethe's love did not wane; it outlived Christiane's youth and beauty and was expressed in words of gratitude and affection to the last. Yet at times Goethe must have suffered from her limitations, for in later years Christiane lost her charm and drank somewhat beyond her thirst. Gundolf remarks: "Goethe paid heavily for founding a lifetime relationship on the needs of a passing phase of his life." Goethe once said to Count Reinhard: "First of all I must tell you that my wife never read a line of what I have written. The realm of the mind does not exist for her, she is made for housework. There she relieves me of all worries, that is her domain. But she likes finery, and company, and loves to go to the theater."

This remark may be contradictory to others. But it is obvious that Goethe could not find everything in Christiane. In the choice of this woman we see a consequence of his one-time inability to unite in one object physical and spiritual love. And in his long delay in legitimizing the union with his faithful partner, the mother who had borne him five children and who suffered from the contempt and malice of the small town,

135

we see another proof of his dread of lasting commitments. What later bound him to her was partly habit. Goethe himself once wrote: "It is worth special contemplation that habit can completely take the place of passion; it needs a comfortable presence more than a charming one; then it is invincible. It takes a great deal to break the habit of a relationship; it endures, despite all annoyances; discontent, anger, vexation are powerless against it; it even survives contempt and hatred." In 1810 Goethe wrote a poem, *Das Tagebuch* ("The Diary"), which because of its intimate contents is not included in the general editions of his works. From this poem we learn that even after twelve years of marriage Goethe was unable to deceive Christiane. With drastic humor and self-irony the poem describes his failure with a willing waitress. While the girl, a virgin, lies sleeping by his side, the man, aggrieved at his weakness, thinks of his beloved at home, and these fantasies bring excitement. Here is again proof of the limitations of his sexuality through psychic inhibitions.[2]

Summing up, we may say that the *Römische Elegien* with their elated mood, their feelings of victory and liberation, force us to assume that Goethe found fulfillment for the first time with Faustina and then with Christiane; in other words, not until the age of thirty-eight did he find complete satisfaction, that is, the capacity to focus his entire affective personality from time to time on purely physical love. The young Goethe must be considered fortunate in that he was able to endure congestions through intensive work and genuine sublimation. But of course, this was only possible within limits and for a certain period of time. His flight to Rome led to the change we have described.

To some extent Goethe himself was aware of this change and mentioned it. He called the psychic state of his youth a "loving condition" (meaning obviously "enamored"), and reproached himself with "having perhaps in my youth cherished my inner longings too much." But with progressing

virility he "sought full and final satisfaction" instead. This
step is of great importance in a man's life; it must be experienced, above all, as inner liberation.

There is a proverb: "Man is born twice; the first time by
his mother, a second time by his beloved."

We shall never be able to do justice to a creative person if
we do not consider what psychoanalysis calls his narcissism.
The term is taken from the ancient, mythological figure of
Narcissus who fell in love with his own reflection in the water.
Narcissism means a universal human quality, varying in degree,
a kind of self-love, a concentrating on one's own personality,
such as can best be observed in children. Narcissism is love
of one's own person in the physical and spiritual sense, of the
own personality, the ego and its products and powers. No
artist would preserve his thoughts, his emotions, and his daydreams, if he did not love and value them as part of his self.
The creative person lives for his own self, he concentrates on
his ego and his work; he himself is always, secretly or openly,
the center of his work. Thus, aware or not aware, all production—and literary production most of all—is self-portrayal,
autobiography.

During the period of our development love and praise by
our surroundings teach us to love ourselves; make us vain. But
there are also affronts to narcissism, consequences of reproof
and unfavorable comparisons. There is no reason to doubt Frau
Rath's story, as reported by Bettina: "From earliest youth,
everyone's eyes were fastened on him. Once somebody was
standing at the window with his mother when the boy came
across the street with several friends. They noticed that he
was walking along very gravely, and pointed out to him that
his stiffly erect posture distinguished him peculiarly from the
other boys.—'That's the beginning,' he said, 'later on I'll be
distinguished in all kinds of ways.'"

As his mother's darling, as favored pupil of the father who

admired his talents, the young Goethe could give his narcissism full rein. As a young, immature man, he was outwardly vain and foppish. Self-confident even as a youth, he said of himself: "I have never known a more presumptuous person than myself. . . . I never believed that there was anything to be achieved, I always thought I already had it. Had somebody set a crown upon my head, I would have thought it my due."

In his middle age we find an opposite reaction. Goethe shrouds himself, becomes unpretentious. He wrote to Schiller: Out of a certain realistic tic, out of his innermost being sprang his fault to conceal from the eyes of the people his existence, his actions, and his writings.

I always like to travel incognito, I like to choose the more modest suit of clothes rather than the better one; when talking to strangers or acquaintances, I prefer the trivial topic and the less important expression (the less effective phrase), to behave more frivolous than I am, to put myself, as it were, between myself and my appearance.

At an advanced age [Kretshmer says of the old Goethe] this trait [of self-complacency] contributes in a very refined, subdued, and stylized manner to the bearing of the connoisseur of living, the sage and the prince of poets; there is a slight suggestion of a solemn pose, of egotism and the role of handsome man; a bearing which comprises the youthful narcissism as well as the need to protect the oversensitive inner life, and which blends them into the total of a spiritualized personality.

We do not want to speak here of that part of narcissism which loves "what one represents," but of that which loves "what one is," the narcissism of the personality. What I have in mind is Goethe's active love for his ideal, his self-education, his life which in so many respects was consciously directed toward certain ideals that he himself called it a work of art.

This desire to point the pyramid of my existence, whose basis was given me and founded for me, as high as possible into the air, this desire outweighs everything else and permits hardly a moment's forgetfulness. I must not delay, I am quite on in years, and perhaps fate will break me in the middle and the Tower of Babel will remain blunt and incomplete. People shall say at least that it was boldly planned; and if I live, my powers, by God's grace, shall reach the top. (Goethe to Lavater, 1780)

And in *Wilhelm Meister* he wrote: "To develop my own self, just as I am, that was obscurely my wish and my purpose since youth." Instead of "obscurely" we can also say "unconsciously."

As a writer, he says, he never asked: What does the great mass want, how could I serve the common good? Instead, "I have always tried to gain greater insight for myself, to make myself better, to enhance my own personality. . . ." No matter if the poet lost, as long as the human being gained by it.

In other creative artists we find their work to be the sole object of narcissistic love; for Goethe, his personality was always the main object of all his strivings. His ego, his development, his self-formation, was his main work. We only have to see with what energy he had sought in Strasbourg to make himself immune from his nervous weaknesses, his sensitivity to loud noises, his vertigo, etc. At parade he walked next to the drummer; he climbed the cathedral tower to the top; evenings he visited graveyards, and mornings anatomy classes—all in order to conquer his weaknesses. Is not this inner voice reminiscent of the constant admonitions of his pedagogically inclined father?

He was thorough and conscientious in his official duties. His versatility, his thirst for knowledge, his ambitions command our admiration. There was no event of the day, no work of art, no product of literature that found him uninterested, even in his advanced age. He made valuable contributions to natural science. A universality, still possible in those days, for which the father had sowed the germ, characterized his unique personality. He himself describes his life's work as "a collective being that bears the name of Goethe."

He felt his life to be permeated by "a mildly systematic

plan." Even Goethe's grandfather had been narcissistic in this narrower sense. Too delicate for the smith's trade of his forebears, he had become a tailor. His aim was to reach the top of his profession; he educated himself by traveling, and wrote his name in the French fashion, with an accent on the "e": Goethé; the self-complacent man felt this addition necessary. Kaspar Goethe's narcissism, self-confident but sensitive, was of a nobler kind. He, too, strove toward self-improvement, attached some importance to cosmopolitanism and outward appearance, and did not neglect "what one has," material possessions, a home appropriate to his standing, and collections. He did not reach this goal for himself, he reached it only in his son. "It is a pious wish of every father," Goethe observed in *Dichtung und Wahrheit*, "to see realized in his son everything that he had missed; it is almost like living one's life over again, using to best advantage the experiences of the earlier existence."

Goethe's father retired comparatively early and could devote himself entirely to the education of his children. Goethe himself devoted the development of his personality and his work to the world! Thus the education of his son August may well have been stinted; Goethe reproached himself that August never had come to know the categorical imperative. If the children of men of genius do not succeed, or turn out badly, it is not necessarily hereditary taint or exhaustion of germ plasma; the narcissism of the fathers should not be forgotten as an explanation.

The ideal of perfecting his personality lighted Goethe's way like a pillar of fire. As he grew older, this ideal became more and more conscious, his personality spread its wings more fully, his appearance became most imposing and towering. If we look at the impression of Goethe on his own people— indeed, on the civilized peoples of the whole globe—we will find that an intimate knowledge of his work is far rarer than the strong image of his personality. It is the image of a man who inspires reverence, a man mighty in the realm of the mind, whose face, whose figure, whose eyes above all, have become dear and sacred to mankind. (E. Engel)

The people sense in him the embodiment of the people's soul, the ancestor of mankind; the figure of Goethe actually appears in dreams as the symbol of the father—and psychoanalysis deserves the credit for having established this fact.

A genius, a heroic personality like Goethe, represents for countless human beings the image of the father; they transfer upon it all the feelings of admiration, gratitude, and respect with which they once paid homage to their real fathers.

1932

NOTES

1. In both father and son these traits are reaction formations to the anal instinct, a universal human drive of varying degree, and therefore of varying influence on the manifestations of character. In this connection Ernest Jones includes productivity and pleasure in creating, fondness for the graphic and plastic arts, refined and discriminating artistic taste, love of orderliness bordering on the pedantic, proclivity for collecting, striving for perfection—all traits found in Goethe. On the other hand, we know that pregenital anality is, so to speak, the counterpole of overt genitality. It is the anal instinct from which stems the ascetic strivings, the rejection of the unclean, even in the moral sphere. Sexual activity depends in no small degree on the overcoming of the anal instinct. The fear of infection, especially, has its origin partly in the anal phase of development. Such persons often spend at least some period of their life in sexual abstinence.

2. We can refer to these inhibitions as castration fear, for which there is much remarkable data in Goethe.

◘ MARCEL PROUST

Caroline Wijsenbeek

In a cork-lined room with closed windows, away from sound and sight, wrapped up in flannels and taking the day for the night, Marcel Proust at the age of 35 begins to write the work which will make his name immortal. Only at rare intervals will he seek contact with the friends whose company once seemed indispensable to him and he now lives as much in self-imposed retreat from the world, as formerly the *grand monde* were the only surroundings where he seemed to feel at his ease.

We ask ourselves what was the past which changed the elegant, much sought-after frequenter of Paris salons into the invalid sequestered from human intercourse.

Marcel Proust was born in 1871 as the son of a Roman Catholic physician and a Jewish mother. His father had a great reputation among his colleagues and did good work in the field of public health. His mother belonged to that numerically very small and very refined Jewish group, which in the time of Marcel's youth was fully assimilated into the cultural French milieu in which it lived.

From his early youth Marcel was a sickly child, given to fits of hay fever and asthma, and hypersensitive in his nervous reactions.[1] His mother gave him all-loving care to that excess

143

which delicate children seem to claim and which in their later lives may become of such far-reaching influence. Marcel adored his sweet looking, tender mother with an adoration that wanted her all to himself. And in the self-confession he gave to the world in *A la Recherche du Temps Perdu* ("Remembrance of Things Past") he speaks of the anxiety of sleepless nights when his mother's absence became unbearable, and of her night kiss which brought the peace that passes all understanding. His ambivalent attitude toward his father, whose conscious good will he appreciated at times, but whom he chiefly experienced as a rival for his mother's love, impaired still further his harmonious development. The father's indulgence for the little boy's desire to keep his mother with him in the night, withholding the expected punishment for the gratification of his wish to do away with the father, may well have had its weighty consequences also.

Contrary to his father's wish Proust insisted on becoming an author; and he took further revenge upon his father in the medical personages of his work who may excel in their profession, but show the one-sided practical intelligence that Marcel disdained above everything.

Already at school he showed an aptitude for writing and was one of a group of gifted boys who all later on contributed to the literature of their time. Bergson, whom he personally knew, had a decided influence upon him, although he never fully accepted his teaching. Perhaps he was most indebted to Ruskin in these early years; not only for his love for Gothic art, but also his aesthetic theories, which show the latter's influence. Proust translated the *Bible of Amiens* and *Sesame and Lilies* into French and added copious notes in which he gave expression to his own views upon art and beauty and on the collaboration of religious thought and love of sensual beauty.

The salons which Proust frequented gave him an opportunity of hearing good music in which he delighted, and of forming one of the staunchest friendships of his life, that with the composer Reynaldo Hahn. The circle of young aristocrats and the artists admitted to their exclusive milieu gave him an opportunity of satisfying his thirst for artistic enjoyment and for animated discussions on the subject.

As a young man Proust was cherished and admired in the highly cultured circles where he was a regular guest and where his eccentric attitude, his over-politeness, and hypersensitiveness with regard to the slightest look or intonation, only seemed to enhance his popularity. He had many friends whom he sought to bind by charming kindness and generosity; but he lived in a continual fear of having hurt and thus risked losing them. The vast correspondence of these years with its very characteristic alternating tones of pleasure and pain, shows that his own feelings also were exceedingly vulnerable and he seems at times to have lived in great tension and anxiety concerning these social relations. It is as if he knew himself that he was not capable of giving or receiving love in the full sense of the word.

The passivity of his attitude, the suffering meekness and humility alternating with sarcasm and pitiless remarks betray his underlying revolutionary feelings, his obstinacy in revolt, his hardness under an apparent willingness to efface himself before others. Characteristic also is the tendency of giving much too costly presents, of exorbitantly praising the work of his friends, even when he knows it to be much inferior to his own and of little real value.

When he is 32 his father dies and three years later his mother. Then follows the seclusion from all earthly things, until the moment of his early death. Refusing to see his brother, the physician, who might have alleviated the terrible sufferings of his last days, having put himself on a diet of starvation, when he feels that the liberation through death is drawing near, he repeats the parting from the mother and the feelings of hatred for the father which were the dominant chord in the disturbed polyphony of his life.

Marcel Proust had never been able to overcome that period of his childhood in which he loved his mother to the exclusion of everybody else. The love for her persisted in its primitive phase when she provided the infant with everything he needed; that phase in which the child feels himself and his mother as a perfect unity. This experience of love remained "Paradise Lost" throughout his life. He continued to maintain the infantile attitude in which nobody and nothing can exist outside himself and in which the outward world has no reality except in so far as it is the reflection of himself. "Man is that being who cannot get out of himself," he says, "who only knows others within himself and, when he says the contrary, lies . . . we are irremediably alone." He was never able to attain fully that stage of development in which the libido reaches out for the object, and in his attempt to find sexual relations of an object-character he never succeeded in getting beyond the homosexual stage.

The absence of direct reality in his love relations is exemplified also in the increased "charm" of the beloved the moment associations to works of art are suggested. When Swann in his married life has ceased to love the once so fervently desired Odette, but for the few occasions when she is able to arouse his jealousy and suspicion, she becomes dear to him when he sees in her a likeness to Botticelli's women portraits or when her hand suggests that of the angel in the painter's "Magnificat." And the memory of *"La jeune fille en fleurs"* against the background of the sea, the rocks and the sands as one of the little poetic group among whom his craving for love erred, enhances Albertine's personal attraction which in her captivity no longer exists for him.

Fixated in the primitive relation to his mother, all his later loves are repetitions of the only reality in love he ever knew. He will always have the tendency to keep the beloved all to himself, that he may be guarded against the anxiety of her absence, and on the other hand this absence with its uncertainty and painful tension will be a *conditio sine qua non* for the preservation of his love. He identifies alternately with the mother and the child; his infantile satisfactions are of an oral character or consist in gazing at the beloved object especially in her sleep when she has lost consciousness, is concentrated within her body and unable to escape him in thought or look. Proust recognizes this character of his love, when in the rightly famous pages on "seeing Albertine sleep" he says that he never experienced anything similar since the distant nights of Combray, when 'his' mother bent over his bed and came to bring him peace in a kiss." The only real communion, the only oneness with another life bestowed upon him, was that with his mother and instead of the development into higher, more diversified forms, there was, as he grew older, only the yearning for the return to the blessedness of his childhood.

As long as his mother lived he repeatedly tried to fulfill their common desire and become an author. He succeeded in finishing the two Ruskin translations and in writing a volume of short stories *Les plaisirs et les jours* ("Pleasures and Regrets") which contains many of the themes of his later work and a promise that did not escape the best writers of his time. He was convinced that life had meant to bestow on him the vocation of expressing in terms of art the message which would be the expression of his individuality, but insurmountable barriers seemed to make it impossible for him to live up to his vocation.

It was as if the mundane life he led, with its many distractions and its filling of his days with charming nothingness, prevented him from taking up serious work. The very fact, however, of his being dominated by what was alien to his brooding self-concentration and his thirst for an understanding of "true reality" is indicative of a flight from himself into that which is loud enough to drown the inner voice. But moreover, a vocation is of a holy character and he on whom it is bestowed must be worthy to be its bearer. Was there not in him the unconscious murderous wish against his father; was there not the underlying tendency to inflict upon his mother the anxiety which all his childish illnesses caused her and the choice of this means of keeping her in bondage; was there not also that form of his sexual life with its uncertainty, its incompleteness and anxiety that never allowed him a moment of full satisfaction and was a source of continual worry and deception to his mother? One of the very characteristic utterances of his feeling of guilt is when he says that sons are not always like their fathers; . . . they achieve in their faces the profanation of their mothers. Also, the scene between the composer Vinteuil's daughter and her girl friend celebrating their homosexual relation with acts that profane the father is an eloquent expression of his horror of himself. The redemption of the father through the birth of his glorious compositions is a clear exemplification of Proust's own attitude toward his work, and when in his last volume he tries to understand the profound connection between his own psychic experience and the work of art that was its fruit, the thought of that same momentous night comes back to him when the "abdication" of his parents made his guilt feeling find an expression in a decline of health and will and led to the daily postponements of the task he set himself. The removing of the repression on the day when the fulfillment of his vocation becomes possible "not only illuminates the blind gropings of [his] mind, but also the aim of [his] life and perhaps of art." Words in which he shows the psychoanalytical understanding of the meaning and function of art.

Consciously Proust may have wished to become an author

all the time; consciously he may have tried to soothe himself by considering his good will and his hopeless attempts; unconsciously he knew that feelings of such suicidal guilt as he had did not allow him the self-liberation that writing would have been for him. Only if he could punish himself so hard that the ever-present sense of guilt would be satisfied, could he allow himself to give shape to his unconscious life, to expiate his sin by committing it again in fantasies. Unconsciously knowing that there is no expiation for a criminal deed without its repetition in fantasy he excluded the world and its pleasures—he excluded outward temptations and all the sensual beauty that had been so dear to him, and he retired into loneliness, into an ever-increasing invalidism and lived under conditions that were the nearest approach to the time when in the literal sense of the word he and his mother were still one. Then only he found within himself the liberty to follow his vocation.

A la recherche du temps perdu is the expression of the reality of Proust's world, a world that exists only within himself, and in which outward things may find their translation. For not only with respect to his sexual life, but also with regard to everything else outside himself, he is unable to come to a full object relation.

Objects to him, then, have meaning only if he is able to reach a "true reality and diversity" behind their appearance. The outward world as it appears to us is the imperfect image which can be known through the senses and which the intelligence fixes through habit. "Only gross and erring perception places everything in the object, whilst everything is in the spirit." It is interesting to notice in this connection the various aspects one person in the work offers to the different personages: Rachel, the actress whom St. Loup got to know in a *maison de passe* and who became a much appreciated actress is another woman in her lover's eyes than in those of Marcel;

Albertine, a very insignificant, though vicious person to others, is the source of extreme suffering and much valuable thinking to Marcel.

The intellectual concept is that which can be communicated to others, as it is based on the dubious logic inherent in the intelligence and required in the communication of our thoughts. "True reality" has only an intra-psychic life and is that which the unconscious preserves in its hidden treasury. The routine of daily life prevents us from having access to this reservoir of the essential in our experience and it is only through a mechanism which Proust discovered for himself that he is able to revive the past within him. From his first attempts at expressing himself he vaguely knows that there are hoarded in the depth of the psyche experiences and sensuous impressions from the years of earliest childhood onward and that there is a possibility for him to have access to them. He feels that only thus will he understand the essence of things and never once questions his gift of re-creating this inner reality in a form that will give pleasure of an aesthetic character. The doubts that besiege him in his early manhood are mainly connected with his search for subjects of such philosophical or intellectual importance and abstract truth that they are worthy of the Work of Art, never with the question of his ability to transpose the unconscious, once it has been able to reach consciousness, into its equivalent in artistic re-creation.

The first experience in the years of his boyhood of the inexplicable feeling of well-being at the sight of the sun shining on a landscape awakened in him a sense of duty to see clearer into the exaltation that then could only find utterance in his flourishing his umbrella and repeatedly shouting "Zut!" But every time afterward when he could not "succeed in discovering" what lay hidden beyond what he saw, he accused himself of mental laziness. At that time he was an adherent of the theory of participation and declared himself a believer in the Celtic mythical belief that he could liberate "his lost ones" from their captivity within inferior creatures or inanimate things.

The first achievements in giving shape to the "reality" behind the appearance of things concern his vision of the church towers of Martinville during a carriage drive; their steeples, the movement of their lines, and the shifting of the sunlight on their surface beckon him to something that these movements seem to contain. Then it is as if their solidity is torn, a thought rises within him that takes form and he has that feeling of exaltation. As he follows their appearances and disappearances, the variety of their shapes and illumination by the setting sun, he knows that what is behind all this must be analogous to a beautiful sentence: he is able to write his first bit of artistic prose.

The artist can only communicate the truth. Proust knows from now on, when he expresses the connection between two different things "analogous in the world of art to that of the law of causality in that of science" and thus extracting their essence, he will reunite the one to the other, liberating them from the contingencies of time in a metaphor, and will link them together by that indescribable chain of an alliance of words.

In the interview which Proust gave to a critic after the publication of *Du côté de chez Swann* ("Swann's Way") he explains that his psychology is three-dimensional: "I have tried to isolate this invisible substance which is Time and for this indeed the experiment must have duration." Novels of the unconscious he calls his work, not built on a memory feeding on the intelligence and the eyes, which gives of the past only faces without truth, but on "involuntary memory," when a scent, a savor recaptured under quite different circumstances, brings back the past almost in spite of ourselves. Through the co-operation of the actual impression and the revived past the "extra-temporal" reality becomes conscious and it is this process which Proust tries to express in an intelligible form akin to a musical theme. The timeless inner reality is that which the individual may call his own and the shape his vision of it assumes is the style of his artistic work.

It is not in broad daylight, when the exigencies of daily life have their claim upon him, that the artist is able to resurrect his past experience; either a sensuous impression brings it back to the light, or the state between sleeping and waking and, in a peculiar form, the activity of dreaming.[1]

The reviving process which psychoanalysis applies on scientific grounds in its research and its therapeutic work is more or less conscious in the artist as one of the privileges that make him the exceptional human type he is, the other gift being that mysterious power of transposing his inner truth in terms of beauty. Proust himself gives an interesting explanation of the artistic potentialities of those contents of his psyche he is able to reach in obscurity and silence when he says that the truths one has attained in oneself float in an atmosphere of poetry, in the sweetness of a mystery which is nothing else than the token of the twilight which we have to pass, the exact indication of the depth of a work.

Proust was one of the few who not only had the consciousness of their own unconscious, but whose art is a glorification of this inner re-creative process and of its hidden meaning. He knew of the inner freedom which the loosening of repression brings; he also knew of the expiation of unconscious guilt and its need of punishment through the confession of the innermost self and of the pleasure in pain gained by committing the mortal sin again in fantasy, not only for the artist, but also for his readers who, if he but adheres to his inner truth, will be the "readers of themselves." Much of what Freud built into a grandiose structure that would revolutionize human thinking in many fields belongs to the elements of that dualistic world of fancy and thought which Proust created in the search for the *temps perdu*.

The most instructive example of his description of this mental mechanism is the rebirth of his youth in that charming provincial town of Combray.

The famous episode of the *madeleine* soaked in tea describes how a sensuous impression may first awaken the conviction that the unconscious can be revived and that it will yield the essential. This is how he describes the process: "Then I feel flutter within myself something that displaces itself, that would rise, something that had been loosened from its anchor at a profound depth; I do not know what it is, but it mounts slowly, I experience a resistance and I hear the rumble of the distances gone through." While he concentrates himself on repeated endeavors to set free what seeks its liberation, there is a sudden opening up of the unconscious, a revival of his youth in Combray, as in the Japanese shell which, when laid in water, opens and shows a whole town.

What is thus revived is a visual memory linked to a savor, preserved in the unconscious as a "photographic negative," and the *souvenir involontaire* gave it back a positive reality. In its concealment it was subtracted from the influence of time in which it had been incorporated. It has now acquired an existence *en dehors du temps*. In the last volume of his great work, where Proust analyzes his psychological theories, he says how often in life objective reality disappointed him because one can admire only through the imagination and this means the exclusion of the actual object.

There cannot exist any doubt concerning the resuscitation of the past, it is a revelation and yields a "fruitful and true pleasure." It is through involuntary memory that this inner psychic reality may be reached; if conscious thought is applied, it remains hidden in the "great, impenetrated and discouraging night of our soul which we thought of as void and nothing."

Words being the medium of conscious thoughts and the conventional symbols of human contact, they bar the way to what is the individual reality rather than serving as a means of discovering it. "We feel in one world; we think, we name in another; we can between the two establish a concordance, but not fill the gap." Real communication between people is impossible.

"That inexpressible something that differentiates qualitatively what everyone has felt" must be left "on the threshold of the sentences in which we can only communicate with others in restricting ourselves to exterior things common to everybody and without any interest."

There is only one way of giving voice to this inner reality: if words have to be the medium, we must string them together into a metaphor, thus lifting into the more fluent form of the comparison that which conventional speech can only impart in the form of rigid, conscious expression as a compromise of the different voices in the "polyphony of thinking." (Stekel) But better than in a metaphor, reality may be expressed without words when it takes shape in art in a re-creation of the incommunicable.

Thus "landscapes which would have remained as unknown as those there may be in the moon" may become transferable to others. The world is always re-created by the artist; it will last until the next geological catastrophe which an original new painter or a new author will bring about. For every great artist is the creator of a new world, and if science may have led to the conclusion that the individuality does not exist, works of art testify to the contrary. We think in one world and we experience and feel in another, and if we are able to take away the names of things and invest them with the form which they have within ourselves, we have accomplished the only way in which truth, our truth, can be revealed to the world. Reading the "inner book" is already a creative act. His instinct enables the artist to read it; to his instinct he must always listen and have the moral courage to accept its dictates unreservedly, without the restrictive selection of conscious intelligence in its subordination to the purposes of practical life. He must give these findings shape in his art, thus making art into the most real, the most austere school of life, the "last judgment."

Proust is one of the very few who were able to raise this creative process into the conscious, and thus his work is not only the image of his inner self, it is also an exposition of the forces working in the composition of the work of art. But that in an inextricable way theory and poetic creation are bound up together so that the one can hardly exist without the other is one of the instances of duality in Proust's *oeuvre*.

The mechanism of the unconscious, the failure of the intelligence to preserve that which is of real value, but its indispensable co-operation when the involuntary memory claims shape—all that and many more theoretical reflections of other subjects: on repression, the strata of the human personality, on the meaning of the "psychopathology of everyday life," are formulated in such a way that we feel what their discovery means to the artist in his quest for inner reality. Perhaps the most beautiful instance is the picture of the revival of Marcel's grandmother, a year after her death, when in a *souvenir involontaire et complet* he found again living reality. And only then he knew that she was dead. In the superficiality of his mundane life there has been no place for her because linked up with the troubles of memory are the *intermittences du coeur*.[2] "Without doubt it is the existence of our body which to us is like a vase in which our spirituality is inclosed, that induces us to suppose that all our inner possessions, our past joys, and all our sorrows are perpetually our property. Perhaps it is as inexact to believe that they escape or come back. In any case if they remain in us it is most of the time in unknown regions, where they are of no use whatever to us, and where

155

even the most usual feelings are repressed by memories of a different order, excluding all simultaneity with them in the conscious. But when the ambiance of sensations in which they are preserved is recaptured, they have in their turn the same power to expel everything that is incompatible with them, to establish in us only the ego that lived through them." And so in his misery and illness, having experienced the same anxiety and having made the same movement which once brought his grandmother's loving care, the same minute is revived in which she bent over him.

There is, however, another duality in Proust's work which from an artistic standpoint must be looked upon as an imperfection: the best part of the work is the shaping of the unconscious, but there are long, dull, learned pages where Proust acts as the teacher and consequently as that type of man which he violently dislikes. It is as if this identification with his father is too strong for total exclusion from his work and we may ask ourselves whether the fact that he allowed those descriptive, intellectual pages to find their place in the whole is not one of the strongest proofs of his extreme sincerity toward himself. If he had applied the standard of his highest level, they ought to have been impossible. But he is so unrelenting in his demand for inner truthfulness that even what he, in his very keen self-criticism, rejects in himself and condemns as the extremely unartistic follows the dictate of the instinct and must find its place.

The exclusion of conscious volition in the sensations vouches for the truth of the past they revive; evasion by purely intellectual work may have scientific, not artistic value. From these views it must follow that Proust has a very poor opinion of the literature that is satisfied with the description of things, where it is only the conscious attitude toward the present that counts. Thus a "motion picture" is made in which the writer's personality plays no part, while the artist can but write the

book he does not invent, but which exists within himself, so
that he must only translate it: "The duty and the task of an
author are those of a translator."

Proust's lifelong fixation in the unsolved Oedipus complex
and the domination of his life by his yearning for the Paradise
Lost of the relation to his mother make it clear that the pleasure
principle remains with him a factor of major importance.
Always on the quest for pleasure he knows that if ever it is
obtainable for him, he will have to pay a heavy price of sorrow.
Pain is a necessary condition in everything which ultimately
will bring him pleasure, in love and in art. Only then, when
his fantasy is able to inflict sufficient pain, is he able to reap
the reward, fully in his work and only imperfectly in his
love. The whole art of living, he says, is to make use of the
persons who cause suffering to us as of "rungs of the ladder
allowing us to reach the divine form and thus daily to people
our lives with divinities. The perception of such truth makes
me happy; and yet I seem to remember that more than one of
them I have discovered in suffering, others in very mediocre
pleasures."

Over and over again Proust insists on the element of pain as
essential to the lover and the artist; and for the good it promises he is willing not only to accept it, but even to create it.
". . . The cruel law of art is that people must die and that we
ourselves die in undergoing all forms of suffering, that may
grow the grass not of oblivion, but of eternal life, the thick
grass of fruitful works. . . . Whatever it would be that I should
love it will always have its place at the end of a painful pursuit
in the course of which I should first have to sacrifice my
pleasure to the extreme good, instead of seeking for it there."

The uncertainty, the misery, and the occasionally hardly
bearable tension of jealousy is essential to his loves, and it is
enough for him to have, for a moment, the illusion of possession

to kill his once fervent desire. In his work he takes upon himself the mental repetition of all the suffering he went through in fantasy and reality and he even adds all the misery he would have been capable of enduring, had fate been good enough to think him worthy of it. In our short lives, he says, it is only while we suffer that our thoughts, agitated as it were by perpetual and changing movements, cause to rise as in a storm, to a level where we can see it, that whole immensity ruled by laws, which, posted before the wrong window, we have not seen. For the calm of happiness leaves this immensity unruffled and at too low a level; perhaps only for a few great geniuses that movement constantly exists without requiring the agitation of sorrow; besides it is not certain when we contemplate the ample and regular development of their joyful works that we are not too easily led to infer from the joy of the work that of the artist's life, which was perhaps a miserable one.

The joy of giving birth to the work of art in which his unconscious looses its bonds, and above all the price of immortality, of coming generations living in communion with him through his work, is the highest "crown of sorrow."

Happiness in Proust's opinion may be salutary to the body; it is pain that develops the forces of the spirit. It often reveals psychological laws, but always forces us to take things seriously, pulling out again and again the weeds of habit, skepticism, light-heartedness, and indifference. It is indispensable to the artist, although it hastens his death and causes those awe-inspiring, ravaged faces to develop, the faces of the old Rembrandt, the old Beethoven, objects of derision to the world. But he willingly accepts this dumb heartache because it can raise above itself the visible permanence of an image with every new sorrow; he can accept the physical pain it causes for the spiritual understanding it brings. He seems to see some strange, mystic transmutation of bodily decay into luminous spirituality and to seek suffering for its contribution to his artistic perfection. Happiness to him is "useful only in one sense, that of rendering suffering possible, . . . for if we had not been happy, be it only in anticipation, misery would lose its cruelty and consequently its fruit." It is as if in ever-renewed immolation of himself and others who are his creatures and his self-made instruments of torture, he conquers the omnipotence that makes him the god of his own world, in the work of art. On the level of the creative artist the child in him once again believes that pain brings his own reward, because unconscious anxiety requires conscious victory over retributive, avenging powers.

Proust's conception of the psychic meaning of the work of art is thus an approach in terms of emotional experience to the Freudian concept, as it is developed by his school, attributing to it the function of an expiation in fantasy re-enactment of the original sin in a form that affords aesthetic pleasure and in such disguise that others are able unconsciously to live through the same psychic process, thus affording them a temporary freedom from repression together with the satisfaction of their sense of beauty. Perhaps Proust's imperfection as an artist is due to the fact that his entire work did not succeed in presenting a sufficient disguise and perhaps also that is why he desires "when the work shall be finished [that he], mortally wounded, [shall] suffer for long hours, abandoned by everybody before dying," his work not having sufficed to make up for the "indifference with which he saw his grandmother agonize and suffer near him."

But that he also knew of that function of the work of art which is going out into the world of men to win love for the lonely recluse who was its author, appears from the passage on the painter who "perhaps lived in loneliness, not from indifference, but from love of others and whose work perhaps was meant for others as a return to them, that people without

159

seeing him might love and admire him, might speak about him; for a renouncement is not always total from the beginning, when we decide about it with our old soul and before it has worked upon us by reaction, whether it is the renouncement of an invalid, of a monk, of an artist or a hero." In Proust's own renouncement there is that of all these lonely ones together.

And so the artist unites within himself the vulnerability of the child and the omnipotence of the god. When Proust speaks of the re-creation of the world through every great artist he must have felt the revival of the infantile sense of omnipotence. Also, the meaning he attaches to names, their suggestion and their power, his creations in words that rival musical composition and painting in color, vouch for his unconscious belief in the omnipotence of thought. The name may become for him a real sexual fetish: the repetition of the name Gilberte, the juggling with that of Swann, etc. But it is to his gift of suffering and to that other precious gift, to be able to say what he suffers, that we owe Proust's work.

The ideal artist in Proust's work is the composer Vinteuil, the sufferer in silence. At the time when he writes his greatest work his name is hardly known and he lives away from the world in a little village. He is almost ashamed to show his work to the very few people he knows and who might have some understanding of it. He has got only one great love, his daughter, and she betrays him and inflicts upon him her homosexual relations with a girl friend. Never a word of complaint is heard from the artist, who, when this "shame" becomes known to him, retreats even more from human intercourse than before and yearns for death as his only refuge. His sorrow, his hopes, and his love find their sole utterance in musical creation of unsurpassed beauty. Proust does not go into a detailed analysis of Vinteuil's life, but in frequent references to the Beethoven of the last quartets we see that he understood the

composer's profound suffering and his masochism as a powerful element in his artistic creation.

If Vinteuil is thus a personification of one of the most
important aspects of Proust himself, the medium of his art is
that language which Proust considers as the most perfect instrument of human expression. Music is the language that does not
know of conventionalism and the fixity of the word, it is an
eternal flowing and its moments of rest are ever-varying expressions of tension, differing in intensity and possibility of duration. Music is the narcissistic language par excellence; ignoring
the object as a medium for expression, it lives in the inner
hearing only, and the beings it creates, the musical phrases, are
"supernatural creatures" having independent existence. The
composer brings them from the divine world to which he has
access, to shine for some moments on our own.

Who like Proust rejects outer reality must regard music as a
means of communication for which unknown development
would have been possible, if the language of words had not
been a necessary consequence of the development of human
culture. This thought points to his recognition of the infantile
element in music and to his knowledge that critical consciousness is eliminated in this most direct form of unreservedly expressing emotions and sensations.

His favored way of picturing outward things and inward
experience by metaphors reaches its most perfect development
when the metaphor is of a musical character.

Of great interest also is Proust's capacity of composing music
in words; his wording of Vinteuil's sonata and septet, his
description of Chopin's musical phrase are word-music of so
suggestive a character that the musical-minded reader hears the
composition within himself.

Florence Hier in her book *La musique dans l'oeuvre de
Marcel Proust* rightly remarks that the narrator's story in
Proust's entire work is accompanied by music. It is that of

the church bell in Combray, that of the sea in Balbec, that of the restaurant in Rivebelle; in Paris it is the songs, the street cries, and the music of the "salons," it is the sound of the piano to which the hero sits down to play and to muse. And then there is always, deep down within his mind, a background of sonorous memories, songs, musical pieces heard in the past, which rise from the depth to translate in sound the color of his state of mind and body. There seems to be a close affinity between music and life as Proust conceives it.

When in his description of Vinteuil's septet Proust speaks of "the immaterial and dynamic combats" between a phrase that incarnates happiness and another of a painful character in which the former remains triumphant "it is an ineffable joy that seems to come from paradise" and a call, super-earthly and unforgettable, and he asks whether this joy can find its realization for him.

He sees music as the power that gives him access to the secret realities of life, the supreme guide to the understanding of things so precious that they are hidden to the ordinary mortal, and the means of expressing truth in the purest form.

Besides the special quality of the language of music to which we referred before, we venture to think that it is this freedom of expression which music allows to the unconscious and its significance as an ever-flowing undercurrent in life that makes Proust the potential composer he shows himself in his work.

In relation to life and to art there is one question especially that obsesses him: the question of immortality or, as he expresses it, the question of the reality of the eternity of our thoughts. In the moments when he is in touch with the unconscious, when his being is free from the bonds of time and living in the "extra-temporal," his ever-present death anxiety leaves him. But there is such a yearning in him for certainty concerning eternal life, such an anxiety that it might perhaps not exist, that he comes to constructions so utterly unreasonable that they can only be looked upon as rationalizations of his *triebhafte* wishes. When he suggested that the desire to act on the dictates of goodness, scruple, sacrifice can only be explained by our coming from a world entirely different from this one, he accepted a form of mysticism which, in his later years at least, he had entirely dropped. It should be borne in mind that this paradise of all perfection is bound up in his unconscious with the prenatal stage of unity with the mother. "The real paradises are those that one has lost." But throughout his life music for him is of a distinctly religious character and a link to eternity; he considers the joy it gives as "super-earthly, the boldest approximation to the beatitudes of the beyond."

At other times he doubts whether nothingness might be the truth and our dreams non-existent, but then he would have to accept that the musical phrases and the notions that exist in connection with them would have to be void of meaning. This thought is intolerable to him and he turns to the consolation that, if in our death we can take "as hostages the divine captives of music, death with them would have something less bitter, less inglorious, and perhaps less probable."

And so the question arises whether in art there is a deeper reality than in life and whether the emotion music is able to give does not correspond to a certain spiritual reality. Throughout his life he continues to hear in music an appeal; it says that something better and higher than all the treasures, and even than that of love, is capable of finding its suitable expression. The vocation of the artist becomes a religious one, that of revealing to humanity truth, inexpressible in words, and beyond the reach of the intelligence.

With an artist whose work was so fundamentally honest, so unreservedly true to himself as that of Proust, it is only to be expected that the form is organically bound up with the contents. He clearly states in the last volume, where he allows the reader full knowledge of all he knows himself of the genesis of his work, that "style for the author, in the same way as for the painter, is a question, not of technique, but of vision. It is the revelation that would be impossible through direct and conscious means of the qualitative difference there is in the way in which the world appears to us; a difference which, if art were not, would remain the eternal secret of each of us."

If for Proust's style a designation were required, it would have to be called impressionistic. Whether it is in the exquisite representations of the beauties of nature, in the suggestive evocation of concrete objects, in the word pictures of Vinteuil's music—which Proust composed himself—or in that of real composers or again in those devoted to Elstir's painting, or Berma's acting (expecting to hear Berma pronounce the well-known words from Racine's *Phèdre*, Proust says: "At last I shall see them bathe indeed in the atmosphere and the sunshine of the golden voice"), there is always an evocation, never a description. As all these experiences exist only within himself, they are never fixed in rigid outline, but always seem in ever-shifting perspective of time and space, reflecting the psychic strata and the intra-psychic movements. His perception in musical matters is often visual, in painting it becomes musical, and metaphors are the means by which his subjective world can be presented. Speaking of the marines of his painter, Elstir, whose "probity makes him ignorant of everything before setting to work, because what one knows is not one's own," he says that his metamorphoses of sky, sea, and land into each other are "analogous to those which in poetry are called metaphors, and if God the Father had created things in naming them, it was in taking away their names or in giving them others, that Elstir re-created them. The names that designate things always respond to a concept of the intelligence, foreign to our real impressions, that forces us to eliminate from them everything not related to that concept.

Everything of which we want to know and to express the

inner reality is the total of many past impressions reactivated by the actual. Its image, whether it is expressed in the ever-moving medium of music or in the stability of the art of painting, always suggests the inner emotional movement and it is this fluidity that allows participation of others, who, through the artist's magic, live in the sublimation of their own unconscious world.

No wonder that Proust is a lover of that wonderful group of French nineteenth century painters who are known as impressionists and of whom his own painter is the ideal synthesis. No wonder music is the highest human utterance for him and Chopin and Debussy speak in a language which he, as well as his reader, feel to be his own. No wonder also, that, when he rises to his greatest perfection, his phrase has the sound of music and at times suggests color and perspective. For those who feel in impressionist art a more direct utterance of the unconscious than in other more disguised forms of artistic expression, Proust brings the confirmation of their intuitive feeling. The "primal functioning" of the unconscious, which does not know of the restrictive forces of logic and reason, is reflected in a form of art that to a marked degree rejects these conscious factors, and in which the form-giving elements are more than elsewhere of an aesthetic character, i.e. directed to giving pleasure in freeing us from the bonds of outer reality and inner guilt feelings, so that impressionism creates a fairy-land which we experience as a pleasurable reality. The picture of the little river and its waterflowers tells its own tale: the waterlilies on the lake, green from the shadow of overhanging trees, or sometimes, toward the evening, a light blue merging into mauve. A watery flower bed and a heavenly one.

Proust reproaches Elstir for liking one building because it is old and disliking another because it is new; he considers such an opinion to be in contradiction to his impressionism, as it makes him isolate the object from the light in which it bathes.

A little white suburban house, built for well-to-do middle-class people may tear the torrid air in mid-summer with as "acid a cry as the odor of cherries waiting till dinner is served in the darkened dining-room, where the glass prisms, on which the knives rest, project multicolored fires as beautiful as the windows in Chartres." The subject of art is without importance; it is the riches of the unconscious that count, for only they are able to invest the outer world with light and shadow, form and motion that belong to the artist's individual world. What we believe a thing with a definitive aspect is a hundred others just as well; each of these is relative to a perspective not less legitimate than that to other perspectives. "The universe is true for all and dissimilar to everyone," says Proust.

For the artistic achievement the only thing that counts is the indefatigable striving for perfection. The artist's conscience, the super-ego, must in this "last judgment" show a severity appropriate to the requirements of creating a transfigured inner world. Only where there is that reaching out for perfection in the work of art will the task be done and the liberation in death become possible. When Bergotte, the personification of the author in Proust's work, knows that death is near, he is irresistibly drawn to Vermeer's "View of Delft," where he wants to see "a little section of a yellow wall, so well-painted that it was, if one looked at that only, as a precious Chinese work of art, so beautiful, that it was sufficient unto itself"; he feels his vertigo increase but "attaches his eye, like a child, to the yellow butterfly, that he wants to capture, to the precious section of wall. 'That is how I ought to have written,' he said. 'My last books are too dry, I should have put on several layers of color, rendered my phrase precious in itself, as that little section of little wall.'" His last vision is that of the heavenly balance, in the one scale his own life, in the other, the little section of wall. He felt that imprudently he had given the former for the latter. Having passed judgment on himself, he dies before the image of real achievement.

It is said that in his last conscious moments Proust changed in this passage what he only knew on the approach of death, and with it he expresses that the self-imposed duty of attaining perfection, which would have brought him his full redemption and the glorification of his mother through her son, had not been entirely completed.

1941

NOTES

1. One of the doctors in his work gives voice to Proust's appreciation of "nervous" people, "that magnificent and lamentable family which is the salt of the earth. . . . We enjoy the fine music, the beautiful pictures, a thousand beauties, but we do not know what they cost those who invented them in sleeplessness, tears, spasmodic laughter, urticaria, asthma, epilepsy, and death-anxiety, worse than all these to suffer."

2. The *intermittences du coeur* is a concept that assumes successive egos unacquainted with each other. but capable of contact through involuntary memory. In terms of psychoanalysis, these "cessations of the heart" are the consequences of repression and occur under the same psychic conditions.

◘ ROMAIN ROLLAND:

THE PSYCHOLOGICAL BASIS

OF POLITICAL BELIEF

John Cruickshank

The literary critic who considers it a legitimate part of his activity to examine a writer's political beliefs normally carries out his investigation at three different levels. He must obviously begin by establishing and arranging those facts which constitute the subject of his inquiry. This is the easiest of his tasks, though all critics do not possess those analytical and objective powers which it demands. It is an activity performed at the descriptive level, and as such it is confined to a dispassionate repetition of ideas and attitudes already formulated by the writer himself. Yet even this preliminary task has its own difficulties. Simplification and systematization constantly tempt the critic. The unthinking or improvised nature of much political belief is all too easily organized or recast in the interests of clarity and design. Therefore, unless the allurement of neat intellectual categories is avoided, the critic's exposition may be thoroughly misleading.

Even in those cases where description and exposition have

been faithfully and satisfactorily carried out, the achievement is one of duplication and abstraction only. A portion of the writer's thought has simply been repeated as precisely as possible. Furthermore, it has been isolated from its intellectual and emotional context, being reproduced as an independent whole. Such separation, however convenient, clearly leads to artificiality and another type of misleading simplification. The writer's political beliefs did not develop in a void. They were stimulated and modified by contact with other ideas and personalities. They received a certain coloring from the intellectual and emotional climate in which they circulated. At this stage, therefore, the literary critic finds himself obliged to expand the scope of his investigation. He must turn from the recording of facts to the consideration of sources. He must move from the descriptive to the attributive level. Here a new difficulty presents itself. The critic has already described the political thought of his subject. He now proceeds to describe the personal and public changes which accompanied this thought. But on what basis does the critic decide where the points of contact and interaction are placed? To attribute them accurately, and to develop a reliable causal pattern, is a difficult and delicate undertaking. If we grant—as it seems we must—the ability of certain critics to discern influences accurately, a further problem intervenes. Why did a particular set of influences, though equally available to both, produce an effect on writer *A* and produce no effect on writer *B?* Or why was *A* influenced differently from *B?* It is when questions such as these are asked that the attributive type of criticism most quickly breaks down.

There remains a third level from which a writer's political views may be examined. This is the evaluative level. Its dangers are less serious simply because they are more obvious. In assessing the political beliefs of a writer, the critic may be tempted into a displacement of emphasis resulting from a strong emotional reaction to his subject. It is all too easy for his own views to eclipse the thought which he originally set out to evaluate. He may interpose himself to such an extent that the object of his assessment becomes obscured from his own and the reader's view. The result is exploitation rather than evaluation.

It would seem, therefore, that the admittedly unsatisfactory nature of most attempts by literary critics to deal with a writer's political beliefs can be assigned to three main difficulties. At the descriptive level, simplification and systematization may easily lead to deformation. At the attributive level, causality presents problems too often ignored. At the evaluative level, exploitation becomes difficult to avoid and is sometimes even consciously and actively pursued. Nevertheless, these perplexities need not prove inescapable. They do not necessarily inhere in all aspects of the study of political belief. They form part of one approach, but the subject is such as to allow of different treatment. They would seem rather to be an inevitable consequence of limiting the examination of a writer's political beliefs to their content. As long as the emphasis is placed on the substance of thought the problem will remain. An attempt to explore the form of political belief therefore seems worthwhile. Ideas and attitudes are available at any given period. A selection of these ideas and attitudes, conscious or unconscious, is made by the individual. The subject of investigation can therefore become not the content of those ideas which have been selected, but the form of the selecting mechanism which determined their choice. The emphasis shifts to the structure of the individual's mind—to those characteristics of intellect and sensibility which prompted him to accept certain ideas and reject others. The information resulting from a predominantly psychological study is more likely to be accurately presented than that which emerges from an ideological treatment.

Romain Rolland's political thought lends itself particularly to the former approach. Not only has it not been investigated along these lines, but Rolland has suffered more than most from deformation. He was a controversial figure in the First World War, and he remained so until his death in 1944 after a long association with left-wing politics. The "committed" quality of Rolland's writing has made it particularly liable to critical exploitation, even though this commitment aimed at the establishment of truth and justice rather than the furtherance of partisan advantage. It therefore seems necessary to attempt an investigation of Rolland's political attitude from a new standpoint. This can best be done by demonstrating the presence of a consistent pattern in his mental approach to any given question.

Critics have been slow to grasp the fact that Rolland's thought in general, whether on religious, political, or aesthetic questions, is erected on two consistently held principles of *process* and *unity*. His mental activity takes its pattern from these two elements. His awareness of movement, and the emphasis which he places on becoming, give rise to linear and temporal forms. His desire to harmonize and synthesize introduces lateral and spatial movements. On the one hand he travels backward and forward in time, noting change and consistency alike. On the other hand he directs his thinking outward in space, extending his attention on either side of the temporal line and seeking to embrace increasingly disparate elements. The first page of his memoirs testifies to his own awareness of the part which movement played in his development. The manuscript bears this prefatory remark:

Jamais je n'ai mieux senti qu'en confrontant ensemble ces témoignages fixés de tous les âges d'une vie le flux incessant de la vie et de l'être intérieur.

His conscious desire to synthesize is indicated by his dedication of *L'Âme enchantée* to "l'Harmonie, reine des Songes, Songe de ma vie." Evidence such as this, however, is inadequate in itself. It suggests a pattern such as that just outlined, but it does not demonstrate its nature. Therefore, before establishing a relationship between the pattern of his mental processes and the form of his political convictions, it is necessary to examine in more detail the evidence for asserting Romain Rolland's preoccupation with process and unity. By doing so, we shall also obtain a clearer idea of the precise meaning of these terms as applied to his thought.

The extent of Rolland's awareness of movement is most easily shown by indicating the way in which he picked out and approved this awareness in others. The clearest examples are to be found in his views on pre-Socratic philosophy, Hindu religion, and the thought of Rousseau and Goethe. From his writings on these topics there emerges a picture of universal mobility extending from a constantly changing individual self to the rhythmic processes of the cosmos. All phenomena enclosed within these limits, whether geological, biological, psychological, or sociological,, can be correctly interpreted only in the light of a constantly evolving reality.

Rolland found the incessant becoming of individual identity clearly expressed by Rousseau, particularly in the ninth *Promenade:*

Tout est sur la terre dans un flux continuel qui ne permet à rien d'y prendre une forme constante. Tout change autour de nous. Nous changeons nous-mêmes, et nul ne peut s'assurer qu'il aimera demain ce qu'il aime aujourd'hui.

Self-inspection reveals the mobile basis of individual psychology. None of us is a constant and unified "I," but a sequence of selves. We are characterized by self-succession, and any sense of immobility which we may have is simply due to the persistence and regularity of these changes. Now, just as our mind and senses alter, so must the external world as we know

173

it by private experience. The physical world, from the individual's point of view, exists only in relation to his mind and senses, and since these change and develop in accordance with experience and circumstance, so the world which they construct is constantly changing. Each individual creation, whether plant, animal, or human being, is subject to an inescapable law of mobility and, ironically enough, the author of this law is man himself. In his biography of Swami Vivekananda, Rolland emphasized his own assent to certain similar implications contained in the Hindu doctrine of *Maya*. He agrees that the existence which our senses confer on the external world is not absolute and fixed. It is based rather on an indefinable mixture of reality and appearance, certainty and illusion.

It may be argued at this point that to say our senses reveal to us an unstable world may merely amount to declaring them unreliable. The impressions of external phenomena which intoxication produces are not normally regarded as manifestations of objective reality. An attempt must therefore be made to disengage ourselves, as far as this is possible, from an entirely individual and subjectivist standpoint. Otherwise, the alleged changefulness of the external world may simply be attributed to the workings of private illusion.

A possible escape from the charge of solipsism may be found by turning one's attention from the immediate indications of sense to comparisons made in time. Retrospection allows of more objectivity than does direct and immediate scrutiny; one is bound to consider data which, by their temporal distance, present themselves primarily to the mind rather than the senses. Rolland's own training as a historian encouraged him in such an approach. He reached a belief in the objective reality of movement mainly through a study of historical vicissitude and evolutionary biology. He later found confirmation of his own theories in the writings of Goethe. As a young man he had disliked Goethe's work, and it is significant that his subsequent enthusiasm arose from a realization of the mobile aspect of Goethe's thinking. He discovered the Goethe who wrote to Zelter on October 30, 1808: "Kein Mensch will begreifen, dass die höchste und einzige Operation der Natur und Kunst die Gestaltung sei." ("Nobody wants to understand that, in nature as in art, the formative process is the supreme and only process"). Rolland now took as his credo a phrase from the *Westöstlicher Divan*—"Stirb und werde": die and become. He regarded this phrase as summarizing his own view of the world —a world governed by the constant rhythm of evolution and revolution. Development and change, progress and regress, are revealed by historical thinking. Existence involves time, and time involves becoming. In short, Romain Rolland saw process working itself out both in the individual and social spheres— *tempora mutantur nos et mutamur in illis.*

Rolland also considered the evidence for non-human movement to be overwhelming. He pointed out, by way of example, the increasing confirmation in modern theory of those mobile interpretations made by Goethe in geology and botany. Even in pre-Socratic thought these interpretations had been anticipated in a remarkable way by Empedocles, to be repeated and extended in the Darwinian theory of natural selection as modified by De Vries. In an essay on Empedocles Rolland went further, professing a belief in cosmic movement as the source of all becoming in man and nature alike.

It is clear that such emphasis on the idea of movement may lead to complete instability and the worst kind of relativism. Nevertheless, motion and instability are not necessarily synonymous, and Rolland prevents their becoming so in his own case. The mobile element in his intellectual processes is organic, not spasmodic. His ways of thought have nothing in common with the unpredictable mobility of the grasshopper mind, nor does he view movement outside himself in these terms. He quickly grasped the fact that flux and permanence are inextricably linked. Movement requires an object which moves, and this object remains itself in fact and something else only in potentiality. Mobility without permanency is a category emptied of significance, while permanency becomes meaningless without mobility. The movement which Rolland claims as a fundamental feature of the world at large is therefore a movement of certain constant factors, for "development is a perpetual surpassing which is at the same time a perpetual conservation" (Croce).

The second outstanding feature of Romain Rolland's mental processes is his imperative desire to embrace and synthesize constantly increasing fields of knowledge and experience. Association and correlation dominate his thought. His life's work was characterized by reconciliation. He sought to reconcile theory and practice, religion and science, faith and reason, workers and intellectuals, Gandhism and Marxism, France and Germany, East and West—one might extend the list almost indefinitely. His immediate success in most of these fields was not great, for it is the mediator's most common experience to be persona non grata. Yet Rolland persisted, pointing out suggestive and fruitful aspects of common identity underlying superficial distinctions. In an age torn by particularly bitter conflicts in the religious, social, and political spheres, his thinking and his actions were outstanding by virtue of their reconciliatory and constructive nature. His life and writings bear eloquent testimony to his enduring belief in the essential and underlying unity of all living forms in their varied manifestations.

Romain Rolland considered that his belief in a constantly changing universe allowed of rational confirmation. He regarded many of the conclusions of modern science as supporting his views. On the other hand, his doctrine of the unity of being, which is at the basis of all his reconciling activity, was more intuitional than rational—hence less apparently amenable to scientific demonstration. Yet even here he saw encouraging signs. There was, for example, the research institute which Sir Jagadis Chunder-Bose founded in Calcutta, and which sought to prove by scientific experiment the essential identity of all forms of life. Rolland was interested in this venture, seeing in it a potential source of support for his own instinctive conclusions. Nevertheless, he does not seem to refer to any specific confirmation of these conclusions in the researches of Sir Jagadis Chunder-Bose, and in fact the story of how his monistic convictions were formed shows how personal and intuitional their basis was. It is worthwhile recording their origin and growth here, not only because the story is largely confined to unpublished material in Rolland's private diary, but also because it explains the persistent search for unity which characterized his ways of thinking and later shaped most of his political ideas.

Rolland has described himself as having lived two parallel and distinct lives—that of a visible and circumstantial self, and that of an essential, spiritual being, without identity or features, forming the very substance and breath of life. It is this latter self, underlying contingency and differentiation, to which Proust refers as "extra-temporal" being. In keeping with general human experience, Rolland's visible and temporal self normally remained dominant, but certain privileged moments occurred when his deeper self broke through. Two such moments—Rolland speaks of them as "illuminations"—played a particularly important part in the development of his monistic beliefs. The first occurred as he stood on the terrace at Ferney, at the age of sixteen. Here, in 1882, he experienced *un panthéisme fiévreux*, which preoccupied him for five years. Until he read Spinoza, Rolland's pantheism remained feverish and adolescent. Nevertheless, the Ferney experience rendered

177

his mind particularly receptive to the second illumination. This took place in 1887 when he opened the *Ethics* and found, for the first time, an intellectual basis and a philosophical system on which could be grafted his own elusive intuitions. He describes the effect of this discovery in words at once intense and hermetic, recalling Pascal's expression of his conversion in the *Mémorial*.

Rolland based his new-found philosophy on the proposition: "*Je sens, donc . . . il est.*" He did not say, as Gide was later to do in *Les nouvelles nourritures: "Je sens, donc je suis."* This latter statement would have appeared to Rolland to drive a wedge between the self and the world, destroying that unity on which his whole conception rested. He was convinced of the oneness and interdependence of all being, and he expressed it thus in his diary:

Dieu s'appauvrirait, l'Être ne serait plus l'Être, s'il lui manquait une seule sensation: car aucune n'est adéquate à une autre.

This appears as the counterpart, in terms of sensation, of Spinoza's own statement in a letter to Oldenburg:

Si una pars materiae annihilaretur, simul tota extensio evanesceret.

With the passage of time, Rolland began to examine his beliefs more closely. Although personally convinced of the truth of his ideas, he realized that their intellectual demonstration was weak. He therefore revised them at intervals, noting weaknesses and devising alternative solutions. His diary from April, 1887, to January, 1888, notes his attempts to solve three main problems—his relation to other selves; freedom; the nature of the external world. He presents the first problem thus: since he and Suarès, for example, share an essential identity as modes of the same being, why do they not experience fuller mutual understanding, each anticipating in detail the thoughts and actions of the other? Rolland replies to his own question by saying that to expect such a situation would be to demand a compatible contradiction. The category of selfhood must involve a certain measure of personal autonomy. Each individual has his particular role, and as one group of sensations cannot become another group of sensations, neither can one self become another self. Only death which, for Rolland, is the discarding of this circumstantial role, can create that full experience of being all individual selves. This idea of full communion between individuals in death suggests to Rolland certain methods by which, in our present life, a measure of participation in total being becomes possible for individuals. The ecstasy of the mystic, or the hypnotic methods of psychoanalysis, can induce a draining away of personal identity. External suggestion can then operate on the depersonalized subject, replacing his own normal sensations by others. In this way an impression is created of extended being, but a distinction persists between such mental states and that sensation, peculiar to death, of being Rolland plus Suarès plus an infinite number of selves. It is on these grounds that Rolland regarded death, not as the negation of life, but as its fulfillment and consummation.

Rolland turns next to the consideration of freedom. Since the category of selfhood involves the impossibility, in this life, of one self becoming another self, a difficulty arises. Can one be free if selfhood is autonomous? According to Rolland, a satisfactory answer can be given to this question only when one realizes that freedom is not a relationship, but a condition of absolute being. Absolute being, by definition, is the sole source of perfect freedom in his monistic universe, and since we are modes of this being, the extent of our freedom will essentially depend, not on our relationship to other modes, but on the degree of our identification with absolute being. Freedom is thus to be achieved by fulfilling selfhood to the maximum limit, by seeking to embrace the greatest possible amount of existence, without theory or analysis. Freedom is full living, and the mystic is most free by most thoroughly resolving the dissonance of self in the plenitude of being.

The third question asked by Rolland concerns the nature of the external world. According to his new doctrine of sensation he claims to see and feel only spirit (*les âmes*). Can he then affirm the external reality of physical objects? Rolland wishes to answer this question in the affirmative, yet his monism requires him to reject the absolute externality of the physical world, since to do otherwise is to affirm a dualism. He evades the difficulty by reducing his problem to a question of emphasis and viewpoint. Because of the limitations of my individual role, my vision lacks focus and I inevitably regard objects as external since I must view them from the central standpoint of self. Ideally, these objects can only be properly seen from the standpoint of total being—*sub specie aeternitatis*. I base my judgments on the sensations imprinted by objects on my individual self. I cannot yet understand them as they impinge on that divine spirit, that pantheism, which animates both them and me. Therefore, only when I am finally and fully absorbed, by death, into total being shall I lose this inevitable but temporary impression of externality.

Such were some of Romain Rolland's theories at the age of twenty-one. They are no doubt immature and open to those objections which can be advanced against all personal vision. Nevertheless, although tentative rather than conclusive, they established the direction and quality of much of Rolland's future thinking. He continued to speculate, being particularly dissatisfied with his inadequately defined notion of individuality. He later solved some of his problems through contact, in Switzerland, with Rudolf Maria Holzapfel, and through his discovery of the philosophical idealism of India. Hindu thought in particular offered a more satisfactory status for the individual than did the pantheism of Spinoza. Rolland finally evolved a monism which retained a sufficient degree of subsidiary differentiation, and in 1928 he wrote firmly to Hans Leo Götzfried:

La matière est aussi divine que l'esprit. C'est le même Être considéré d'un point de vue différent,

and

Je crois à l'unité de l'Etre. Je crois à l'identité essentielle du sujet et de l'objet.

On this evidence, therefore, one can claim that Romain Rolland saw life as presenting two main aspects: process and unity. He shaped his own thinking in accordance with the picture which he had established, so that the structure of his thought possesses a double movement. It is progressive and it is reconciliatory. This suggests the pattern of the Hegelian dialectic, for his thought moves through opposites to a superior harmony which embraces both. Descotes, in his book on Rolland, goes so far as to claim a direct influence, but it is difficult to find any specific evidence in support of this view.

Given this emphasis on process and unity, the main principles of Rolland's political thinking at once emerge. His social theory is dynamic and progressive. He regards social change as both inevitable and desirable. In some societies the natural rhythm of political evolution must be recognized and implemented. In other societies—for example those faced by the "unnatural" situation of European supremacy and exploitation —the more violent tempo of revolution must be accepted as the only means of initiating a forward movement. In both cases, the goal toward which movement is made will be a fuller realization of equality of rights arising from that underlying unity which a static social theory tends to conceal. All *a priori* theories of social or racial supremacy run counter to that spiritual view of the world which makes unity its basis. Social and racial differentiation, in so far as they exist, cannot affect the undifferentiated spiritual reality which underlies them. These,

181

then, are the broad principles which maintained Rolland's position on the political left. The instinct to keep his thinking mobile and unitary ultimately determined his political attitude.

The double pattern of Rolland's thought—its combination of flexibility with an assimilative tendency—not only decided the general orientation of his political theory, but imparted certain distinguishing features to it. These features, which follow from his preoccupation with process and unity, are: independence of party ties, belief in artistic commitment, tolerance, insistence on the dignity and uniqueness of the individual person. A short discussion of each will complete the picture of how Rolland's mental characteristics molded the contours of his political convictions.

In the first place, Romain Rolland's attitude is characterized by independence and the capacity to change his point of view. His thinking was too flexible to become insistently dogmatic or narrowly doctrinaire. An awareness of movement and a desire to synthesize introduced into his thought a measure of restlessness which rebelled against the limiting demands of group loyalty. He steadfastly refused to join any political party. He preferred to remain unaccountable to a disciplinary system which, on occasions, would inevitably tend to place considerations of party solidarity above truth. Furthermore, an intellectual insistence on the underlying unity of life means that the purest form of mental activity must concern itself with universals. This is another argument for refusing any reduction to the arbitrary dimensions of a prearranged system. And so, Romain Rolland persisted in assuming entire responsibility for his political views, emphasizing at the same time his unwillingness to commit himself to a particular policy of future action.

Rolland's refusal to become a party politician is to be taken as a measure, not of his indifference, but of his deep and serious concern with those problems which political activity seeks to solve. This concern led him to adopt a position which many would regard as suicidal in a serious artist. He attempted, both through his imaginative writings and in articles and manifestos, to exercise political influence. When art and polemics consciously seek to live in harmony, art frequently suffers most from the experiment, and many critics would say that Rolland provides an example. Yet whatever one's point of view, one can understand how the unitary tendency of Rolland's thought shaped his attitude. He believed that no man, whether an artist or not, can abstract himself completely from political and social life. The individual lives within a group of some sort, and those theories which seek to separate him entirely from his social context ignore evident facts. The artist, in particular, possesses special vision and has at his disposal a unique means of communicating his perceptions. A privileged gift for language, which is his by definition, involves him in serious responsibility toward his readers. While he has a clear duty to extend and enrich his own spiritual and intellectual life, he must not allow his attitude to harden into complete egotism and indifference. He should renew his vision mainly in order to communicate it with new and persuasive power to others.

Also, Rolland considered it his civic duty to make his views publicly known, but he regarded his theories as being of little value until he had tested them in a practical way. Although reacting against what he held to be the moral degeneracy of much professional politics, he was not content to remain aloof. It was his constant concern to harmonize theory with practice, and he therefore sought to divert into practical and fruitful channels that objectivity which his independence of party ties made possible.

A third characteristic of Rolland's political thinking is his capacity for tolerance. The virtue of tolerance is a further consequence of mobile and unitary thinking. Both the temporal and spatial movements of Rolland's mind introduce broadness

183

of vision and an awareness of relativity. The relationships which result, based either on similarity or contrast, can only be rightly judged by reference to that ultimate unity which they suggest and which transcends them. Rolland's tolerance therefore arose from his desire to reach an essential unity underlying apparent diversity. He considered that while many systems of belief contain partial truth, no creed offers infallibility. This was the basis of his reconciling activity. He conceived it as his duty not to reject out of hand an alien system of belief. He attempted rather to discover what was true in all creeds, defending and extending their common fund of wisdom. This was the cast of mind which he brought to bear on the tensions and conflicts of the Third Republic in France.

An insistence on the unique importance of each individual is the fourth consequence of Romain Rolland's capacity of mobile and unitary thinking. His monistic beliefs rendered the relationship between man and deity that of the mode to its substance, and a wholly spiritual view of man resulted. It is part of Romain Rolland's significance as a writer on social and political matters that he fought unceasingly for a fully dimensional view of the individual. He was the determined opponent of any force seeking to enslave human personality or diminish the complexity of human needs and aspirations. He realized the presence, in our modern unbalance, of tendencies which threaten to dehumanize human life. It is from this viewpoint that one must judge his tireless campaigning on behalf of colonial peoples; his championship of Gandhi against the British in India; his appeals on behalf of Sacco and Vanzetti, Norris and Patterson; his denunciation of fascism and nazism. In fact, Rolland gave to the fraternal idea its full, logical extension. He accepted the brotherhood of man as a spiritual reality, relegating the brotherhood of some men with common beliefs and interests to the realm of convenience and expediency. Here his awareness of process is again important.

It means that no particular communal grouping can be regarded as final. It allows for man's further growth in spiritual understanding. It recognizes that no terrestrial organization can be a complete substitute for that identity between men which can be fully attained only in the godhead. In a word, it not only realizes the manifest difficulties of the fraternal idea but, despite these obstacles, it emphasizes the need for a sustained effort to approach this ideal more nearly.

1954

CHARLOTTE BRONTË:

A STUDY OF A

MASOCHISTIC CHARACTER

Kate Friedlander

On entering the Brontë saga, we move at once upon highly emotional ground. It has struck me as significant that my attempts to discuss *Jane Eyre* with English friends immediately elicited the question: did I not know of the tragedy of the author's life? A great many biographers are attracted by Charlotte Brontë's personality, much more than by her work. Although at the present time many libraries are inaccessible, I have nevertheless been able to acquire sixteen biographies, some of them consisting of several volumes. In comparison with this it is interesting to note that during the investigation only five biographies of Dickens came to my notice, though there are plenty of books on his work. This disparity is in itself a point of psychological interest, but much more so when one finds in these biographies ardent disputes about facts which could easily be objectively ascertained. One theme especially is made the center of attention: most authors agree that Charlotte Brontë suffered and bore her lot with admirable patience and piety; but there are disputes about what caused her suffering, whether it was fate, the treatment she received from her harsh and cruel father, the loneliness and bleakness of the West Riding landscape, the sadism of her teachers, or the horrible life she had to lead in her situations as a governess. Some of her biographers go so far as to hint at the possible loss of some masterpieces, unwritten under these conditions.

We owe the first biography to Mrs. Gaskell (1857), then already well known as a novelist and a personal friend of Charlotte Brontë, who was commissioned by Charlotte's father to write this work. The book appeared two years after Charlotte's death. Soon after publication Mrs. Gaskell was threatened with two libel actions and invoked the fury of the father at whose request she had written the book. Strange that this should happen to a distinguished writer who had striven hard to collect letters and to ascertain facts! Such passages as were considered objectionable were deleted in subsequent editions and the modified book has remained the standard life, which clearly shows that it was well constructed and that the cause which led to the threatening libel actions was entirely unintentional. Yet, even in the revised edition, a tendency on the part of the author appears which is not compatible with the stating of mere facts. This tendency to paint Charlotte all white and to account rationally for her sufferings must have been the upshot of a strong emotion in the biographer, which also caused the inclusion of the passages whose incorrect and libelous character Mrs. Gaskell had completely misjudged.

What were these much-discussed passages? There is first of all the description of the school which Charlotte Brontë attended from her eighth to ninth year. The bad food, the cruel and indeed sadistic treatment of the children were much insisted upon and made responsible for Charlotte's future development. Considering that most of the mistresses and pupils who were Charlotte's contemporaries were still alive and could have furnished facts, it seems to be a gross mistake that the evidence was mainly based on the description of Lowood orphanage in *Jane Eyre*. Furthermore, Charlotte's father was described as a bigoted, hard, cruel man with frequent fits of temper, who did everything he could to suppress any joy of life in his children. Again, bad and insufficient food, bad housing, etc., were especially emphasized. Evidence was collected from village gossip, mainly from Mrs. Brontë's old nurse, who had been dismissed from the parsonage thirty years before making these slanderous remarks. Another such mistake occurred in relation to Charlotte's brother Branwell; but discussion of this is beyond the scope of this paper.

Apart from these libelous passages, there are also omissions, which are no less significant. Charlotte's homosexual passion for Ellen Nussey, which lasted for six years in unabated strength, is toned down to a girlish friendship; no allusion is made to Charlotte's love for M. Héger, which had a decisive influence upon her life.

This is certainly a strange state of affairs. A distinguished writer makes gross mistakes in compiling the biography of an author whose contemporaries are still alive, and omits every circumstance indicative of conflicts and passions in the soul of an artist whose very hold on humanity lies in the emotions and passions displayed in her novels. But Mrs. Gaskell was not alone in showing this prejudice. Subsequent biographers used the allegations made in the first edition and distorted them further, although they must have been aware of the hue and cry after the book had appeared and of Mrs. Gaskell's apology printed in *The Times*.

We may well be interested in the personality of a novelist whose first book aroused an emotion in the public so strong that an unknown spinster became famous overnight, whose novels after a hundred years are still among the classics of

English literature and whose influence on the public was such that for a century a great many biographers were involved in hotly disputed arguments to maintain the picture of a suffering saint.

Charlotte Brontë was born in 1816, the third daughter of a Yorkshire clergyman. The only son Branwell was born in 1817, the two youngest daughters Emily and Anne in 1818 and 1820. Soon after the birth of the youngest daughter, their father became vicar and the family moved to Haworth Parsonage, near Bradford, where they settled permanently. When Charlotte was five and a half years of age, her mother died of internal cancer, probably after she had been bedridden for some months. An elder sister of her mother's, a rather severe but kind-hearted spinster, came to take care of the motherless children and stayed there until her death in 1843. At the age of eight Charlotte entered the school at Cowan Bridge, which later became the much-abused orphanage of Lowood in *Jane Eyre*, where her two elder sisters, Maria and Elizabeth, had already been pupils for six months. During the one year of Charlotte's stay in the school Maria and Elizabeth died of consumption. From her ninth to fifteenth years Charlotte, now the eldest, was at home together with her brother and sisters under the care of Aunt Branwell and a very devoted maid, Tabby. During this time her father taught Charlotte and Branwell, and Charlotte taught the younger sisters. At the age of fifteen Charlotte went to school again at Roe Head, where she stayed for a year and a half and to which she returned (after having been at home for three years) as a mistress for another two years. Then, suffering from a nervous breakdown, she went back to Haworth Parsonage. In the following year she had two proposals of marriage, both of which she refused. During the next three years she held three positions as a governess, for a few months each, and stayed at home in the intervals. In 1842, when she was twenty-six, she went with her sister Emily to Brussels to be a pupil in the *pensionnat* of M. and Mme. Héger. With a short interruption caused by the death of her aunt in 1843, she stayed in Brussels for two years, the latter part of the time as a teacher. On her return home in 1844 she did not put into practice her old idea of opening a school but remained at home with her father, who was threatened with impending blindness. She never left Haworth Parsonage from that year onward for any length of time. In 1846 she published poems together with Emily and Anne, and shortly afterward, in 1847, *Jane Eyre* appeared, followed in 1849 by *Shirley* and in 1853 by *Villette*. In 1848 Branwell died of consumption, followed a few months later by Emily and a year later by the youngest sister Anne. Charlotte's life, after the publication of *Jane Eyre*, was divided between her literary activities and her care for her father and sisters, occasionally interrupted by a short visit to London, where she met members of the literary world. During that time she had a third proposal of marriage, which she again refused. In 1852, when Charlotte was thirty-six, one of her father's curates, the Rev. A. B. Nicholls, declared his love for her. She married him two years later, lived with him in perfect happiness for nine months, and died in March, 1855, from an illness caused by pregnancy.

Such is the framework of Charlotte Brontë's life. Of her emotional life and experiences I am afraid I shall only be able to develop here those fragments which it will be most important to know in connection with the character traits I want to stress.

Nothing is known about Charlotte's early childhood. Her mother seems to have been a very gentle, refined personality; her father, an Irishman, himself had an astonishing career and was a rather erratic person. But he must have taken great care at least in the tuition of his children, certainly in that of his son and also perhaps to a minor degree in that of his daughters. There is a short account of Charlotte at the age of eight at school, where she was known as a clever little girl who was the most talkative of the sisters. This statement is important, because shortly afterward her main disturbing symptom, extreme shyness in the presence of strangers, which poisoned her whole life, must have made its appearance. During this year at school an event took place which certainly affected her future development, only in a somewhat different way from what is usually accepted. Maria, her eldest sister, died. I do not share the belief of the biographers that the death of a sister, or even the two sisters, in itself could account for the fact that Charlotte could never afterward be happy. By using the material presented in *Jane Eyre* as a manifestation of Charlotte's unconscious impulses and by comparing it with the known facts, we might be able to arrive at something like the truth.

Maria is said to have been very clever, very quiet and patient. She started school half a year before Charlotte and was not in very good health, suffering from the after-effects of whooping cough and measles. E. F. Benson (1932), an objective biographer, states that "Maria was constantly in disgrace, owing to habits common to children who have not sufficient physical control, and was often punished by a junior mistress, called Miss Andrews, in a harsh and excessive manner." These are the facts from which is drawn the picture of Helen Burns in *Jane Eyre*. Helen Burns, representing Maria, Jane's friend from the very first day she entered Lowood, is the subject of the most cruel persecution. Her misdemeanors are not always clearly defined. She is untidy and has dirty habits. This would indicate too that Maria suffered from enuresis diurna. Helen Burns is misused, beaten, has to stand alone in a classroom, so that everybody knows she has done something wrong, and suffers these cruelties without any wish to rebel; she even herself fetches the bundle of twigs with which she is to be beaten. It is this submissiveness and lack of rebellion which outrages Jane and throws her into fits of temper. The whole childhood history of Jane Eyre is preoccupied with the theme of the struggle against inflicted cruelties and a constant repudiation of the attraction of a masochistic fantasy on a deeper level. The more attractive the masochistic fantasy, the more violent the rebellion against the inflicted cruelty.

A very typical phenomenon, which we can usually observe in masochistic patients, occurred also with Charlotte Brontë. She left this school at the age of nine. She had never mentioned anything of her experiences until after the publication of *Jane Eyre*. But apparently every little incident was kept fresh in her memory and burst suddenly forth with passion. From her letters we can see that small occurrences of injustice rankled in her mind for years and appeared then in a somewhat distorted form in one of her novels. It is very significant that Mrs. Gaskell had to admit that Charlotte only once made any allusion to these school days and then only said that for a certain period the food was bad. But a certain reticence in Charlotte's behavior and her reluctance to say more convinced Mrs. Gaskell that the account in *Jane Eyre* was in accordance with the truth.

We are inclined to think that Charlotte's emotion in discussing the subject was felt by the person she was discussing it with and aroused the unconscious fantasies of the hearer. We find over and over again that in her letters Charlotte intimates by some remark that she is suffering, though hardly expressing what has caused her state of mind; and the biographer at once speaks of her suffering at that period as a reality caused by her circumstances.

The death of her sister Maria had probably impressed Charlotte in many ways. It undoubtedly revived the feelings of guilt connected with the death of her mother, which occurred at the height of the oedipal phase. Furthermore, in so far as she identified herself with Maria, it must have impressed her as being the result of "dirty habits." Apparently she tried to defend herself against the onrush of feelings of guilt by defaming the school, and especially the mistress to whose persecutions she ascribed Maria's death. But most important for our theme is the likelihood that the event revived an old masochistic fantasy of great intensity, probably connected with Charlotte's relationship to her mother, and the struggle against yielding to this fantasy seems to have been at the root of her constant unhappiness.

An incident in Charlotte's later life shows a repetition of the same conflicts. When she was a mistress at Roe Head, she had taken her youngest sister with her as a pupil. One day Anne caught a cold and started to cough. Although Charlotte was on very good and friendly terms with Miss Wooler, the headmistress, on this occasion she created a scene in which she behaved quite unreasonably and accused the headmistress of having caused her sister's illness by her inattention. Miss Wooler had understanding enough to excuse Charlotte's excitement and the difference between them was made up, but Charlotte remained in a very depressed state of mind and six months later suddenly left the school, as she stated in a letter, "because I cannot bear it any longer." Clearly it had been on her responsibility that Anne had come to the school and she had been in as good a position to notice her sister's illness (which, incidentally, was really only a cold) as the headmistress. But again she had to defend herself against her feelings of guilt by means of the accusation against Miss Wooler, to whom she continued to remain hostile.

Charlotte's masochistic attitude and her hostility toward women is shown clearly in her position as a governess. As soon as she enters a new family her letters convey the impression that she is being badly treated by her employer and the children. Her actual accusations are that her employer does not understand her and does not try to do so, that she is not as amiable to her as she appears to be to other people, and sometimes also that she is coarse and uneducated. Charlotte had three situations as a private governess and felt unhappy in each of them, hating to go there in the beginning and always very apprehensive as to her employer's behavior. The slightest unfriendliness or coolness at once hurt her deeply and as she writes in one of her letters: "I find it so difficult to ask either servants or mistress for what I want, however much I want it. It is less pain for me to endure the greatest inconvenience than to request its removal. I am a fool. Heaven knows I cannot help it." All her letters are full of sharp sarcastic criticism of her employers and their children, but she always has something good to say about the man in the house.

I think it is important in this connection to say something about Charlotte's personal appearance and behavior. She is described as of small, slender stature, with a pleasant though not pretty face, a rather large nose and a somewhat crooked mouth. She was always very neatly dressed and looked a little bit quaint, but very feminine. She was extremely shy and could not talk easily, was very often even unable to answer when she was addressed. Sometimes suddenly, when she was excited, she would break out with all her repressed accusations. It is easy to imagine her behavior if one knows her novels, because she presents a good picture of herself as Jane in *Jane Eyre* and Lucy Snowe in *Villette*. It is also very easy to imagine how provocative this little person, with her clever searching eyes, her constant silence, and her suffering expression, must have been for her less educated employers, who must have guessed the contempt she felt for them.

It seems clear that the occupation of governess was uncongenial to Charlotte. "No one but myself," she writes, "is aware how utterly averse my whole mind and nature is to the employment." She did not like children at all and was constantly on her guard to repel their "rude familiarities" as she called the demonstration of their affection. Yet from very early onward it was her plan, to which she adhered with a high degree of tenacity, to call this the chosen profession for herself and her sisters, although educational problems did not play the slightest part in their discussions. But the first possibility of opening a school of her own was rejected, instead of which she went for further studies to Brussels. On her return home she decided not to put her old plan into action, but to remain at home with her father, who was threatened with impending blindness. A half-hearted attempt was made to take some boarders at Haworth Parsonage, but no pupil ever answered the prospectus and the whole scheme was at last abandoned.

Certainly Charlotte's wish to be independent, about which we shall presently hear more, was one factor in her taking up the school scheme so early, namely at about her twelfth or thirteenth year. But it cannot wholly account for the choice of a profession which she consciously detested and for which she had no qualification other than the necessary intellectual capacity. It seems much more likely that unconscious factors played the determining part in this choice. We remember that her masochistic fantasy was revived at school in connection with the death of her sister Maria, with whom she had apparently identified herself. We have also seen how hard she was fighting against yielding to that fantasy, which she felt to be so very dangerous. Nevertheless the attraction of the fantasy was strong, and where could she have more possibility for indulging in it and for living out a sadistic fantasy than in the profession of a schoolmistress? Her constant dissatisfaction and her hatred of her various situations as governess and schoolmistress are probably the expression of a defense against yielding to the masochistic pleasures which were amply provided for her. The attraction ceased to work when she was not to be employed any more, but would be free of oppression and her own mistress. Very important evidence of the unconscious attraction of the teaching profession is expressed in all her novels. Nearly all the love scenes in her novels take place between teacher and pupil, as if she could not imagine that a passion between a man and a woman could arise out of a different situation. Of course there are important alterations. The teachers are men, the relationship is pleasurable and a sexual one, only occasionally are there scenes in which the inhibition of exhibitionism causes acute embarrassment. The counterpart in life was Charlotte's great and unhappy passion for M. Héger, her teacher in Brussels. The relationship to her father, who we may assume was her teacher and who was certainly the teacher of her brother Branwell, is here interwoven with the attitude of dependence between pupil and teacher as an expression of the masochistic fantasy which probably originated in her early relationship to her mother.

So far I have tried to show some justification for my belief that Charlotte's constant sufferings were the expression of this masochistic fantasy. Her descriptions in her novels of psychic pains, of the effect of injustice and cruelty on a sensitive mind, in short her descriptions of every unhappy feeling and relationship, are very beautiful and genuine. We have also seen that the intensity of this fantasy was such that it imparted itself not only to her friends but also to the public and to subsequent biographers.

But this fantasy forms only one side of Charlotte's personality, that part which, as being an expression of a direct instinctual drive, has impressed itself most on her surroundings. Let us get a glimpse of her character which is somewhat different from the usual picture.

Charlotte did not succeed in reaching her aim of opening a school, not because she was unable to do so, but probably because that aim lost its attraction. But whenever she was a pupil or a teacher she was successful and earned the highest praise for her work. Her intellectual abilities and her tenacity in achieving a task were among the outstanding features of this remarkable personality. Though constantly suffering, or, as we say, constantly having some instinctual gratification of the passive masochistic type, her activity was strong enough to attain positive achievements of a high order. From a very early time, she developed the idea that women should have a profession and not simply wait for a husband. In this conception she was fifty years in advance of her time. She saw two openings for herself: that of literary activity and that of a teacher. We have seen the fate of the latter and I want only to add that the plan of opening a school was always strengthened when her hopes of a literary career were disappointed. Although she never expressed openly her intention of becoming a writer, the school scheme seems to have been a second best.

For the development of her activities, especially her literary career, the relationship to her brother and father and, naturally, the particular way in which she coped with her penis envy are of paramount importance.

Although more than five years old when her mother died, the only recollection Charlotte had of her mother was seeing her playing with Branwell, her younger brother. I believe that the traumas which decisively formed Charlotte's character were not so much the deaths but the births of her brother and sisters. Branwell, only a year younger than herself, was the only son in a family of six children and the declared favorite of his father, and in him that ambitious man invested all his hopes. He was a very clever and very good-looking boy and his education was undertaken solely by his father. When the girls went to school, Branwell stayed at home. There is nothing known about Charlotte's early relationship to Branwell. But between the ages of nine and fifteen she shared daydreams with him, some of which were written down. They had a country called Angria and their heroes fought there. Charlotte's hero was the Duke of Wellington, with whom she identified herself and who remained her hero throughout her life and appeared over and over again in her novels. Apparently in these daydreams with her brother Charlotte represented a boy and her relationship to her brother was a homosexual one.

When Charlotte returned from Roe Head at the age of sixteen, these literary activities were taken up again and poems as well as prose works were poured out in great quantity. Branwell still shared her full confidence and wrote himself at great speed. One of the prose works of that time, *The Spell*, has been preserved and is said to be of no literary value whatsoever. Charlotte always wrote under a male pseudonym, her *nom de plume* being at this time "Lord Wellesley." When twenty, she sent a poem of hers to Southey, then poet laureate, for criticism, while Branwell at the same time asked the opinion of Wordsworth. His letter was never answered at all, while Charlotte, who had for once abandoned her pseudonym, got a very discouraging reply, containing the remark that "literature cannot be the business of a woman's life." She commented bitterly on this phrase in her letters and stopped her literary production altogether. During this time the school scheme came into the foreground. Only four years later did she start writing again, and then she sent the beginning of a Victorian novel to Wordsworth. Again she was discouraged and in her answer to Wordsworth's letter, who seems to have alluded to the author as probably being a woman, ironically and very cleverly evaded the question, stating that the sex of the author was no concern of his. Again her literary activities stopped entirely and the school scheme was taken up until as late as 1846, which was nearly two years after her Brussels experience.

At that time certain events had happened which must have

worked together to free Charlotte's talent. She had been passionately in love with M. Héger, a married man, and for two years afterward she was miserably unhappy. But this experience alone was not sufficient. A novel which she then wrote (*The Professor*) was published only after her death and does not yet show her particular quality of writing. Probably the fate of her brother Branwell was more important. He had not fulfilled the hopes which he had promised. Having been unsuccessful in writing, he developed an interest in painting, and there was a plan that he should be sent to the Royal Academy in London. A portrait of his three sisters, which he painted at that time, is in the National Portrait Gallery. It is not known why this plan did not succeed. But instead of going to the academy he became a clerk in the Manchester Railway, and this incurred Charlotte's bitter criticism and sarcasm. He began drinking; once more he had a position as a tutor, but was dismissed on account of an attempted love affair with the wife of his employer and returned home, in 1846, where he led an idle life, drinking and making scenes and becoming generally unmanageable. He died in 1849 of consumption. Charlotte showed her contempt openly and, although she was his best friend and companion, sharing all his literary activities as long as he was still brilliant, she hated him now so much that through these last years of his life she did not even talk to him. But it was when Branwell's decline and her separation from him had taken place that she started to write again, this time successfully.

The immediate starting point was that by chance she found in her sister Emily's desk a collection of the most startling poems. Although Emily was deeply wounded by this intrusion into her privacy, Charlotte succeeded in persuading her to publish them, as the gentle Charlotte always imposed her will successfully on her sisters. And now she did something which is utterly mysterious, if ulterior motives are not taken into account. Instead of publishing Emily's poems alone, she made a collection of Emily's, Anne's, and her own poems. One cannot doubt Charlotte's critical faculties for a moment. Even if she had lacked objectivity toward her own work—she had no poetical faculty—she must have been aware of the inferior quality of Anne's production. By this act she entirely crushed any success Emily's very beautiful lyrics might have had and we can assume that that was her unconscious wish. Only two copies of the collected poems, which were published under the names of Currer, Ellis, and Acton Bell, were sold.

But this disappointment did not stop her literary activity. The sisters set to work again and Charlotte wrote *Jane Eyre,* which was published in 1847 and which made Currer Bell immediately famous. Even after the great success of her novel she took great care to keep her pseudonym and she was furious whenever there was any discussion as to the sex of the author.

Apparently Charlotte, with all her expressed femininity, considered writing to be a male activity. Rational reasons alone cannot account for her emotional outbursts if she was identified as a woman, certainly not after *Jane Eyre* had conquered the public. After all, Jane Austen was in high esteem at the time. This behavior is inconsistent with her rational views on the ability of women and her claim for equality.

We have seen that her literary activity was very closely linked with her relationship to her brother. She shared this activity with him, fantasying that she was a man too. Her contempt for him when he was weak appears as contempt for an individual who has lost his manliness and with whom she could therefore no longer share her fantasy of being a man. While formerly the identification with her brother seemed all-important, it looked now as if his loss of manliness had given her the power to fulfill a masculine task. The identification was too easily disturbed by the disappointments which reminded her of her femininity. Her contempt for her brother was shown in such a demonstrative way that one could think she wanted all the time to assert that it was *his* fault and not *hers* which had made him destitute. We have seen this defensive mechanism at work in her hatred against women whom she accused of being guilty of the death and illness of her sisters.

We get some confirmation of the conception of her castration wishes against her brother from her attitude to brother-figures in novels and in life. St. John Rivers in *Jane Eyre*, the curates in *Shirley*, the admirers of Ginevra Fanshawe in *Villette* —all these she treats with contempt, sharp irony, and sarcasm, as impotent and ridiculous individuals of whom she is the master. In reality she had a very happy time for a year amusing herself at the expense of one of her father's curates whom she called Celia Amelia on account of his womanish appearance.

But from the relationship to her brother alone the fantasies connected with her penis envy do not become clear. We only see that as long as she was sharing his fantasies she was unproductive, but that his decline freed her or aided her in the desexualization of a masculine activity, while at the same time she lost her brother as a love object. We can furthermore suspect the strength of her castration wishes from the way in which she had to defend herself against her feelings of guilt.

We get further information about Charlotte's fantasies connected with her penis envy from her relationship to her father and to father-figures. On the whole one does not hear much about her relationship to her father. The reason can probably be seen in the fact that she is very reticent about her life with her father and covers up her dependence on him under her sense of duty. It is taken for granted in literary circles that her male heroes, especially Paul Emanuel in *Villette*, are formed after the image of M. Héger. Certainly. But what force drove Charlotte to fall hopelessly in love with a married man of her father's age, who had never made her even the slightest advance? We can see other intimations of the stormy power which forced her to repeat the Oedipus conflict so openly in her relationship to the families in which she was governess. I have already mentioned that she always expressed contempt for the wife and children and admiration for the man.

There is one item which I am inclined to think very significant as evidence of her still sexualized relationship to her father. The first intimation which we get of her awakening love for M. Héger is expressed in a letter which she wrote when she had returned to Brussels after the death of her aunt, who had been a mother-substitute for so many years. "I returned to Brussels after aunt's death against my conscience, prompted by what then seemed an irresistible impulse. I was punished for my selfish folly by a withdrawal for more than two years of happiness and peace of mind." It seems likely that her aunt's death revived the conflict about her mother's death, which we can assume to have been feelings of guilt on account of her Oedipus wishes. She fled from the temptation of living alone with her father and acted out the whole conflict with the professor in Brussels as a less dangerous object. Not only did her love for M. Héger then start, but suddenly a sharp hostility developed toward his wife, with whom she had been on very good terms before; there were allegations that Mme. Héger was persecuting her in the most elaborate manner. There is some evidence of jealousy on Mme. Héger's part after Charlotte's departure, when she wrote love letters to M. Héger; but the picture of Mme. Beck in *Villette* seems at least exaggerated and influenced by paranoid ideas. I am fully aware of the fact that the direct Oedipus conflict was a superficial layer behind which the old and very strong attachment to her mother was hidden. Her hostility against women was strengthened by her wish to defend herself against her homosexual wishes and the old masochistic attachment breaks through in the suffering to which she feels herself exposed in her relationship to these women. But in the present context I want to stress a peculiarity in her relationship to these beloved father-figures and I want to demonstrate it by examples from her life and novels.

I have assumed that Charlotte was driven away from her home after her aunt's death by fear of the revival of her old sexual relationship to her father. But when he was threatened with blindness she remained with him, although that meant giving up her school scheme. Various signs show that it was not her sense of duty alone which then kept her in the parsonage. I think we can get an inkling of what her father's blindness meant to her from her unconscious admission of it in *Jane Eyre*. Jane loves Rochester with a passion which is a mixture of a passive masochistic devotion and an active wish to master him. She leaves him when she hears about his first marriage and comes back, called by a spiritual voice, after Rochester has become blind and has lost his right hand through an act of his insane wife. These are Jane Eyre's own words: "Mr. Rochester continued blind for two years, . . . perhaps that was the circumstance which knit us so close. For I was then his vision, as I am still his right hand. Literally I was (what he often called me) the apple of his eye. He saw nature, he saw books through me."

Another example from *Villette*, which I will again quote verbatim, will show another aspect of a man's impending blindness and will enable us to construct the underlying fantasy.

The professor, Paul Emanuel, is in a very bad mood and nobody dares to come near him to give him a message. Lucy is sent as a last resort. She enters the classroom in fear. She ventures eventually to get near the desk. Close to him she is not afraid any more. She gives her message. He will not hear. She lays his bonnet on the desk. He will not obey the summons she has to impart: "Knowing well it would *not* do, I gently pushed the bonnet towards his hand. Thus impelled, it slid down the polished slope of the varnished and unbaized desk, carried before it the slight steel-framed 'lunettes,' and, fearful to relate, they fell to the estrade. A score of times ere now had I seen them fall and receive no damage—*this* time, as Lucy Snowe's hapless luck would have it, they so fell that each clear pebble became a shivered and shapeless star.

"Now, indeed, dismay seized me—dismay and regret. I knew the value of these 'lunettes': M. Paul's sight was peculiar, not easily fitted, and these glasses suited him. I had heard him call them his treasures: as I picked them up, cracked and worthless, my hand trembled. Frightened through all my nerves I was to see the mischief I had done, but I think I was even more sorry than afraid. For some seconds I dared not look the bereaved professor in the face; he was the first to speak.

"'La!' said he: 'me voilà veuf de mes lunettes! I think Mademoiselle Lucy will now confess that the cord and gallows are amply earned; she trembles in anticipation of her doom. Ah, traitress! traitress! You are resolved to have me quite blind and helpless in your hands!'

"I lifted my eyes: his face, instead of being irate, lowering, and furrowed, was overflowing with the smile, colored with the bloom I had seen brightening it that evening at the Hôtel Crécy. He was not angry—not even grieved. For the real injury he showed himself full of clemency; under the real provocation, patient as a saint. This event, which seemed so untoward—which I thought had ruined at once my chance of successful persuasion—proved my best help. Difficult of management so long as I had done him no harm, he became graciously pliant as soon as I stood in his presence a conscious and contrite offender."

The blindness seems to signify that by the action of the woman the man loses his manliness, becomes castrated. At the same time this action forms a firm union between man and woman which cannot be dissolved any more. Now it also becomes clear in what way the impending blindness of her father fitted into Charlotte's fantasies and therefore knitted her closer to him.

Her behavior in life toward such men was not very different from that of the heroes in her novels. Thus, she admired Thackeray very much and he was favorably impressed with *Jane Eyre*. The first meeting took place. Charlotte was so shy that she was not able to talk and the acquaintance ended in disappointment. She said in a letter afterward that the effort to talk was torture. She chiefly listened and found his talk cynical, harsh, and contradictory. Next time she met him her shyness seemed to have worn off. She wrote to her friend Ellen: "He made a morning call and sat about for two hours. Mr. Smith alone was in the room the whole time. He described it afterwards as a 'queer scene' and I suppose it was. The giant sat before me: I was moved to speak to him of some of his shortcomings, literary of course: one by one the faults came into my mind, and one by one I brought them out, and sought some explanation or defense. He did defend himself like a great Turk and heathen; that is to say the excuses were often worse than the crime itself. The matter ended in decent amity; if all be well I am to dine at his home this evening." She did dine there, and Thackeray, who was apparently very much looking forward to presenting this sharp and brilliant little lady to an illustrious set from London literary society, was bitterly disappointed. Again she did not talk, was not to be roused from her stupor, and left early.

Of more importance to her was her attitude to the man whom she afterward married. The Reverend Mr. Nicholls, a curate of her father's, had known her for eight years when he came into her room one afternoon to declare his love. From a letter to Ellen: ". . . His manner you can hardly realize nor can I forget it. Shaking from head to foot, looking deadly pale, speaking low, vehemently yet with difficulty he made me for the first time feel what it costs a man to declare affection when he doubts response." She promised an answer and wrote a refusal next day, after having had a frightful scene with her father, who was most insulting about his curate, whom he otherwise highly respected. Owing to the hostility of Mr. Brontë, which it is quite interesting to note, the situation grew intolerable for Mr. Nicholls, and he made up his mind to leave for good. Then an incident happened for which it is again best to quote Charlotte's own words: "It seems as if I were to be punished for my doubts about the nature and truth of poor Mr. Nicholls' regard. Having ventured on Whit Sunday to stop to the sacrament, I got a lesson not to be repeated. He struggled, faltered, then lost command over himself, stood before my eyes and in the sight of all the communicants, white, shaking, voiceless. He made a great effort, but could only with difficulty whisper and falter through the service. I suppose he thought this would be the last time, he goes either this week or the next. I heard the women sobbing round, and I could not quite check my own tears. What had happened was reported to Papa; . . . it excited only anger and such expression as unmanly driveler."

From this moment Charlotte had made up her mind to marry him and in time she managed a very interesting compromise. She soothed her father by arranging that Mr. Nicholls should stay in Haworth Parsonage and that he should take over most of her father's duties. So she had to leave her father only for her short honeymoon and she then experienced what she herself called the only happy time in her whole life, being wholeheartedly devoted to her husband and living only for his health and comfort. She emphasizes his motherly care for her during her last illness.

I think that the fantasy which is the basis of these incidents in her real life as well as of her creation in her novels may be interpreted like a similar one which Fenichel describes. The man becomes irresistible after he has been robbed of his manliness, while the woman herself becomes the penis, the instrument without which the man cannot exist any more. The woman becomes "literally the apple of his eye." This fantasy, which we may consider a driving force in Charlotte's activities, has of course pregenital forerunners: there is, for instance, her strong exhibitionism, the inhibition of which was so tormenting to her. The fantasy "the apple of his eye" also allows the development of feminine wishes, as the woman becomes the instrument of a strong man: in her short married life Charlotte was very happy and satisfied.

Now one can understand why the relationship to her brother was disturbed when he failed in life. He was no longer the strong man whom she helped to write novels. She regarded his failure as a result of her castration wishes and reacted to it with feelings of guilt, at the same time losing him as a love object. In order to have a satisfactory relationship to a man—either in fantasy or in reality—it was necessary for her that the man should remain strong and powerful in spite of her castration wishes. The interruption of her fantasy with her brother must have helped her at least partly to desexualize her literary capacity.

If we link this fantasy with the masochistic fantasy already described, a very interesting picture results: the personality of a mild, gentle woman who is able to impose her will at all times. I believe that the attraction of Charlotte Brontë's novels for the public is to be found in their passionate expression of these very fantasies.

I hope I have shown that the personality which now emerges before us, the personality which was hidden behind the suffering, shyness, gentleness, and piety, behind the very feminine attire, is somewhat different from the first impression conveyed by most of her biographers. We see now a woman with what one usually calls a masculine brain, very clever, very sharp, with a high degree of critical faculty and a great tenacity in achieving her aims, who is able to impose her will, gently perhaps, on her whole environment, on her sisters as well as on her father, on women as well as on men, a woman who, quite by herself, living most of her life in an isolated village with very little social contact, succeeded in becoming famous.

Whenever the theme of the so-called masochistic character is discussed, the difficulty arises of its great variety of types. In my experience, this combination of masochistic fantasy, father-fixation, and special development of penis envy is by no means rare; the result is a typical and interesting personality. In recent years I have analyzed three female patients with a similar psychic structure, of whom one, by the way, was a very gifted artist. To summarize this type in a few words, I would say that under cover of acute sufferings and difficulties a masculine activity can be carried out. It depends, of course, on the degree of desexualization of this activity how far these women are really successful in their achievements. We have here a series ranging from the mere aggressive impulse to rob the penis to the positive value of a Charlotte Brontë. It might perhaps be more correct to call such personalities phallic characters with a masochistic fantasy rather than masochistic characters.

1941

▣ THOMAS WOLFE:

OF TIME AND NEUROSIS

W. M. Frohock

Tom Wolfe's great poem rises out of our national neurosis, and his characteristic anxiety state is one that most of us have experienced in some measure. Much of America is still rural. Most Americans feel that they have rural origins. Yet our centers of education and culture, through which in the process of our growth we naturally pass, are as a rule urban in spirit and sensitive to the metropolitan influence. Thus in the case history of the educated American there is a record of the emotional adjustment by which the two cultures—urban and rural—were more or less successfully brought to terms. The city is always moving ahead and the country always catching up, so that the young man coming out of the country to the city crosses not only a gap of miles but also a gap of years. We live as if in two centuries at once and belong entirely to neither; and the boy who comes from the back-eddy of Maine and arrives on the campus of a New England university wearing his first "college cut" suit knows as well, by instinct, what Wolfe is talking about as if he had been born in the hills of North Carolina. I who write this have been reading Wolfe

over again in a place within sight of the village where I was
born, and I think I know now better than ever before what
is at the root of Tom Wolfe's vision of life.

Home is the place where you were once and where you
really belonged, even though as you remember it you were
not always happy there; a part of you which should have
been permanent. a place to which you could return after a
long stay somewhere else. But it turns out not to be the place
where, as Frost says, when you return they have to take you
in. It is not in their power to take you in. You have been away,
having gone with the premonition that you could not come
back, and when you try to return the place has changed and
you have changed (O Lost!) and nothing is as it has been.
You are, in many senses, the victim of time.

If you are from the South, the feeling may be so much
the stronger because you are more aware of the differences.
(To find a southerner who is not conscious of being a southerner is rare, whereas your Yankee, for instance, has pretty
much to migrate from New England to discover that the whole
world is not populated by people like himself!) And Wolfe
was from North Carolina. Yet the difference was one of degree
and not of kind. The breath-taking titles, themselves—*Look
Homeward, Angel; Of Time and the River; You Can't Go
Home Again*—point to the vast predicament in which a man
finds himself trapped and frustrated because everything ebbs,
flows, shifts, and refuses to be seen whole; even *The Web
and the Rock* juxtaposes an image of permanence with an
image of change. And however much his being from the
South dramatized this predicament for Wolfe, the predicament
is general. It is a paradox that a nation with as short a history
as ours should be as obsessed as we are with the flight of time.

Wolfe himself saw the predicament as something general
and at the same time extremely personal. The major part of
his effort as an artist went into trying to fix the illusory shift-

ings of memory before they should become lost. Again and again he spoke of his purpose as being to set down, in the time he had, his vision of life. Now, after twenty years of controversy since *Look Homeward, Angel* precipitated the sterile debate which centered so often about such questions as whether Wolfe was "magnificently abundant" or "merely garrulous," the scope of his vision remains the central question about him. As he wrote to his old teacher, Mrs. Roberts, he had the Dantesque ambition to create a universe; he did not dodge the question, nor can the serious reader evade it. Every writer of course creates a universe, in the sense, at least, of having to give his characters a world in which to breathe and live. But Wolfe was self-conscious about doing it. He had the characters to people his universe ready at hand. His concern was to give them a habitation, and this habitation is central to his vision.

One might say that he should have written of his ambition to *re-create* a universe, which would have been more appropriate to the process of recording a vision of the past as viewed through the distorting lens of violent and tortured temperament. "The world I create," he wrote to Mrs. Roberts, ". . . is always inside me." In another connection he wrote that the process of writing a novel was very much as if a great black cloud had gathered inside him and suddenly burst. He never hid—how could he?—the very evident fact that he was writing about himself; the unnecessary little foreword to *Look Homeward, Angel,* in which he defends his method on the somewhat preposterous grounds that there is much of Swift in *Gulliver,* serves only to show how well Wolfe knew what he was doing and how apprehensive he was, as he would always be apprehensive, of what the critics might say. His material was his own experience, as every new fact we learn about him, every new letter published, every anecdote, drives home. Under the name of Eugene Gant or George Webber, the figure of Tom Wolfe always stands in the center of his vision.

How completely different from Dos Passos, who was writing at about the same time and, to a great extent, about the same America! Dos Passos' great strength in *U.S.A.* is his ability to maintain his own detachment. As the result of a discipline which can be traced through his earlier books, Dos Passos can give his reader the feeling that the events which make up his fiction would have taken place just as surely if there had been no novelist at hand to note them down. His ability to establish his perspective—which he finally achieves by the device of presenting his autobiography as a sort of comment on the fiction—has a great deal to do with the success of his great trilogy. Wolfe is the diametrical opposite. The events of his story derive their meaning entirely from their effect upon the central, autobiographical character.

As Dos Passos depends essentially on a discipline which originated in France during the middle years of the nineteenth century, Wolfe seems to go back all the way to the English Romantics. Given the nature of his talent, it is probably just as well that he grew up out of reach of literary modes, that he read more of Virgil than of the little magazines at Asheville, that no one made him give up reading Melville to read Henry James, that he went to the state university, and that he reached the literary hot-frame of Harvard only after he was a man grown. He seems never to have played the sedulous ape or to have submitted himself to the current literary disciplines or to have acquired the writer's suspicion of himself, of the accuracy of his own senses, or of the validity of his report on them, which marks so much of the literature of our time. He never acquired the constraining awareness of the importance of technique which has conditioned men like Dos Passos. Literary sophistication simply was not his line: who else could have written, with anything like Wolfe's unawareness of the ludicrous side of what he was doing, his endless variations on lines from Shakespeare? One of his major sources of strength was that he was so completely and miraculously out of date. "I began life," he wrote, again to Mrs. Roberts, "as a lyric writer." He ended life as nothing else.

Romantic lyric poetry—and we are agreed that Wolfe's poem is romantic in many ways, including the way of revolt —is the poetry of youth. The greatest praise we give to a poet who in mature years writes lyrics of freshness and originality is that he "seems so young." This strikes me as one of the most helpful keys to Wolfe; his vision of life and the world in which he makes his characters live are the vision and the world of a very young man.

He felt himself so wretchedly, so miserably, and so magnificently alone. Despite all his use of the second person plural, Eugene Gant and George Webber never escape the feeling that their enterprises are personal and special, their cases unique. There is a story about Wolfe, that once when he was riding downtown after a baseball game he suddenly alarmed a subway car by screaming, "The bastards are ambushing me!" According to this story—which for all I know is apocryphal—Wolfe had been talking to a friend about literary critics, but the world's series crowd on the subway did not know this, did not know Wolfe and probably had not read his books, so that his outburst occasioned no little surprise. Now no one who has read his Wolfe faithfully would, or should, have been surprised in the least. The point is that we were all bastards—there was Tom Wolfe and then there were all the other people who were not Tom Wolfe and they were aliens. He went alone.

If his great feeling of loneliness was not pathological, it was at least exaggerated. He hated many things because they were not himself: Negroes (much of the time) and Irish Catholics (or at least the Boston Irish) and Brahmins and Jews. Eugene Gant and George Webber are repelled, immediately or eventually, by most of the people with whom they come in contact. The record of the autobiographical character's inability to establish satisfactory communication with other human beings suggests a fundamental difficulty, a failure to understand and to be understood, which may in turn be related to the state of compulsive frenzy in which Wolfe appears to have done much of his writing. With Wolfe, as with Céline, the other novelist of our time who approaches Wolfe in this matter of being repelled by people, one cannot help feeling that the drive to write, and to keep on writing at whatever cost in prolixity and reiteration, is tied up with some sort of despair of ever being fully understood.

Yet the exaggeration, painful as its results may be at times both to Wolfe and his reader, seems only the magnification of one aspect of the time-neurosis which so generally affects Wolfe's vision and which indeed afflicts so many of the rest of us. We live, by circumstances of our birth and culture, in two periods at once and are completely at home in neither. If we do not, as Eugene Gant did, envy the English family which appears in *Of Time and the River* simply because for all their stuffiness they were so thoroughly at home where they were, or if we do not envy a man like Morison, who is so sure of being understood that he converses always in ejaculations and fragments of sentences, the underlying feeling of being aliens and not understood is certainly not foreign to us: transplantation implies that for a long time the plant will not take root firmly. Wolfe comes by the feeling of isolation very honestly indeed.

Since I began a desultory sort of discussion of a few recent American novelists, trying to show how some who were writing in the 1930's had broken with the traditional novel as we have known it, Wolfe's figure has frequently returned to plague me. My argument, originally proposed in an article on

Steinbeck and reiterated in one on Dos Passos, is that in Wolfe and Dos Passos there is a culmination of the long tradition of the novel dominated by the desire to fix the past, to catch hold of the ceaseless flow of events long enough to preserve them in a work of art—a novel which in mood and tone is essentially lyrical and nostalgic—whereas we have recently seen a new type of novel which, by its preoccupation with violence, its disregard for time, its great concentration, its essential moods and attitudes, is very closely allied to tragedy. A writer like Hemingway comes to view his central characters as heroes whose tragic stature is established through an act or acts of violence, and makes violence a source of a new literary discipline. Steinbeck, when he is at his rare best, shows an acceptance of life as conflict, and the events of his novel rush toward an inevitable catastrophe. Erskine Caldwell destroys his effectiveness very often by wavering between a mood of tragedy and a humorous realism which, for want of a better term, I have to call journalistic. Faulkner, as André Malraux puts it, at times combines the atmosphere of tragedy with the peripetia of a detective story. But Wolfe threatens to break down such pretty—and, I hope, plausible—classifications.

Wolfe is without doubt a very violent writer, and violence is one of the materials of tragedy. There is in his work an atmosphere which, if not really tragic, is something like what Unamuno called the tragic sense of life. His characters are important to him, not the kind of nonentities which Dos Passos consistently creates, and they achieve a stature which Dos Passos' characters are not intended to have. Despite the interminable length of Wolfe's novels—which certainly do not aim at delivering a maximum impact in one place at one time—these other aspects of his work may be enough to break down the distinction between the lyrical-nostalgic and the tragic novel. And if they are, there goes my ball game.

I argue, however, that the game is not lost, because the

exaggerated feeling of man's loneliness which permeates
Wolfe's work, and which conditions his whole somewhat neurotic vision of life, prevents that vision from being a truly
tragic vision. At this point, a comparison with the work of
André Malraux becomes almost inevitable.

Wolfe and Malraux, better than any other contemporaries
who come to mind, have caught up and made their own the
feeling of man's solitude. Malraux's early jungle tale, *The
Royal Way*, is full of this great loneliness which, as it does in
Wolfe, goes hand in hand with an almost overwhelming
awareness of the imminence of death. In Malraux' other novels
(*The Conquerors, Man's Fate*) the principal characters are
beset by the problem of breaking through this loneliness into
a feeling of community with their fellows. In the act of killing by stealth, Tchen, in *Man's Fate*, is somewhat less bothered
by the fact of murder than by the solitude which terrifies him
as he commits it. Most of the other characters in the book
experience something similar. But some of them, at least, overcome this feeling of isolation. They go down, but they go in
the knowledge that their fate is *man's* fate. And this is precisely
the book which made European critics so aware of the possibilities of the tragic novel. Malraux proceeded, in *Days of
Wrath*, to write a novel—little known in America—which in
its mood, its highly compact and concentrated form, its insistence on struggle, its atmosphere of violence, comes as near to
being pure tragedy, I believe, as a novel can come. This is a
story of a man imprisoned by the Nazis, whose strength to
undergo imprisonment and torture and finally to escape comes
from his discovering that even in the solitude of a Nazi prison
no man is ever completely alone. In a preface to the book,
Malraux insists that man's loneliness and man's essential solidarity are equally important; they may not be separated.

This awareness of there being two faces to the medal, which
Malraux reaches in his mature work, is what Wolfe seems

to me never to have attained. He never convinced himself that no man is an island. Wolfe's feeling of solitude—together with his awareness of the erosions of time and the imminent presence of death—appears, in comparison with Malraux' later work, as a badge of immaturity. Not that this condemns him; many writers as great as and greater than Wolfe have been immature in this sense. But their achievement has little to do with tragedy; and neither has his. The feeling of loneliness, and of the individual's being so bafflingly penned within himself, prevents it. The first person singular, as has often been remarked, is not the appropriate pronoun for tragedy.

It would be pointless, of course, to worry such a question of what Wolfe was not, and of what he did not do, unless in the process we got a fresh view of what he was and of what he did. But consideration of Wolfe's chronic immaturity—moral and aesthetic—throws emphasis on the question of the degree to which the immaturity of his personality warped the vision of life which is our subject.

For all the lore about Wolfe—and many strange yarns are abroad about him—we really know little about him as a private person. The letters published to date are mostly literary, and, in a way, formal. The Wolfe legend is doubtless as undependable as it is picturesque; he probably was never so colossally incapable of telling the unembellished truth about himself as many stories (such as the one about his persistent complaint that he was starving like Chatterton in a garret, when actually he lived where he did only from inertia) made him sound. I have never been able to down in myself the suspicion that Wolfe's books made him look like one of the people—Stendhal was another—who spend their lives trying to see themselves as they are without ever quite penetrating the thick wall of self-delusion. We will never know what to think of such matters until his letters are all collected and published,

219

as they should ultimately be, and there is an opportunity to compare what he says of himself with the account provided by a scrupulously careful and minutely detailed definitive biography.

But meanwhile we *can* see how other people looked to him.

His ability to make incredible things seem credible is itself almost incredible. It is only when one goes back to *Look Homeward, Angel* that the Aeschylean family of the early book shows itself for what it is and the whole Pentland-Gant clan becomes implausible if not preposterous. W. O. Gant as Agamemnon home from the wars to die, Eliza as Clytemnestra (her refusal to admit that there is anything wrong with the old man being a kind of murder), Helen as Electra when she is not doubling as Cassandra, Eugene as the wretched Orestes . . . one feels that Wolfe cannot really have intended these things, and yet, vaguely, there they are! The people, if hardly the setting, of an *Oresteia*. The family taint on which Eliza sometimes, and Helen always, dwells is the Curse upon the House. And on first reading, or if one has read *Look Homeward, Angel* and no more, one accepts these things unthinkingly; the Gant-Pentland tribe seems plausible indeed when taken by itself.

But when one gets out of Altamont into the wider world of *Of Time and the River*, he begins to see that too many people are closely like the Gants and the Pentlands; there are simply too many queer ducks. Robert Weaver, drinking himself to pieces and already showing marks of the insanity "that will destroy him"; Francis Starwick, prey of a diabolical absence of passion; George Thornton, in the quiet depths of whose eyes "the fatal madness which would destroy him was already legible"; Bascom Pentland, the crazy uncle in Boston married to the crazy wife; the inordinately vulgar John T. Brill—with so many such people around it is impossible not to feel that we have strayed into some gallery of eccentrics.

At times it seems as if everyone Wolfe writes about is abnormal, or else downright insane. And after we have seen these people we look back at Altamont and are much less impressed by the extraordinary population of *Look Homeward, Angel;* the Aeschylean family now appear as only the first in a long succession of crackpot figures. There is small doubt that something in Wolfe's vision has warped them. All of them are a little like the policemen who pick up Eugene and his friends for drunken driving in a little South Carolina town.

And these huge creatures evoked for Eugene a whole history of this earth and people, monstrous, savage, and unutterable—a congruent and unspeakable legend which he knew, and all of them knew, down to the roots, and which he could not speak about and had to speak about, somehow, or die. For in these men there was evident not only the savage and mindless energy of the earth itself, with all that was wild, sensual, fecund, cruel and good-natured— the whole weather of life—but there was also evident the fear, the shame, the horror that had crushed them beneath its ocean weight of nameless and cowering dread, and broken or destroyed their souls.

Applied to a squad of country cops, this is evidently and clumsily out of proportion, but the fact is that Wolfe saw most of his characters in some such light. And because of this extravagance which works to prevent the appearance of any group of reasonably life-size characters in his books by which to measure the out-size of the others, those others, the important ones, lose something of their stature, even in *Look Homeward, Angel* and *You Can't Go Home Again.*

I had better open an apologetic parenthesis here to explain that, to my taste, *Look Homeward, Angel* and *You Can't Go Home Again* are by far the best parts of Wolfe's long novel. These two books, describing the preparation of Eugene's departure, and the later discovery that, as he had suspected before leaving, true return was impossible, haunt me, in spite of what

I have been saying about them, as no other books written in
America have ever done. But the other two, the story of what
happened to Gant-Webber between the departure and the
attempted return, seem to me less important. Possibly this is
because what happens in the first and last books of the series
is what happens, in some degree, to every American, whereas
what happens in the middle volumes is more special, to the
extent that some of the things that occur in *The Web and the
Rock* could happen only to a rising American novelist. Possibly there is another reason: it is also true that *Look Homeward, Angel* was the work of an unknown with whom the
editor could exert the authority of experience, and *You Can't
Go Home Again* was edited after Wolfe's death left the editor
with a relatively free hand, whereas the middle volumes were
products of years when Wolfe had become extremely sensitive
on the subject of editing. But whatever the reason, the second
and third books are spotty. Pick up any copy of *Of Time
and the River* and hold the page-edges to the light; the darkened sections are sure signs that the book has been read as
if it were an anthology. After the first time, one does not
voluntarily read his way through the 900-odd pages of this
book again. One goes directly to certain parts—some of the
best things Wolfe ever wrote—like the death of Eugene's
father, the race between the trains, the station stop in Troy,
the visit to Joe Pierce's icebox. As novels, that is to say *as
wholes,* the middle books do not seem to me to stand with
the other two.

Reading *Of Time and the River* directly after *Look Homeward, Angel* throws a revealing light on the people of the
latter book. The Gants and Pentlands become not tragic but
queer; not people working out their destiny, but frustrate
victims of time. Their violence, instead of being the inevitable
result of forces which drive them in a given direction, is
merely the inevitable result of frazzled nerves. A typical case

of this, perhaps the most eloquent that Wolfe ever invented, is the struggle between Eugene and his brother Luke, which takes place in their mother's living room. There is no point to the fight, nothing is at stake; doing physical damage to each other will accomplish no more than the temporary relief of the exasperation. This is violence without significance. Compare it with the fighting in *The Grapes of Wrath* or with the last chapter of *For Whom the Bell Tolls* and the distinction is clear. These are eccentrics clawing at each other; they are frustrated even in the attempt to do lasting harm; and this is the best proof possible that the people Wolfe sees, as he sees them, are not tragic figures.

Straightway we also doubt the reality of the places where Wolfe makes them move. Originally we accepted Altamont without question, but just as we suspect that the people are distorted as soon as we leave Altamont for Cambridge, so we also suspect Altamont itself as soon as we can put it in the new perspective. Wolfe's New England makes Altamont a never-never land.

. . . New England, with its harsh and stony soil, and its tragic and lonely beauty; its desolate rocky coasts and its swarming fisheries, the white, piled, frozen bleakness of its winters with the magnificent jewelry of stars, the dark firwoods, and the warm little white houses at which it is impossible to look without thinking of groaning bins, hung bacon, hard cider, succulent bastings and love's warm, white, and opulent flesh.

Harsh New England certainly is and there is no exaggerating the stoniness of its soil. Its beauty is lonely and can be tragic if you want it to be. And so forth. But New England is above all the homeland of shortage and worry, of industries that move out and of young people who emigrate because New England cannot support the children it spawns, and of old people who stay on to grub what living they can from the farms and—along the main roads—from the tourists. There is indeed a school of New England romanticists who write stuff of the "succulent bastings" sort, and there are apparently readers for it, but the difference between Wolfe's New England and the New England of people like Professor Robert P. T. Coffin is that Wolfe seems actually to believe that his New England exists. It doesn't. Here where the wind is always north-northeast, as Robinson says, care is the rule—not plenty and not sensuousness. Those cozy little white houses have but one warm room in them during the winter and upstairs the chamber-pots are frozen before morning; the succulent bastings are in the writer's mind; and love's flesh is rough with goose-pimples.

Wolfe's New York is probably better. New York is at least so various that nothing said of it can be convicted of falsehood. But here again, as Wolfe watches the gray-faced, hostile millions stream through the subways, he is an outsider. There is always something about him that suggests that he is again looking in at the cozy little white houses. The intimate sentiment of New York, which Dos Passos has in spite of all the Sandburg-Millay romanticism of the big city permeating *Manhattan Transfer*, is not in Wolfe.

It is in the nature of his talent that he should see things from the outside only, and be forced always to guess what is inside them; his vision is the vision of the outsider; and this again is a part of the national neurosis out of which, I am arguing, his vision rises and which warps it. Thus the question naturally arises, after we have finished looking at his middle books, whether his view of Altamont is not the vision of an outsider also. Did this youth of sixteen ever read all the books Wolfe talks about, or are these the reading experiences of a mature man, garnered at the University of North Carolina and at Harvard and thrown back in memory to be associated with the wrong age? And did the still younger lad, delivering papers in Altamont's Niggertown, experience all its alien mystery then, or are these also the emotions of a later age thrown back upon adolescence? All these things in *Look Homeward, Angel* sound much more like a relatively mature novelist, deep in his first work at the age of twenty-four, when he has left Altamont far behind him—as if they were a confused reconstruction of memories. No growing youth was ever quite so full of literature, never felt anything with quite such transcendent keenness, any more than the Gant-Pentland family was ever quite so monstrous as Wolfe makes it look. The reconstruction of the past is a notoriously tricky enterprise and Wolfe has been tricked in it.

Thus, just as we were saying a bit earlier that the first person singular is not the appropriate pronoun for tragedy, so also we have to add that the perfect is not the appropriate tense. Recollection of tragic events does not make tragedy. To get the full force of the tragic situation we need to feel contemporaneous with it; the author has to show the action as it takes place, not as it is rebuilt in retrospect. And so Wolfe's novels are not tragic, not only because they are so exclusively personal but because his attitude toward his material, with special respect to time, is not a tragic attitude. It is dominantly emotion recollected.

But not emotion recollected in tranquillity. Wolfe's poetry is not calmly and quietly intense; his main theme is the theme of being lost in America, and it is treated by a poet who is still lost. His perspective of America itself is out of joint: distances and spaces are magnified, a trip from New York to North Carolina becomes a journey "down the continent"; much of his America is an abstraction. He has some of the naturalistic pantheism, the feeling that man and the soil are intimately bound together in essence, which marks so much Western literature since Zola and which makes him sound occasionally like Jean Giono, just as he has at times some of the enthusiasm for being American, if not the faith democratic, of Walt Whitman. Now and again he shows a feeling for, though not much knowledge of, the history of our people—the feeling that this land is something apart because the dust of his ancestors is mixed with its dust. But mostly his complaint is that these things do not mean more to him than they do, that he really has no place and "no door where he can enter," and that meanwhile he is being swept along by the stream of time. The answer to his eternal question is not the answer of Whitman and Crane and Paul Engle. The one thing that he can be sure of, the one door that must open for him, is death.

Wolfe is the writer of our century who has written the most eloquently about death—the death of Grover, the death of Ben, of Old Gant; and of the overwhelming imminence of death everywhere. As each individual submerges beneath the river of time, something of Wolfe himself is lost; they were part and parcel of his consciousness. More surely than anything else the thought of death looses that remarkable flow of his language—the unearthly torrent of words which has always been the delight of some of his critics and the bane of the rest—and also the extraordinary resources of his rhetoric.

The rhetoric is essential. One reads much more about Wolfe's breadth of vocabulary and his obviously sensuous pleasure in words, and of what someone has called his multitudinous garrulity, than about the way he used his gift. He has the distinction of being the one writer of his generation who truly dared pull out all the stops. Dos Passos cannot compete with him in this respect, because Dos Passos' method of seeing and recording impressions calls for finding the perfectly right word, and the perfectly right word is obscured if associated with a half-dozen approximately right words; and besides, the completely successful word for Dos Passos needs the least possible rhetorical support: where each word stands completely for an impression the only real linkage needed is that of consciousness, proximity to the word which denotes the preceding impression in the series. Hemingway cannot compete because his instinctive emotional key, subdued and uneloquent, will not permit, and because his favorite characters are frequently talkative but rarely eloquent people.

Wolfe and his characters, on the other hand, have the native eloquence of an old-time political orator. He needs every resource of rhetorical structure to support the great weight of his enormous enumerations, which are as heavy as Dreiser's. It is extraordinary how often the rhetoric of his own sentences is identical with the drunken rhetoric which he puts in the sonorous mouth of the old man Gant, the great difference of course being that Gant has the rhetorical structure he needs, but not the words to go with it; whereas Wolfe has the words.

The hands had given to the interminable protraction of his living death a kind of concrete horror that it otherwise would not have had. For as his powerful gaunt figure waned and wasted under the ravages of the cancer that was consuming him until he had become only the enfeebled shadow of his former self, his gaunt hands, on which there was so little which death could consume, lost none of their former rock-like heaviness, strength and shapely power. Thus, even when the giant figure of the man had become nothing but a spectral remnant of itself, sunk in a sorrow of time, awaiting death, those great, still-living hands of power and strength hung incredibly, horribly, from that spectral form of death to which they were attached.

The words are here. And so also are most of the things against which the manuals of English continually warn: prolixity, punning, cliché, repetitiousness, and the rest. What saves it? It seems to me that in passages like this Wolfe skates determinedly around the edges of the hackneyed, rescuing himself each time through the presence of the particular word which redeems the rest and keeps the phrase from being irremediable cliché: in the first sentence "interminable protraction" saves the hackneyed "living death"; in the second, the appearance of the verb "waned"—entirely unexpected and acquiring from its context a meaning it never quite had before —stands in relation to the other verb, "wasted," as "enfeebled" stands to the rest of what would otherwise be the deadly cliché, "shadow of his former self." Such rhetorical repetitions as "spectral remnant," which picks up the earlier "shadow," and "spectral form," which in turn picks up "spectral remnant," are the sources of a freshness which is all the more perceptible because on analysis we are convinced that it comes from reviving what, except in the hands of Thomas Wolfe, would be entirely beyond hope of resuscitation.

All of this is related to Wolfe's habit of taking up some of the most familiar lines of the literary heritage and making them new and strange by the changing of a word or so: "It was unbelievable that an old cancer-riddled spectre of a man should have so much blood in him." I can remember offhand three separate places where he plays variations on the old man with so much blood in him. Despite our awareness that Wolfe abuses this device—as for that matter he abuses, sooner or later, most other rhetorical devices—its value to him is palpable. The essence of this sort of thing we find in Shakespeare himself, in such lines as

> . . . the feet
> That fourteen hundred years ago were nailed
> For our advantage to the bitter cross

wherein a word like "bitter," common as dirt itself, of its own strength lifts an ordinary prose discourse into poetry. Wolfe's gift is of the same kind. The result is the sort of boldness which allows him to get away with the obvious—note the repeated pun on Gant's name in the passage above, and the association of "rock-like heaviness" with the hands of a man who has always been a stonecutter. This is the kind of eloquence that

Wolfe brings to the themes of time and of death, time's child.

It is impossible to read Wolfe and like him without becoming something of an anthologist. And since each reader of Wolfe has his own favorite selections, I am offering here only one example of his poetry of time:

> . . . it is not the slow, the punctual sanded drip of the un-numbered days that we remember best, the ash of time; nor is it the huge monotone of the lost years, the unswerving schedules of the lost life and the well-known faces, that we remember best . . .

This sort of stuff is the poetry of a theme on which John Dos Passos, with a poet's discipline turned to his special uses, was writing the prose.

This is not meant to deny that often Wolfe let go to print much that should never have gone. Those of us who like him believe that there was a god in him, but a very unruly god who gave him no peace and at times went away without warning, as people sometimes go away and leave a radio with the switch turned on playing in an empty tenement. He was an enthusiast who had, as old Gant had, "a tragic consciousness of time," and of death. Like the people in *Look Homeward, Angel* he was a fanatic, and time and death were his obsessions. Consequently, in those moments when the god is absent he sounds like a hysterical woman who insists on feeling unloved, while life slips away without anything really stable appearing amid the flow of existence—a hysterical woman whose life is a great conspiracy to frustrate her.

Much that he wrote proves what has been said so often by critics who were hell-bent to show what really needed no demonstration, i.e., that he did not know how to compose, and is evidence of the compulsive frenzy in which he wrote. It was often more important to him to finish saying something and get on to saying something else, than to take care for the nicety of the saying. Edward Aswell has done his best to dispel the legend that Wolfe never rewrote, and other critics have examined Wolfe's style closely and found a change appearing in the later work; but there remains abundant proof he did not rewrite enough. Words obsess him, and rhetoric sweeps him away. Such things as Francis Starwick's having a "rather womanish" voice almost *ad infinitum*, the appearance of words like "octopal" in and out of acceptable context on so many occasions, the inability to stop ringing the changes on lines like the one about the old man with all the blood in him, the multiple repetitions of such an intuition as that Uncle Bascom's head is like Emerson's—and so on indefinitely— simply mar his work. They also testify to the great truth of Wolfe's own remark that at times when he wrote it felt as if a great black cloud had discharged itself inside him. Wolfe knew his weakness; he was haunted by the example of Flaubert, and grateful to Maxwell Perkins for assuring him that it was not necessary to be "the Flaubert kind of writer." He finally changed from Scribner's to Harper in order to prove to his detractors that he, and not Maxwell Perkins, was the one who put the books together. Our criticism of him will become more cogent as we give over arguing about this incontrovertible weakness and go on to define, as precisely as we can, Wolfe's great strength.

A long time ago the French philosopher Diderot, busy with a discussion on institutions among the savages of the South Seas, paused a moment to remark how contrary to common sense it seems, in a world where time is always at work and change is the rule, to base marriage on the assumption that love is eternal. Years later his countryman, Musset, picked up the theme in a famous poem, *Le Souvenir*, in which he added a new ingredient: how sad and how poignant that the eternity of the love we swear is, of necessity, an illusion. The difference between the two points of view is probably the essential difference between the eighteenth century and the nineteenth;

Diderot's reflection was prompted merely by the fact that he was having a certain amount of trouble with his wife—a situation which he managed somehow to take pretty much in stride—whereas Musset, frustrated in his various attempts to realize a completely satisfactory love, generalizes his predicament into an essential aspect of man's fate. This mood is Wolfe's, leaving out love or substituting for it the whole complex of man's emotions. It puts him in the tradition of Proust . . . and of Dos Passos, a very central and important tradition since it reflects in literature the great discovery of the relativity of all things which is our inheritance from the nineteenth century. But the tradition itself does not need to be eternal, and the feeling we have that after Proust and Dos Passos and Wolfe there was left, *circa* 1930, very little to be said about it, is probably the best indication we have that by that ·date the nineteenth century was over.

The theme of time's revenges had run out. The mood of the novels we could have during the thirties would change from lyrical to tragic.

1948

HÖLDERLIN: GREATEST OF "SCHIZOPHRENICS"

F. L. Wells

Hölderlin is the most conspicuous if not the only individual in history whose international and posthumous repute is unmistakably combined with this psychiatric classification. A sketch of his career is given, followed by some consideration of how it bears on the problem of schizophrenia. Schizophrenia is only by courtesy a diagnostic entity since it denotes a symptom-complex which, comparably to aphasia or even fever, is observable over an indefinite nosologic area. The Kraepelinian nomenclature had from this standpoint a sounder descriptive basis. The distinctiveness of the preschizophrenic personality has been exaggerated; so far as this is concerned, Hölderlin's psychosis could as well have been benign-affective. The roles of psychogenesis and of predisposition (*Anlage*) in these conditions are very comparable to the development of a photographic exposure.

Among persons who reach the age of twenty in a culture like ours, the chances of being hospitalized under a disorder

233

of the schizophrenic type are of the order of one in a thousand. The chances that anyone will before the age of thirty make a mark that brings him enduring and international repute are very much less—one in twenty million is no ungenerous estimate. As there is little likelihood of positive relation between these two attributes, the chances of their meeting in the same person may be figured as of the order of one in twenty billion. That would still allow for some coincidence in recorded history and there seems to have been certainly one, the subject of these remarks. The nearest other possibility is the Italian Tasso, but it is already too remote a possibility to figure here. Nor need one consider those distinguished representatives of contemporary arts who seem to find amusement and not a little profit in schizophrenic make-believe.

Those who interest themselves in the roster of neuropsychiatric complexes associated with high accomplishment can well note the relative absence from them of what we today know as schizophrenia, in the sense of the older *dementia praecox*. It is a natural absence, for as is implicit in its older and in some ways preferable name, it tends to manifest itself early, before many avenues to fame have fully opened. Only in poetry and music could one look hopefully for parallel cases. There is, however, no lack of those who complete higher education, rarely, indeed, going on to a brief professional career.

In the present instance, the breakdown occurs in an individual whose status a century after his death is partially attested by some seven feet of shelf space in the local university library, with commentaries in English, French, German, and Italian. "With Hölderlin, rhapsodic verse may be said to reach its zenith, not only in Germany, but in modern literature as a whole." This judgment, uttered by a British critic, condenses the evidence for the title of these remarks. Rhapsodic verse is a restricted field, and Hölderlin does not therefore claim rank in German literature with Goethe, Schiller, or perhaps Lessing; but within that field, not Goethe himself is more esteemed.

Johann Christian Friederich Hölderlin was born on March 20, 1770, at Lauffen, a town on the Neckar, a tributary of the Rhine, in Württemberg, south central Germany. Stuttgart is the nearest large city of the region. Along a hundred-mile stretch of this otherwise notable river, nearly all his life was spent. Some ancestry has been traced as far as the fourteenth century. Such mental instability, as noted there, seems rather of a cyclothymic character; on the other hand, there is record of an indirect descendant with similar symptoms, who died in 1909 in the same clinic at Tübingen which had cared for Hölderlin. Hölderlin's father appears to have been a solid citizen, local *Klosterhofmeister, geistlicher Verwalter;* his mother, who endured a life of uncommon tragedy, a woman of notable character and charm. One sister died in infancy, another grew up normally.

The father died when Hölderlin was something over two years old, and the mother soon remarried. By this marriage there was one surviving son, Carl Gock. Between this half-brother and Hölderlin there developed a close and enduring friendship; Carl Gock largely supported him during his long disability. The family moved to Nürtingen, a town some fifty miles up the Neckar and there, when Hölderlin was nine years old, the stepfather also lost his life. The possible effects of these occurrences on the growing child are not neglected by early biographers, but the remaining siblings seem to have escaped them. In this early period he is already described as dreamy, craving affection—aspirations satisfied in fancy life— "profoundly hurt by the innocent funmaking of playmates that calls him back to reality." Destined by elders for the priesthood, he entered at fourteen years a boarding "Latin school" in the neighboring town of Denkendorf. The great restriction here imposed on the liberty of the pupils made a difficult transition from the freedoms (laxities?) which had characterized Hölderlin's home life. Recorded is the profile (cluster?) of ability *good;* industry *very good;* morals *excellent;* with an excess of language over mathematical aptitude. After some two years he transferred to a similar institution at Maulbronn, some thirty miles to the northwest, where one again meets with comment on the development of fancy life, sympathy-craving, and liking for solitude. At this time there came the first of three noteworthy involvements with the opposite sex. The object was Luise Nast, sister of a close school friend. The brother was sympathetic, but after two or three years the attachment dissolved, ostensibly from lack of economic prospects.

At nineteen he entered the university at nearby Tübingen, where he attracted the friendship of such budding philosophers as Hegel and Schelling. Some broader if relatively abstract social interests seem to have developed at this time, as in the progressing French revolution; it appears that Hegel organized a sort of discussion club about social issues, in which Hölderlin was active and often spoke at meetings. At twenty-one, possibly on rebound of separation from Luise Nast, came a second attachment to a professor's daughter sixteen years of age, described as of a somewhat lackadaisical personality. It is recorded as intense while it lasted, burned out in about a year, nominally continued two or three years longer.

At twenty-three, financial circumstances compelled his leaving Tübingen for employment in the capacity of that singular combination of tutor and nursemaid, misleadingly termed *Hofmeister.* In respect to this and other positions of the sort that he held, the record emphasizes that he liked children and was liked by them, "knew how to win their hearts." His charge, however, turned out something of a problem child, and this plus the boy's somatic illness created a situation that could not be managed in the home, so that, after about a year's tenure, and with expressions of marked satisfaction and regard, he was released with three month's pay. He sojourned for eight months in Weimar and Jena, where, through his close association with Schiller, he had also some contact with Goethe, but unfortunately with no very favorable mutual impressions. The money ran out, and he returned to his mother's establishment in Nürtingen. Meanwhile he had qualified for the priesthood; he received several offers but accepted none. (Apart from rationalizations, it is very doubtful if his temperament or theology would have adapted themselves properly to the duties of a parish priest.)

A year later, in December, 1795, began his fateful association with the home of the Frankfurt banker, Gontard. The children were a boy of eight and three younger girls. As a tutor he seems to have been reasonably successful with his primary responsibility, the boy, and there is a letter written by one of the girls in after years, remarking that "no tutor was so good to us children as Hölderlin." There soon sprang up in Hölderlin a heavy attachment to the banker's young wife, who is the Diotima of Hölderlin's verse. No competent opinion believes that there was any somatic involvement; but the feeling was clearly reciprocated, with Gontard's general attitude rather complaisant than otherwise. As is the case with other passages in Hölderlin's life, there are conflicting and sensational accounts of what happened; but the best opinion is that he gradually arrived at a decision to leave the place, which he did, decorously enough, in 1798. There was for about two years considerable exchange of letters, with frequent meetings.

After leaving Frankfurt, he went to Homburg, where his chronically straitened circumstances received some help from a more prosperous friend and fellow-countryman, Isaak Sinclair. At this time there seem to have been in his mind some rather grandiose schemes, in particular the foundation of a literary journal, suggestive of a keyed-up episode; also there were further offers of ecclesiastical employment, which he declined. Like Chatterton in his garret, he endured cold and hunger, being finally compelled, greatly depressed, to seek again the support of his mother in Nürtingen. Later in the same year he was in Stuttgart, where there was a period of overactivity, both literary and social; after which he took another tutorial assignment, at an estate in Hauptwyl, Switzerland. Markedly favorable first impressions again hint at a somewhat excited phase; but a change in the employer's domestic affairs caused a termination of this employment, without prejudice, at the close of 1801. He then made a difficult winter journey to Bordeaux, France, for an assignment in the family of the Hamburg consul.

About the following months, probably the most critical of all from a psychiatric standpoint, we are substantially in the dark. Duties seem to have been vaguely defined, and may have been found intolerable, but it is really not known why he left, in the spring of 1802, or what happened on the return journey. About June 10, 1802, he turned up in Nürtingen, destitute and semidelirious. Just about this time there occurred the death of Diotima, after a short illness; but the chronology excludes this from the precipitating role that some accounts have sought to assign it. He was cared for as a sick man, and it is now that the first record appears of anything specifically schizophrenic; an observation by the philosopher Schelling, who visited him, that in the presence of mental clearness, he neglected his person *"bis zum Ekelhaften."* He improved considerably, but for the most part occupied himself no longer with essentially creative work, but with rather uneven translations of Sophocles, which can properly be regarded as evidence of failing powers. Here his friend Sinclair re-enters the picture, with sufficient influence and good will to arrange that Hölderlin should take an essentially sinecure post as a sort of secretary-librarian to the landgrave of Homburg, Sinclair himself paying the modest salary. Everyone was friendly in the new atmosphere, and for perhaps a year all went well; but in the spring of 1806 his conduct became uncontrolled, with episodes of such violence (as for example smashing a piano which a member of the landgrave's household had given him) that the townspeople insisted on his sequestration. It is regrettable to record that, at the age of 36, he was "railroaded" to the clinic at Tübingen on the pretense of visiting the university town to see about the purchase of some books. The remainder of his history belongs to the psychosis. He was seventy-three when he died.

The clinical picture that has come down to us is no stereotyped form of the disorder. Splitting phenomena, such as hallucinations and delusion formation, are singularly absent. There appear few of those oddities and eccentricities of conduct, *Verschrobenheiten*, for which so important a place is claimed in the typical picture. Failing to improve at the Tübingen clinic, he was taken, after about a year, to be cared for in the home of a specially intelligent local artisan, Zimmer by name, where he remained until his death over thirty-five years later. After Zimmer died, he was cared for by a daughter of the household, toward whom the accounts speak of a childlike gratitude. His quarters were in a turreted portion of the house, long since shown to visitors as the *Hölderlinturm*. University students also lived in the house; with them Hölderlin sometimes associated, by invitation, for a smoke and/or drinks of beer. Other students were less friendly, occasionally mocking him when he was out of doors, to which he responded by throwing stones and dung at them. Prominent in the accounts is a tendency to address visitors by honorific titles, which Waiblinger, one of his closest personal observers, looks on as a device for further self-isolation. On the other hand, there is record of his having once behaved with marked presence of mind in rescuing a child seen to be in danger at an open window. His old-time fondness for children persisted, but they were naturally less disposed to respond. His liking for honorific titles included himself; "He likes to be addressed as Herr Bibliothekarius," writes Bethge, "because this shows that he has managed to amount to something in the world." It is recounted that he once flew into a rage persisting for days, upon a friend's addressing him as *Herr Magister* simply. His formerly active correspondence now involved only short letters to his mother, nothing after her death, which occurred in 1828. Böhm speaks of a general timidity, especially fear of death; of a continued motor activity, talking, pacing about, or playing the piano, whose sounds were modified by his uncut fingernails on the keys. At times he sang.

He continued to compose simple verses, probably for the most part on the request of visitors for some souvenir. It may be noted that these are again in rhyme, with which his career had begun, but which he had altogether abandoned in the Diotima period. Little or no poetic merit can be attached to them, though it must be said that to the casual reader they occasionally make a greater show of grammatical coherence than does much of the work on which his fame rests.

His health was well preserved; it is recorded that at seventy-two he violently ejected from his apartment a distinguished visitor who had irritated him. During the following year he failed progressively, and died quietly on June 7, 1843, a respiratory disorder being assigned as the precipitating cause.

Hölderlin's psychosis was authoritatively classified in 1909, in the local and current nomenclature, as *Dementia praecox catatonica;* and in terms of this nomenclature, there is no reason to question it. The later designation of schizophrenia also stands or falls with the concept itself. But no psychosis of which Hölderlin's was typical would ever have acquired the

name of schizophrenia. It was not dominated by the characteristic schizoid traits. It was much nearer what the older term
described it to be: a deteriorative condition, of comparatively
early onset, intellectually rather colorless, and characterized
largely by motor symptoms (violence). The current characterization of Hölderlin as schizophrenic is a minor accident of
semantics.

If the Kraepelinian terms were overspecific for the state
of knowledge, so Bleuler's conception has not maintained a
properly precise meaning. Semantically, schizophrenia (like
epilepsy, for that matter) stands about where fever stood in
the beginnings of medicine, where aphasia and amnesia stood
perhaps half a century ago. All these are names for superficial
symptoms. Illnesses which show them may be known by them
until the illnesses are better understood. Only the very uninformed today use fever as the name of a disease; but aphasia
and amnesia are still popularly used in this way. The Kraepelinian categories, confessedly symptomatic and incomplete,
yet expressed a specific and overt differentiation which schizophrenia as a diagnostic entity often obscures, as in the present
case. As the designation of a mental mechanism, schizophrenia
is a step in advance; as the name of a mental disease, it is as
though we should begin speaking of fever without its
adjectives.

The influence of Kretschmer has led to some interest in
Hölderlin's body-build as related to his personality and psychosis. Anthropometric data could hardly be anticipated, and
are limited to a body-height measurement just short of six
feet. The information available has not produced agreement
on relatively simple issues; Treichler is more impressed with
asthenic, Böhm with athletic, components. It is at least agreed
that pyknic features are subordinate. Such portraiture as has
come down to us seems to support Böhm rather than Treichler, as does the much-quoted comparison of Hölderlin as a

young man to "Apollo striding through the hall." The considerable progress in the study of body-build vs. personality that has accrued through the work of Sheldon gives further point to the issue. So far as can be made out at this range, Hölderlin's "temperament index" would have better fitted an "asthenic" (ectomorph) body-build than an "athletic" (mesomorph), and it is reasonably certain that there was a greater amount of mesomorphy than would by hypothesis be associated with this degree of (Sheldon's) cerebrotonia. Sheldon and Stevens make the point, which seems to be well taken, that marked disjunction between body-build and temperament index is likely to be associated with adjustment difficulties. Hölderlin's history would be consistent with such a view; so cerebrotonic a mind should not have been in so mesomorphic a body.

To what extent are we now justified in looking on schizophrenia (*dementia praecox*) in general, and on Hölderlin's psychosis in particular, as an adaptive process? It is all but axiomatic that when the environment reaches a critical degree of difficulty, adaptive behavior breaks down. The temper tantrum, the catastrophic behavior formulated by Goldstein, are simple examples. During the past half-century, and stemming largely from the Breuer-Freud work on hysteria, there has been growing interest in the adaptive component, not to say adaptive nature, of more systematized mental disorders. Among these may be specially reckoned hysteria and the psychoneuroses, the manic-depressive group, and those now known as the schizophrenias. As such, they are regarded as ways to escape normal adaptive functions. One may first raise the question of whether there are types of environmental stress leading specifically to a deteriorative psychosis rather than to affective disorders or psychoneurosis, as, for example, the loss of parents previously mentioned. Here one must realize that frustration is not in the event, but in the experience. Event is what happens; experience is what happens to you. When one speaks in psychiatry of a threat to security, the essence is not a function of the event, but of the one to whom that event is a threat. That Hölderlin broke down (*a*) under his particular environment, and (*b*) with schizophrenia, must indeed be looked on as in essential part a function of predisposition, of *Anlage*. The question is only in how great a part. The generality of observed relations between event and reaction is altogether too tenuous and capricious for any other position in respect to these mental disorders. Case after case externally more favored has traveled if anything more readily the same psychotic road; case after case less favored has more than met the challenge. When Hölderlin finally went under, in the spring of 1806, the externals were as favorable to him as they had ever been.

But this is very different from saying that he would have broken similarly in any case. Suppose he had, in times of peace, been born into the culture of our contemporary northeastern seaboard, had completed Shady Hill School, graduated from St. John's College, and after a term of Guggenheim Fellowship, attained the promotional ladder of a good university? His intellectual talent was easily equal to all these; the critical question is whether under such circumstances he would have become more detached from reality than many a scholarly eccentric who is well tolerated, not to say esteemed.

A further question concerns the relation of the prepsychotic personality to the psychosis: does the psychosis represent essentially an exaggeration; or is the prepsychotic personality (supposing always that a distinctive one can be made out) simply a sign of greater vulnerability to the psychosis, somewhat as a leptic body-build is more vulnerable to stomach ulcer?

In a broad way it is understood that those who later develop schizophrenia lack aptitude and/or interest for social contacts (also contact sports), i.e., are of shut-in personality, though the concept can well be refined. Thus on other grounds, distinction has arisen between a trait-complex of shyness, which craves social contacts but is inhibited in making them, and a basic asociality which neither needs nor desires them. Among normal adults closely observed, this distinction is reasonably clear; and Hölderlin's case is apposite to examining its relation to the prepsychotic personality of such disorders.

Later research has confirmed the original impressions of asociality, basic or reactive, in the schizophrenic as compared with the normal, but finds a similar trait-complex in the benign-affective disorders also. For this and other reasons, it is impossible to make out that Hölderlin's personality corresponded to a specifically preschizophrenic type. The most satisfactory reference point is afforded by Bowman's data; and, according to these, Hölderlin's pre-Bordeaux personality is if anything closer to the affective disorders. The dual basis of the shut-in personality (shyness, basic asociality) has not differentiated along schizophrenic or benign-affective lines. One difficulty is that any person as mentally active as Hölderlin could, and probably would, build for himself a series of defenses such as Hölderlin's quasi nature-love, to make him relatively independent of his fellow men. The ensuing picture might be hard to distinguish from basic asociality, but this is probably what happened in Hölderlin; he withdrew from normal contacts not because they did not matter but because they hurt. The children in his environment were less likely than the average adult to wound these sensibilities; the liking that he evoked from them testifies to genuinely amiable qualities in him, when not inhibited as above.

Biographers stress a quality whose name has no precise English equivalent, *Ehrgeiz*. It denotes not merely a high aspiration level, but a concern to be treated in accord with a status-complex. Thus it expresses in Hölderlin not indifference to his fellows, but regard for them; need for their good opinion and

support against insecurity feelings. Note that this is not a concern for his fellow man as such; it is a concern for his fellow
man as an instrument against his own insufficiencies. Compare
Bleuler's remark on the "passionate striving of the autistic
schizoid, to draw people to him"; that is a defensive isolation-
ism masked by idealization of humanity in the abstract. On the
other hand, if the schizophrenia of Hölderlin were a logical
sequence of an earlier schizoid personality, we should look
in his earlier poetry for a somewhat critical attitude toward
the universe, and what is found is the substantial opposite;
more self-pity perhaps than self-criticism, but very little projection upon the environment. Compared to the spirit of
Hälfte des Lebens, An die Parzen, the *Abendphantasie* and the
like, the Shropshire Lad was an embittered cynic.[1] There is
always appeal to repressions and compensations, but this is
demanded by a hypothesis, not by the evidence.

It would have been as consistent with what we know of
Hölderlin's prepsychotic personality if he had gone into a
series of circular attacks.[2] Nor is a schizoid personality any
more a subclinical schizophrenia than a night's sleep is a subclinical hyoscine narcosis. Jaspers well recognizes this distinction between *Persönlichkeit* and *Prozess,* as does Prinzhorn
with his metaphor of the balloonist and the mountaineer; both
see the same view but the climber can get down on his own
two feet, the other not. There is no reason to question the
generally accepted view of the schizophrenic psychoses as
Anlage-determined, but they must be allowed to operate on a
delayed-action basis, as do certain epilepsies, for example.

The photographic film offers a more familiar comparison.
Development can bring out nothing that is not latent there;
but, according to the developer's composition, strength, and
duration of action, it may bring out the *Anlage* of the expos-
ure-image thinly or densely, and give varying emphasis to
lights and shadows. Thus it is reasonable to think that under

a Shady Hill-St. John's-Guggenheim development, Hölderlin's schizophrenia might have been so thin as to be hardly discernible, whereas it was brought out heavily by the Denkendorf-Frankfurt-Bordeaux composition. But the image latent in the film (genes) was that of a deteriorative psychosis. The more regrettable is the then state of psychiatry; to literature, the remote chance of another *Schicksaalslied* or *Menons Klagen* would have been worth several electro-shocks.

1946

NOTES

1. Another instructive comparison is with the career of the American writer, Lovecraft (1890-1937). Personal amiability appears at least equal to Hölderlin's, the schizoid background not less marked; fantasy life (with its distinctive macabre dynamic) was if anything more marked, but there was no deteriorative outcome. "Those who knew him salute not only his curious genius, but his magnificent spirit; as a writer he stands among the best in his field; . . . as a man he had no contemporary equal, for even as Oliver Alden was the last Puritan, so Howard Phillips Lovecraft was the last gentleman." (Derleth and Wandrei, *Howard Phillips Lovecraft: Outsider.*)

2. It is also safe to say that the extensive commentaries on the schizoid component in his writings could be as well reconciled with such an event. Etymologically, schizophrenia does not have the deteriorative implications in which usage has involved it. Swedenborg's illness was characterized by schizoid traits more than was Hölderlin's, and the clinical resemblance of the two is remote.

THE CHARACTER OF
JEAN JACQUES ROUSSEAU

Charles Kligerman

The Confessions of Jean Jacques Rousseau reveal important genetic factors in his character development. A psychoanalytic study of this material, while not fully explaining his genius, can show how these factors played a vital role in some of the major events and literary productions of his life.

The *Confessions* were written during the period 1765-1770, toward the close of his life when he was traveling from country to country, harassed, and clearly in a paranoid state. Rousseau freely admits that much of the early material is untrustworthy, due to the caprice of his memory. Some critics have suggested that he was guilty of deliberately falsifying important events. Rousseau nevertheless takes great pains to speak with utmost candor of the ridiculousness and humiliation of his masochistic perversion, exhibitionism, petty thefts, and sexual inadequacy. Allowing for the masochistic and exhibitionistic components of this self-revelation, one wonders what further motive Rousseau could have had for confabulation. In any case, verity is not essential in the psychoanalytic examination of character. In autobiography, as in free association, confabulations assume even greater importance in understanding the fantasy life of the author. However, the famous "oak tree incident" will, because of its historical interest, be more critically examined.

The *Confessions* and other works of Rousseau were previously studied by René Laforgue, who published a penetrating article in 1930. Laforgue noted that Rousseau, whose mother died during his delivery, identified himself with her and developed a latent homosexual organization, often close to consciousness. To atone for his mother's death, he had to yield the woman to the father figure, and to castrate himself both "morally" and "fantastic-psychically." By the latter, Laforgue apparently referred to Rousseau's chronic suffering from psychosomatic involvements of the urinary tract and other organ systems. Rousseau was constantly playing the fool in a series of triangular relationships in which, through guilt, he renounced the woman to the other man. I feel that in these instances Rousseau identified himself with the woman, but the two formulations are not mutually exclusive. Laforgue also notes Rousseau's tendency to infantile regression. He was seemingly sexually potent in a few relationships with permissive parental figures like Madame de Warrens ("Mama") and Claude Anet. Significantly, too, his nickname for Thérèse le Vasseur, whom he ultimately married, was "Aunt." Laforgue traces Rousseau's masochistic perversion to a beating he received at the age of eight from Mademoiselle Lambercier. The exhibitionism is regarded as an attempt to approach girls and at the same time to maintain a feminine attitude. Laforgue's formulation appears in the main valid; however, I believe much more emphasis should be placed on the masochistic features of Rousseau's character, and the one beating received from Mademoiselle Lambercier at the age of eight is insufficient to account for the origin of this difficulty.

Jean Jacques Rousseau was born in Geneva in 1712. His father, Isaac, a watchmaker, had worked abroad several years away from his wife. His homecoming was followed by Jean Jacques' birth and the mother's death. The nature of his surrogate mother-child relationship from his birth is unknown. Rousseau speaks tenderly of his nurse Jacqueline and of a good aunt who sang him nursery songs. Suggestive of an early oral conflict is the fact that in later years he made a special point of exhorting the women of France to feed their babies at the breast. Rousseau tells us that he was an indulged, over-protected child, but strictly disciplined and not allowed to play with other children in the street.

Other clues to his psychosexual development include an early screen memory in which Rousseau urinated into the kettle of a woman neighbor absent in church. This is followed by many evidences of preoccupation with urethral and anal erotic activities. He recalls the backside of Mademoiselle Lambercier "which by an unlucky fall was exposed to the view of the king of Sardinia." In adolescence he exposed his own backside to servant girls. In middle life he manifested increasing libidinal fixation on the urinary tract with which he had much real and hypochondriacal difficulty.

Rousseau gives rich and ample evidence of the markedly obsessional nature of his character. He mentions repeatedly his timidity, hesitancy, awkwardness, indecisiveness, fantastic ruminations, and strange compulsions. We know from Freud's description of the wolf-man, who like Rousseau developed somatic delusions and a paranoid state, and also from the studies of the masochistic character by Wilhelm Reich, that such persons frequently reach the genital level with a weakly exhibitionistic organization which breaks down with regression to the anal and urethral level. The specific fear which influences this regression appears to be dread of being beaten on the penis. Thus the buttocks are proffered instead, with the additional idea of being loved passively by the father. But the fantasy of playing the passive role in coitus *a tergo* like a castrated, mutilated woman appears particularly repugnant. Rousseau states that in childhood ". . . my aversion for lewdness went so far, since one day I walked through a hollow in the road at Petit Sacconez; I saw on both sides cavities in the earth and was told it was there the people did their pairing. When I thought of it, it came to my mind that I had seen dogs in a similar situation, and my heart revolted at the remembrance." Like the wolf-man, Rousseau conceived of human coitus as that of dogs where the horrible castration of the passive participant is plainly visible. The solution is to be beaten by a phallic woman whose illusory penis denies the fact of castration.

Rousseau's father appears to have been a psychopathic character. He drank, brawled, was inconsistent, of violent temper, and fond of wandering. Despite the varied ministrations of female relatives and nurses, this inadequate father seems to have furnished the only fairly constant relationship with the young Jean Jacques. The relation consisted of seductiveness, overprotectiveness, severity, and finally abandonment. Rousseau tells us almost initially: "In me he thought he saw her he so tenderly lamented, but could never forget that I had been the innocent cause of his misfortune, nor did he overembrace me. . . . 'Ah,' exclaimed he with agitation, 'Give me back my wife; at least console me for her loss; fill up, dear boy, the void she has left in my soul. Could I love thee thus wert thou only *my* son?'"

Quite early Rousseau was taught by his father to read, and every night after supper they would read romances which had belonged to the mother. Often they would become so enraptured as to read the entire night. Rousseau shows the degree of his erotic stimulation in the statement, "I soon acquired by this custom . . . a too intimate acquaintance with the passions.

An infinity of sensations were familiar to me, without possessing any precise idea of the objects to which they related—I
had conceived nothing—I had felt the whole."

It seems clear, as Laforgue noted, that Rousseau early developed a passive feminine attitude toward his father, taking the
mother's place, filling the void in his father's life. He also
developed the pattern of building up high degrees of painful
tension without discharge in end-pleasure, which is so characteristic of the masochist.

Rousseau next turns to a conflict which I believe is imperative to the dynamic understanding of his character formation.
This was his relationship with his brother, who was seven
years older. This brother was the only real rival for the father's
affection; but Rousseau states, "The extraordinary affection
they lavished on me might be the reason he was too much
neglected: this certainly was a fault which cannot be justified.
His education and morals suffered by this neglect, and he
acquired the habits of a libertine before he arrived at an age
to be really one. . . . One day I remember when my father
was correcting him severely, I threw myself down between
them, embracing my brother whom I covered with my body,
receiving the strokes designed for him; I persisted so obstinately
in my protection that, either softened by my cries and tears, or
fearing to hurt me most, his anger subsided and he pardoned
his fault."

In this episode, Rousseau demonstrates a reactive solicitude.
We can easily imagine the brother's attitude toward him: after
enjoying the mother's exclusive love for seven years, he was
deprived first of her life, then of his father's affection by the
little newcomer. There must have been intense mutual resentment which at least in the case of Jean Jacques was repressed
with the reaction formation of pity and tenderness. It is not
accidental that he soon declares: "How could I become cruel
or vicious when I had before my eyes only examples of mild-

ness . . . ?" Throughout the *Confessions* Rousseau refers constantly to his timidity, mildness, lack of aggression, and abhorrence of cruelty.

Further insight is given in the classic essay in which Freud traced the derivation of beating fantasies. When these occurred in men, he found that the men were generally masochistic perverts, and that behind the fantasy of a neutral child being beaten were fantasies of the man himself being beaten by women (mother figures). Freud showed that this was a defense against an earlier fantasy of being beaten by the father. This reconstruction was in turn a punishment for similar wishes toward sibling rivals, and stemmed from a passive feminine wish to be loved by the father. To quote Freud:

In the male fantasy—as I shall call it briefly, and, I hope, without any risk of being misunderstood—the being beaten also stands for being loved (in a genital sense), though this has been debased to a lower level owing to regression. So the original form of the unconscious male fantasy was not the provisional one that we have hitherto given: "I am being beaten by my father," but rather: "*I am loved by my father.*" The fantasy has been transformed by the process with which we are familiar into the conscious fantasy: "*I am being beaten by my mother.*" The boy's beating fantasy is therefore passive from the very beginning, and is derived from a feminine attitude toward his father.

Freud was not able to demonstrate in men the earliest stage of sadistic rivalry toward the sibling, but felt that it might be found by a fortunate observation.

We are now in a position to recapitulate Rousseau's psychosexual development. He reached the genital level with a strongly bisexual libidinal orientation expressed toward women in a weak phallic-exhibitionistic manner. Presumably due to fear of being beaten on the penis, but especially because of the father's seductiveness, he emerged with a passive feminine attitude to the father and a great deal of hostile rivalry toward his brother. This hostility was repressed and replaced by the reaction formation of solicitude, along with anal and urethral regression. The episode of being beaten appears to be a fusion of the two preliminary phases postulated by Freud: (1) sadistic (Father loves me and is beating the child whom I hate); (2) masochistic (I am being beaten [loved] by my father). The stage was now set for phase three. The beating administered by Mademoiselle Lambercier transformed the fantasy into "I am being beaten by my mother," which protected it against the painful passive homosexual and castrative implications, and much of the work of repression. In the shift from infantile urinary exhibitionism to adolescent gluteal exhibitionism with a beating fantasy, Rousseau became a perverse masochistic character.

During adolescence Rousseau was able to gratify his perversion to some extent in masturbatory fantasies, for he states, "In my crazy fancies during my erotic passions and while I was committing extravagant acts, I borrowed the help of the other sex in my imagination." At the height of his adolescent turmoil he lost self-control to the point of exposing his buttocks to passing girls in the hope that one "more resolute than the others" would spank him, but he invariably lost courage and fled. In this way he was caught and released by the Piedmontese who at once played the role of the terrifying and forgiving father. After this Rousseau restrained himself from giving overt expression to his masochistic impulses and strove to suppress the humiliating fantasies. He affirms, ". . . During the whole of my life, though frequently laboring under the most violent agitation, I could never, in the course of the most unbounded familiarity, acquire sufficient courage to declare my folly, and implore the only favor that remained to bestow. That has happened only once, when a child, with a girl my own age; even then it was she who first proposed it." This inability to accept his perversion was probably responsible for both his subsequent misery and his creative productiveness.

The events of Rousseau's life corroborate that his sense of guilt was largely displaced from the father to the brother. He had an otherwise unexplainable habit of being led astray by a series of gay young men of rather psychopathic temperament. His first brother surrogate was his cousin, Bernard, whom he protected against bullies. Later came Verrat, Bacle, Venture de Villeneuve, Grimm, and others. Even his enemy, Dominic, was able to manipulate him through guilt. Many of these "brothers" were able to provoke him into defiant behavior toward "fathers" and authority in general. With Grimm, Rousseau comes close to a frank avowal of homosexual love.

His attitude toward authority was one of provocation, hostility, and defiance. He reacted with intense hatred to being beaten by Monsieur Lambercier (in contrast to Mademoiselle Lambercier), ran away from his masters, left his homeland, deserted his religion (but could not accept the new one), turned French but insulted the French, and rejected the king of France. The incidents are numerous. Much of this is a counterphobic attitude against castration anxiety as shown in the comical "aqueduct" incident in which he diverted the flow of water from Monsieur Lambercier's big tree to his own little tree. But most of it seems due to his intense dread of accepting anything from men for fear of being pushed into the passive, masochistic, castrated role. As a result he complains frequently that he does not seem able to learn from men.

Rousseau's neurosis was split into three components: first, a deep passive masochistic attitude toward his father with a defiant provocative overcompensation; second, strong hatred of his brother with intense guilt, a reaction formation of tenderness, and a latent homosexual defense; third, conscious but suppressed masochistic impulses toward phallic women. His shaky defense was bolstered by further regression to infantile dependence, as in his relation with Madame de Warrens, and by hypochondriacal somatizations, often almost delusional ("polyposis of the heart").

The celebrated "oak tree incident" Rousseau regarded with justification as the turning point of his life. In 1749 Rousseau, then thirty-seven, was settled in Paris as a struggling musical hack, known to the intellectual salons, but had yet made no notable achievement. He was living with the illiterate Thérèse le Vasseur, by whom he presumably fathered five children, all of them immediately consigned to foundling homes. His two greatest friends were the German, Grimm, to whom he was passionately attached, and the encyclopedist, Diderot, who had befriended him. At this point Diderot, following the publication of his somewhat slanderous *Lettre sur les aveugles*, was jailed by the state in the dungeon at Vincennes. Rousseau became almost frantic. He wrote letters to Madame de Pompadour, the power behind the throne (phallic mother), imploring her either to release Diderot or jail him instead. This plea was ignored.

Finally, to Rousseau's unbounded joy, Diderot was permitted to stroll in the jail garden prior to his ultimate release. Rousseau hastened at once to see him and was deeply affected by Diderot's ravaged state. He then visited Diderot frequently, walking because of his poverty the five miles from Paris to Vincennes. One stifling summer day, to slow his pace in the heat, he read *Mercure de France*. He noticed an advertisement by the Academy of Dijon offering a prize for the best essay on the question: "Has the progress of the arts and sciences contributed to corrupt or to purify society?" This touched off a remarkable sequence of events. In a letter to Monsieur de Malesherbes, he states:

If ever anything resembled a sudden inspiration, it was the movement which began in me as I read this. All at once I felt myself dazzled by a thousand sparkling lights; crowds of vivid ideas thronged into my mind with a force and confusion that threw me into an unspeakable agitation; I felt my head whirling in a giddiness like that of intoxication. A violent palpitation oppressed me; unable to walk for difficulty of breathing, I sank under one of the trees of the avenue, and passed half an hour there in such a condition of excitement that when I arose I saw that the front of my waistcoat was all wet with my tears, though I was wholly unconscious of shedding them. Ah, if I could ever have written a quarter of what I saw and felt under that tree, with what clearness should I have revealed all the contradictions of the social system, . . . with what simplicity should I have demonstrated that man is naturally good and that it is through institutions alone that men have become wicked!

When Rousseau reached Diderot he was almost in a "delirium." He recounted his experience, his ideas, received some suggestions, and the result was the prize-winning essay which made him famous.

The oak tree incident repeated dramatically Rousseau's childhood conflict. His sibling (Diderot) was being beaten by father (the state) and Rousseau reacted with the same attempt at substitution which, being denied, increased his guilt. Occurring at a time when his homosexual feelings were close to the surface with Grimm, his dependence on Thérèse was shaken by her pregnancies, and the exertion in the hot sun had decreased his physiological reserve, his defenses were apparently lowered to the point where the repressed, passive masochistic longings toward the father, and the violent aggression toward the brother threatened to break through and overwhelm him. It was essentially a state of panic. Rousseau was able to save himself by projecting the whole conflict—not, however, before considerable modification of the infantile fantasies by his frantic ego into the thesis that man is noble in his primeval state, equal with his siblings, and corrupted by civilization (= authority = father). His ego, resting on the weak defense of masochistic fantasy, received such a shattering blow that it was forced to retrench, and from that moment Rousseau became a paranoid character.

The steps involved in this process may be schematically represented as (1) the id wish to be loved (beaten, castrated) by the father, and the destructive wishes toward the brother; (2) a reaction formation of defiance of the tyrannical father, and solicitude for the brother. The economic failure of the masochistic fantasy necessitated further preconscious elaboration into (3) displacement of the father authority to the state, social institutions, civilization, as wicked and tyrannical. All men are brothers and equal.

Since the intensity of the conflict had reached such a pitch that it threatened to break into consciousness, the stability of the last formulation was further strengthened by denial of the ego of its own part in the process; by hasty withdrawal of the ego boundary the final result appeared as something real in the external world, as a hallucinatory experience or "inspiration." In this way Rousseau was able to deny his own hostile impulses and to project them to the social order, and thus to assert that "man is naturally good" (free of aggression).

In the elaboration of this first essay Rousseau worked with fanatical fervor, dictating while lying in bed. He speaks of an "effervescence" of the mind which lasted the next five years. For the remainder of his life outright psychosis was staved off by hypochondriacal defenses, by a flood of literary productions which continued to externalize the conflict, and by constant withdrawal from personal relationships into a series of isolated retreats. The hermitage furnished by Madame d'Epinay was the first of a series of such havens. This intrauterine ideal had previously been enjoyed by Rousseau in his idyllic relation with "Mama" de Warrens, and is undoubtedly the utopian

THE CHARACTER OF JEAN JACQUES ROUSSEAU

dream of his ideal society: a noncompetitive paradise of non-sexual siblings, scarcely aware of each other, under the indulgent eye of Mother Nature. However, the paranoid turn in his character prevented him from enjoying this tranquility. The latter portion of the *Confessions* is a pitiful, almost monotonous repetition of the same pattern. Rousseau would find a haven, antagonize his friends and neighbors, be forced to flee. With the physiological deterioration of his declining years he became progressively incapable of testing reality. His last days were spent in a misery of torturing the aging Thérèse by accusing her of infidelity with a stable boy.

The thoughts developed by Rousseau in his prize-winning essay and repeated in his subsequent writings fit so closely the structure of his character and its mechanisms of defense that it seems quite unlikely—as some have alleged—that he stole the idea from Diderot. The unconscious would not be fooled by such a maneuver; however, both Rousseau and Diderot state that the latter suggested minor changes which Rousseau attributed to his own lack of skill in writing. In addition, the "great inspiration" lends itself to little secondary elaboration. Great "revelation" bears a sacrosanctness that brooks little tampering because too close an examination would threaten to expose its defensive nature. So much energy is concentrated in the projected fantasy that little is left for the integrative task of preconscious elaboration. The first discourse preserves much of the wild state in which it was conceived, while Rousseau's later works carry the ideas further with finer organization. Rousseau shrank from reviving the ego state of the original experience, stating rather lamely in the *Confessions* that he had previously described it in a letter.

The shift from a masochistic to a paranoid state is a most logical step. Probably it does not happen more often because most masochists, unlike Rousseau, are able to diminish the conflict and tension by perverse gratification. In "A Child Is Being Beaten" Freud tells us that ". . . the second phase, the unconscious and masochistic one in which the child itself is being beaten by the father, is incomparably the more important, not only because it continues to operate through the agency of the phase that takes its place; but we can also detect effects upon the character which are directly derived from its unconscious setting. People who harbor fantasies of this kind develop a special sensitiveness and irritability toward anyone whom they can put among the class of fathers. They allow themselves to be easily offended by a person of this kind, and in that way (to their own sorrow and cost) bring about the realization of the imagined situation of being beaten by their father. I should not be surprised if it were one day possible to prove that the same fantasy is the basis of the delusional litigiousness of the paranoiac." So far as I know, this extension has not been affirmed, but in this autobiography is a confirmation of Freud's great intuition.

In attempting to summarize the effect of Rousseau's psychopathology on his creative work, it seems clear that the change in his personality at the time of the oak tree incident coincided with the sudden flowering of his productivity. Previously he had floundered, an inconsistent, poorly integrated, masochistic character, awkwardly pursuing a fragmentary career; yet somehow he was able to be sufficiently gratified to maintain a tenuous equilibrium, shattered by a sudden failure of repression, replaced by a projective defense to ward off panic. Rousseau was thus more efficiently integrated by a paranoid type of thinking with some degree of consistent systematization.

Had Rousseau's "system" been a common paranoia, it would have quickly become a delusional system which would have provided a stable internal solution interesting only to psychopathologists. But the content of his peculiar conflicts, namely, a special need to deny both his sibling hatred and his passive masochistic attitude toward fathers, coincided with the urgent historical development of the eighteenth century—the breakdown of authoritarian monarchism and the rise of the capitalist bourgeoisie with the new ideology of the equality of men. There was enough correspondence between Rousseau's inspired defensive elaborations and the social ferment of the period to give his ideas external validation which undoubtedly played a great role in preserving his total integration.

The restless wanderer who could identify with no leader or group was a harbinger of the era which followed. Thus in the *Discourse on the Origin of Inequality* he states his ideal as ". . . man in a state of nature, wandering up and down the forests, without industry, without speech, and without home, an equal stranger to war and to all ties, neither standing in need of his fellow creatures nor having any desire to hurt them, and perhaps not even distinguishing them one from another; let us conclude that being self-sufficient and subject to so few passions, he could have no feelings or knowledge but such as befitted his situation. . . ." In our own experience such complete autism with "so few passions" and no object libido is found only in schizophrenics or infants. But Rousseau was not a schizophrenic. "Paranoid character" is a phenomenological label which in Rousseau's case covered a series of fluctuating ego states in a loosely organized personality. The reader of the *Confessions* is deeply impressed by Rousseau's lifelong ability to relate to new people with powerful affection which was returned by them with a protective tenderness that was often astonishingly generous. These libidinal attachments he was unable to sustain because his sense of guilt evoked masochistic fantasies so intense that he became paranoid or fled. Rousseau wanted to be a loving person, but was too afraid of his feelings. He imbues his "natural man" with an almost complete lack of affect, which spares him the painfulness of fantasy.

For such a natural man to survive, the very quality necessary is the one Rousseau most explicitly denies him—purposeful aggression toward the environment. Indiscriminately linking such constructive achievements as speech and industry with such destructive realities as war and sadism, Rousseau intuitively perceives that both stem from the same basic tendencies. He undervalues the sexual because he denies the aggressive instincts. Elsewhere in this discourse he takes issue with Hobbes on the wicked (aggressive) nature of man and insists on compassion as a "natural virtue" (instinct).

The primitive state of man which Rousseau glorifies would seem to be a classless, leaderless society—leaderless, because it depends on Rousseau's concept of natural law as a gift of Mother Nature, who watches over the savage and feeds him with her bounty. It is essentially a benign, desexualized maternal authority under whom all siblings are equally loved and favored. In his denial of the passive, masochistic attitude toward his father, Rousseau projects his aggression to the tyrant, and regresses to mother for protection. If punishment is to be meted out, mother will do it. A man who consigns his own five children to foundling homes conceives of the world as a foundling home—a protected environment where the siblings are equal, the maternal authority remote, and personal relations reduced to a minimum. In his later discussion of "general will," he speaks of the alienation of the individual: ". . . each man in giving himself to all, gives himself to nobody."

In *The Social Contract* his approach is different. Realizing that the primitive state is forever lost, he sets himself the task of reconciling corrupt modern society with an ancient ideal by appropriate compromises. To do this he destroys the analogy between family and state. His reasoning, pursued at length in *The Discourse on Political Economy* and continued in *The Social Contract*, is that the benign father maintains authority only until the child can fend for himself, and he is violently opposed to any extension of paternal authority in the state. In place of such authority he substitutes the abstraction of the general will, which binds men together into a sovereign body, and is infallible. He never describes the sanction for this general will, but it is implicitly derived from natural law (maternal authority).

In this work, more than in any of his other political writings, Rousseau rises above his neurosis and gears his ideas to reality. Faced with the practical problem of giving detailed description of the mechanism of the state, he demonstrates his genius in the adroit manner in which he outlines the various possibilities. Contrary to popular belief, Rousseau did not favor democracy ("a government for gods") but an elective aristocracy; however, it is not this for which he is remembered, but for his denial of royal authority, and the ideas of general will.

Rousseau's *Weltanschauung* is almost directly antithetical to Freud's hypotheses. Whereas Freud maintained that instinctual life is innate and partially sacrificed in the development of culture, Rousseau felt that natural man was relatively free of instincts and that civilization had corrupted him. Rousseau, with Comte and most sociologists, ignored the link between family and state, maintaining that the laws of man and the laws of groups are fundamentally different, a thesis which Freud challenged. Although Freud wrote about a patriarchal culture, his basic principles can be applied to Rousseau's concept. Rousseau did not get rid of the family; he merely removed the punitive father and substituted a remote depersonalized Mother Nature, or the Goddess of Liberty. The general will is an expression of identification of the members of the group with the mother.

The impact of Rousseau was profound. He influenced the Enlightenment, the French and American revolutions, the romantic movement, and subsequent developments in sociology, politics, and education. More than any other man he expressed the turbulent revolutionary spirit which arose in Western Europe in the eighteenth century. It may seem ironic that a deeply dependent, paranoid character, however gifted, became a prophet of modern democracy. By denying his instincts Rousseau helped forge the desexualized "debating society" which has become characteristic of Western liberalism, and which has helped make democratic political systems so unpsychological and so vulnerable to emotional eruptions. As Freud believed, only by the thorough biological study of man, and consistent adherence to the reality principle, can a meaningful science of politics be constructed.

1951

ANDRÉ GIDE:

REBEL AND CONFORMIST

John D. Mitchell

The late André Gide was throughout his long life a prolific and distinguished writer in nearly all forms of *belles lettres*. He enjoyed singular world-wide recognition for his literary works throughout his life, including the award of the Nobel Prize for Literature. His daring innovations in forms of the novel influenced a generation of writers both in his native France and abroad. Alongside his iconoclasm in seeking new modes of literary expression, he set himself the task of becoming a master of the French language. With persistent scholarly endeavor and study of the rules and the traditions of that most precise and authoritarian language, he ultimately achieved a perfection of style and lucidity. There is reflected in André Gide's work and his approach to his work, innovation and submission, the pattern of the writer's life.

André Gide never espoused a religious faith, but he was patently attracted to religion. At one period in his life he embraced the dogma of Marxism, but later rejected authoritarian Communism. His marriage would seem never to have been consummated, but he had a child out of wedlock, whom he publicly acknowledged. No other literary figure—including Oscar Wilde—has in the history of the arts been so compulsive about telling the world about his homosexuality.

The journals, autobiography, novels, articles, plays, essays, and translations of the works of other writers provide an exceptional opportunity for applied psychoanalysis, for the minutiae of thoughts, fantasies, actions, and reactions—particularly in the journals—are set down over an extended period with Protestant honesty and a painful candor. A parallel reading of his journals and his autobiography is most rewarding for insights into the dynamics of the personality of André Gide, creative writer and genius in art.

For coming to a deeper understanding of André Gide, rebel and conformist, one may turn first to the revealing childhood experiences reported in his autobiography *Si le Grain ne meurt*.

Gide was an only child of Protestant parents. As an only child and as a child frail in health, his parents were protective. Their wealth enabled them to be more protective than parents of lesser means with a similar child. Gide as a child lived pretty exclusively in a world of adults. The adult world of seeming giants and oversized furniture and objects is a fearful and frustrating world for any child. Given the opportunity, a child seeks out objects and things of a size commensurate with his diminutive stature, and he seeks companionship with his contemporaries. For a child in this world of Gullivers, there is comfort and reassurance in peer companionship—if it be only with one other child.

As an only child without a brother or sister or relatives contemporary with his age, Gide's contacts with other children his age were meager and fleeting. One early association was with the son of the concierge, which culminated in infantile sex play. Gide does not clearly indicate whether parental discovery of this led to a dissolution of his friendship or whether the family simply for other reasons moved to another

apartment. In any case the omnipotent parents, without explanation, terminated a human relationship for Gide. It is not idle speculation that the Protestant insistence on sin and retribution, the evil inherent in sex could have prompted the child Gide to make the infantile assumption that the enforced cessation of this friendship was punishment from above for his sexuality.

Under the watchful eye of an adult, Gide sought companionship with another little boy of his age in the public gardens. Though overtly the association was slight, the identification was emotionally very intense. When Gide missed the little boy and overheard the little boy's nurse tell his adult companion that the boy had gone blind, Gide went about for days with his eyes closed in order to discover what his friend was experiencing.

The seasonal movement of the family from Paris to its estates in Normandy, to the homes of his paternal and maternal grandparents, militated against Gide's establishing any long-term companionship with children his own age. Gide was forced by circumstances to seek the gratification of contact with human beings from his mother and father, and mother and father surrogates.

Such a situation aggravates and intensifies the omnipresent and universal oedipal conflict. What was the nature of Gide's relations with his mother and his father within the family constellation? On the basis of Gide's own recapitulation of memories of his father, the father was a taciturn man of a studious nature. Gide's father would seem to have almost dwelt apart in his study, and it became an event when the child Gide was invited in to visit with his father.

The mother, however, would seem to have been a greater source of affection. Gide was almost fearful of his aloof father. Nevertheless, the mother was more of the authoritarian. Gide tells of the conflict between his parents in the matter of the administration of authority. Gide's father was of the opinion that any order or admonition given the child ought to be explained to the child in detail within his comprehension. To the contrary, Gide's mother was firm in insisting that the child show unquestioning obedience. Gide concludes in his autobiography that he as an adult is of the opinion that his mother's concept of the parental authority was the right one! It seems safe to assume from that that the mother's will prevailed most often over that of the father.

Thus, during Gide's formative years, the father, as a result of his retiring nature and his early death, is for Gide a shadowy figure. Whereas the father is in the background, the mother, reinforced by a companion mother figure, Anna Shakelton, is decidedly in the foreground. The mother figures become not only an almost exclusive source of gratification intensified by the lack of childhood companions but also the authority figures administering fiats without explanation.

In the autobiography, Gide dwells at length and lovingly on the personality, interests, and talents of Anna Shakelton. His memories of her are told with an even greater vividness than any of those of his mother. Anna Shakelton was a kind of companion to Gide's mother and something of a tutor to him as a small child, by no means an unusual thing in a European family of means. She was a spinster of Scottish nationality; her many years of residence with the family had welded her into the family constellation. Anna Shakelton seems to have been a woman of many and varied accomplishments. She was at home in many languages, and she left behind her many translations of literary works in several foreign languages. They were never published. During his preschool years, she was a constant companion to Gide, an only child and a lonely one. Together they collected and identified the flora and fauna of the Norman estates of the Gide family.

Anna Shakelton seems to have had some talent and inclination for music. While still a small child, Gide's instruction in music and the playing of the piano was begun. The man who was his mentor in music was a brilliant pianist and minor composer. He was a frequent visitor in the Gide household. Following the death of Gide's father, he was the sole male visitor during the extended period of mourning of Gide's mother. Evidently, Gide's mother had some qualms even in regard to his visits during her period of being an unattached widow. All of which Gide reports in his autobiography.

Gide's mother and Anna Shakelton used to play duets together. Likewise, Anna Shakelton and the musician began playing duets together. Gide sets down in his autobiography that an older relative of the family reported to his mother one day that he had surprised the musician making advances toward Anna Shakelton. It is easy to see how closely identified with music were Gide's mother and most particularly the mother substitute, Anna Shakelton. Assuming the child's desire to monopolize the mother figure, it is easy to realize the impact the report of the musician's advances had on the mind of the sensitive child.

Gide reports frequently in his journals that in adult life he was incapable of playing the piano if anyone was around and might hear him. Guests in the country house at Cuverville would prevent him from playing. Yet he would spend hours for days on end perfecting his Chopin, Beethoven, Albeniz. He notes with concern his fear that his practicing distracts him from his real metier, writing. His intense study of music, almost an addiction, led to his being able to perfect his reading of musical scores until he could *hear* the music. This is no mean accomplishment, for it is an achievement rare among professional musicians. This was one of the feats of genius of Toscanini, and it is spoken of with awe by other musicians. For a non-professional musician to pursue music with such intensity is extraordinary; for such a devotee of music to be without the need of an audience is indeed unusual. (One prolonged period of playing the piano actually resulted in Gide's straining the ligaments in his hands and incapacitated him from playing the piano for some days.) For such a talented and persistent student of the piano to be immobilized by the possible presence in the house of as few as one or two friends is astonishing and merits closer scrutiny.

Obviously, there is a sexual aura about Gide's compulsive need for "making music" at the piano and his immobilizing anxieties if other people were within the house. Gide's wife, a cousin, would seem to have merged somewhat with the figures of his mother and Anna Shakelton. Reading between the lines would seem to suggest that Gide was able to spend hours of devotion to the piano with Em, his wife, present in the house at Cuverville. It is interesting to note, too, that after the death of his wife, in 1938, Gide no longer touched the piano.

There are other items which would seem to bear out the contention that Gide both identified himself with and attempted to move toward the female, the mother figure, represented by Anna Shakelton. Gide had been from his earliest years a serious student of languages. During his forties, when there is often a decline in new intellectual endeavors, Gide hired a teacher to guide his study of English. His conscientious study of the language took him beyond Shakespeare to a mastery of Spenser's *The Faerie Queene*, a poetic work which is not without difficulty for students native to the English language. Gide is noted for his translations of works in other languages. From the journals, one learns that Gide's writing was almost a titanic struggle against inhibiting emotions. He informs us that writing, his writing, left him spent, emotionally and physically. His perfectionism in writing is almost fantastic. Albeit it has resulted in a miracle of style.

Here again Gide seems not only to be emulating Anna

271

Shakelton but attempting to reach her, the female, the mother figure. To play the piano in the presence of others was to expose himself in a forbidden sexual act. As was true with his musical performance, so too was his writing unconsciously involved and confused with sexuality. Before submitting his writing to a larger public through publication, he invariably, as he reports in the journals, would seek out the approval of a close friend, usually Copeau. Such testing always left him enervated, disturbed, a victim of nights of insomnia. How supersensitive he admitted he had always been to criticism! It is noteworthy that Gide was never highly critical or destructive of his contemporaries' works, for unconscious identification of his writings with sexuality made him fearful of counter-aggression and therefore defensive.

Through a study of Gide's aptitudes, talents, and intense preoccupations, it has been noted how strongly Gide unconsciously identified himself with Anna Shakelton, clearly his mother once removed. Having identified himself with a female figure, despite his own masculine sex, it was likely that he would in his life be psychosexually maladjusted. The mother had become invested with authority, and it was inevitable for Gide that in his own search for authority, he would identify himself with the authority figure he had known as a child. Overt efforts on Gide's part to reach the female sexually provoked anxiety. As a result of the early death of the father, Gide's oedipal conflict would seem not to have had a resolution through identification with the father. The incest taboo of Western civilization made for inhibitions, reinforced by an inculcated Protestant attitude toward sexuality as sin.

Gide's unconscious attempts to resolve his inner conflicts suggest that he sought sublimation of the movement toward the female through deep involvement in art forms closely identified with the mother and the mother substitute. The results have been exceptional accomplishment in literature, for which he won deserved recognition. As can be seen in his journals, it was at great cost to him personally.

How much the use of applied psychoanalysis in a study of André Gide's life and works enables us to explain the mystery of genius is hard to say. Too little is known as yet of the nature of the process, and the degree of influence of heredity, social and cultural environment. Had Gide's childhood been more propitious, his genius might still have expressed itself in literature, with even greater accomplishment, fraught with less anguish and conflict between rebelling and conforming. Nevertheless, the fact that André Gide has left a detailed record of his life and his literary labors enables us to understand him better with the use of psychoanalytic insights.

1959

◙ NOTES ON THE
ENVIRONMENT OF A
GENIUS

K. R. Eissler

It is all too easy, when one is working on a subject that requires attention to a mass of details, to lose sight of the forest because of the many trees.

Thus after having finished a biographical study that centered in a detailed investigation of the decade that Goethe spent in Weimar before his departure for Italy, I raise the question whether in the environment in which Goethe grew up as a boy, features are observable that can be brought into meaningful connection with Goethe's later geniushood. In the following I wish to present summarily those which impressed me as the most significant. The reader may, however, consider that each group of features I list would require in itself a detailed discussion in order to demonstrate its full effect upon the growing child. That such a discussion cannot be presented here is obvious.

1. A reality factor which, though not unique, was still rare enough and undoubtedly of import to the boy's development

was his father's freedom from any professional obligations. Johann Kaspar Goethe (1710-1782) was the third son of his father, Friedrich Georg Goethe (1657-1730), a tailor who after the death of his first wife in 1700 had married a wealthy widow, Cornelia Schellhorn (1668-1754). It may be noteworthy that his parents were relatively old (the father fifty-three, the mother forty-two) when he was born.

In view of Johann Kaspar's later relationship to his son it may be worthwhile to spend a few words on his own father's relationship to him. The father—in contrast to Johann Kaspar—was a professionally restless, active, and successful man who rose from poverty to considerable wealth. Johann Kaspar was his favorite son, whom he wished to enable to enjoy the niceties of life which he himself had been denied. This mechanism, so frequently observed in the parental relationship to children, led to a careful planning of Johann Kaspar's education. He was sent to the best universities and acquired comprehensive juridical experience in the major centers of the empire which would have warranted a promising career as a lawyer. However, the statutes of his native city, Frankfurt am Main, made this impossible, because, since he was the bearer of the title of Imperial Counselor, he was barred from private practice. Neither did he succeed in a political career, partly because he insisted on being appointed as a civil servant rather than elected, as was the established procedure.

Thus he spent his years in writing a book on his Italian journey, on the administration of his property, his extensive collections and library, his avocations, and, above all, on the education of his two children. It is important to note that he was an extremely industrious and zealous person; although he did not work for a living, he was by no means a man of leisure. Because of this amalgam of earnest zeal with unconstrained activities he probably was a propitious subject of identification for the future genius, whose colossal output also required a combination of play activity and self-discipline.

The father's life was so organized that he could regard the rearing and education of his children as his main and principal function. He was hardly distracted by other activities from full concentration on his son, who at an early age was given the opportunity of sharing the main part of his father's daily activities and thus of familiarizing himself thoroughly with the adult world. The line of demarcation that separates a father's life from that of his son was thinner and less distinct than usual in Goethe's childhood and this must have had a relevant bearing on the later adult, who took it as a matter of course that he could be proficient in any activity in which he might become interested, whether this were the writing of poetry, administering the finances of a principality, serving as ambassador to foreign courts, or supervising the construction and management of a silver mine, engaging in the experiments of the physicist, the administration of a university, or a score of others, each single one of which it would have taken a lifetime for an ordinary person to become proficient in. This boldness, this urge to penetrate into all fields of human knowledge and activity, and the corresponding expectation of proficiency were certainly based—aside from the inherited store of endowment—on the fact that the paternal world was not kept apart as a mystery, but the child was invited into partnership, the strong, authoritarian father focusing his existence on the welfare of his son.

But Johann Kaspar must have had a surprisingly subtle feeling for the phaseal needs of the child. Toward the infant he had behaved quite differently. It is recorded that once when he held the infant in his arms and let him see the moon the baby fell back suddenly, as if struck by something, and became so beside himself that the father had to blow air into him so that he should not choke to death. Here Johann Kaspar behaved in a quite maternal way, replacing milk with breath.

It is important to take notice of this benign, tender, actively maternal behavior, which gradually changed so that later the father emerges as the stern representative of law and order. Maternal imagery surrounding a preoedipal father appears quite distinctly in Goethe's poetry. The blending of the image of a benign preoedipal father with that of a law-enforcing and prohibitive oedipal father was a fortunate prerequisite for the relationship between ego and superego on whose proper co-operation in the adult personality largely depend the intensity and quality of creativity.

When, from puberty on, Goethe's personality was, with short interruptions, geared to maximum creativity, no minor share in this outcome was the result of Johann Kaspar's centering his life in the upbringing of the boy and acting by his intuitive bent in accordance with his son's needs. This bent comprised an unusually large emotional area, and it would require a study in itself to find out how it happened that Johann Kaspar was capable of treating the infant initially in a grandfatherly, maternal way without going on to dote on a child as seductive as the little boy must have been. This would have, as clinical observation shows, been most pernicious. It goes to the father's credit that he switched to an entirely different pattern, which was appropriate for a boy in the oedipal and latency phases.

A study of Johann Kaspar may reveal that here was a father who found the consummation of his life in his son's greatness. Initially, either through a fortuitous combination of external circumstances, against his will and wish, or through silent co-operation with adverse conditions, a gap was created in his life inasmuch as breadwinning activities were impossible. His dealings with his son, which at the outset may have meant no more than an attempt at filling the gap left by the lack of an occupation, quickly became the absorbing center of his whole life.

To a certain extent he was continuing here his father's relationship to himself, but I think he went far beyond this. His son was not to serve primarily narcissistic needs dictated by a superego demand, nor was he to realize the fulfillment of an id wish that had remained unfulfilled in his own life, although such mechanisms probably played their subordinate role; but the center of his existence moved, suddenly or gradually, into that of his son. Consequently a relationship seems to have emerged that was almost free of ambivalence. He did not use the son selfishly for purposes of self-aggrandizement and apparently was capable of acknowledging his son's genius without grudge or jealousy. I presume that the relationship was *au fond* a twofold one. (1) The son was an extension of his own self, as can perhaps also be deduced from the coincidence of the onset of progressive deterioration in the father with the son's permanent departure from Frankfurt. (2) The son was the father's most beloved object, on whose care, nurture, and growth unambivalent solicitude, watchfulness, and affection were spontaneously expended. It was this combination of wholesome narcissism and strong object love that was characteristic and unique in the relationship. At times this combination led to conflicts between father and son which have more frequently than not been misunderstood by Goethe's biographers. These conflicts never led to the son's being injured but served as optimal stimuli for the growth of masculine behavior. If the father's behavior had ever resulted in a conflict-free relationship on the son's side, this would have had an emasculating effect, and under such conditions the father would not have served the best possible purpose.

The following passage may serve as an illustration of the twofold relationship. "He [my father]," wrote Goethe, "esteemed my natural gifts all the more as they were wanting in him, for he had acquired everything only through inexpressible diligence, perseverance, and repetition. He often assured me, early and late, in seriousness and in jest, that with my talents he would have behaved quite differently and would not have managed them so carelessly."

We observe here the father's unqualified acknowledgment of his son's superiority, combined with the reservation of a niche in which paternal superiority is left safeguarded.

Nevertheless, one should not suppose that Goethe's education stood completely under his father's domination. From Goethe's own account in *Dichtung und Wahrheit* one might easily get the impression that his father had been almost his only instructor of importance. I presume that in the form of reality events the poet wanted here to express the psychological truth that he owed to his father's way of rearing him a major part of his later successes. Yet these reality events were slightly different from the way the poet recalled them. Documentary evidence reveals the participation of a number (at least sixteen up to the time of Goethe's departure to Leipzig at the age of fifteen and two months) of persons who contributed substantially to his education.

2. If an episode, to be presently discussed, has been correctly recorded and was typical of the way the infant was raised, then the conclusion becomes stringent that he was most skillfully protected against traumatization at a time when the human being is particularly vulnerable to portentous injury.

The infant tossed in his sleep because of nightmares—at least, so his grandparents, parents, and nurse believed. They stood around his cradle and watched his mien for signs of unrest. When he awoke he cried pitifully and sometimes with such vehemence that he lost his breath and made them fear for his life. The parents rigged a small bell and when the infant became restless in his sleep they rang the bell and rattled, with the intention of making him forget the dream immediately upon his awakening.

Whether the parents interpreted their observations correctly, and whether their measures had the imputed effect, may be questioned, but it is conceivable that pleasant external stimulation has an antitraumatic effect at a moment of emergency in the infant's life. To the earliest phases of development psychoanalysis has appointed primal repression. In the biographical study to which I have referred I raise the question whether the unconscious worked in Goethe otherwise than is commonly assumed. If these parents, out of an unusual affinity to the exigencies of infantile life, intuitively dealt with situations of strain that were impinging upon the dawning mind by providing the kind of stimuli that proved an antidote against the poison of trauma, then we may presume that the phase of primal repression led in this infant to a result different from that in a child who is left to his own devices in such or similar situations. I am aware of the low credibility of such a hypothesis. The minimum, however, that can be deduced is the beneficial effect the constantly present loving care, attention, and eagerness to help must have had upon the infant. Indeed, there was great need of such care, since the mother had been in labor for three days and the infant was born "black and without sign of life."

3. I introduce a more comprehensive subject by setting forth external events that facilitated phase-adequate development of the boy.

When the boy was five years and eight months old, Johann Kaspar felt free, his mother having died in the previous year, to carry out an old plan of his to rebuild the house in which he and his mother had lived for over two decades. The building operation lasted about eight months. The children's accustomed world was uprooted. First they continued to live in the house and witnessed the tearing down of parts of the building; later they were moved to the quarters of friends. The immediate contact of boy and father must have been even more weakened when he was sent temporarily to a public school.

All this brought him in touch with a new world he had not known before when living in his accustomed environment. This new world contained much of the "mean, bad, even vile" of which he had been ignorant before.

At a time when he had gone past the peak of the oedipal phase and had entered the latency period, he was temporarily exposed to a disorganizing stimulation, and the educational pressure of the protective environment was decreased for a short time. When an intense oedipal situation approaches the point of internalization, the danger that an abrupt internal reorganization in the child will leave permanent and grave traces in the adult personality looms high. The interval of low educational external pressure, of excitation by forbidden (aggressive and sexual) external stimuli, occurring just at the time of transition granted the boy a respite, delayed the onset of internalization, and thus reduced the intensification of reaction formations that otherwise would have set in.

I cite a few dates to indicate how difficult a time the boy must have gone through: March 26, 1754, death of the paternal grandmother, to whom the boy had been close; six months later, September 9, birth of a sister; in April, 1755, the tearing down and rebuilding of the house is starting; October to November the new building is finished; middle of December, death of the sister; March 29, 1756, a dead child is born.

This sequence of events might, in a different child, have precipitated intense psychopathology. However, the boy appears to have been relatively well protected against traumatization. When writing about this period the aging poet will speak almost exclusively about the fears, dangers, and inconveniences of the building operation; each detail and each reaction he sets forth probably stand for principal, deep-going psychological processes elicited by tragic events. The poet's recollection decades later recalls the superb result of sublimation: "It was at this time that for the first time I really became aware of my native [lit., father] city." Thus the house and the town function here again as age-old symbols of the female body or the world at large, or symbolize basic psychological processes.

At the age of nine years and eight months an event took place that made the father appear in a new light. During the occupation of Frankfurt (1759-1762) by the French, the Count Thoranc was billeted in the house of Goethe's father, who felt intensely against the French intruders and could not reconcile himself to the presence of this high dignitary in his house. He became depressed and failed in his customary supervision of the children. When the French proved victorious in a battle in the vicinity of Frankfurt, from which he had hoped liberation would come, he let himself be so far carried away as to hurl a very offensive remark against the count, who decided to punish the affront with severity. Only by the skin of his teeth did the father escape a disastrous situation. Yet the boy had witnessed the strong father in a helpless and humiliating situation, in which he depended on the intercession and clemency of others. The image of the humiliated but greatly loved father also played a significant role in Freud's life. A solitary blemish on the idealized image of the father seems to be an enormous spur toward later activity and ambition in male psychology. An out-and-out humiliated, incompetent father and a superb, completely blameless, perfect father are the two extremes that, as far as external factors correlated with the father are concerned, prove to have the most damaging effect upon a son's maturation. I do not wish to dispute the oedipal aspect of the episode with Count Thoranc (the psychological root of Goethe's great admiration of Napoleon may go back to it) when I call attention to the death of Hermann Jakob, Goethe's younger brother, on January 13, 1759. The French marched into the city on January 2, and the Thoranc episode may have been partly the product of a fantasy at the bottom of which lies the death of a brother.

The occupation of Frankfurt by the French changed the whole atmosphere of the city. A troupe of actors had moved in with the army. Goethe became familiar not only with the French theater but also with the ways of the actors. He moved in a sensuous climate, and now outside of the sexually repressive home, he had a chance to observe a sexually far freer way of life.

The father's degradation at the time of prepubertal transition with its consequent retrenchment of paternal authority, the subsequent easing of the general, strong environmental pressure and the access to a less austere and more eroticized group —all these are reality events which, if anything, worked against a traumatic intensification of pubertal conflicts.

This phase of relative freedom, which might so easily have led to a deterioration of the boy's morals, ended in the Gretchen adventure, his first serious infatuation, in the course of which he unwittingly became entangled in the ill-doings of a malfeasant group. When this whole affair exploded, the environmental pressure was raised again to full pitch and the boy, now fourteen and seven months old, was put under the supervision of a tutor. The damage that may be caused by long-lasting lack of discipline was forestalled.

In the two foregoing examples we can see how fate provided an assemblage of circumstances that proffered the kind of support most needed by the boy at critical turns in his development. This, of course, in no way diminishes the importance of the part played by his own ability to use for maximum profit that which, if it had occurred at a different time or had had to be met by a less resourceful subject, might have produced most undesirable effects.

It seems that external circumstances had their share in preventing the boy's fixation to particular forms of psychopathology. External events of a sort likely to evoke neurotic behavior changed with such as are apt to evoke delinquency, or vice versa. Such sequences, given the proper subjective prerequisites, will greatly help prevent the formation of a rigid character and will favor fluidity of structure.

The psychological consequences of this harmony between the dynamics of external reality and phaseal needs of the boy were far-reaching. I wish to stress only one. It helped greatly in the acquisition of the adult's capacity to keep activity and passivity in proper balance. A conflict centering in the polarity of these strivings makes many falter and so often destroys the creative potential. The external influences in Goethe's instance seem to have been so subtly balanced that fixations to active or passive attitudes were prevented and his ego preserved not only the capacity of deriving pleasure from both but also of making use of either of them singly or of both simultaneously in accordance with the task on hand. The mechanics of the creative "spell" depend greatly on the smooth and undisturbed interplay between the active and passive strivings.

4. The mental development of a child depends, it goes without saying, on the opportunities offered to establish contacts with the culture of his time. This boy had no dearth of such opportunities. It is not necessary to enumerate or discuss in a psychological examination of this sort the cultural media, the books and cultural values, which the boy became familiar with and readily and eagerly absorbed and integrated. This factor is a static or mechanical one that usually spells injury when absent, and when present is not relevant in a psychological investigation.

a. However, a less mechanical and more relevant factor also belonging to external stimulation ought to be mentioned. This concerns the broad psychological spectrum by which Goethe as a boy was surrounded, and which provided him with experiences that familiarized him with the main categories of psychopathology.

His father was a compulsive, narcissistic personality with

broad sublimations, rather unsensual, with an inclination toward
stubbornness, insisting on fulfillment of duty and endowed
with a warm heart behind a stern front. The mother was
impulsive, seductive, gay, jovial, merry, permissive, and abound-
ing in a capacity to enjoy life, in many respects the opposite
of Goethe's father. The sister, fifteen months younger than
the boy, was the admiring and faithful companion of his
childhood years. She was heterosexual mirror image and object
in one. She was in earlier years a gay and bright, enchanting,
seemingly unneurotic girl, whose influence made feminine attachments an ineradicable part of Goethe's life and thus protected him forever against the danger of manifest homosexuality.

There was a fourth element represented in the boy's environment. His father had been since 1755 the guardian of Balthasar
Clauer (1732-1796), a schizophrenic (hebephrenic?) young
man who, with short interruptions, lived with the family and
was quite attached to the children. Here the boy was in
contact with the open manifestations of the primary process,
a psychosis. Thus his experience was not geared to one single
type of psychopathology, but the breadth of human variability
became an integral part of his early daily environment.

b. The psychotic young man had a far-reaching effect. He
felt best when he could do what he had done during his
academic years prior to the onset of his illness, and was grateful
when he had the opportunity to write from dictation, as he
had done during his academic courses. Goethe made use of
this opportunity when his father did not need the scribe. Thus
at an early age he was already habituated to seeing the stream
of his fantasies and thoughts become fixed in the material form
of symbols.

If we consider how critical for many a creative personality
is just that moment when the mental image must be transposed
into a material form, then we shall not underrate this unique
situation, of a boy in the latency period with the privilege of

taking the transformation of his thoughts into objective symbols as a matter of course. Perhaps it was also of psychological significance that the fantasies which were partially the product of the primary process in his mind were channelized into material form through the primary process of the mentally diseased, his senior, who here became reduced to a subservient automatic tool.

5. When investigating the external reality in which an overtowering mind developed, the psychoanalyst expects or, perhaps, would even like to discover some unique features. Our daily clinical experience makes us reluctant to attribute all the manifestations of such unusual creativity as Goethe possessed entirely to constitutional factors and to the inherited endowment. The presence of these factors, although we are well-nigh ignorant about them, remains undisputed, whatever external factors may be revealed by an investigation. Almost all those I have so far set forth may, indeed, impress us as being perhaps related to specific details in which Goethe's genius emerged, but they may nevertheless strike us as superficial and unrelated to the fact that here creativity ran in such torrents as even to go beyond the excessive demands we put up before being willing to consider a man a genius. Only with regard to the last point—the unusual use to which the boy put the schizophrenic scribe, passionate of sorts, in order to concretize or objectify his fantasy life—have we come upon a reality factor that will strike us as indeed unique and possibly of great bearing on his later fabulous geniushood. How often, indeed, has even the most talented boy of eight or nine had an adult at his side who was willing and eager faithfully to write down the fantastic as well as the reasonable that might cross his mind?

This impression of uniqueness, related to later geniushood, is transmitted even more markedly in a type of episode that occurred serially for a while in the boy's life.

The mother was a passionate storyteller. Not only was she

ingenious in invention but quite ready almost to believe in the fairy tales and other stories she narrated. She resented any distraction from the evening gatherings at which a gradually larger crowd gathered around her. The boy participated intensely in his mother's recitals. Anger and sadness changed in accordance with the vicissitudes of the various characters. At times he became so excited that he openly declared what he thought should or should not happen. When then the mother stopped, and postponed the denouement to the following evening, the boy devised by his own imagination the further course of events. These imaginings he regularly confided to his paternal grandmother, who lived in the household, in a back room. From her, in turn, the mother learned what the boy's anticipations were. "Thus there was a secret diplomatic traffic between us that neither betrayed to the other" (Bettina Von Arnim).

The mother had the superb idea of following, when she resumed her stories the next evening, the wishes the boy had expressed to his grandmother. "With glowing eyes he looked forward to the fulfillment of his boldly constructed plans and he greeted the elaboration of them with enthusiastic applause" (Bettina).

At first hearing one feels at once that such an experience must be fateful for a child. Each analyst will impute consequences to it in accordance with his own bent, and all such suggestions will probably be correct, for such a constellation is bound to affect profoundly all provinces of the personality. One may think of the triumph the boy experienced, the penetration into the mother, the uniting with her, the consequent separation, the receiving from her and giving back, the omnipotence of mastering her, the relief of feeling of guilt, the immense stimulation of fantasy life, the encouragement to objectivation, the gratification of oedipal wishes without the price of guilt, the harmony between him and her, and the unending feeling of being loved and understood by her.

There are certainly many more alternatives, which it does not seem necessary to enumerate. There is, indeed, virtually no issue of child life that could not be brought into association with this situation, which is truly drenched in meaning and could have stemmed from the friendly pen of an author who was writing a novel about the education of a poet.

There is no reason to believe that this episode which Bettina reported in her book was not transmitted to Goethe somewhere in her many letters, yet just this episode, which strikes me as the most engaging and charming among all that were told her by his mother, was omitted by the aging poet, and there is no evidence that he ever intended to include it in his autobiography. Did the aging man feel embarrassed when he heard the truth about what must have lived on in him as the image of a very gift of the gods, such as no other poet had ever received in his childhood?

It is, of course, futile to speculate whether Goethe remembered the episode, although I personally feel inclined to assume it. Be this as it may, the residue of this incredibly extensive provocation and gratification of early belief in omnipotence was to be seriously jolted when it became evident that adult artifice and deception were at the bottom of this first manifestation of the daemon that would accompany him through the rest of his life.

A benign destiny had conjured up here an assemblage of circumstances that was not far removed from a situation in which he would find himself innumerable times as an adult. There was the crowd eager to be entertained and responding with joy to the tales that were offered by the enraptured mother. Did the little boy, when, as must have been the case, he felt himself to be the source of his mother's inspiration, seem to himself like a god who inspires the bard? Did he here experience actively as a child what he so often would have later to submit to passively as an adult when he was seized by spells of inspiration?

6. I wish to set forth a few external conditions that must have had a significant bearing on the boy's Oedipus conflict or his reaction to it:

Johann Kaspar Goethe, the poet's father, was born in 1710, and his mother, Katharina Elisabeth, in 1731. Thus the age difference between mother and son was three years less than that between the parents. This numerical distribution itself would suggest that the mother felt closer to her first-born son than to her husband.

The father was a man who emphasized order, duty, and authority, who preferred the didactic to the playful and therefore aroused awe and respect rather than love and affection in his wife, who had not yet developed into full womanhood when she married him at the age of seventeen. Thus, quite understandably, the bulk of her tender feelings was directed toward the charming son. Yet, however much she may have idolized him, in early years the father's authority was not questioned by her preferences, and she did not disturb important identificatory processes.

The boy seems to have been aware of the mother's being closer to him than to the father. At least, as an adult he wrote about her: "A mother, almost still a child, who only with and in her two oldest grew up to consciousness." Thus he was spared a mental frustration that has blackened the outlook on life of almost every mortal.

The protection against undue frustration, so far as it can be provided by external factors, can be observed also with regard to another source from which most infants suffer traumata. Freud has pointed out the effect it probably had upon Goethe that all his siblings born after Cornelia died at an early age.

Hermann Jakob lived from November, 1752, to January, 1759; Katharina Elisabeth from September, 1754, to December, 1755; Johanna Maria from March, 1757, to August, 1759; and Georg Adolph from July, 1760, to February, 1761. In 1756 a child was born dead. All the evidence squares with Freud's reconstruction that Goethe's unconscious reaction to his oldest brother's death was as follows: "I was a child of fortune; . . . destiny removed my brother, so that I did not have to share my mother's love with him."

Neither was Cornelia a rival. Her death at the age of twenty-six and a half was borne by the mother with surprising equanimity.

Everything one knows about Katharina Elisabeth's relationship to her son bespeaks absence of ambivalence. The situation was most favorable from the start. Like her mother, she had married at the age of seventeen; both married men considerably older. But her mother twice gave birth to boys who died as infants, and the third child, the poet's mother, was the first child that survived. When Goethe was born he was believed to be dead and the mother's fate seemed to repeat itself. Bettina reports the mother's account of the despair when it seemed that the newborn could not be brought to life. "Your grandmother," she continued, "stood behind the bed; when you first opened your eyes, she exclaimed: '*Rätin, er lebt!*' [lit., "Mrs. Counselor, he lives," italics by Bettina]. 'At that moment my maternal heart awakened and has lived since then in continuous elation until this hour,' she told me in her seventy-fifth year."

This "*Rätin, er lebt*" seems to have been the center of her story, which was frequently recited with the expression of great joy. Here we observe the usual narcissism of the bearing mother multiplied and dramatized. The infant is born dead, and in the midst of the greatest despair the grandmother's jubilant outcry—implying envy, admiration, and identification with her daughter—is the first messenger of the happy tidings. It is not her infant's first cry that the mother remembers, but her own mother's ecstatic outcry. The newborn apparently was experienced as an object, a kind of hero who provided her with victory over her mother.

The newborn refused to suck his mother's breast and a wet nurse had to be engaged. At her breast he drank "with strong appetite and delight." When it turned out that the mother had no milk she concluded that in refusing her breast the infant "had been more intelligent than all of us."

Here the mother's narcissism had been seriously threatened from three sides—the infant's refusal, the wet nurse's superiority, her own physical inability to suckle—and still she succeeded in compensating for all this by forming a myth that idealized her newborn and thus turned defeat into victory. One may easily suspect that the mechanism of denial was here at work. It is, however, questionable whether this happened to a significant extent, for this mother, without known exception, served her son faithfully the rest of her life and bore frustrations and sacrifices without really experiencing them as such.

If there was ambivalence on her side in that relation, it was so deeply repressed that it could not reach the infant. How much this meant in terms of adult object relations, I wish to discuss briefly.

The unambivalent relationship Goethe's mother maintained to her son was probably one of the most consequential external factors in his life. In speculating about the psychological consequences of this environmental condition I always return to the conclusion that here is to be found the external source that contributed to Goethe's profound attachment to the world.

The demands that are put on the psychic apparatus of a genius of Goethe's dimensions are not to be compared with anything an ordinary person has to bear. No wonder that in many instances of highly creative minds, sanity gives way to permanent insanity. To discuss the relationship between extreme endowment for creativity and psychosis would require a long discourse. Suffice it to say that Goethe might have suffered such a fate—there were actually episodes when his friends were deeply concerned about his mental health—if he had not been protected against a final break with reality, not only by his sheer inexhaustible creativity, which essentially is the very antipode of psychosis despite their apparent affinity, but also by unusually strong ties to the world of objects. One receives the impression that basically Goethe was a uniquely unambivalent personality. But from where then stem the unquestionable manifestations of ambivalence? How can one reconcile this impression of basic unambivalence with contrary manifestations?

A satisfactory answer would lead afar. Yet this much may be said: artistic creation requires a certain degree of ambivalence toward objects. And this ambivalence that is the inescapable prerequisite of great creations can be found in Goethe, too. The most apt formulation appears to me that Goethe was fundamentally in such firm contact with the world that he could safely indulge, so to speak, in the luxury of marked ambivalence. It was, however, an ambivalence that almost never touched upon this strikingly huge store of undisturbed, basic positive contact with the world. His ability always to find his way back to the real world, despite all conflicts, frustrations, and the well-nigh fugue states into which he was thrown by creative processes, was, I seriously believe, also the consequence of the undivided, total way in which his mother had turned toward her child. Apparently a healthy child that from early on has had contact with an unambivalent object over a long period of time is later protected against the insidious effects of even marked ambivalence.[1]

I shall later set forth some evidence that a rather unexpected reality factor gave the boy relative protection also against a

293

regular source of trauma or long-lasting discouragement such as the biological inferiority a boy observes when he compares himself to his father.

Thus we encounter the surprising situation that in the three oedipal aspects in which most children suffer severe traumata (oedipal defeat by the father, sibling rivalry, biological inferiority) this boy's reality was structured in such a way as to provide the maximum primary relief. In other words, reality, so far as the oedipus conflict was concerned, imposed the smallest possible psychological strain on the growing child. Unavoidably I connect this rarely encountered triad of circumstances with Goethe's later creativity, which, as said before, even measured in terms of geniushood, was supreme. I assume this connection, although external reality factors and later psychological vicissitudes cannot be strictly correlated. The same reality structure might, in a different child, have favored the development of an unsufferable, arrogant, insipid personality.

I am inclined, however, to consider this reality structure as the most favorable one for a psychobiological unit that by natural endowment and inheritance carries the potential of maximum creativity. This generalization is based on my opinion, shared by many others, that Goethe represents the ideal model of creative man, an opinion that cannot here be justified. Instances of genius who grew up under the opposite circumstances are well known. Winston Churchill wrote: "It is said that famous men are usually the product of unhappy childhood. The stern compression of circumstances, the twinges of adversity, the spur of slights and taunts in early years, are needed to evoke that ruthless fixity of purpose and tenacious mother-wit without which great actions are seldom accomplished"; and his biographer is right in suggesting that the author was thinking of himself when he wrote thus about his ancestor, the first Duke of Marlborough.

Indeed, in studying the biographies of men such as Newton

or Churchill, one encounters a frightful array of external circumstances that are considered by psychoanalysis and psychiatry as most detrimental to adequate development, and prove, in general, to lead to severe psychopathology. It is possible that these apparently adverse reality factors contributed greatly to the later genius of those who had to suffer them, that later genius evolved, not despite them, but possibly even because of them. It would not be surprising if it turned out that some constitutions with inherent genius endowment require, for later maximum realization, conditions that severely frustrate infantile and childhood wishes and others that provide gratifications abundantly. Of course, it can be only the matter of an unequal distribution of traumata and gratifications in the instances of these two types, for traumata as well as gratifications are indispensable occurrences in the development of any child. But in the one case one may say the whole development stood under the sign of repeated traumata as if a superior power conjured up all imaginable adversities upon the one luckless child (in Newton's case a posthumous and premature birth, separation at age three from the mother because of her remarriage, and a sudden uprooting of his accustomed way of living at twelve when his stepfather died) and in the other as if such a power had provided up to the last detail all that is congenial, favorable, auspicious, and timely.[2]

This is a summary, as regards the external environment, of the exceptional and possibly relevant in Goethe's childhood that can be meaningfully connected with his later genius. I have not considered the boy's own contribution and responses, which formed out of these favorable circumstances the superb life he lived. I have intentionally omitted the sociological factor, such as the wealthy, upper middle-class background, which provided the atmosphere of relative leisure and near luxury.

Among the factors enumerated there is none, with the exception of the dictation to the scribe and the mother's telling stories invented by the boy, which, taken singly, will not be discovered in other lives; yet all of them together are to be considered a unique assemblage of lucky coincidences.

If his father had been distracted by a profession, if a younger brother had survived, if the mother had been older—any change in one of these details would have upset the splendid harmony, wisdom, and balance that pervade the physical and psychological reality by which the boy was surrounded, and would have cast a shadow, a scruple, on the creative potential.

By all this I do not mean to suggest that the child's life was an easy or conflict-free one. Goethe's life, if anything, particularly from the onset of adolescence on to the end of the third decade, was unusually rich in intense conflicts. It is my hypothesis that the reality factors in Goethe's environment were structured in such a way as to facilitate his dealings with conflict-arousing stimuli. If the environment had been of such a kind as to eliminate conflict, the result would have been a shallow personality without great creative potential. The boy's curiosity and intelligence, the whole bent of his personality as far as it can be reconstructed, show depth and capacity to experience conflict, but also resources to meet them. Without the conflicts that deeply shook the inmost personality he would never have been capable of drawing into his artistic creations the whole gamut of passions, the whole cosmos of human conflicts; none of them had been omitted from self-experience.

Whereas in general the spontaneous "tendency to conflict" is a malignant etiological factor of psychopathology, most difficult to combat therapeutically, it is a prerequisite of genius-hood. Summarily it can well be stated: without conflict, no creativity. Do we have in the genius's spontaneous tendency to conflict a force that is unrelated to environmental factors, but is a manifestation of his particular differentiation or perhaps even part of his endowment?

Clinical observation teaches that the pathological tendency

to conflict occurs frequently—but by no means exclusively—in patients whose childhood stood under the influence of an unusually pathological parent or of parents whose personalities were particularly discrepant, a factor leading often to marked discord or regular disagreement. In such instances the frequency of traumatization is at least a supporting or aggravating factor, if not the principal etiologic one.

Traumata, although injurious, are unavoidable parts of the child's development. In properly raising a child one tries to limit the effect of injuries, to help the child in undoing their detrimental effects, and to make the child so strong that it can bear without damage severe and even extraordinary strains. The problem is to have the child's ego develop in such a way that strains which under ordinary circumstances have a traumatic effect, that is to say, reduce the efficiency of ego functions, will stimulate or energize ego functions, elicit the evolvement of new ones, or lead to the synthesis of already existing ones.

A traumatic conflict absorbs energy and imposes burdens on or retards development. In Freud's scheme of the traumatic neurosis this becomes quite evident. There an external strain works appreciable destruction on an ego function and the ego must then concentrate, as its principal task, on mere repair, that is, the ego is highly fortunate when it can achieve the restoration of the *status quo ante*, without gaining any structural accretion. If, however, the ego has enough energy at its disposal to bind all the processes that are set into motion by the intruding potentially traumatic stimuli, then the resulting conflict can be used for creative purposes.

I discuss the problem here only in terms of psychic economy. For obvious reasons this is much easier than to consider the dynamic and structural and genetic aspects.

In view of my description of Goethe's environment as one that offered such rich compensations and was protective against severe traumata, the question may arise how it was possible that even under such favorable conditions a tendency to conflict, so conspicuously strong in Goethe, could emerge at all. No doubt, in order to explain the intensity of that tendency in Goethe one has to have recourse to biology, as did Greenacre in her study, *The Childhood of the Artist*. But quite aside from such a recourse, environmental factors are to be considered, and one must not forget that even under optimal conditions the range of conflict-arousing external stimuli remains broad. There is the wide area of the prohibition of incest, which, of course, entered this boy's life as it does that of any other.

Aside from this, the historical record does not suggest by any means that the boy's environment was of a kind often found in our days in progressive families who deliberately aim at keeping conflict and trauma away from the child. "Unfortunately," Goethe wrote about his childhood, "the pedagogical principle still prevailed of stripping children at an early age of all fear of the ominous and unseen and to habituate them to the horrible." Thus when at night time the children, driven by anxiety, stole from their bedroom to find solace in the company of the servants, their father came to meet them in the disguise of a kind of specter in order to scare them back into the room. Goethe rightly adds that a measure which doubled the children's fear was of no avail. His mother, however, promised to give them delicious fruit each morning if they curbed their fears. "It succeeded and both sides were content."

Here we see how the internal conflict-arousing stimulus is joined by an additional external one of the same quality and how both are pleasantly assuaged by the gratification of instinctual impulses. It was only natural that the fearsome was attributed to the father and the gratifying to the mother.

If this recollection of Goethe's is representative of his childhood and therefore perhaps typical, one may feel inclined to cite it as an indirect confirmation of some claims made in the foregoing, for in this instance again his environment afforded the condition that was needed for a wholesome reduction of conflict to the bearable. It afforded, indeed, a solution that was almost ideal, for, without destroying the child's contact with the ominous, it led to his mastery of anxiety.

Yet still one wonders whether the unavoidable conflicts inherent in the oedipal situation, and quite generally in the inner processes that gradually change the untamed infant into a civilized being, suffice to explain Goethe's tendency to conflict, which was unusually intense.

Faust, who, after all, is a comprehensive projection of the poet's self, is characterized by his constantly being in a state of conflict, which can be resolved only in the last moments of his earthly existence. Was there in the boy's environment something quite specific that favored a heightened tendency to conflict?

I believe that this external factor becomes visible when incidents of birth and deaths that occurred in his home are marked in relation to his age at the time of their occurrence. In the following series, the first figure gives Goethe's age in years, the second the approximate number of months. The exclamation point signifies an incident of childbirth: 1;3!—3;3!—4;7—5;1! —6;3—6;7!—7;7!—9;4—10;0—10;10!—11;6. If one considers that periods of pregnancy usually combine with heightened tension in the child, it becomes clear that time periods lacking in conspicuous occasions for conflict were rather short in this boy's life. It becomes shockingly clear that this child grew up in a world of constant pregnancy and death; that the biology of life, so to speak, took care of the boy's familiarization with the tragic aspect of human existence.[3] The hypothesis that the tendency to conflict originated in this area stands in strange contrast to the sparseness of the poet's references to this subject. Whereas he writes profusely and with frankness about

Cornelia, the only surviving sister, there is only one short reference to his other siblings in *Dichtung und Wahrheit*. Yet in puberty he projected a novel in which "six to seven" siblings, separated from one another and dispersed all over the world, write one another about their feelings and vicissitudes. "Six to seven" is the appropriate term when six live and one dead infant were born.

In *Wilhelm Meisters Wanderjahre*, the novel in which in his old age the poet revealed some of what he had held back all his life, the main character, who stands for Goethe, writes in a letter to his wife of a gruesome childhood episode in which five boys are drowned, which is the number of siblings whose deaths the boy had witnessed.

At any rate, it is not a question here of what effect the problem of the dead siblings had on Goethe's work. The point is that in the closest part of his environment great calamities took place, that the love and affection and encouragement he received are only one aspect of his environment. Simultaneous and parallel with his being immersed in a constant stream of affection, he was probably kept constantly in tension and conflict by the bewildering observation and experience of pregnancies and deaths. It is puzzling, in view of extensive clinical observation that would, if anything, bespeak the opposite, how it came to pass that this boy could ever develop into the person that Goethe ultimately became. However, if we assume that this mother perhaps did not withdraw her libido from her firstborn son during her pregnancies and while her many children went through their death struggles, if we assume that the boy was never given, even for a moment's time, a realistic reason to doubt his mother's love, and that these parents when the many calamities occurred did not truly mourn or grieve because they had the feeling that this one child richly compensated them for the loss of so many others, then it may become understandable that the closeness to pregnancies and deaths did not, in this instance, lead to a devastating tendency to conflict but to a truly constructive one.

From the seventh year of his life an episode is reported that shows the boy fairly well solidified in himself. When in November, 1755, a terrible earthquake almost destroyed Lisbon and other Portuguese cities (sixty to a hundred thousand people were reported to have lost their lives) this was discussed all over Europe with great excitement from the religious point of view. It became the topic of sermons and for the first time in his life the boy was drawn, as Goethe later described it, into doubts about God's wisdom and justice. His mother, however, told Bettina that when the boy was asked his opinion, upon his return from a sermon, he said: "In the end everything may be much simpler than the preacher thinks, for God will know well that the immortal soul cannot suffer any damage through an evil fate."

Here we see the boy expounding in a precocious way views that cannot possibly have been integrated by him but which in the form of secondary elaborations served excellently as defenses against anxiety. Here he apparently did not depend on the accidental good luck of circumstances but seemingly generated out of himself a very effective rationalization. The idea of the soul's invulnerability stood him in good stead throughout his life and found its beautiful realization in the solution the aged poet found for his tragedy of *Faust*.

Conflicts such as the oedipal one and others are unavoidable, and a boy who later will be an active member of the cultural community has to go through their throes. The course conflicts will take and the result they may produce in the child— whether they will traumatize or be stimuli to maturation—all this depends to a large extent on inner complications. These I wish to disregard in order to turn again toward external reality. The difficulty encountered in this investigation is that no particular reality or environment can be stringently correlated with well-defined courses that developmental processes will take or with well-defined clinical end results. It can only be a matter of statistical approximations of the type: given a certain constitution, a particular reality structure will have the optimal chance of leading to a particular end result.

Although the following is nothing but a repetition of well-known propositions, it still may be necessary to restate them. The manifestation of inherited, constitutional, psychological traits may in general be favored or impeded by environmental factors. Some such traits manifest themselves in a variety of environments that are quite different one from another. Such traits are more or less environmentally independent, if not completely resistant to external influences. In severe instances of psychopathology one obtains the impression that viability is possible only if the psychobiological organism grows up in a very special environment, that is to say, only one environmental setup will lead, for example in the presence of a schizophrenic constitution, to a condition free of psychotic manifestations. Children endowed with such constitutions will develop into schizophrenics in almost any of the kinds of environment in which children of our times are expected to grow up. Yet an expert child analyst may well be capable of devising an environmental setup that will preserve the child from later disease.

In the instance of Goethe I surmise the following relation between constitution and environment as regards later geniushood. One has to assume that the constitutional requisites of creativity were extremely strong. He would have developed into a person with remarkable creative abilities under a large number of different environmental setups. Yet—and this is the principal point—is the spectrum of environments that would have led to precisely that creative maximum which is actually observed in Goethe, just as large or approximately as large? Would any other than the actual environmental setup have brought to manifestation the total constitutional creative potential? It is my impression that the constitutional factor related to Goethe's creativity was environmentally resistant to a large extent, but that only one very special environmental setup could lead to the maximum realization of his genius.

Kroeber has demonstrated very convincingly on a statistical basis the dependency of genius manifestation on environmental factors. The relative scarcity of genius is probably not based only upon the relative infrequency of those gene combinations that are necessary for geniushood, but perhaps even more upon the extremely small chance that such a combination, itself rare, will meet just the one unique environmental setup that is necessary for its maximum realization.[4]

The boy Goethe was bound to go through the throes of the Oedipus conflict, the effect of which, as in the case of all authors and poets, can also be demonstrated in his works and in his later life. But the fact that his mother felt closer to him and gave preference to him over his father, plus the other factors that have been enumerated, checked the capacity of the Oedipus conflict to produce that aggravation or hopelessness that so often becomes a boy's undoing. Some or all of these reality factors may have been relevant to the boy's possession of that energy surplus with which counteraction against the destructive effect of the usual childhood conflicts was possible, and which guaranteed maximum realization of the genius potential.

I wish to present two examples of how Goethe dealt with the one part of the Oedipus conflict, namely, the relationship to the father.

Leschnitzer has the merit of having been the first one to describe analytically the family romance that is to be discovered in Goethe's *Dichtung und Wahrheit*.

Goethe had got the idea into his head—from playmates, he claimed—that his ostensible grandfather had not been his father's father but had been willing to act *in loco patris* for a son begotten of his wife by a nobleman. Did not, so the friends reasoned, all the wealth come from the grandmother, whereas all other members of the family were unmoneyed? When the boy heard these remarks, he dismissed them with a show of indignation but started all kinds of investigations in order to discover a physical similarity between his father, or even himself, and members of princely families.

In view of the frequency of such ideas about descent it is probable that, under the guise of insinuations coming from others, Goethe was recording his own original fantasies and that Leschnitzer is right in recognizing in them a genuine family romance.

Regarding the interpretation I should like to add one remark. What impresses me as unusual—although possibly it may often have been observed clinically by others—is the inclusion of the father in the family romance. In my experience and that of many others the family romance builds up a barrier between the child and the parents; one might easily expect that Goethe's family romance would have been such as to separate him from his father, whose function as representative of authority caused him particular pain at that time. Goethe's insinuation, however, that not only he but also his father was of princely descent may easily be understood as the effect of affectionate closeness. Yet the unequal distribution of onus and privilege in assigning to himself the honor of noble ancestry but to his father the burden of illegitimacy shows the ambivalence that gave birth to the fantasy.

The second example of Goethe's dealing with the father-relationship aspect of the Oedipus conflict concerns the development of Goethe's genitality. It seems almost certain that the first time Goethe had sexual intercourse was at the age of about thirty-nine. The reasons for that delay and how beneficial—even necessary—it was for his creativity and his establishment as Germany's greatest lyrical poet are not a subject of this paper. The relevant facts of the episode for present purposes are these: During his second sojourn in Rome (June 7, 1787–April 23, 1788), Goethe started a sexual relationship with Faustina, daughter of the innkeeper Agostino di Giovanni. From his correspondence with the Duke of Weimar, it can be proved with some accuracy that this must have occurred in January, or February, 1788. It is, now, a very surprising fact that at that time he was very close to the same age as that at which his father was married—to be exact, Goethe was three months older. The conclusion suggests itself that his father's marriage was unconsciously looked upon by Goethe as the time of his first intercourse. Thus one interpretation may be formulated as follows: "My father did not have the privilege of sexual enjoyment until he was thirty-nine years old; why should I have that privilege at an earlier age?" The delay in genital gratification would thus be the expression of a supreme loyalty to his father. It is indeed a maximum sacrifice when a young man, out of respect and loyalty to his father, voluntarily (or not so voluntarily?) renounces for the years when the sexual urge is at its peak, the full establishment of his virility.

Yet a more subtle investigation shows that Goethe's age at the time of his first intercourse coincides almost to the day with his father's age when he begot his first child. I find it impossible to devise a more satisfactory hypothesis to account for this choice of date by Goethe than that it meant to his unconscious the celebration of a kind of self-generation performed in identification with his father.[5] Thus interpreted, the delay of the first intercourse and its final performance express the deepest love, respect, obedience, and loyalty to the father and simultaneously a complete abrogation, namely, the thought: "Not you are my father, not you have begotten me, but I am my own father."

It is most striking that an action in the service of the reality principle—the delay of intercourse favored Goethe's maximum creativity—simultaneously expressed to the fullest the deepest feeling of love and its very opposite. I do not think it is right to correlate such an act with ambivalence, as we are prone to do. Ambivalence usually creates a schism in the ego, increases conflicts, and in cases of great intensity leads to feelings of guilt and the corresponding desire for self-punishment.

Little of this is found in Goethe. Skipping over details and some intervening phases, it can be briefly said that he continued the adjustment that had begun in Italy, started the relationship with Christiane upon his return to Weimar, and indulged for a few years in a rich heterosexual life. Therefore I feel more inclined to stress the tremendous synthetic value of the act under discussion. Ambivalence toward his father was, of course, present in Goethe, and only, as I think, at the end of his life did this ambivalence vanish.

But side by side with this area of conflict between love and hate, there was the deepest love and respect untainted by any contrary impulses. The relevant and unique psychological fact is Goethe's freedom, or, better, capacity to synthesize the gratification of these more or less isolated, mutually contradictory strivings into a perfect, reality-adequate action. This unusual characteristic of his psychic economy, in which one is inclined to discover something like innate wisdom, is one of the psychological points that made him so very different from other mortals.

A host of problems beset, of course, the reconstruction and interpretation that I propose, not the least being the old problem of time representation in the unconscious. If I am right, the image of the father in Goethe's unconscious would have been highly structured in terms of time. We cannot suppose that Goethe consciously kept track of a correspondence between age-related events in his father's and his own life.

But instead of discussing any or all of the many problems that attract our attention in this connection, I prefer to turn to another one. For this purpose I must first report a piece of historical research on my own.

In a not very well-known booklet about Goethe's father, the author, Von Der Schulenburg, refers to a passage in the diary kept by Johann Christian Senckenberg (1707-1772), the famous physician who, except for brief interruptions, practiced medicine in Frankfurt from 1732 till his death. This diary has not yet been published, but according to this author Senckenberg wrote in it that Johann Kaspar Goethe, Goethe's father, "had only him, Senckenberg, to thank that he was able to marry."

In none of the standard biographies of Goethe is this entry from Senckenberg's diary recorded.

The first question the reader will ask is as to the reliability of the informant. Since Senckenberg left a voluminous diary with a huge mass of references to almost everyone who played a role of any importance in the Frankfurt of his day, his reliability has been tested repeatedly by scholars concerned with other subjects and usually has been judged affirmatively with regard to the factual information the diary records. Senckenberg was a very righteous person who measured his fellow men in terms of the loftiest standards and he was inclined toward a black-white concept of human behavior. Accordingly, his personal judgment, his evaluation of motives, may often have been prejudiced or erroneous. But that misinformation as to facts should come from him is highly improbable.

The next question, of course, is in what way did Senckenberg make it possible for Goethe's father to marry? The first hypothesis suggested by most people I consulted was that perhaps Senckenberg acted as an intermediary between Johann Kaspar Goethe and Johann Wolfgang Textor, father of Katharina Elisabeth. This interpretation can be easily refuted.

307

(1) Johann Kaspar was in no need of intercession in his behalf. Although the Textor family held a higher place than Goethe's in the social hierarchy of Frankfurt, Textor had several daughters and little money and is generally believed to have been delighted to give his oldest daughter in marriage to a wealthy citizen. (2) Senckenberg despised Textor for many reasons and would for this reason alone almost certainly not have taken upon himself such a mission. (3) According to Schulenburg, the passage does not say that Senckenberg made it possible for Johann Kaspar to marry *a particular woman,* but only refers in general terms to *the fact of marriage* per se.

Schulenburg himself suggests that Johann Kaspar had become infected with syphilis while traveling through Italy as a young man, and that Senckenberg had by his treatment made it possible for him to marry. However, there is no evidence for Schulenburg's assumption and it is probable that he was the victim of a fashion rather prevalent a few years ago, namely, to attribute to almost anyone who showed psychopathology a syphilitic infection. The state of dementia in which Goethe's father died at the age of seventy-two seems to have been an arteriosclerotic condition and the clinical evidence does not favor the diagnosis of general paresis.

When a physician says that he made it possible for a patient to marry, then there is a good chance that he refers to a treatment that removed an obstacle to the successful performance of intercourse. There are the alternatives of psychic or physical impotence. I was not successful in ascertaining specific instances of Senckenberg's medical practice, but it goes without saying that at that time, too, many symptoms of psychogenic origin were regarded as physical and treated as such. Thus it would be possible that Johann Kaspar was suffering from psychogenic impotence, and sought and received help from Senckenberg. However, if a man discovers that he is impotent, would he, if he sought medical help at all, wait until he intended to marry? Whatever his premarital experiences might have been, it is a deficiency which might deter him from marriage altogether or which he might expect marriage itself to cure him of.

The information as it stands now suggests most strongly, among the alternatives I can think of, a physical infirmity, of which a phimosis is the most probable. However, the question may be raised again why a man under such circumstances would wait for necessary treatment until marriage. Instead of further speculation I set forth the contemporary example of Louis XVI, who even married despite an incapacitating phimosis and who only submitted to surgery seven years after his wedding. Reasons abound, of course, why a man at that time, and even today, might hesitate to have a circumcision performed. Johann Kaspar may easily have been one of those who accepted the idea of circumcision only when the decision could no longer be postponed.

Further, the question is to be raised whether Senckenberg performed such operations at all. This also cannot be answered precisely. At that time medical practice was divided between Medicus and Chirurgicus. Senckenberg's name never shows up on the list of surgeons, but in his function as *Stadtphysikus* (a physician in a municipal appointment) he had to examine the surgeons when they applied for licenses. Minor surgery was probably practiced by him.[6]

About Johann Kaspar's premarital life only one adventure is known. This is one he reports himself in his *Viaggio in Italia* and apparently it did not lead to physical contacts. When he was twenty years old, Senckenberg, in the diary referred to, called him "a morally pure young man throughout."

The least that can be said is that from Johann Kaspar's biography no fact is known that would indicate he had a love relation before marriage or would militate against the assumption that he suffered from an incapacitating phimosis and that he submitted to surgery as an adult in order to marry. An experienced psychosomaticist may discern in his character some traits that confirm the suggested medical diagnosis: his life is characterized by the fact that he had the best possible opportunities in terms of natural endowment and environmental conditions, but was incapable of using them to his advantage.

Thus we would be confronted with the very surprising fact that when Goethe postponed intercourse until the age of thirty-nine he was prompted by what was not, as it might easily seem, a fantasy about his father's sexual life, but what his father's actual sexual development had been.

If the many reconstructions I have ventured are correct, we should, of course, like to know what the boy's knowledge was of his father's past. We can be certain that he observed the shape of his father's penis. Yet it is hardly possible that he drew the correct conclusions from its anatomical appearance as to when his father's heterosexual relations began. By identification alone, after all, essential parts of a person's past may find effective representation in the mind of the identifying subject.

I regret that I have to leave this important topic at that. I shall now discuss what I have suggested before, that reality also spared the boy the trauma that the male child ordinarily suffers when, comparing himself with his father, he becomes aware of his biological inferiority.[7]

The psychological effects of perceiving the father's circumcised penis when the boy's penis is uncircumcised may be ranged under two main headings. One reaction will be still essentially identical with the well-known pattern: the greater size of the father's penis will arouse envy, aggression, and anxiety in the boy. But a second reaction is also possible: because of the relative shortening and incompleteness of the father's penis, the boy may, in comparing his father's organ with his own, develop a feeling of superiority and of being physically better endowed for virility than his father who may even impress him as being castrated. These two types of reaction do not exhaust the many alternatives one will have to think of.[8]

The intensity of the boy's reaction will have to be assessed much higher even when one considers in what disrepute circumcision has been held in Central Europe. From abundant clinical observations the conflicts are known that are correlated with devaluation of the father by the son, but these conflicts are built around the core of the paternal sexual superiority and derive their significance precisely from that core. In patients, of course, fantasies or acting out are frequently observed that are related to pretended sexual superiority over the father, but this is based on compensation or denial of the very opposite feeling. In Goethe's instance, however, we would encounter a remarkable reversal of conditions. Here, paradoxically, reality provided the little boy, in the most relevant context, with a position of partial superiority over his father. Reality thus provided him with what others, if need be, would have had to create in fantasy by a special effort. This is also true of the two other oedipal components which I considered earlier: the mother's preference for the boy over his father, and the boy's victory (by survival) over his siblings. These contents are also clincially well-known in the shape of fantasies. Yet it probably makes an essential difference whether such contents are provided by reality or whether psychic energy has to be invested in denial and the formation of opposites in order to reach the equivalent position in fantasy.[9]

The possibility thus looms that when Goethe postponed genital relations until he had reached the age his father had when he married, he was not being led by a mere fantasy to the effect that marriage and first intercourse coincided in his father's life, but that he was responding to what had been an external reality. If this is correct, it is striking. The role fantasy plays in the life of every human being can hardly be overrated. Fantasies are like catchalls into which everything can be thrown that is useless for a person's immediate dealings with reality. They may then serve gratification or defense or repression or rationalization. Yet they may drain off valuable forces, that might better be spent in direct handling of reality. By means of introversion a person may become well-nigh completely incapacitated to act realistically.

Fantasies, in turn, may, however, be the stimuli toward action. Perceiving the difference that exists between the true shape of reality and his own fantasies, a person may be spurred to give reality a shape that will bring it into focus with the content of his fantasies. But in this instance, too, fantasy is a detour, though a detour that carries rich dividends.

Thus in Goethe's life what would otherwise seem, in the decisively important area of genital development, to have been an identification based on fantasy, turns out, if my research and interpretations are correct, to have been an identification based on a most subtly perceived reality. Is this just an interesting psychological observation related to what may in essence be a coincidence, or are we here confronted with a principal issue in determining whether high endowment develops into mere talent—close though it may come to genius, still talent— or into its true potential or full geniushood? [10]

There is another example of genius in whom it seems probable that apparent fantasy was almost identical with early reality. It has always struck me that Freud, the oldest son of his father Jakob's second and probably preferred wife, held exactly the same place as the biblical Joseph, who was the first-born son of Jacob's second and preferred wife, Rachel, and who later became the famous interpreter of dreams. We know that Freud had consciously formed a Joseph fantasy about himself —belatedly as it would appear from his report. Is it possible that the *exquisiteness* of his *Interpretation of Dreams*—a book unique not only for its originality but also for the fact that in the six decades since it was written not one relevant discovery had been added by any one of the many minds devoted to the subject—rests genetically on accidental factors of childhood that repeated the environment of the biblical son of Jacob?

All the more should this be true of the genius of art. After all, the artistic task of the genius is to create a new reality. As long as artistic reality strikes us as spurious, as a figment or a fantasy, art has not reached its goal. Hamlet, after all, is more real than, or, at least, as real as, anyone whom we know in the narrow confines of external reality. We know him better and can say more about him and are on more intimate terms with him than with most of our friends and acquaintances. He is also more meaningful to us than they because he is in his own way more perfect than what blind nature can create. Only when art reaches this level of solidified, bona-fide reality should we speak of the work of a genius.

From where does the genius derive this faculty for creating a new world that in its reality value transcends external reality? Is it perhaps the case that the work of the genius, as well as his inner life, is based less on fantasy but rather more on a reality? Or, in other words, are the genius poet's fantasies, conscious and unconscious, derived, possibly unwittingly, from a reality, and is that why they bear that fulminating power that later endows the work of art with its characteristic appearance as a new reality?

The motto of the second part of *Dichtung und Wahrheit* is: "What one wishes for in youth, one has abundantly in old age."

No wronger assertion, it seems, could be put at the head of an autobiography. "What is *feared* in youth one has abundantly in old age" would be an apothegm truer to human destiny as it is actually observed. Yet still, for Goethe, there was a truth deeper than the apparent wrongness in his assertion.

It has been observed by most of Goethe's biographers that, quite aside from all the works he left, his life itself appears like a work of art. Indeed, were we capable of keeping the two, his life and his work, apart, we could hardly decide which is more beautiful. It can be easily shown that every sector of his life was typical and paradigmatic (most movingly observable in his adolescent crisis), but this ideal-type quality of his actions is simultaneously incomparably individual, in a sense more intense than that which is conveyed by such hackneyed statements as that "every person is an individual." It is difficult to define this true uniqueness which most of Goethe's biographers, like most of his contemporaries that were close to him, found so strikingly apparent.

I have thought it necessary to mention this general principle of Goethe's life, for geniushood is usually measured by the yardstick of achievement, but in Goethe's instance there is still something added which cursorily may perhaps be called the geniushood of his life.

Georg Simmel expressed the idea that Goethe's life shows a trend which everyone would follow if he were able to pursue, or surrender to, the pure humanness that abides in all of us. From this viewpoint Simmel is right when he says that Goethe's life shows that supreme geniushood is combinable with "the simply normal." Goethe's motto regarding youth and old age expresses in the simplest form a harmony that, present in his own development, is absent in the lives of most people, who, by trauma and Ananke, are drawn away from what Simmel called "pure humanness." The usual life we study is the mutual permeation of pure humanness and human dross that leads to psychopathology such as neurosis, psychosis, perversion, or crime—categories in terms of which it is just not possible to account for what made Goethe's life unique.

What I have called metaphorically the dross of human existence was not alien to him. He presented it with keen insight in his writings. It slumbered in him as it does in others. But with one exception it never became an integral part of his life. For reasons that have not yet been understood the genius forms out of what leads in others to disorder and disease, the marvels of his creations. Thus the true genius cannot be measured in those terms with which we commonly approach psychopathology. Admitting their special position, it still is reasonable to ask: do they grow in relative independence of their environment? They need, of course, an environment. They have to be fed, they have to learn a language and acquire skills, all of which clearly depend on environment.

But does that particularity that makes them totally different from the rest grow independently of the environment? The final answer will have to wait until the great debate between environmentalists and hereditists has come to a close. Yet I have thought it interesting enough to set forth that at the beginning of his life, which like perhaps no other has aroused the interest of so many inquisitive minds, we find the infant in contact with two parents that phenotypically were well within the bounds of the average, yet on closer scrutiny reveal themselves (as much as this can be explored from the historical record) as unique in one respect, of certainly no minor relevance—by the total absence of ambivalence toward their child.

Appendix

Of the several points I have marshaled in support of my general view of the role of Goethe's immediate environment in shaping his genius, the one most weakly supported by evidence is the point that Goethe's father was circumcised. To be sure, this detail of Goethe's environment is not decisive for the main point of my thesis but only adds further evidence to a state of affairs that can be well documented in other contexts. A reader, however, who has not become convinced of this

315

particular conclusion will probably remain dubious about its validity also in view of what follows. Accordingly, even at the risk of compounding such skepticism by adding material that may itself seem farfetched at first glance, I venture to present some evidence which seems to me to favor my assumption.

I have previously cited Louis XVI as a historical example of how a phimosis was dealt with in the eighteenth century. This was not an instance chosen at random, for it probably was known to Goethe. Zweig, in *Marie Antoinette: The Portrait of an Average Woman*, reproduces the report on this matter sent to Madrid by the Spanish ambassador to the French court and no detail of the physical disturbance and its consequences was omitted. Further, the court in Vienna was fully informed. The unhappy king's brother-in-law, the future Austrian emperor, had a leading role in counseling and arranging for the operation.

The planning of marriages, the scanning of marriage prospects, was, after all, an important part of court policies, and it is just about as unlikely that the ducal court at Weimar was unaware why the dauphin's marriage had remained childless for so long as that the fact of the childlessness itself should have gone unnoticed. It is almost certain that Louis' impotence was for years a matter of ridicule and gossip. Thus Goethe, the most intimate friend of Karl August, Duke of Weimar, must have known what the state of affairs was.

In the biographical record covering the years that followed his departure from his native city in 1775, Goethe made a remark, important in this context, about the famous Diamond Necklace Affair in which the queen, Marie Antoinette, became implicated. On the basis of the first news that came out of France, it seemed as if the queen had been involved in the fraud. Goethe wrote: "Already in the year 1785 the Necklace Affair had made an indescribable impression on me. In the immoral abyss of city, court, and state that opened up

316

here, there appeared before me, specterlike, the most horrible consequences, whose apparition I could not for some time get rid of; withal I comported myself so strangely that friends with whom I was just then sojourning in the country when the first news about it reached us, confessed to me later, long after the revolution had broken out, that at that time I appeared to them as if out of my mind."

Goethe's occasional hyperexcitability is well known. After the spasmodic years of the *Sturm und Drang* period had faded out, this excitability occurred less often, but still manifested itself in certain situations, for example, (1) when he was suddenly exposed to stimulation without forewarning, as when his son, who he did not even know was present, played a prank on him and put his hands before his father's eyes from behind; (2) when personal events of manifest grave emotional importance took place, such as the departure from Weimar in 1823 of the famous piano player Maria Szymanowska (1795-1831), whom he adored.

Political events did not affect him strongly as far as I know, and though I think Heinrich Meyer goes too far when he says that "Goethe cared excedingly little about the vicissitudes of countries and states," it must have been a personal factor that made him behave in an apparently insane manner and not concerned about the first harbinger of a political cataclysm. Another remark of Goethe's about the Necklace Affair is known. He said to Eckermann in 1831: "The Queen, so closely intertwined with the vexatious Necklace Affair, lost her dignity, yes her respect, and thus she had lost in the people's opinion the position of being inviolable. Hatred does not harm anyone, but it is contempt that brings men low."

Here Goethe is quite outspoken. The news of 1785 had aroused his contempt for a queen. But why should loss of respect for the Queen make him act as if he were insane?

Marie Antoinette (1755-1793) was not a newcomer in his

317

life. In 1770 while he was a student in Strasbourg he owed her indirectly a great service. Having left Vienna after being married to the dauphin by proxy, she stopped in Strasbourg, where she was entrusted to the care of the dauphin's emissaries. The official act took place in a building especially erected for this purpose. In small rooms adjoining the principal one, there were on exhibit tapestries woven after Raphael's famous cartoons, and Goethe spent much time there. These copies had "quite a decisive effect" on him. He became acquainted here with "the right and the perfect. . . . I went and came and came and went, and could not get my fill of seeing; indeed a futile striving tormented me because I should have liked to comprehend that which incited my interest so extraordinarily."

Yet as delighted as Goethe was by the decorations in the small rooms, just as much was he struck with horror by those in the main hall. These were much larger, richer, and more splendid tapestries, woven after painting of the modern French school. The style itself Goethe would also have taken to his heart if it had not been for the subject. These tapestries represented all the abominations of the myth of the golden fleece, such as Creüsa in her last agony and Jason with the assassinated children.

Apparently, Goethe's reaction to the tapestries was so violent as to alarm his friends. That a representation of Jason, whose marriage was so ill-starred, should have been chosen to celebrate the nuptials of the dauphine, was "a crime against taste and feeling." In vain they sought to persuade him that it is not everyone's business "to look for meanings in the pictures," and that neither Marie Antoinette nor anyone else would read any far-fetched significance in this choice of hangings. Goethe continued to argue: "It is, indeed, not otherwise than if the most ghastly specter had been sent to meet this pretty, and, as one hears, gay lady at the border."

318

Still one must wonder whether outrage at the bad taste in the choice of subject is itself enough to account for the alleged vehemence of Goethe's reaction. In his own words, the blunder "put me wholly beside myself," and his friends tried to hustle him out of the pavilion lest there be trouble.

What seems to have struck Goethe as most offensive was a tapestry that had as subject "Jason Taming the Bull." It is descibed in an official catalogue as follows: "In a public place, in the middle of a large crowd struck by terror, Jason advances alone slowly toward the two white bulls, which shoot fire from their nostrils. He stretches against them a leafed twig. To the right the king is seated on an elevated throne, Medea at his side. He is surrounded by his court."

It seems to me there is more than a hint in the very detailed account Goethe himself gives—indeed, in the very fact that he goes into such detail—of the precise way in which the tapestry was hung. According to him, most of the tapestry was hidden by the red velvet that covered the back of Marie Antoinette's throne, so that neither Jason advancing toward the bull nor the bull were visible, but only its tail "curled forth." Now, in fact, as can be seen in the reproduction of the tapestry, the bull's tail is not "curled," but, rather, outstretched. If one imagines how it appeared, isolated, standing forth whitely, the conjecture seems to me inescapable that Goethe saw it as an erect penis.

It is to be observed, further, that Goethe used this incident to illustrate the forebodings that pictures may elicit. Accordingly, he connects his feelings on this occasion with the horrible end the queen later suffered. We shall, however, see that all this can be interpreted quite differently if one also tries to account for Goethe's "insane"-like reaction of 1785. After all, it is not reasonable to assume that Goethe really had any premonitions in 1770, and the fact that the passage just cited above was written long after Marie Antoinette had fallen as a victim of revolution makes his assertion more than suspect.

The dauphine's passage through Strasbourg is historically confirmed, the plan of the pavilion is preserved, and the tapestries, correctly described by Goethe, can still be seen in Baden-Baden.

The decisive question here is: did Goethe as a young student really have the reaction which he described when he wrote *Dichtung und Wahrheit* as an old man? In the text he goes on to refer to a grave accident that killed many people in Paris at a fireworks display in celebration of the dauphin's wedding. Again the ghastly pictures in the pavilion stepped before Goethe's mind. The accident had still other consequences. Goethe and his circle loved practical jokes, and he wrote a friend in his native city a letter dated from Versailles pretending that he had witnessed all the royal wedding celebrations. When the friend heard of the accident he feared Goethe, whom he believed to be in Paris, had been killed. Since Goethe actually did make a journey at that time, if not to Paris, and no letters of his reached Frankfurt, he was, for a while, believed dead, thus causing fright and anxiety. Such dire consequences of his desire to mystify others made him forswear practical jokes of this sort. Yet he was not always faithful to his oath. "Real life often loses its sheen so much that sometimes one has to touch it up again with the varnish of fiction." Some authors believe that Goethe actually carried out this practical joke which he reports in *Dichtung und Wahrheit*, relying on a letter of July 7, 1770, from Renatus Senckenberg, a student in Göttingen, to Bernhard Crespel, a Frankfurt friend of Goethe's and of the victim of Goethe's alleged practical joke. The letter contains a sentence in which Renatus expresses his agreement with Bernhard, who had desired to see the dauphine after the night of her first intercourse. There is no word about Goethe or any indication that Crespel's desire was precipitated by Goethe's alleged pretense of having gone to Paris. As far as

I know there is no evidence that Goethe actually carried out this prank.

I surmise that this whole episode belongs to "the varnish of fiction," as Goethe's last words about it put it. The story of the mystification sounds to me as if it was following a literary model. While he was at work on that part of *Dichtung und Wahrheit* that contains the account of his stay in Strasbourg (1811), Goethe was reading the *Novelle* of Matteo Bandello (c. 1480-1561). Bandello's stories are rich in all sorts of unusual events, but I have not discovered a story that might have served as a pattern of a kind I was looking for, unless a somewhat strained relationship is established to Bandello's thirty-third story of the second part. This story became famous as a literary predecessor to *Romeo and Juliet*. The connection with Goethe's account is so slight that it would hardly be worth considering if it were not that Goethe was engaged in a translation of Shakespeare's play at that time. In both stories a voyage takes a central place. More about Bandello later. Let us now try to investigate the psychoanalytic meaning of the two episodes Goethe reported in connection with Marie Antoinette.

In the episode of 1785 it makes no great difference whether or not Goethe's report about his reaction was true. Whether he actually was told by friends that he behaved in an insane-like manner upon receiving the news of the Necklace Affair, or whether this was a poetic embellishment, we can be certain that by including it in a biographical report he at least intimated that the news provoked in him an extremely strong emotional reaction. Accordingly, taking the report about his feelings in 1770 as he gives it, I find it suggestive of the following interpretation.

The small rooms with Raphael's tapestries were in Goethe's imagination Christian, good, beautiful, right, and perfect. The large hall with its tapestry was pagan, cruel, unbecoming for a bride, and frightening, the whole imagery leading to the perception of an erected penis. The specter that is sent to meet the bride then would refer to the frightening experiences that await an innocent girl on her wedding night.

From Renatus' letter we know in what direction a young man's fantasy went at that time. Quite generally one finds that king and queen stand for father and mother in the imagery of a person who grows up in a monarchy. Events in sovereign families have oedipal implications. In the case of Renatus it was the voyeuristic desire that was excited, as if he wanted to say: "I wish I could have had an opportunity to watch my mother when she was deflowered by my father."

Goethe's reaction, then, reflected the anxiety with which he regarded the bride's ordeal. The innocent bride is not prepared to endure the cruel things father will do to her during the wedding night, with the frightening specter of the erected penis.

Yet we know that when Goethe wrote about Strasbourg as an aging man he was aware not only that the attractive girl, whose marriage took place under the most auspicious circumstances, had later been executed, but also that her marriage was not consummated for seven years. The specter then assumes a different meaning. First the bride is excited by being made to believe she will be gratified by a potent male, and then she is exposed to the humiliation and disappointment of having married a man who is impotent. Significantly Goethe mentions the fatal mishap at the celebration in Paris and not the tragic end of the queen. If the Medea-Creüsa imagery on the other hand for poetical reasons adumbrates the many tragic events that lay in store for the queen, beginning with the fatal accidents at the wedding celebration and ending in her public execution, then one asks why Goethe added the reference to the erected penis. This detail is close to indelicacy and almost improper if viewed within the total context. It is certainly not meant in a facetious or satirical way in view of the strong reaction the young man allegedly showed.

The reaction of 1785 is less difficult to interpret. The news that reached Goethe would have meant to him that a mother figure, sexually unsatisfied by her defective husband, did not bear her frustration with dignity but sought compensatory pleasures in a profligate way that exposed her husband to ridicule. Oddly enough this comes close to the way Goethe described Wilhelm Meister's mother in the first draft of his famous novel *William Meister's Lehrjahre*, which was his first autobiographical endeavor. In no other work of his than in that early draft can there be found a more intimate description of his own early childhood, and it is very striking to find just there a very negative presentation of the principal character's mother. She is cold and on bad terms with Wilhelm's father, has a lover, and is most unkind to her children.

The aging poet must have found himself in a peculiar situation when he wrote of his experience with Marie Antoinette of four decades before. Here the son and the daughter of Europe's two most powerful sovereigns were being married, a most auspicious alliance. The intense emotional ties of Goethe to nobility in his later years are well known. The higher a person stood in the feudal pyramid, the greater was Goethe's adoration. Psychologically this penchant of his, so often quite wrongly criticized, was expressive of how alive his Oedipus complex was, an indispensable prerequisite of creativity in a genius of Goethe's type. This inclination toward a strong emotional responsiveness to nobility must already have been latently present when he was young. Therefore the impending nuptials of the emperor's daughter to the future king of France and the bride's renowned beauty must have elicited strong oedipal reactions in him. He probably envied the dauphin and felt attracted toward the dauphine. Looking back at that episode from the position of old age, he may have felt that as a young man he had been duped and cheated, for as things turned out all his envy and jealousy had been superfluous. The dauphin was unmasked as having been impotent as a man and most unsuccessful as a king, and the dauphine was now known to have been a coquette. This sounds like a repetition of past childhood experiences, when the gradual recognition of foibles and weaknesses in the admired parents leads to the child's disappointment and the humiliating feeling that life has played on his credulity.

Possibly Goethe's reading of Bandello's story of Gerardo and Elena, where a fantastic complication ends in joy and happiness, and the contrast of it with *Romeo and Juliet,* where the sweetness of life turns into the greatest bitterness, enhanced impressions he had gained in his own life. Accordingly, he may have felt induced to describe himself in a situation in which he himself had been the victim of a mystification as someone who had actively mystified others.

In my reconstruction these two episodes as reported in Goethe's autobiographical writings contain confirmatory evidence of the circumcision of Goethe's father. It is, after all, most strange that Goethe reacted in this peculiar way to a woman of whom he knew at the time he was writing of her that she had lived with a husband who for the first seven years of his marriage had not been able to carry out his marital duties because of a phimosis.

The following episode reported by Goethe in *Dichtung und Wahrheit* may be looked at as another indirect evidence for my thesis:

Once, when his father, as was his habit, was shaved by a barber on a Saturday evening Wolfgang and Cornelia sitting behind the store recited verses in a low voice. These verses were by the poet Klopstock whose books they were not permitted to read. Cornelia, however, carried away by the passion of reciting, suddenly raised her voice to such an outcry that "the good surgeon was startled and spilled the soap basin over father's chest. There rose a great turmoil and a stern inquisition was held, particularly in view of the misfortune that might have occurred had the process of shaving already been under way."

This humorous anecdote looked to me in the past like a cover memory of the aging Goethe ridiculing castration fear. However, with the idea of Goethe's father's circumcision in mind, I am more inclined to interpret it as an intimation that his father actually had suffered such "misfortune" which the anecdote reduces to an "almost" event.

1959

NOTES

1. Combined with a core of basic, close, and unambivalent contact with the world there is also encountered in Goethe a core of solid sense of identity. Problems regarding the sense of identity can, of course, be found in Goethe, as probably in everyone who thinks about himself and his position in life. But there is no indication that his role playing, his pleasure in costume and disguise, his interest in and contempt for impostors, grew out of a weakness of sense of identity or a doubt about identity. To crawl for a while into another shape may be a sign of strength or weakness. Out of exuberance and abundance he was a man of many shapes, but never out of a basic dissatisfaction or a weakness of sense of identity.

2. Tentatively I suggest that the former type leads to specialized genius and the latter to the generally creative genius such as is manifest in Goethe. The benevolent sway of events continued throughout Goethe's life. With progress of age, he of course increasingly participated actively in the formation of his destiny, but he was only continuing by effort and plan that which had been begun by external fortunate coincidences.

3. I omit the effect of childhood disease and the little alleviation children got in those times from medical care. At the age of nine the boy was blind for days from a severe attack of smallpox. Application of heat was recommended. This only increased his suffering. Still he had the will power and endurance not to scratch or rub the affected areas.

4. I have simplified the problem in various ways, two of which I wish to mention. The constitutional aspect alone is vastly complicated and it is probably not justifiable to speak simply of "the constitutional factor." Also, I did not consider here the historical situation, which is not really included in the concept of environment. Goethe was aware of the debt a genius owes the historical situation when at the age of seventy-five he said he was happy not to be eighteen at that time in view of the development the world had taken since his youth.

5. In my own clinical experience I have encountered the wish or fantasy of self-generation only once, in a schizophrenic patient. However, it seems to occur with some frequency. Freud wrote referring to the relation of a certain type of man to his mother: "All his [the son's] instincts, those of tenderness, gratitude, lustfulness, defiance and independence, find satisfaction in the single wish *to be his own father*." (Italics by Freud)

6. In the play *Die Räuber* by Schiller, Goethe's contemporary, the remark is made about a circumcised man that the *barber* has his foreskin.

7. I did not find anything in Goethe's works that could meaningfully be connected with imagery of a circumcised father except perhaps his enduring interest in the figure of Moses (see Leschnitzer, 1949), who was, after all, the uncircumcised father figure among the circumcised. The preoccupation with the Moses figure would then have been because it contained those features that compensated for the defects of his real father. However, such reasoning may rightly be regarded as farfetched in view of the universal interest in the Moses figure and its many aspects, which fascinated the greatest minds. After all, the perception of the father's circumcised penis may have shed its effect upon the boy's development without intruding into particular details of his later writings.

8. I am inclined to connect with the father's circumcision Goethe's ambivalence toward the Jews; his interest in Frankfurt's ghetto, in the Old Testament, in Jewish folklore, vs. his strong anti-Semitic feelings.

9. I must add that the feelings of virile superiority evidently did not reach an intensity which would have led to contempt for the father, at least during the formative years. There is, however, in the early draft of *Wilhelm Meister* an episode in which a professional actor whose last name is varyingly Bendel or Bengel (the latter meaning literally club or uncouth fellow, but also connoting penis) is devastatingly ridiculed in contrast to Wilhelm Meister, who evidently represents Goethe in the novel and who as an amateur actor attains the highest levels where Bengel miserably fails. Also the earliest preserved letter of Goethe to his sister, written at the age of fifteen, contains a passage that sounds like a symbolic reference to an impotent penis. The context, however, may suggest contempt of a phallic mother figure.

10. In the present stage of psychoanalytic research into creativity, I cannot warn enough against the frequently observed procedure of minimizing the difference between genius and talent and approaching both as if they were essentially the same, or reducing their differences to purely quantitative relations. Such a tendency is often noticeable also when the differences between psychosis and neurosis are discussed. Early psychoanalytic investigations erred on this score, as can be observed in Jung's first publication on the subject. The reader will expect at this point a definition of genius. However, oddly enough, although there is general agreement about a certain number of persons, few though they are, that they are geniuses, no satisfactory definition of genius has as yet been produced.

□ DOSTOEVSKY

AND PARRICIDE

Sigmund Freud

Four facets may be distinguished in the rich personality of Dostoevsky: the creative artist, the neurotic, the moralist, and the sinner. How is one to find one's way in this bewildering complexity?

The creative artist is the least doubtful: Dostoevsky's place is not far behind Shakespeare. *The Brothers Karamazov* is the most magnificent novel ever written; the episode of the Grand Inquisitor, one of the peaks in the literature of the world, can hardly be valued too highly. Before the problem of the creative artist analysis must, alas, lay down its arms.

The moralist in Dostoevsky is the most readily assailable. If we seek to rank him high as a moralist on the plea that only a man who has gone through the depths of sin can reach the highest summit of morality, we are neglecting a doubt that arises. A moral man is one who reacts to temptation as soon as he feels it in his heart, without yielding to it. A man who alternately sins and then in his remorse erects high moral standards lays himself open to the reproach that he has made things too easy for himself. He has not achieved the essence of morality, renunciation, for the moral conduct of life is a practical human interest. He reminds one of the barbarians of the great migrations, who murdered and did penance for it, till penance became an actual technique for enabling murder to be done. Ivan the Terrible behaved in exactly this way; indeed, this compromise with morality is a characteristic Russian trait. Nor was the final outcome of Dostoevsky's moral strivings anything very glorious. After the most violent struggles to reconcile the instinctual demands of the individual with the claims of the community, he landed in the retrograde position of submission both to temporal and spiritual authority, of veneration both for the czar and for the God of the Christians, and of a narrow Russian nationalism—a position which lesser minds have reached with smaller effort. This is the weak point in that great personality. Dostoevsky threw away the chance of becoming a teacher and liberator of humanity and made himself one with their jailers. The future of human civilization will have little to thank him for. It seems probable that he was condemned to this failure by his neurosis. The greatness of his intelligence and the strength of his love for humanity might have opened to him another, an apostolic, way of life.

To consider Dostoevsky as a sinner or a criminal rouses violent opposition, which need not be based upon a philistine assessment of crime. The real motive for this opposition soon becomes apparent. Two traits are essential in a criminal: boundless egoism and a strong destructive impulse. Common to both of these, and a necessary condition for their expression, is absence of love, lack of an emotional appreciation of (human) objects. One at once recalls the contrast to this presented by Dostoevsky—his great need of love and his enormous capacity for love, which is to be seen in manifestations of exaggerated kindness and caused him to love and to help where he had a right to hatred and revenge, as, for example, in his relations with his first wife and her lover. That being so, it must be asked why there is any temptation to reckon Dostoevsky among the criminals. The answer is that it comes from his choice of material, which singles out from all others violent, murderous, and egoistic characters, thus pointing to the existence of similar tendencies in his own soul, and also from certain facts in his life, like his passion for gambling and his possible admission of a sexual assault upon a young girl. The contradiction is resolved by the realization that Dostoevsky's very strong destructive instinct, which might easily have made him a criminal, was in his actual life directed mainly against his own person (inward instead of outward) and thus found expression as masochism and a sense of guilt. Nevertheless, his personality retained sadistic traits in plenty, which show themselves in his irritability, his love of tormenting, and his intolerance even toward people he loved, and which appear also in the way in which, as an author, he treats his readers. Thus in little things he was a sadist toward others, and in bigger things a sadist toward himself, in fact a masochist, that is to say the mildest, kindliest, most helpful person possible.

We have selected three factors from Dostoevsky's complex personality, one quantitative and two qualitative: the extraordinary intensity of his emotional life, his perverse instinctual predisposition, which inevitably marked him out to be a sadomasochist or a criminal, and his unanalyzable artistic endowment. This combination might very well exist without neurosis; there are people who are complete masochists without being neurotic. Nevertheless, the balance of forces between his instinctual demands and the inhibitions opposing them (plus the available methods of sublimation) would even so make it necessary to classify Dostoevsky as what is known as an "instinctual character." But the position is obscured by the simultaneous presence of neurosis, which, as we have said, was not in the circumstances inevitable, but which comes into being the more

331

readily, the richer the complication which has to be mastered by the ego. For neurosis is after all only a sign that the ego has not succeeded in making a synthesis, that in attempting to do so it has forfeited its unity.

How, then, strictly speaking, does his neurosis show itself? Dostoevsky called himself an epileptic, and was regarded as such by other people, on account of his severe seizures, which were accompanied by loss of consciousness, muscular convulsions, and subsequent depression. Now it is highly probable that this so-called epilepsy was only a symptom of his neurosis and must accordingly be classified as hystero-epilepsy, that is, as severe hysteria. We cannot be completely certain on this point for two reasons, first, because the anamnestic data on Dostoevsky's alleged epilepsy are defective and untrustworthy, and secondly, because our understanding of pathological states combined with epileptiform seizures is imperfect.

To take the second point first. It is unnecessary here to reproduce the whole pathology of epilepsy, for it would throw no decisive light on the problem. But this may be said. The old *morbus sacer* is still in evidence as an ostensible clinical entity, the uncanny disease with its incalculable, apparently unprovoked convulsive seizures, its changing of the character into irritability and aggressiveness, and its progressive lowering of all the mental faculties. But the outlines of this picture are quite lacking in precision. The seizures, so savage in their onset, accompanied by biting of the tongue and incontinence of urine and working up to the dangerous *status epilepticus* with its risk of severe self-injuries, may, nevertheless, be reduced to brief periods of absence, or rapidly passing attacks of vertigo or may be replaced by short spaces of time during which the patient does something out of character, as though he were under the control of his unconscious. These seizures, though as a rule determined, in a way we do not understand, by purely physical causes, may nevertheless owe their first appearance to some purely mental cause (a fright, for instance) or may react in other respects to mental excitations. However characteristic intellectual impairment may be in the overwhelming majority of cases, at least *one* case is known to us (that of Helmholtz) in which the affliction did not interfere with the highest intellectual achievement. (Other cases of which the same assertion has been made are either disputable or open to the same doubts as the case of Dostoevsky himself.) People who are victims of epilepsy may give an impression of dullness and arrested development, just as the disease often accompanies the most palpable idiocy and the grossest cerebral defects, even though not as a necessary component of the clinical picture. But these seizures, with all their variations, also occur in other people who display complete mental development and, if anything, an excessive and as a rule insufficiently controlled emotional life. It is no wonder in these circumstances that it has been found impossible to maintain that "epilepsy" is a single clinical entity. The similarity that we find in the manifest symptoms seems to call for a functional view of them. It is as though a mechanism for abnormal instinctual discharge had been laid down organically, which could be made use of in quite different circumstances—both in the case of disturbances of cerebral activity due to severe histolytic or toxic affections, and also in the case of inadequate control over the mental economy and at times when the activity of the energy operating in the mind reaches crisis pitch. Behind this dichotomy we have a glimpse of the identity of the underlying mechanism of instinctual discharge. Nor can that mechanism stand remote from the sexual processes, which are fundamentally of toxic origin: the earliest physicians described copulation as a minor epilepsy and thus recognized in the sexual act a mitigation and adaptation of the epileptic method of discharging stimuli.

The "epileptic reaction," as this common element may be called, is also undoubtedly at the disposal of the neurosis whose essence it is to get rid by somatic means of quantities of excitation which it cannot deal with psychically. Thus the epileptic seizure becomes a symptom of hysteria and is adapted and modified by it just as it is by the normal sexual process of discharge. It is therefore quite right to distinguish between an organic and an "affective" epilepsy. The practical significance of this is that a person who suffers from the first kind has a disease of the brain, while a person who suffers from the second kind is a neurotic. In the first case his mental life is subjected to an alien disturbance from without, in the second case the disturbance is an expression of his mental life itself.

It is extremely probable that Dostoevsky's epilepsy was of the second kind. This cannot, strictly speaking, be proved. To do so we should have to be in a position to insert the first appearance of the seizures and their subsequent fluctuations into the thread of his mental life; and for that we know too little. The descriptions of the seizures themselves teach us nothing and our information about the relations between the seizures and Dostoevsky's experiences is defective and often contradictory. The most probable assumption is that the seizures went back far into his childhood, that their place was taken to begin with by milder symptoms, and that they did not assume an epileptic form until after the shocking experience of his eighteenth year—the murder of his father. It would be very much to the point if it could be established that they ceased completely during his exile in Siberia, but other accounts contradict this.[1]

The unmistakable connection between the murder of the father in *The Brothers Karamazov* and the fate of Dostoevsky's own father has struck more than one of his biographers, and has led them to refer to "a certain modern school of psychology." From the standpoint of psychoanalysis (for that is what is meant), we are tempted to see in that event the severest trauma and to regard Dostoevsky's reaction to it as the turning point of his neurosis. But if I undertake to substantiate this view psychoanalytically, I am bound to risk the danger of being unintelligible to all those readers who are unfamiliar with the language and theories of psychoanalysis.

We have one certain starting point. We know the meaning of the first attacks from which Dostoevsky suffered in his early years, long before the incidence of the "epilepsy." These attacks had the significance of death: they were heralded by a fear of death and consisted of lethargic, somnolent states. The illness first came over him, while he was still a boy, in the form of a sudden, groundless melancholy, a feeling, as he later told his friend Soloviev, as though he were going to die on the spot. And there in fact followed a state exactly similar to real death. His brother Andrei tells us that even when he was quite young Feodor used to leave little notes about before he went to sleep, saying that he was afraid he might fall into this death-like sleep during the night and therefore begged that his burial should be postponed for five days.

We know the meaning and intention of such death-like seizures. They signify an identification with a dead person, either with someone who is really dead or with someone who is still alive and whom the subject wishes dead. The latter case is the more significant. The attack then has the value of a punishment. One has wished another person dead, and now one *is* this other person and is dead oneself. At this point psychoanalytical theory brings in the assertion that for a boy this other person is usually his father and that the attack (which is termed hysterical) is thus a self-punishment for a death wish against a hated father.

Parricide, according to a well-known view, is the principal and primal crime of humanity as well as of the individual. It is in any case the main source of the sense of guilt, though we do not know if it is the only one: researches have not yet been able to establish with certainty the mental origin of guilt and the need for expiation. But it is not necessary for it to be the only one. The psychological situation is complicated and requires elucidation. The relation of a boy to his father is, as we say, an ambivalent one. In addition to the hate which seeks to get rid of the father as a rival, a measure of tenderness for him is also habitually present. The two attitudes of mind combine to produce identification with the father; the boy wants to be in his father's place because he admires him and wants to be like him, and also because he wants to put him out of the way. This whole development now comes up against a powerful obstacle. At a certain moment the child comes to understand that an attempt to remove his father as a rival would be punished by him with castration. So from fear of castration, that is, in the interests of preserving his masculinity, he gives up his wish to possess his mother and get rid of his father. In so far as this wish remains in the unconscious it forms the basis of the sense of guilt. We believe that what we have here been describing are the normal processes, the normal fate of the so-called Oedipus complex; nevertheless it requires an important amplification.

A further complication arises when the constitutional factor we call bisexuality is comparatively strongly developed in the child. For then, under the threat to the boy's masculinity by castration, his inclination becomes strengthened to deflect in the direction of femininity, to put himself instead in his mother's place and take over her role as object of his father's love. But the fear of castration makes *this* solution impossible as well. The boy understands that he must also submit to castration if he wants to be loved by his father as a woman. Thus both impulses, hatred of the father and being in love with the father, undergo repression. There is a certain psychological distinction in the fact that the hatred of the father is given up on account of fear of an *external* danger (castration), while the being in love with the father is treated as an *internal* instinctual danger, though fundamentally it goes back to the same external danger.

What makes hatred of the father unacceptable is *fear* of the father; castration is terrible, whether as a punishment or as the price of love. Of the two factors which repress hatred of the father, the first, the direct fear of punishment and castration, may be called the normal one; its pathogenic intensification seems to come only with the addition of the second factor, the fear of the feminine attitude. Thus a strong bisexual predisposition becomes one of the preconditions or reinforcements of neurosis. Such a predisposition must certainly be assumed in Dostoevsky, and it shows itself in a viable form (as latent homosexuality) in the important part played by male friendships in his life, in his strangely tender attitude toward rivals in love, and in his remarkable understanding of situations which are explicable only by repressed homosexuality, as many examples from his novels show.

I am sorry, though I cannot alter the facts, if this exposition of the attitudes of hatred and love toward the father and their transformations under the influence of the threat of castration seems to readers unfamiliar with psychoanalysis unsavory and incredible. I should myself expect that it is precisely the castration complex that would be bound to arouse the most universal repugnance. But I can only insist that psychoanalytic experience has put these relations in particular beyond the reach of doubt and has taught us to recognize in them the key to every neurosis. This key, then, we must apply to our author's so-called epilepsy. So alien to our consciousness are the things by which our unconscious mental life is governed!

But what has been said so far does not exhaust the consequences of the repression of the hatred of the father in the Oedipus complex. There is something fresh to be added: namely, that in spite of everything, the identification with the father finally makes a permanent place for itself in the ego. It is received into the ego, but establishes itself there as a separate agency in contrast to the rest of the content of the ego. We then give it the name of superego and ascribe to it, the inheritor of the parental influence, the most important functions. If the father was hard, violent, and cruel, the superego takes over those attributes from him and, in the relations between the ego and it, the passivity which was supposed to have been repressed is re-established. The superego has become sadistic, and the ego becomes masochistic, that is to say, at bottom passive in a feminine way. A great need for punishment develops in the ego, which in part offers itself as a victim to fate, and in part finds satisfaction in ill-treatment by the superego (that is, in the sense of guilt). For every punishment is ultimately castration and, as such, a fulfillment of the old passive attitude toward the father. Even fate is, in the last resort, only a later father-projection.

The normal processes in the formation of conscience must be similar to the abnormal ones described here. We have not yet succeeded in fixing the boundary line between them. It will be observed that here the largest share in the event is ascribed to the passive component of repressed femininity. Moreover, it must be of importance as an accidental factor whether the father, who is feared in any case, is also especially violent in reality. This was true in Dostoevsky's case, and we can trace back the fact of his extraordinary sense of guilt and of his masochistic conduct of life to a specially strong feminine component. Thus the formula for Dostoevsky is as follows: a person of specially strong bisexual predisposition, who can defend himself with special intensity against dependence on a specially severe father. This characteristic of bisexuality comes as an addition to the components of his nature that we have already recognized. His early symptom of death-like seizures can thus be understood as a father-identification on the part of his ego, permitted by his superego as a punishment. "You wanted to kill your father in order to be your father yourself. Now you *are* your father, but a dead father"—the regular mechanism of hysterical symptoms. And further: "Now your father is killing *you.*" For the ego the death symptom is a satisfaction in fantasy of the masculine wish and at the same time a masochistic satisfaction; for the superego it is a punishment satisfaction, that is, a sadistic satisfaction. Both of them, the ego and the superego, carry on the role of father.

To sum up, the relation between the subject and his father-object, while retaining its content, has been transformed into a relation between the ego and the superego—a new setting on a fresh stage. Infantile reactions from the Oedipus complex such as these may disappear if reality gives them no further nourishment. But the characteristics of the father remain the same, or rather, they deteriorate with the years, and so too Dostoevsky's hatred for his father and his death-wish against that wicked father were maintained. Now it is a dangerous thing if reality fulfills such repressed wishes. The fantasy has become reality and all defensive measures are thereupon reinforced. Dostoevsky's attacks now assumed an epileptic character; they still undoubtedly signified an identification with his father as a punishment, but they had become terrible, like his father's frightful death itself. What further content they had absorbed, particularly what sexual content, escapes conjecture.

One thing is remarkable: in the aura of the epileptic attack, one moment of supreme bliss is experienced. This may very well be a record of the triumph and sense of liberation felt on hearing the news of the death, to be followed immediately by an all-the-more-cruel punishment. We have divined just such a sequence of triumph and mourning, of festive joy and mourning, in the brothers of the primal horde who murdered their father, and we find it repeated in the ceremony of the totem meal. If it proved to be the case that Dostoevsky was

339

free from his seizures in Siberia, that would merely substantiate the view that his seizures were his punishment. He did not need them any longer when he was being punished in another way. But that cannot be proved. Rather does this necessity for punishment on the part of Dostoevsky's mental economy explain the fact that he passed unbroken through these years of misery and humiliation. Dostoevsky's condemnation as a political prisoner was unjust and he must have known it, but he accepted the undeserved punishment at the hands of the Little Father, the czar, as a substitute for the punishment he deserved for his sin against his real father. Instead of punishing himself, he got himself punished by his father's deputy. Here we have a glimpse of the psychological justification of the punishments inflicted by society. It is a fact that large groups of criminals long for punishment. Their superego demands it and so saves itself the necessity for inflicting the punishment itself.

Everyone who is familiar with the complicated transformation of meaning undergone by hysterical symptoms will understand that no attempt can be made here to follow out the meaning of Dostoevsky's attacks beyond this beginning.[2] It is enough that we may assume that their original meaning remained unchanged behind all later accretions. We can safely say that Dostoevsky never got free from the feelings of guilt arising from his intention of murdering his father. They also determined his attitude in the two other spheres in which the father-relation is the decisive factor, his attitude toward the authority of the state and toward belief in God. In the first of these he ended up with complete submission to his Little Father, the czar, who had once performed with him in *reality* the comedy of killing which his seizures had so often represented in *play*. Here penitence gained the upper hand. In the religious sphere he retained more freedom: according to apparently trustworthy reports he wavered, up to the last moment of his life, between faith and atheism. His great intellect made it impossible for him to overlook any of the intellectual difficulties to which faith leads. By an individual recapitulation of a development in world history he hoped to find a way out and a liberation from guilt in the Christ ideal, and even to make use of his sufferings as a claim to be playing a Christ-like role. If on the whole he did not achieve freedom and became a reactionary, that was because the filial guilt, which is present in human beings generally and on which religious feeling is built, had in him attained a super-individual intensity and remained insurmountable even to his great intelligence. In writing this we are laying ourselves open to the charge of having abandoned the impartiality of analysis and of subjecting Dostoevsky to judgments that can only be justified from the partisan standpoint of a particular philosophy of life. A conservative would take the side of the Grand Inquisitor and would judge Dostoevsky differently. The objection is just; and one can only say in extenuation that Dostoevsky's decision has every appearance of having been determined by an intellectual inhibition due to his neurosis.

It can scarcely be owing to chance that three of the masterpieces of the literature of all time—the *Oedipus Rex* of Sophocles, Shakespeare's *Hamlet*, and Dostoevsky's *The Brothers Karamazov*—should all deal with the same subject, parricide. In all three, moreover, the motive for the deed, sexual rivalry for a woman, is laid bare.

The most straightforward is certainly the representation in the drama derived from the Greek legend. In this it is still the hero himself who commits the crime. But poetic treatment is impossible without softening and disguise. The naked admission of an intention to commit parricide, as we arrive at it in analysis, seems intolerable without analytical preparation. The Greek drama, while retaining the crime, introduces the indispensable toning-down in a masterly fashion by projecting the hero's

341

unconscious motive into reality in the form of a compulsion by a destiny which is alien to him. The hero commits the deed unintentionally and apparently uninfluenced by the woman; this latter element is, however, taken into account in the circumstance that the hero can only obtain possession of the queen mother after he has repeated his deed upon the monster who symbolizes the father. After his guilt has been revealed and made conscious, the hero makes no attempt to exculpate himself by appealing to the artificial expedient of the compulsion of destiny. His crime is acknowledged and punished as though it were fully conscious—which is bound to appear unjust to our reason, but which psychologically is perfectly correct.

In the English play the presentation is more indirect; the hero does not commit the crime himself; it is carried out by someone else, for whom it is not parricide. The forbidden motive of sexual rivalry for the woman does not need, therefore, to be disguised. Moreover, we see the hero's Oedipus complex, as it were, in a reflected light, by learning the effect upon him of the other's crime. He ought to avenge the crime, but finds himself, strangely enough, incapable of doing so. We know that it is his sense of guilt that is paralyzing him; but, in a manner entirely in keeping with neurotic processes, the sense of guilt is displaced onto the perception of his inadequacy for fulfilling his task. There are signs that the hero feels this guilt as a super-individual one. He despises others no less than himself: "Use every man after his dessert, and who should 'scape whipping?"

The Russian novel goes a step further in the same direction. There also the murder is committed by someone else. This other person, however, stands to the murdered man in the same filial relation as the hero, Dmitri; in this other person's case the motive of sexual rivalry is openly admitted; he is a brother of the hero, and it is a remarkable fact that Dostoevsky has attributed to him his own illness, the alleged epilepsy, as though he were seeking to confess that the epileptic, the neurotic, in himself was a parricide. Then, again, in the speech for the defense at the trial, there is the famous joke at the expense of psychology—it is a "knife that cuts both ways"; a splendid piece of disguise, for we have only to reverse it in order to discover the deepest meaning of Dostoevsky's view of things. It is not psychology that deserves to be laughed at, but the procedure of judicial enquiry. It is a matter of indifference who actually committed the crime; psychology is only concerned to know who desired it emotionally and who welcomed it when it was done. And for that reason all of the brothers, except the contrasted figure of Alyosha, are equally guilty, the impulsive sensualist, the skeptical cynic, and the epileptic criminal. In *The Brothers Karamazov* there is one particularly revealing scene. In the course of his talk with Dmitri, Father Zossima recognizes that Dmitri is prepared to commit parricide, and he bows down at his feet. It is impossible that this can be meant as an expression of admiration; it must mean that the holy man is rejecting the temptation to despise or detest the murderer and for that reason humbles himself before him. Dostoevsky's sympathy for the criminal is, in fact, boundless; it goes far beyond the pity which the unhappy wretch might claim, and reminds us of the "holy awe" with which epileptics and lunatics were regarded in the past. A criminal is to him almost a Redeemer, who has taken on himself the guilt which must else have been borne by others. There is no longer any need for one to murder, since *he* has already murdered; and one must be grateful to him, for, except for him, one would have been obliged oneself to murder. That is not just kindly pity, it is identification on the basis of a similar murderous impulse—in fact, a slightly displaced narcissism. (In saying this, we are not disputing the ethical value of this kindliness.) This may perhaps be quite generally the mechanism of kindly sympathy with other people, a mechanism which one can discern with especial ease in the extreme case of

343

the guilt-ridden novelist. There is no doubt that this sympathy by identification was a decisive factor in determining Dostoevsky's choice of material. He dealt first with the common criminal (whose motives are egotistical) and the political and religious criminal; and not until the end of his life did he come back to the primal criminal, the parricide, and use him, in a work of art, for making his confession.

The publication of Dostoevsky's posthumous papers and of his wife's diaries has thrown a glaring light on one episode in his life, namely the period in Germany when he was obsessed with a mania for gambling, which no one could regard as anything but an unmistakable fit of pathological passion. There was no lack of rationalization for this remarkable and unworthy behavior. As often happens with neurotics, Dostoevsky's burden of guilt had taken a tangible shape as a burden of debt, and he was able to take refuge behind the pretext that he was trying by his winnings at the tables to make it possible for him to return to Russia without being arrested by his creditors. But this was no more than a pretext; and Dostoevsky was acute enough to recognize the fact and honest enough to admit it. He knew that the chief thing was gambling for its own sake—*le jeu pour le jeu*.[3] All the details of his impulsively irrational conduct show this and something more besides. He never rested until he had lost everything. For him gambling was another method of self-punishment. Time after time he gave his young wife his promise or his word of honor not to play any more or not to play any more on that particular day; and, as she says, he almost always broke it. When his losses had reduced himself and her to the direst need, he derived a second pathological satisfaction from that. He could then scold and humiliate himself before her, invite her to despise him and to feel sorry that she had married such an old sinner; and when he had thus unburdened his conscience, the whole business would begin again next day. His young wife accustomed herself to this cycle, for she had noticed that the one thing which offered any real hope of salvation—his literary production—never went better than when they had lost everything and pawned their last possessions. Naturally she did not understand the connection. When his sense of guilt was satisfied by the punishments he had inflicted on himself, the inhibitions upon his work became less severe and he allowed himself to take a few steps along the way to success.

What part of a gambler's long-buried childhood is it that forces its way to repetition in his obsession for play? The answer may be defined without difficulty from a story by . . . Stefan Zweig, who has incidentally devoted a study to Dostoevsky himself [and who] has included in his collection of three stories *Die Verwirrung der Gefühle* one which he calls *Vierundzwanzig Stunden aus dem Leben einer Frau* ("Twenty-Four Hours in a Woman's Life"). This little masterpiece ostensibly sets out only to show what an irresponsible creature woman is, and to what excesses, surprising even to herself, an unexpected experience may drive her. But the story tells far more than this. If it is subjected to an analytical interpretation, it will be found to represent (without any apologetic intent) something quite different, something universally human, or rather something masculine. And such an interpretation is so extremely obvious that it cannot be resisted. It is characteristic of the nature of artistic creation that the author . . . was able to assure me, when I asked him, that the interpretation which I put to him had been completely strange to his knowledge and intention, although some of the details woven into the narrative seemed expressly designed to give a clue to the hidden secret.

In this story, an elderly day of distinction tells the author of an experience she has had more than twenty years earlier. She has been left a widow when still young and is the mother of two sons, who no longer need her. In her forty-second year,

345

expecting nothing further of life, she happens, on one of her aimless journeyings, to visit the rooms at Monte Carlo. There, among all the remarkable impressions which the place produces, she is soon fascinated by the sight of a pair of hands which seem to betray all the feelings of the unlucky gambler with terrifying sincerity and intensity. These hands belong to a handsome young man—the author, as though unintentionally, makes him of the same age as the narrator's elder son—who, after losing everything, leaves the rooms in the depth of despair, with the evident intention of ending his hopeless life in the Casino gardens. An inexplicable feeling of sympathy compels her to follow him and make every effort to save him. He takes her for one of the importunate women so common there and tries to shake her off; but she stays with him and finds herself obliged, in the most natural way possible, to join him in his apartment at the hotel, and finally to share his bed. After this improvised night of love, she exacts a most solemn vow from the young man, who has now apparently calmed down, that he will never play again, provides him with money for his journey home, and promises to meet him at the station before the departure of his train. Now, however, she begins to feel a great tenderness for him, is ready to sacrifice all she has in order to keep him, and makes up her mind to go with him instead of saying goodbye. Various mischances delay her, so that she misses the train. In her longing for the lost one she returns once more to the rooms and there, to her horror, sees once more the hands which had first excited her sympathy: the faithless youth had gone back to his play. She reminds him of his promise, but, obsessed by his passion, he calls her a spoil-sport, tells her to go, and flings back the money with which she has tried to rescue him. She hurries away in deep mortification and learns later that she has not succeeded in saving him from suicide.

The brilliantly told, faultlessly motivated story is of course complete in itself and is certain to make a deep effect upon the reader. But analysis shows us that its invention is based fundamentally upon a wishful fantasy belonging to the period of puberty, which a number of people actually remember consciously. The fantasy embodies a boy's wish that his mother should herself initiate him into sexual life in order to save him from the dreaded injuries caused by masturbation. (The numerous creative works that deal with the theme of redemption have the same origin.) The "vice" of masturbation is replaced by the mania for gambling; and the emphasis laid upon the passionate activity of the hands betrays this derivation. The passion for play is an equivalent of the old compulsion to masturbate; "playing" is the actual word used in the nursery to describe the activity of the hands upon the genitals. The irresistible nature of the temptation, the solemn resolutions, which are nevertheless invariably broken, never to do it again, the numbing pleasure and the bad conscience which tells the subject that he is ruining himself (committing suicide)—all these elements remain unaltered in the process of substitution. It is true that Zweig's story is told by the mother, not by the son. It must flatter the son to think: "if my mother only knew what dangers masturbation involves me in, she would certainly save me from them by allowing me to lavish all my tenderness on her own body." The equation of the mother with a prostitute, which is made by the young man in the story, is linked up with the same fantasy. It brings the unattainable within easy reach. The bad conscience which accompanies the fantasy brings about the unhappy ending of the story. It is also interesting to notice how the façade given to the story by its author seeks to disguise its analytic meaning. For it is extremely questionable whether the erotic life of women is dominated by sudden and mysterious impulses. On the contrary, analysis reveals an adequate motivation for the surprising behavior of this woman who had hitherto turned away from love. Faithful to the memory of her dead husband,

347

she had armed herself against all similar attractions; but—and here the son's fantasy is right—she did not, as a mother, escape her quite unconscious transference of love onto her son, and fate was able to catch her at this undefended spot.

If the mania for gambling, with the unsuccessful struggles to break the habit and the opportunities it affords for self-punishment, is a repetition of the compulsion to masturbate, we shall not be surprised to find that it occupied such a large space in Dostoevsky's life. After all, we find no cases of severe neurosis in which the autoerotic satisfaction of early childhood and of puberty has not played a part; and the relation between efforts to suppress it and fear of the father are too well known to need more than a mention.

1928

NOTES

1. Most of the accounts, including Dostoevsky's own, assert on the contrary that the illness only assumed its final, epileptic character during the Siberian exile. Unfortunately, there is reason to distrust the auto-biographical statements of neurotics. Experience shows that their memories introduce falsifications, which are designed to interrupt disagreeable causal connections. Nevertheless, it appears certain that Dostoevsky's detention in the Siberian prison markedly altered his pathological condition.

2. The best account of the meaning and content of his seizures was given by Dostoevsky himself, when he told his friend Strakhov that his irritability and depression after an epileptic attack were due to the fact he seemed to himself a criminal and could not get rid of the feeling he had a burden of unknown guilt upon him, that he had committed some great misdeed, which oppressed him. In self-accusations like these, psychoanalysis sees signs of a recognition of "psychical reality," and it endeavors to make the unknown guilt known to consciousness.

3. "The main thing is the play itself," he writes in one of his letters. "I swear that greed for money has nothing to do with it, although Heaven knows I am sorely in need of money."

WALT WHITMAN:

LOVER AND COMRADE

Paul Lauter

Walt Whitman's relations with his reader were both personal and didactic: he wished to invite comradeship and also to inculcate certain precepts. Revelation of hard-won personal insight and assertion of moral and metaphysical "truths" intersect to provide Whitman's poetry with its distinctive quality. It would therefore seriously distort Whitman to view his work solely as the product of either motive; however, it is useful to distinguish and to explore the psychological and programmatic impulses and their connections, if for no other reason than to clear the ground for an integrated reading of *Leaves of Grass*. The primary purpose of this paper is to organize the rich background material—for clarification of Whitman's relations with and attitudes toward real men and women, and as a kind of prologue to a study of the imaginative comradeship he established with the readers of his book.

Whitman idealized women as madonnas, pure and wise beyond the ken of men, but from earliest childhood he was terribly insecure in the presence of girls. George Whitman

349

commented on Walt's youth: ". . . I am confident I never knew Walt to fall in love with young girls or even to show them marked attention. He did not seem to affect the girls." Shyness toward women, originating partly in his feeling that social situations inevitably implied sex, precluded any lasting heterosexual relationship. Brought up among lower-class working people, Whitman was further inhibited by his ignorance of "polite" society, from which he was excluded until after he had achieved a type of fame. For these reasons he never fit into the mixed-company drawing-room, always preferring the men's smoker,[1] or, if forced to join society, adopting the pose he himself pathetically described:

You ought to be here with me a day or so—(likely one day would be enough *for you*, as there is no city excitement or fashions—no sogering & no balls or theatres—but quite a lot of *gals*, & some real nice ones—I take an old man's liberty of *kissing them all* (especially the handsome ones) when I go around where they are.

Whitman could, as Professor G. W. Allen has pointed out, hold up his end in conversation—but only in small groups of intimate friends. Whitman's letters to Peter Doyle, a man whose opinions he knew were close to his own, make apparent his ill-defined sense of social inferiority and permit us to understand the often crude overcompensation of the "free old hawk."

I talked too, indeed went like a house afire. It was good exercise—for the fun of the thing. I also made love to the women, and flatter myself that I created at least one impression—wretch and gay deceiver that I am. The truth is Peter, that I am here at the present time mainly in the midst of female women, some of them young and jolly, and meet them most every evening in company, and the way in which this aged party comes up to scratch and cuts out the youthful parties and fills their hearts with envy is absolutely a caution. You would be astonished, my son, to see the brass and coolness and the capacity of flirtation and carrying on with the girls—I would never have believed it of myself. Brought here by destiny, surrounded in this way and, as I in self defense would

modestly state, sought for, seized upon and ravenously devoured by these creatures—and so nice and smart some of them are, and handsome too—there is nothing left for me, is there, but to go in. Of course, young man, you understand it is all on the square. My going in amounts to just talking and joking and having a devil of a jolly time carrying on—that's all. They are all as good girls as ever lived.

The bluff exaggeration, the self-doubt, the quick apology for implying sexual contacts, the obvious inexperience and naiveté are all perfectly typical of Whitman.

Although he could not cope with women, Whitman continued to believe them the more perfect sex: "Charley I think sometimes to be a woman is greater than to be a man—is more eligible to greatness, not the ostensible article, but the real one." This persistent view springs from a deep reservoir of typically Victorian sentimentality:

We know that humanity is by no means perfect—even the "better half" of humanity. But if goodness, charity, faith, and love reside not in the breasts of females, they reside not on earth. The man who attacks the good name of "the sex," attacks the last resort of the finer virtues which adorn his nature. Retired from the stern conflicts of the world—from the chaffering, grosser strife—women seem to be selected by Providence, as the depositories of the germs of the truest Truth and the fairest Beautiful. In their souls is preserved the ark of the covenant of purity.

Indeed, Whitman's woman is so extraordinary that she will assume all the functions usually reserved for man beside retaining her own divine duties: "A woman is to be able to ride, swim, run, resist, advance, [re?] fuse, shoot, defend herself, sail a boat, hunt, rebel—just as much as a man." In his insistence upon woman's equality Whitman reaches the pitch of fervor, to say nothing of the heights of bombast, usually reserved by feminists for themselves: "Why should there be these modesties and prohibitions keeps [sic] women from strong actual life—from going about there with men."

He was not satisfied, however, with American femininity; even the frontier women, in whom he placed his hopes, could not fit his requirements:

I am not so well satisfied with what I see of the women of the prairie cities. . . . The ladies . . . are all fashionably drest, and have the look of "gentility" in face, manner and action, but they do *not* have, either in physique or the mentality appropriate to them, any high native originality of spirit or body, (as the men certainly have, appropriate to them.)

Whitman's ideal would have to emulate his paternal great-grandmother, his paragon of womanhood:

Sarah White, my great grandmother Whitman, lived to be 90 years old,—she was a large, strong woman, chewed tobacco, opium &c. . . . She would sit with her feet up before the fire, just like a man—was every way decided and masculine in her behavior.

And in another reference to her:

She smoked tobacco, rode on horseback like a man, managed the most vicious horse, and, becoming a widow in later life, went forth every day over her farm-lands, frequently in the saddle, directing the labor of her slaves, with language in which, on exciting occasions, oaths were not spared.

But such a woman is little more than a man who has mysteriously acquired the ability to bear children. Thus Whitman's ideal evolves from his desire to reduce as far as possible the barrier between the sexes,[2] the barrier which so continuously troubled him.

Maintaining such an impossible standard, and burdened by his fear of sexuality, Whitman could hardly have been expected to find the perfect mate for himself. Invariably he turned to the one female on whom he could depend, with whom he could feel secure, for as he loved to relate, ". . . George like me is the son of my mother." Whitman was indeed close to his mother: "We have been great chums; always next to each

353

other." Until she died he wrote to her at least once or twice a week whenever he was away from home, her home. Their letters are gossipy and intimate, discussing people's health, the vegetables he eats, his new shirts, her household difficulties, mutual friends (mostly older, motherly women). In an early story Whitman makes much of his hero's correspondence with his mother, announcing that "strange as it may seem to most men, she was also his confidential friend." His eternal dream was to build a small shanty in which he and she could peacefully live out their lives together. Mrs. Whitman seems always to have provided warmth and sympathy for Walt, a sense of contact and belongingness. In the intense depression subsequent to his paralysis she remained a rare spark of happiness: "I have tacked your picture up on the wall at the foot of the bed—the one I like—it looks as natural as can be—& is quite company for me—as I am alone a good deal. . . ." In Whitman's early stories the mother is invariably a sweet, put-upon woman, who strives to protect her son from the injustices of an unfriendly world.

Louisa Whitman thus provided the pattern for all mothers; other mothers, in turn, served Whitman as substitutes for his own beloved. Whitman sought out motherly women like Abby Price for comfort and warmth; to them he could write and talk about his little daily chores and annoyances, obtaining in return the affection and assurances of maternal love he required. Whitman's need for maternal love also induced him to glorify the mother. He is quoted as saying: "I know of nothing more beautiful, inspiring, significant: a hale old woman, full of cheer as of years, who has raised a brood of hearty children. . . ." Of the angelic sex, mothers are the Thrones, Powers, and Dominions: "Mothers precede all. Put in a poem the sentiment of women (mothers) as preceding all the rest. ? Let this lead the poem of women." As an individual led him to the group, so the group leads him to the abstraction—motherhood, the crowning achievement of woman: "The best part of any man is his mother. . . . But any mother of any baby has a right to be proud." The overwhelming force of this mother-love produces a kind of superficial mother-cult:

Behold a woman!
She looks out from her quaker cap, her face is clearer and more
    beautiful than the sky.
She sits in an armchair under the shaded porch of the farmhouse,
The sun just shines on her old white head. . . .
The melodious character of the earth,
The finish beyond which philosophy cannot go and does not wish
    to go,
The justified mother of men.

This passionate attachment to the mother Whitman elsewhere transmuted into much more effective images of the sea. But while in poems such as "Out of the Cradle Endlessly Rocking" his devotion was a poetic asset, it proved a social liability, for it was still another element inhibiting normal relations with women.

Whitman seems, in fact, to have attempted to establish some type of alliance from time to time during his life; but all attempts, if they really developed, were unsatisfying and transient. The information we have about his love life is scattered, fragmentary, and contradictory. For example, a certain "Ellen Eyre" is purported to have written the following to Whitman on March 25, 1862.

I fear you took me last night for a female privateer. It is time I was sailing under my true colors—but then today I assume you cared nothing piratical though I would have joyfully made your heart a captive. . . . I trust you will think well enough of me soon to renew the pleasure you afforded me last p.m. and I therefore write to remind you that this is a sensible head as well as a sympathetic heart, both of which would gladly evolve with warmth for your diversion and comfort. You have already my whereabouts and hours. It shall only depend on you to make them yours and me the happiest of women.

355

While "Ellen Eyre" seems to have existed—"Frank Sweeney
. . . (is the one I told the whole story to about Ellen Eyre)"—
the original of the letter has never been found. Moreover, the
"affair," if such indeed it was, must have ended almost as it
began, for the unanimous testimony of Whitman's Washington and New York friends was that he was never "bothered up
by a woman." Other similarly mysterious amours—Will Wallace's "Frenchy," ³ the girl whose story Whitman never quite
tells Traubel, the imaginary southern belle—crop up from time
to time, but the conflicting evidence indicates only rare attempts
and invariable failures. Whitman's "love affairs" have been
exaggerated by sentimentalist critics who wish to find a broken
heart behind every poem, and excessively minimized by some
psychological analysts who wish to establish his homosexuality.
But the very ambiguity and obviously attenuated nature of
any relationships verify only Whitman's wish to establish some
sort of tie with a woman and his inability to do so on any full
and permanent basis.

In spite of this failing, or perhaps because of it, Whitman
considered marriage the ideal refuge for a lonesome spirit.
Thus in real life he would not abide "free love"—relations with
women were difficult enough, but relations without the comforting sanction of marriage were unthinkable. Besides, marriage offered particularly attractive prospects:

Whatever may be the care and mishaps of married life, it is probably undeniable that "if there's bliss to be found on earth," (a
questionable find!) it must be in the domestic circle. . . . How
many blissful hours must be spent by fathers, in the blessedness
of mere *presence* of affectionate children! How much of happiness
is going on—(a cheerful thought that almost cancels the sad evidence of misery we see towering on every side!)—that is dreamed
of by no mortal mind—seen by no mortal eye—except the few
participants in it. . . .

Those who do not marry "at best live single and imperfect

lives, losing the healthy, beautifying power which God intended them to find in the family relations, isolated units in a world whose essence is association." And Whitman recognized himself as one of those "isolated units," although he hid behind the generalized "authors":

Of all the calamities of authors—of all the infelicities of genius—it strikes us that their domestic difficulties are the worst. Take all else from a man and leave him a good and faithful wife and he can never be called unhappy no matter what may be the fluctuations of fortune. But take that comfort, consolation, and safeguard away and he becomes "poor" indeed—a vessel without a rudder, beaten here and there, at the mercy of the wind and waves.

Despite his loneliness, despite the bliss which he thought marriage afforded, Whitman remained a bachelor, sometimes fighting hard to continue single. Each time the possibility of marriage arose, his fear of intimacy with women overcame his expressed program and very probable desire. The heaviest siege laid against his bachelorship was that of Anne Gilchrist, a refined, educated, upper-class Englishwoman whom Rossetti had introduced to *Leaves of Grass* in 1869. Mrs. Gilchrist, like a number of other women, loved with an undisguised passion the virile, athletic poet she discovered in *Leaves*. Assuming equivalence of Whitman and his eidolon, she wrote to him in the same spirit she found in the poems:

In May, 1869, came the voice over the Atlantic to me—O, the voice of my Mate: it must be so—my love rises up out of the very depths of the grief & tramples upon despair. I can wait—any time, a lifetime, many lifetimes—I can suffer, I can dare, I can learn, grow, toil, but nothing in life or death can tear out of my heart the passionate belief that one day I shall hear that voice say to me, "My Mate. The one I so much want. Bride, Wife, indissoluble eternal!" It is not happiness I plead with God for—it is the very life of my Soul, my love is its life, Dear Walt. It is a sweet & precious thing, this love; it clings so close, so close to the Soul and Body, all so tenderly dear, so beautiful, so sacred; it yearns with such passion to soothe and comfort & fill thee with sweet tender joy; it aspires as grandly, as gloriously as thy own soul. Strong to soar—soft & tender to nestle and caress. If God were to say to me, "See—he that you love you shall not be given to in this life—he is going to set sail on the unknown sea—will you go with him?" never yet has bride sprung into her husband's arms with the joy with which I would take thy hand & spring from the shore.

A month later she wrote: "I am yet young enough to bear thee children, my darling."

Whitman must have been flattered by the homage offered him, and titillated by the boost to his manly ego. But as pleased as parts of the letters may have made him, the suggestion of permanent ties, responsibilities, and worst, social and sexual intercourse, horrified him. As much as he would have liked to believe he was the man Mrs. Gilchrist thought him, he could not; he immediately recognized that the situation could end only pathetically. At first he hoped that by not writing, by closing his eyes to the siren, she might go away. But Mrs. Gilchrist persisted, and her second letter apparently convinced Whitman that he would have to face the threat. Thus on November 3, 1871, he replied in a letter which pathetically reveals his inability to share, and perhaps even to appreciate, the nature and the depths of Mrs. Gilchrist's passion:

I wish to give it [writing to her] a day, a sort of Sabbath, or holy day, apart to itself, under serene and propitious influences, confident that I could then write you a letter which would do you good, and me too. But I must at least show without further delay that I am not insensible to your love. I too send you my love. And do you feel no disappointment because I now write so briefly. My book is my best letter, my response, my truest explanation of all. In it I have put my body and spirit. You understand this better and fuller than anyone else. And I too fully and clearly understand the loving letter that it evoked. Enough that there surely exists so beautiful and delicate a relation, accepted by both of us with joy.

Mrs. Gilchrist, however, could not recognize that the "mate" of the poems did not exist, and she continued to implore Whitman to call her to him. But the "mate," growing desperate, and hoping to reorient the friendship on a less personal level, replied:

DEAR FRIEND

Your late letter has just reached me—& I write at once to at least say specifically that both your letter of Sept. 6 and that of Oct. 15 safely reached me—this that comes today being the third.

Again I will say that I am sure I appreciate & accept your letters, & all they stand for, as fully as even you, dear friend, could wish—& as lovingly & *bona fide*.

And thus the correspondence dragged on, Mrs. Gilchrist writing animated, passionate love letters, and Whitman replying only rarely, and then with the impersonal notes that became his trademark. When she finally came to the United States, despite his desperate efforts to head her off, she was, inevitably, disappointed. She found her Walt a sick, shy old man, who was not and never could have been the phallic wonder of the poems.

In spurning Mrs. Gilchrist (and her attempt must stand for the others), Whitman denied many of the principles he had affirmed for his program, for he rejected a healthy mother of three, a potential wife and companion, and above all the sexual fulfillment he insisted upon. But it was not unusual for Whitman to fear and repudiate in personal life what he emphasized so strongly in theory, for "program" served frequently to compensate for shortcomings of personality—even if we were ignorant of Whitman's difficulties with women, we might suspect his virility because of the very way in which, even outside "program" poems, he overemphasized it. Moreover, Whitman's "program" was by no means necessarily a program for Whitman (though in later life he began to assume it was). He himself hardly recognized that the "Children of Adam" poems were, in their ritualistic, mechanical, and abstract way, love bleats. When they were reacted to in kind, he became confused and unresponsive. Receiving the following letter, he had scrawled " ? insane asylum" across the envelope:

. . . Know Walt Whitman that thou hast a child for me! [Just what Whitman had been claiming.] A noble perfect manchild. I charge you my love not to give it to another woman. The world demands it! It is not for you and me, *is our child*, but for the world. My womb is clean and pure. It is ready for thy child my love. Angels guard the vestibule until thou comest to deposit our and the world's precious treasure. Then oh! how lovingly will I cherish and guard it, our child my love. Thine the pleasure my love. Mine the sweet burden and pain. Mine the sacrifice. Mine to have the stinging rebuke, the shame, I am willing. My motives are pure and holy. Our boy my love! Do you not already love him? He must be begotten on a mountain top, in the open air. Not in *lust*, not in mere gratification of sensual passion, but in holy ennobling pure strong deep glorious passionate broad universal love. I charge you to prepare my love.

I love you, I love you, come, come, Write.

Horace Traubel recalls this conversation:

I said to W.: "Why did you write '? insane asylum' there?" He asked: "Isn't it crazy?" "No: it's Leaves of Grass." "What do you mean?" "Why—it sounds like somebody who's taking you at your word." He said: "I've had more than one notion of the letter: I suppose the fact that certain things are unexpected, unusual, makes it hard to get them in their proper perspective: the process of adjustment is a severe one." I said: "You should have been the last man in the world to write 'insane' on that envelope." Then I added: "But the question mark saves you. . . . You might as well have written 'insane' across Children of Adam and the Song of Myself." He said: "Many people do." "Yes," I replied: "they do—but you don't." He assented by a nod of his head: "I suppose you are right."

Whitman recognized the force of sexual drives, even if he did not (or could not) accede to them: "There are certain propensities and passions inherent in our nature which will have vent in one shape or another, despite all the combined legislative wisdom of communities." This was not detached, scientific observation, but was based upon his experiences with his own highly sexed nature. Sex, in fact, became central in Whitman's apprehension of life:

I look at the girls—at the childless women—at the old maids, as you speak of them: they lack something: they are not completed: something yet remains undone. They are not quite full—not quite entire: the woman who has denied the best of herself—the woman who has discredited the animal want, the eager physical hunger, the wish of that which though we will not allow it to be freely spoken of is still the basis of all that makes life worth while and advances the horizon of discovery. Sex: sex: sex: whether you sing or make a machine, or go to the North Pole, or love your mother, or build a house, or black shoes, or anything—anything at all—it's sex, sex, sex: sex is root of it all: sex—the coming together of men and women: sex: sex.

Such carnal incantation vibrates somewhere between mysticism and fustian, the poles of his sexual poems.

On a deeply personal level this crucial bodily function becomes the source of mystical experience. Klaus Mann and Schyberg both point out that in his private life Whitman's "eroticism merges with his religious emotion" in a way not unusual among mystics: ". . . sensual enchantment is transformed into metaphysical divination: the delirium of the mortal flesh mysteriously contains and guarantees the immortality of the soul." A sexual experience (albeit autoerotic) precipitates the central mystical revelation of "Song of Myself":

I mind how once we lay such a transparent summer morning,
How you settled your head athwart my hips and gently turn'd over
    upon me,
And parted my shirt from my bosom-bone, and plunged your
    tongue to my bare-stript heart,
And reach'd till you felt my beard, and reach'd till you held my
    feet.

Swiftly arose and spread around me the peace and knowledge that
    pass all the argument of the earth,
And I know that the hand of God is the promise of my own,
And I know that the spirit of God is the brother of my own,
And that all the men ever born are also my brothers, and the women
    my sisters and lovers,
And that a kelson of the creation is love, . . .

More theoretically, Whitman rejected, on the one hand, repression, which led to "disease and depletion," "morbidity," "inefficient maturity," and "snickering pruriency"; and, on the other, the "sexual voluptuousness" of wit. He celebrated neither the forbidden nor the sentimental. Taboos are silly, sensuality disgusting; the only proper attitude is open and hygienic, for procreation is the end of sex, procreation by which man attains the divine function of creativity. Whitman shows little interest in sentimental literature, but is fascinated by Lucretius' book on love, particularly with his detailing of the best positions for conception:

The time will come when the whole affair of sex—copulation, reproduction—will be treated with the respect to which it is entitled. Instead of meaning shame and being apologized for it will mean purity and will be glorified.

Sex equals "copulation" and "reproduction"; hardly romantic.

This didactic Whitman dipped more toward fustian in his celebration of sex—however functional it might be. *Franklin Evans* (his early "temperance" novel) indicates that glorification of sex was rooted largely in wish-fulfillment: the novel is like an adolescent daydream, with its voluptuous and varied love affairs—its moralizing seems intrusive among the creations of a highly sexed, but frustrated temperament. Similarly, the sexual advances of his Adamic poems were claims on those faceless, athletic women beyond his range of experience who in imagination would accept and complete him. Wooing took two stages: the ritual of virility, shaking the plumes of manliness, the sexual advance, and consummation itself. Nothing of "sentimental" lovemaking, of affection, of social responsibility interfered with the mating ceremony—the male displayed, boasted of his prowess, and conquered. Strides the poet into the bower as Adam:

Lusty, phallic, with potent original loins, perfectly sweet,
I, chanter of Adamic songs,

Through the new garden the West, the great cities calling,
Deliriate, thus preclude what is generated, offering these, offering
myself. . . .

"Know," he calls, in another of the Adamic poems, "I am a man,
attracting, at any time, her I but look upon, or touch with the
tips of my fingers." Then he closes:

I draw you close to me, you women,
I cannot let you go, I would do you good,
I am for you, and you are for me . . . .

It is I, you women, I make my way,
I am stern, acrid, large, undissuadable, but I love you,
I do not hurt you any more than is necessary for you,
I pour the stuff to start sons and daughters fit for these States,
I press with slow rude muscle,
I brace myself effectually, I listen to no entreaties,
I dare not withdraw till I deposit what has so long accumulated
within me.

"Healthy" functionality undercuts sensuality, passion, even
"love"—despite the almost ludicrous "but I love you." Still,
however manly his asserted program, Whitman's attitudes
toward heterosexual relations remain essentially adolescent.

Beneath the clamor of virility, puberty whispers on in his
poems: the overwhelming discovery of the body and sex; the
high-pitched celebration; the dreams of glory and myriad conquests; the idealization and generalization of women; and the
escape from the binding mores of society. Suddenly, there
bursts upon the boy's serenity the new world of sex:

The no-form'd stings that sights, people, objects sting me with,
The hubb'd sting of myself, stinging me as much as it ever can
any one,
The sensitive, orbic, underlapp'd brothers, that only privileged
feelers may be intimate where they are,
The curious roamer the hand roaming all over the body, the bashful
withdrawing of flesh where the fingers soothingly pause and
edge themselves,
The limpid liquid within the young man,

The vex'd corrosion so pensive and so painful,
The torment, the irritable tide that will not be at rest,
The like of the same I feel, the like of the same in others,
The young man that flushes and flushes, the young woman that
 flushes and flushes,
The young man that wakes deep at night, the hot hand seeking to
 repress what would master him,
The mystic amorous night, the strange half-welcome pangs, visions,
 sweats,
The pulse pounding through palms and trembling encircling fingers,
 the young man all color'd, red, ashamed, angry. . . .

The body is freshly discovered and celebrated:

O my body! . . .
Head, neck, hair, ears, drop and tympan of the ears,
Eyes, eye-fringes, iris of the eye, eyebrows, and the waking or
 sleeping of the lids. . . .

And so caressingly down. Dreams—ever a new Female, ever
a new success:

O to be yielded to you whoever you are, and you to be yielded
 to me in defiance of the world!
O to return to Paradise! O bashful and feminine!
O to draw you to me, to plant on you for the first time the lips
 of a determin'd man.

The man of the world, hearty, magnetic, freely scattering his
seed, but also the shamefaced boy—vision and reality:

O hotcheek'd and blushing! O foolish hectic!
O for pity's sake, no one must see me now! my clothes were stolen
 while I was abed,
Now I am thrust forth, where shall I run?
. . . .
I feel ashamed to go naked about the world,
And I am curious to know where my feet stand—and what is this
 flooding me, childhood or manhood—and the hunger that crosses
 the bridge between.

The woman is never Jane or Jill, never a special lover, but

always a woman, women, "whoever you are." Love must be universal:

By "love" as I have used the term . . . I do not mean the sickly sentimentality which is so favorite a theme with novelists and magazine writers. What I would inculcate is that healthy, cheerful feeling of kindness and good will, and affectionate tenderness, a warm-heartedness, the germs of which are plentifully sown by God in each human breast . . .

And sex must be impersonal:

That I infuse you with grits and jets of life,
I am not to be scorned:—I Compell;
It is quite indifferent to me who [you] are.

I will go stay with her who waits for me, and with those women
    that are warm-blooded and sufficient for me,
I see that they understand me and do not deny me,
I see that they are worthy of me, I will be the robust husband of
    these women.

No wonder the author of *Lady Chatterley's Lover*, the champion of personal intimacy, cried out against "A Woman Waits for Me," from which the above quotation comes:

He might as well have said: "The femaleness waits for my maleness." Oh, beautiful generalization and abstraction! Oh, biological function.

"Athletic mothers of the States—" Muscles and wombs. They needn't have had faces at all.

Faceless as she is, the woman who waits "contains all, nothing is lacking." Perfect, naked, entirely responsive she (or they, it is the same) is the forever-fleeting ideal of adolescent dream:

They are tann'd in the face by shining suns and blowing winds,
Their flesh has the old divine suppleness and strength . . .

Together the poet and his ideal will escape to a mountain's heights:

O that you and I escape from the rest and go utterly off, free and
  lawless,
Two hawks in the air, two fishes swimming in the sea not more
  lawless than we. . . .

To escape utterly from others' anchors and holds!
To drive free! to love free! to dash reckless and dangerous!
To court destruction with taunts, with invitations!

But it was only from himself that Whitman had to escape,
and only into his poems that he could.

As a record of adolescent love the "Children of Adam" poems
are remarkable, in fact almost unique in our literature. Frequently flatulent and bombastic, they never contain the tenderness we have come to associate with mature love; that tenderness, the attitude of the lover, Whitman reserves for his
poems to men. As an intellectual, programmatic construct,
". . . a Cluster of Poems the same *to the passion of woman-love*
as the *Calamus-Leaves* are to adhesiveness, manly love," they
fail because Whitman did not know and could not fully imagine the same passion for women that he did for men. But the
very adolescent braggadocio serves as a perhaps too-imitative
correlative to what the poems are: unconscious disclosures of
a frustrated, yearning, oversexed boy. And as revelations of
what they seek to hide these poems are as fascinating, if not
always meritorious, as any other part of *Leaves*.

Alarmed and frustrated by women, Whitman turned to men
for companionship and love. In notes for a proposed lecture,
"To Women," he confirmed his dissatisfaction with heterosexual
relations and his need for man friends:

I desire to say to you, and let you ponder well upon it, the fact
that under present arrangements the love and comradeship of a
woman, of his wife, however welcome, however complete, does not
and cannot satisfy the grandest requirements of a man's soul for
love and comradeship.—The man he loves, he often loves with

more passionate attachment than he can bestow on any woman, even his wife.—Is it that the growth of love needs the free air— the seasons, perhaps more wildness more rudeness? Why is the love of women so invalid? so transient?

To women he could offer the compassion and interest of a friend; to men alone the passion and devoted intensity of a lover. To Whitman came the terrible realization that what he had to have was not merely the respect or admiration, not only the friendship, but the love of those to whom he was drawn; that the meeting of eyes could not be casual, and that a smile must have the personal, secret meaning of lovers.[4]

Whitman called this emotion "adhesiveness," which he defined as "love, that fuses, ties and aggregates, making the races comrades, and fraternizing all." But this was a programmatic interpretation of a far more immediate and throbbing passion. One of the phrenologists, from whom Whitman borrowed the term, indicated its carnal overtones: "Those in whom it is large [i.e. the organ of adhesiveness], feel an involuntary impulse to embrace, and cling to any object which is capable of expressing fondness." Another showed its extreme emotional force:

Those who have adhes. *very large*, or predominant, instinctively recognize it in each other; soon become mutually and strongly attached; desire to cling around the objects of their love; take more interest and delight in the exercise of friendship than in anything else; . . . dread an interruption of friendship as the greatest of calamities. . . . Their friends may be *few*, but will be *dear*, . . . their social intercourse delightful beyond description; their separation painful, in the extreme; their loss, agonizing, almost beyond endurance; and the interruption of friendship, a frequent source of partial derangement.

A kind of physicality and all but overwhelming power similarly characterized Whitman's "adhesive" passions.

Touch was all important to him: bodily contact with men not only satisfied his need to "feel" reality, but consummated his worship of the male physique. He was throughout his life impelled to hug and kiss his men friends. To Harry Stafford he wrote: "Dear son, how I wish you could come in now, even if but for an hour & take off your coat, & sit down on my lap." And Traubel relates a tender moment with Whitman:

W. said: "Come, kiss me for good night." He was still lying down. I reached over him and we kissed. He took my hand—pressed it fervently. "I am in luck. Are you? I guess God just sent us for each other."

This physicality was by no means solely a sublimation of sexual desires, but was motivated also by the drive for the warmth of human contact, which requires satisfaction as much as hunger or thirst. Moreover, for a man as feminine in his perceptions as Whitman, it was a way of showing his affection. Thus in the famous scene of the twenty-eight men bathers, Whitman projects himself into the watching woman. Physical contact also provided Whitman with one of his basic symbols of man for man love: the lovers with their arms thrown about each other's necks or waists.

Besides physical contact, Whitman searched in his relations with men for a substitute to replace his own rejected father,[5] adopted "sons" through whom he would perpetuate himself, but above all for companions and lovers. In view of Whitman's passion for marriage and a family, one can understand his attempts to surmount his inability to have real sons by "adopting" as his own the young soldiers, horse-car drivers, farmers he everywhere met. To these he was a spiritual and intellectual father, introducing them to literature, guiding their taste and attitudes. In another way he was a mother (really the more natural role for him), buying their clothes, nursing them, cooking for them. And in return he received the affection of sons for a father:

. . . i hope the day may come wen i can do for yo some gud in return, for father yo donte know how i do love you i donte know wy it is i am more attached yo than en ny one that i was acquainted with.

Or from another of his boys:

You will allow me to call you Father wont you. I do not know that I told you that both my parents were dead but it is true and now Walt you will be a second Father to me won't you. for my love for you is hardly less than my love for my natural parent I have never before met with a man that I could love as I do you Still there is nothing strange about it for "to know you is to love you" And how any person could know you and not love you is a wonder to me.

Thus Whitman not only satisfied his latent paternalism, but entered a wedge against oblivion, for through his "sons," as in his *Leaves*, he could gratify his need for self-perpetuation.

But filial affection was not sufficient unto Whitman's "adhesiveness." That he required a fuller, more intense response than "sons" could supply is indicated by his relations with Peter Doyle. They met abruptly, informally, mutually attracted:

We fell to each other at once. I was a conductor. The night was very stormy,—he had been over to see Burroughs before he came down to take the car—the storm was awful. Walt had his blanket—it was thrown round his shoulders—he seemed like an old sea-captain. He was the only passenger, it was a lonely night, so I thought I would go in and talk with him. Something in me made me do it and something in him drew me that way. He used to say there was something in me had the same effect on him. Anyway, I went into the car. We were familiar at once—I put my hand on his knee—we understood. He did not get out at the end of the trip—in fact he went all the way back with me.

They rode together frequently, drawing closer as, in the months that followed, Whitman adopted Doyle. Separation, as the phrenologists predicted, brought agony to Walt and letters to Doyle:

I think of you very often, dearest comrade, and with more calmness than when I was there. I find it first rate to think of you Pete, and to know that you are there all right and that I shall return and we will be together again. I don't know what I should do if I hadn't you to think of and look forward to.

More than father-son affection or mere abstract Platonic attachment, this is passionate, perturbed love, love that is terribly dependent—but, at last, mutual:

Pete there was something in that hour from 10 to 11 o'clock (parting though it was) that has left me pleasure and comfort for good—I never dreamed that you made so much of having me with you, nor that you could feel so downcast at losing me. I foolishly thought it was all on the other side. But all I will say further on the subject is, I now see clearly, that was all wrong.

Thus Whitman's attachments developed in passionate perturbation, but never, so far as one can tell, in carnality.

Rather, these friendships permitted him, like many others whose instincts force them toward their own sex, to channel his impulses into socially commendable outlets, particularly into charitable work among men. He himself recognized the inner compulsion which drove him to work in the hospitals as something akin to that passionate manly love which possessed him:

Then came the War. "I was no spring chicken then." His consecration "was no youthful enthusiasm—no mere ebullition of spirits—but deliberate, radical, fundamental." Here he paused, turned his face towards me, passed his fingers, spread, over his heart. "Deliberate? more than that: it was necessary: I went from the call of something within—something, I cannot explain what—something I could not disregard." Whether for good or bad he "could not pause to weight it." "There's something in the human critter that only needs to be budged to reveal itself: not always observed: it is a folded leaf: not absent because we fail to see it: the right man comes—the right hour; the leaf is lifted.[6]

This need joined with Whitman's compassion to direct him toward his hospital activities (which, incidentally, began in New York long before the Civil War). In such work he could prac-

370

tice his principle of sympathy, which in his program required action to relieve misery, and at the same time sublimate the smoldering yearning for lovers that might otherwise have consumed him.

In his hospital labors Whitman played out his more feminine impulses. He realized that his own place was that of sympathetic companion rather than trumpeting prophet and leader:

Arous'd and angry, I'd thought to beat the alarum, and urge relentless war,
But soon my fingers fail'd me, my face droop'd and I resign'd myself,
To sit by the wounded and soothe them, or silently watch the dead.

He gave up the male role of leader and soldier and assumed the, for him, more suitably feminine role of nurse. For as Burroughs saw:

With all his rank masculinity, there was a curious feminine undertone in . . . his voice, the delicate texture of his skin, the gentleness of his touch and ways, the attraction he had for children and common people.

Whitman himself did recognize his femininity, insisting that he took after the women in his family, and claiming that *Leaves of Grass* is "essentially a woman's book," that its "cry is the cry . . . of the woman sex. . . ." From this female perspective, he formulated what Bychowski calls a "truly feminine cult of manliness and the phallos":

The expression of a perfect made man appears not only in his face —but in his limbs—the motion of his hands and arms and all his joints—his walk—the carriage of his neck—and the fleck of his waist and hips. Dress does not hide him. The quality he has and the clean strong sweet supple nature he has strike through cotton and woolen—To see him walk conveys the impression of hearing a beautiful poem.—To see his back and the back of his neck and shoulderside is a spectacle. Great is the body!

371

Again and again in the poems Whitman revels in the delight of a man's supple body:

The negro holds firmly the reins of his four horses, the block swags underneath on its tied-over chain,
The negro that drives the long dray of the stoneyard, steady and tall he stands pois'd on one leg on the string piece,
His blue shirt exposes his ample neck and breast and loosens over his hip-band,
His glance is calm and commanding, he tosses the slouch of his hat away from his forehead,
The sun falls on his crispy hair and mustache, falls on the black of his polish'd and perfect limbs.[7]

Whitman was conscious of the ambiguity, perhaps of the perverseness on which this feminine ardor bordered. His irrational outbursts against Symonds' innocuous questions about "Calamus" indicate his testiness on the subject when, after the fires had burnt out, he could sense their darker implications:

I said to W.: "That's a humble letter enough: I don't see anything in that to get excited about. He don't ask you to answer the old question. In fact, he rather apologizes for having asked it." W. fired up. "Who is excited? As to that question, he does ask it again and again: asks it, asks it, asks it." I laughed at his vehemence: "Well, suppose he does. It does no harm. Besides, you've got nothing to hide. I think your silence might lead him to suppose there was a nigger in the woodpile." "Oh nonsense! But for thirty years my enemies and friends have been asking me questions about the Leaves: I'm tired of not answering questions." [8]

Such self-doubt is registered more directly in the poems. Mourning his lost love, the poet admits, "I am ashamed—but it is useless—I am what I am," and asks, "I wonder if other men ever have the like, out of like feelings?" But these terrible doubts could for him be answered only by the affection, the presence of "my lovers, my dear friends." For in his lonely life it was to these young men that Whitman had to turn for consolation and love.

Pathetically, his special friends never really fathomed Whitman's ardor, appeared in fact confused and bashful before it. His correspondence with Tom Sawyer reads like a piteous mirror-image of the Anne Gilchrist affair. Here Whitman was the active, passionate one:

Dear comrade, you must not forget me, for I never shall you. My love you have in life or death forever. I don't know how you feel about it, but it is the wish of my heart to have your friendship, and also that if you should come safe out of this war, we should come together again in some place where we could make our living, and be true comrades and never be separated while life lasts—and take Lew Brown too, and never separate from him, or if things are not so to be—if you get these lines, my dear, darling comrade, and anything should go wrong, so that we do not meet again here on earth, it seems to me (the way I feel now) that my soul could never be entirely happy, even in the world to come, without you, dear comrade. (What I say is pretty strong talk I suppose but it is I mean exactly what I say am writing have written) And if it is God's will, I hope we shall yet [live] meet, as I say, if you (could) feel as I do about it—and if it is destined that we shall not, you have my love none the less, whatever should keep you from me, no matter how many years. God bless you, Tom, and preserve you through the perils of the fight.

Whitman continued to write, asking repeatedly why Sawyer did not answer. Finally, a note from Tom, probably written for him by some more literate member of his outfit:

Dear Brother
   As you have given me permission, I have taken the liberty to address you as above. And I assure you I fully reciprocate your friendship as expressed in your letter and it will afford me great pleasure to meet you after the war will have terminated or sooner if circumstances will permit.

How this letter must have torn Whitman; how ironical that he would one day reply to Mrs. Gilchrist: "I too send you my love." Later, however, Sawyer replied, apparently in his own person:

Dear Brother I hardly know what to say to you in this letter for it
is my first one to you but it will not be my last I should have
written to you before but I am not a great hand at writtin and I
have ben very buisy firming my tent for this winter and I hope you
will forgive me and in the future I will do better and I hope we
may meet again in this world and now as it is getting very late
you must ecuse this short letter this time—and I hope to here from
soon I send you my love and best wishes.

This was the best Whitman could expect from his shy, uneducated boys; clearly a passionate nature could little be satisfied
by such replies.[9]

However much love Whitman showered on his young men,
he could never obtain full reciprocation, full satisfaction of his
yearning for the one perfect comrade: "Why is it a sense comes
always crushing on me, as of one happiness I have missed in
life? and one friend and companion I have never made?" Not
finding in life his desired ideal, Whitman had to turn to the
unknown audience of his poems for final love and consummation: "Poemet embodying the idea I wander along my life
hardly ever meeting comrades. . . . For I have not met them
Therefore I have put my passionate love of comrades in my
poems." Thus in "Calamus" Whitman opens the face of love to
his reader.

The "Calamus" group, although not strictly ordered, incorporates many of the characteristics of traditional sonnet
sequences. The poet cannot write without his lover near him.
His lover answers his doubts, contents him with his lot merely
by his presence, and shows him that the root of all philosophy
is love. The poet wishes to be remembered only as a lover and
a celebrator of love, discounting other kinds of fame as superficial. Always qualifying these love lyrics, however, is the fact
that they are directed to men, for the kind of love essential to
such poetry Whitman could experience only in relations with
men. It is therefore necessary for the poet to lead us away from

the trodden paths and the prying eyes—the Calamus emotion avoids public display. Whereas he would stride off with his women defying society to do its worst, with his men, secretly and shyly, he slips out to where he can permit the smoldering fires to flame. He does not any longer "compell," but warns:

> Whoever you are holding me now in hand,
> Without one thing all will be useless,
> I give you fair warning before you attempt me further,
> I am not what you supposed, but far different.

Still behind the admonition is the desirous lover tenderly beckoning the new person to join him at the pond side where grow the "Calamus" roots of manly love: "Passing stranger! you do not know how longingly I look upon you."

From this remote backwater emerges Whitman's Democracy, the Democracy of comrades, expanded from the intimate "Calamus" love to the adhesive join of the coming republic:

> Come, I will make the continent indissoluble,
> I will make the most splendid race the sun ever shone upon,
> I will make divine magnetic lands,
>> With the love of comrades,
>> With the life-long love of comrades.
>
> I will plant companionship thick as trees along all the rivers of America, and along the shores of the great lakes, and all over the prairies,
> I will make inseparable cities with their arms about each other's necks,
>> By the love of comrades,
>> By the manly love of comrades.

> For you, these from me, O Democracy, to serve you ma femme!
> For you, for you I am trilling these songs.

It was not only for Democracy, however, that Whitman trilled, but for Walt Whitman—had he sung nothing but ditties like this last, he would never have survived his adulators. For us

Whitman's most affecting Leaves are those in which he does not try to convert love to program, those which spring directly from his troubled breast:

Scented herbage of my breast,
Leaves from you I glean, I write, to be perused best afterwards,
Tomb-leaves, body-leaves growing up above me above death,
.   .   .   .
You are often more bitter than I can bear, you burn and sting me,
Yet you are beautiful to me you faint-tinged roots, you make me
    think of death,
Death is beautiful from you, (what indeed is finally beautiful except
    death and love?)
O I think it is not for life I am chanting here my chants of lovers,
    I think it must be for death . . . .

Baffling, balking life is cast aside as the "usual adjustments and pleasures," while "adhesiveness" merges with death, with delicious desirable death. For only in death and beyond death can Whitman embrace the ideally responsive camerado, the reader who will wholly accept and complete his song:

When you read these I that was visible am become invisible,
Now it is you, compact, visible, realizing my poems, seeking me,
Fancying how happy you were if I could be with you and become
    your comrade;
Be it as if I were with you. (Be not too certain but I am now
    with you.)

1959

NOTES

1. He wrote to Nelly O'Connor in November, 1863: "I find my New York boys the same gay-hearted joyous fellows, full of friendship & determined to have pleasure. We have been together quite a good deal. They have given me little supper parties, Men only. With drinks &c. of course we have great times."

2. Carpenter and Bucke recognized this and, thinking a third sex actually possible, tried to justify it in various writings. Their primary

example, of course, was Whitman himself, whose "bisexuality" seemed to them to presage the eventual desired fusion.

3. Will Wallace to Whitman: "I am surprised at your frenchy leaving you in such a deplorable state, but you are not alone. I had to dismiss mine to save the reputation of the hospital and your humble servant."

4. I do not suggest that Whitman had any overt homosexual experiences; there is no evidence whatever to indicate that he was, in our sense of the word, a homosexual. I do assert, however, that he sought from men the kind of day-to-day warmth and intimacy usually found by a man in relations with a woman. The debate about Whitman's sexual nature has been considerably muddled by failure to distinguish between urge and practice and by the application of twentieth century psychological abstractions to nineteenth century realities.

5. His relations with Walter Whitman were always strained. In the early stories, desperately autobiographical in meaning, the sensitive, artistic son is frequently pitted against a harsh, tyrannical father-figure. Walt was in effect adopted by some of his early preceptors in the newspaper trade.

6. Traubel, *Walt Whitman in Camden*. Note the image of the folded leaf, crucial in the "Calamus" poems.

7. "Song of Myself." Contrast Whitman's descriptions of the male and female forms in "I Sing the Body Electric." The woman's body is never really described, while the man's is detailed with loving tenderness.

8. Traubel, *Walt Whitman in Camden*. With this should be compared a note Whitman wrote to himself, presumably sometime in 1870: "Depress the adhesive nature/ It is in excess—making life in torment/ Ah this diseased, feverish disproportionate adhesiveness."

9. Whitman expressed in his letter to Sawyer another of his favorite desires—to set up housekeeping with his boys. To Doyle he wrote: "My darling, if you are not well when I come back I will get a good room or two in some quiet place, and we will live together and devote ourselves altogether to the job of curing you, and making you stronger and healthier than ever."

377

HONORÉ DE BALZAC— A DISTURBED BOY WHO DID NOT GET TREATMENT

E. C. M. Frijling-Schreuder

These remarks on the life and creative activity of the great French writer Honoré de Balzac (1799-1850) are meant to illustrate, how careful we have to be in making predictions about the future development of children who have been exposed to early neglect, especially if they are seen in a transitional phase, e.g. puberty.

Let us form an anachronistic fantasy: Balzac's parents go with their eldest child to a child guidance clinic, as they have good reason to do. Their boy has been sent home at the age of fourteen from a very strict Roman Catholic institute, the Collège Vendôme, in a rather pitiable condition: extremely emaciated, and in a continuous stupor; he does not react when spoken to and scarcely speaks.

His history is that of an unwanted, unloved child. The eldest of four children of a young mother and a much older father, twenty-one and fifty-three years of age respectively, he is placed with a nurse immediately after his birth and left in her care, without any contact with his parents, until the age of three. A younger sister, Laure, is placed with the same family. These children for whom nobody cares are objects of pity in the village. On his return home at three years of age, Honoré is made the object of his mother's ambivalence, punished for the faults of the other children, and already soliciting punishment.

In his letters and in his works he often returns to this period and to the persecution to which he felt exposed—cut off from all tenderness. There is his beautiful description of a neglected child: "As I was always expecting further suffering, as martyrs expect a further stroke, my being expressed a sad resignation under which the grace and vivacity of a child were smothered. My attitude was taken for a symptom of idiocy and justified my mother's somber predictions. I stayed in the garden to play with the little stones, to look at the insects or at the blue sky."

One of his most pregnant screen memories is the following: He is in the garden, looking dreamily at a star, forgotten by the governess. His sisters have turned on a tap. He is accused of having inundated the garden and is severely beaten. When he says that he was looking at a star, his mother is sarcastic: it is impossible that so dull a boy should have an interest in nature. Entrance to the garden is thenceforth forbidden.

When a boy throws a stone at him and he comes home bleeding, his mother's comment is: "That damned child will always give trouble." Perhaps her ambivalence is heightened by her unhappy marriage. Her youngest son, though formally accepted by her husband, was fathered by another man, and this child, Henri, is the spoiled one.

At eight years old Honoré is sent as a dull and unmanageable boy to a severe Roman Catholic institute, the Collège Vendôme. Once more he is completely cut off from his family, never visited by his parents, never allowed to go home for the holidays. Even in these severe surroundings he is an outcast, and spends much time shut up in a cupboard under the stairs. There in secret he reads anything he can lay his hands on. Neither in his lessons nor in other tasks does he get any good results. His life is a sequence of punishments, new failings, new punishments. At home he sought consolation in nature; now, after his first communion, he takes refuge in religion. Later he says that religious ecstasy helped him in his writings to see the inner meaning of things.

He is a fat, dull boy, ungifted for play as well as for learning. Dancing lessons lead only to ridicule. Only his contacts with the other boys are not too bad. In his fifteenth year comes the crisis with the extreme emaciation which leads to his return home. At that moment his parents are living in the country. In a remarkably short time Honoré improves, even getting better results at a school in the neighborhood. But soon the family moves to Paris, and Honoré is again sent to a boarding school, where history repeats itself: the boy does not work, and is once more continuously punished.

His mother's extreme ambivalence may be illustrated by a few sentences from a letter written to her sixteen-year-old son: he has had a bad mark, and is not allowed to come home for a feast-day. "I cannot tell you how you pain me. You, to have the lowest mark for that paper! You understand that a boy like you cannot take part in a festival. I intended to come for you early tomorrow morning, and we would have had lunch and dinner together. Think of how sad I shall be tomorrow." In this whole letter there is not a word of pity for the boy, and the mother writes as if he were five years old instead of sixteen.

To return to our fantasy: what would our diagnosis have been if we had seen the boy at this time? I think something like this: Severely disturbed development in a boy who has suffered from a disturbed parent-child relationship, with a rather sad prognosis without treatment.

For years Balzac's development seems to bear out this diagnosis. He is given two years of hard work and spare living in Paris to prove that he can be a writer. His work is a deception. He returns to his nagging and domineering mother and his lamenting grandmother. He begins a connection with his mother's friend, Madame de Berny, a woman twice his age, which of course gives rise to much scandal in both families. But she is for many years a very lenient friend to him; she believes in him and stimulates his activities. His relations with women are disturbed, and he does not even try to hide them from Madame de Berny. He begins a relation with the Duchesse d'Abrantès, the widow of General Junot. She too is much older than he, but whereas Madame de Berny was a wholesome influence in his life, she is a decadent, addicted to opium. Both women seem to be part of his family romance. Madame de Berny was the daughter of a musician at the Court of Louis XVI, and the Duchesse d'Abrantès had as a child known Napoleon.

Balzac feels how near he is to asocial conduct. His *Code des gens honnêtes* ("Code of the Honest") is rather a glorification of the master-thief than of honesty. He seeks, as does the thief he describes, "a quick way of becoming rich," and it is this wish that drives him into his unsuccessful enterprises which cost his mother and his friends so much. It will remain typical of his friendships that they cost the friends a great deal of money.

When he is thirty his novel, *Le Dernier des Chouans*, is accepted, and from then on his fame in the literary world increases.

Balzac's love life remains very unsatisfactory. His work, so far as is evident from his letters, is often a heavy burden, endured only to meet his most pressing creditors. Even in his lifetime his work was very famous, but what his contemporaries write about his person is very contradictory: he is described as fat and as extremely meager, as dirty and in rags and as a dandy. At one moment he owns horses, valets, a house full of valuables and bric-à-brac, then he travels to the south of France with 98 francs for his sole wealth and he is not able to raise the money for a voyage to Geneva where his wealthy Polish-Russian friend, Madame Hanska, is waiting for him.

He works for twenty hours a day, alternating with periods of dawdling in the mansions of his noble friends. He lives in extremes of hope and vitality. But the undertone remains that he brings ruin to everyone and to himself. Only his sister Laure is an exception. His mother and his friends he provokes endlessly. He plays on jealousy in every love relation. With his last friend, Madame Hanska, whom he married shortly before his death, he has carried on a correspondence (*Lettres à l'étrangère*) for many years before they meet for the first time, but at that meeting he is more occupied with her niece than with the long-awaited union with his friend.

It is easy to point out the bad consequences of the sadomasochistic relation with his mother in Balzac's love life, but how is it possible that such a disturbed personality can be so magnificently and abundantly creative?

For the creative artist variation between feelings of grandeur and of insecurity may be normal. Balzac's pronounced bisexuality may be a typical trait, too, fostered in his case by the very strong and ambivalent tie to his mother. As Van der Leeuw has pointed out, this identification with the omnipotent mother may be one of the sources of creativity.

What can Balzac's life history teach us about the future of neglected children with a disturbed early parent-child relationship? What in Balzac's early history could have led to a more hopeful prediction about his capacity for sublimation?

In evaluating the disturbance of the mother-child relationship we did not allow for the cultural factors. In a healthy middle-class twentieth century family the placement of the child immediately after birth would be a sign of severe disturbance. In nineteenth century France it was a sign of prosperity to have a wet nurse for the child, and such a placement would not in itself be a sign of a bad mother-child relationship. Moreover, the tie between child and nurse might remain of importance throughout life. But Balzac's feelings about his early placement are the same as would be those of a child of our own time. He feels it as a proof that his parents do not love him, and there is no tie to his foster family in later life. This leads us to a very general thesis: what is normal in a given culture may become a traumatic experience if it is felt as a symbol of a heightened ambivalence.

An important beneficial factor in Balzac's youth was his continually good tie to his sister Laure. The capacity for object love and the sense of responsibility for her as a three-year-old child may be taken as a good prognostic sign.

Because of the importance of the mother-child relationship we sometimes tend to minimize the importance of the other objects in the child's life. Balzac's father was over fifty when Balzac was born, and he was certainly not a father who was very much involved with his family. Yet he was a very vital figure, and one of Balzac's biographers writes of long walks Balzac took with his father, who discoursed on hygiene and politics or about nature. But the young Balzac, as we know, was away from his eighth till his fifteenth year, and on his return his father was sixty-eight!

Balzac senior was an entirely self-made man, the only one among his brothers and sisters who could read or write, the only one who had any social success. One of his brothers was condemned to death as a murderer and young Balzac must have known about this. Balzac senior came to Paris without a penny in his pocket, but he attained some fame as an administrator. His appointments varied from clerk to secretary of the *Conseil*

384

du Roi. In one of his many functions he was inspector of the Paris hospitals. He certainly did well for himself in his official capacity, but he had his social interests also. He wrote several pamphlets, among them one on the lot of the unmarried mother. His personality was characterized by an enormous vitality.

Now this vitality may have been the most essential point. In *Creative Writers and Day-Dreaming* Freud puts forward as the essential feature in literary art that the artist is able to give his inner conflicts a form that is acceptable to others.

Kris speaks of the artist's free contact with his unconscious, but adds another point which is in my opinion very important. He explains that the artist is very prone to regression, with at the same time an unusual ability to neutralize libidinal and aggressive energy in creating his work of art. In his creative capability the artist has his own unconscious conflicts at his disposal. Though they may hinder him in many areas of his life as they do less gifted people, he can use them in his work in such a way as not to hinder but to foster it. The identification with the omnipotent mother may lead to a disturbed sexual life, but in Balzac it led to his giving birth to two thousand imaginary people. His bisexuality enabled him to express himself in the creation of female and male characters in his novels with the same liveliness.

His own conflicts led to the creation of criminals, perverts, misers. Whereas his wastefulness was a great problem in Balzac's life, in his novels he is repeatedly fascinated by the character of the miser. Eugénie Grandet's father is one of the most renowned of these character studies, but they figure in quite a few of his other novels as well. The real ability of the artist does not lie in his rich fantasy life. As Freud put it, the flight into fantasy may lead to neurosis. The artist's real ability lies in his capacity to neutralize the energy bound to his unconscious conflicts into the energy necessary for the creation of his work of art, This neutralization is unstable, and is reversible at any moment. The artist needs great reversibility of his psychic energy, and he must be able to use this reversibility deliberately. So far his mental processes are comparable to the state of mind analysts use in free-flowing attention, a vibrating with the unconscious processes of our analysands which we can at any moment handle consciously. Let us add that this is possible only by reason of our own analysis, whereas in the artist it is a spontaneous condition in the field of his specific ability.

Balzac's writing was done under a most ascetic regime. He started work at midnight, went on until 6:00 A.M., then breakfasted and talked with his publishers until 9:00 A.M., and wrote from 9:00 A.M. till 6:00 in the evening; he went to bed at 8:00, to start work again at midnight. He stressed the purity of this life by wearing a white monk's habit. Generally he was writing two or three novels at the same time, but in spite of his high productivity he did not take his work lightly. On the contrary, even if a book was finished in two or three weeks, he might rewrite the same page seven or more times. Such an exhausting period of work would last for one or two months; then he took up again his life of pleasure, in which the writing was replaced by the acting out of his fantasies.

Let us return to our fantasy once again. Could we, if we had examined the fifteen-year-old Balzac, have diagnosed his genius? I do not think so. Even if the brilliance of his intellect had come to the fore in the psychological examination, for instance in the level of abstract thinking, the staff discussion would have pointed out of how little avail such brilliance is in a severe character neurosis, and his hopelessly bad school results would perhaps have added to our pessimism. Not without reason might we have made such a diagnosis as this: severe character neurosis in a boy of unharmonic build, with a sadomasochistic mother-child relationship; and then we should have missed the essential. In the discussion, his capability for object love in the good relation with his sister Laure might have come up, his interest in reading, his immediate contact when he met with real interest, and the reversibility of his symptoms.

We see this reversibility exhibited later on in his quick recovery from his exhausting work at the houses of his friends. The many contradictions in his contemporaries' writings about him also suggest a great degree of reversibility in his symptoms.

In general the prognosis of early neglect is the more somber in the degree to which the child's capacity for sublimation is disturbed. For children who show a shallow character with a lowered I.Q. our prognosis is worse than for those who still show some affective response and a normal use of their intellectual abilities. But in Balzac's youth the use of his intellectual abilities was severely disturbed. During his whole latency he was seen as dull and clumsy, and only later in his very retarded puberty is some change visible. This might warn us to be very wary of a too-rigid prognosis. His retarded adolescence may partly explain why his capacity for sublimation developed so late in life.

The normal loosening of the ties to the parents in puberty was in Balzac's case very incomplete. His longing for a better mother-figure led to his relation with Madame de Berny, and the steadiness of her love may have had a very favorable influence. Balzac says: "Je ne vis que par le coeur, et elle m'a fait vivre" ("I live only through love, and she has made me live").

Only after a long period in which he continually acted out his oedipal conflicts did his productivity reach its full creative level.

At the same time his creativity and his fame may be responsible for the very fact that his asocial development did not lead to final failure. In this context I would draw attention to Greenacre's view that it is the narcissistic gratification of creativity which compensates the artist for much neurotic suffering.

Sublimation and neutralization often have a connotation of

duty, of making a virtue of necessity. But one essential feature in the neutralizing process is the capacity to enjoy the development of abilities; in this sense it is closely related to the pleasure of functioning, the *Funktionslust,* of the young child in the development of his ego functions, for instance, the control of motility. Though Balzac as a child was much hampered in his activities by his nagging mother, and is described as a very clumsy boy who avoided play as much as possible, there must still have been some stimulation of this pleasure in functioning, this *Funktionslust,* to give rise to later sublimation. For Balzac this may be found in his long communions with nature, his long roamings about the country, sometimes with his father. This love of nature and religious ecstasy led to the cosmic emotional experiences or, to use Greenacre's term, the "collective alternates" which made him partly independent of the lack of love.

The last point I should like to raise is an aesthetic one. We said that the artist has the ability to use his unconcious conflicts in his work. But sometimes they seem to overwhelm him and to express themselves directly in the product. This might lead to an analytic contribution to literary criticism, viz., that where the unconscious is expressed too directly the artistic purpose fails. We can illustrate this from Balzac's writings. His psychology is colored by two fantasies: the dream of absolute love which he paints in such characters as Madame Hulot (*Cousine Bette*) or the still more tragic Père Goriot. On the other hand his novels are peopled by drive-ridden characters: Baron Hulot, Grandet, Cousine Bette, etc. It is as if he had to project his insatiable hunger for love as well as his insatiable egotism. This is the way in which a neglected child sees the world, a child who, just because of his insatiable need for love, cannot believe in the existence of real object love. Though as a whole this conflict is expressed in such a way that it excites our empathy, this is no longer true when Balzac inflicts on us his philosophy of life. He then uses a mixture of his father's materialism and his mother's occultism which leaves us untouched. This too-direct projection of the disturbed discussions in his parental home leads to bad artistic results in an artist who had the capacity for bringing the whole of his epoch to life.

The question whether in Balzac's fifteenth year we could have predicted that he would be capable of great artistic productivity, we answered in the negative. We pointed out some favorable prognostic signs: his good relationship with his sister Laure and his very early sense of responsibility toward her, his interest in books, his vitality, and the reversibility of his symptoms.

Our second question was: How is it possible that in adulthood Balzac's severe character neurosis did not hinder his creative ability, a question which arises in relation to many artists. In other words, the same conflicts which lead to character neurosis can be used by the artist in the field of his abilities in creation. To explain this, Freud speaks of the tolerance of the intelligence in the artist (*Die Duldung der Intelligenz*) toward the unconscious, and, in his Leonardo study, of a great proneness to repression in combination with great possibilities of sublimation. To indicate the fields of free functioning Beres speaks of dissociation, Kris of several degrees of neutralization, and of the reversibility of the process of neutralization, so that conflictual material can be used in conflict-free functioning, but on the other hand the creative process remains in a very unstable equilibrium which is easily disturbed.

Our third point was about an aesthetic criterion, the supposition that aesthetic pleasure is disturbed when the artist's unconscious conflict is expressed too directly in his work.

But the main trend of my presentation is simply this: the fact that we find a history of early neglect in so many cases of asocial character formation does not give us the right to come to the opposite conclusion that from a typical anamnesis we could predict a typical outcome for later life.   *1963*

A PSYCHOANALYTICAL

STUDY OF

EDGAR ALLAN POE

Lorine Pruette

The life of Edgar Allan Poe might be considered an unhappy record of that "disaster" which "followed fast and followed faster" this man of brilliant capacities till it drove him into opposition with most of the world, deprived him of the love he so inordinately craved, paralyzed his creative abilities, seduced him to seek a vague nepenthe in the use of drugs and stimulants, and, its relentless purpose achieved, cast him aside, a helpless wreck, to die from the darkened tragedy of a Baltimore saloon. Without further following such an anthropomorphic conception of fate, we must be impressed that both environmental circumstances and natural inheritance seem to conspire to cast the young poet in a role that is both somber and wild, with a beauty that chills even more than it saddens.

The psychoanalyst who seeks to probe into the earliest details of life to find there the causes of many of the associations and complexes, which even then shadow forth the developments of later years, will be troubled in the case of Poe with both scanty and conflicting data. The attempt has been made in this paper to follow those accounts which seem to be stamped with the strongest degree of authenticity or, at any rate, probability.

Edgar Poe was born in Boston, January 19, 1809, while his parents were playing in a local theater. They were at that time very poor, so that his birth, in spite of distinguished ancestors, may be considered lowly, both from the standpoint of wealth and of the social status which players then occupied. Yet from his paternal grandfather, a general of Revolutionary fame, he boasted of high lineage, and he consistently asserted his pride in being descended from a woman at once so beautiful and so noble as his mother, who both honored and was honored by her profession. Such assertions as these suggest that he spoke quite as much to assure himself as to convince others. While the reality allowed him full right to take pride in his descent, yet circumstances so contrived to cloud over that reality as to make his proud and sensitive spirit constantly alert against the possibility of an indignity.

The father of Poe was a victim of consumption, as was later his cousin-wife. Soon after the father's death, the mother died in abject want in Richmond, leaving her three small children to the mercy of strangers. Edgar was then two years old. The orphans were adopted by different families and seem to have known very little of each other. The elder brother, William, was, to quote from the words of a cousin, J. P. Poe, "a man of taste and genius, and wrote many fugitive verses, which have been lost, but which are said to have exhibited poetical power of a high order." He was not averse to the flowing bowl, and after his rejection as a lover, went to sea, where through recklessness he got into a sailor's scrape; he died at the age of twenty-six, leaving behind him the reputation of great but wasted talents. The youngest child, Rosalie, was so hopelessly dull that she could never attain proficiency in anything at school; she was utterly incapable of procuring her own main-tenance, and after the family which had at first taken her in ceased to befriend her, she led for many years a precarious existence till she was finally admitted to a charitable institution in Washington. There she was credited with many eccentrici-ties; she died at the age of sixty-four. Samuel Poe, a notable oddity of Baltimore, is said to have been the poet's uncle. His father, educated for the law, found such an existence unbear-able, and after several rebellions separated himself from his family, marrying the English actress, Elizabeth Arnold, and adopting her profession. These facts seem to indicate a decided neurotic taint in Poe's paternal inheritance. This inferior nerv-ous system predisposed many of the family toward flights from reality, alcoholism being their favorite form of erethism. Practically nothing is known of Poe's maternal inheritance, Elizabeth Arnold having been an orphan born at sea. She is said to have been extremely talented in singing, acting, and painting. Edgar inherited her artistic ability, was very clever at drawing and passionately fond of music. Along with these gifts of the muses he inherited also those characters which were to bring him at last to an end sadder and more terrible than even that of his young actress mother, starving in Richmond.

A few weeks after Mrs. Poe's death, the Broad Street theater where she had been acting was consumed in the awful con-flagration of Christmas Eve, 1811. The death of so many dis-tinguished people caught in this fire trap sent a thrill of horror through the United States and was discussed in hushed tones by the Virginians for many years thereafter. The story of this event and the sight of the burnt building where his beauti-ful mother had so often graced the stage must have had a powerful effect upon the dawning imagination of young Edgar, so that even at this early age there appeared to him the trilogy which so possessed his mind in after years—death, love, and beauty.

Now a tubercular father and cousin, an eccentric uncle, a drunkard brother as well as many relatives known for a "too free use of the bottle," and an imbecile sister, coupled with the peculiar genius of the poet himself, his sensitiveness to the effects of stimulants and temporary fits of insanity toward the last of his life, form fairly conclusive evidence that there was in the Poe family a decided organic inferiority. The lesion on the brain from which Edgar suffered in later life may have been either the result of syphilitic infection or apoplexy, or caused by an inherited inferior brain for which, according to Lombroso, genius is an over-compensation.

On the death of his mother, Edgar was adopted and baptized into the family of John Allan, a Virginia planter. From the childless wife of Mr. Allan the boy received considerable affection, though it is improbable that she was ever able to give any real understanding to her brilliant foster son. The adoptive father seems to have regarded him with an ambivalent feeling of good and ill will. In early years he was undoubtedly proud of the boy's beauty and precocity, and delighted to have him in to entertain guests after dinner by reciting long passages of poetry. The strain of such occasions must have been severe to the sensitive, excitable child. It was in such festive gatherings that he is said to have acquired, at an early age, the taste for alcohol which was later to play such a sinister part in his undoing. Dr. Bransby, under whom he studied in England for five years, described him as "a quick and clever boy" who "would have been a very good boy if he had not been spoilt by his parents," who "allowed him an extravagant amount of pocket money, which enabled him to get into all manner of mischief." His early boyhood, then, was passed as the spoiled child of indulgent parents, who gave him pocket money rather than love and sympathy. Poe himself, in speaking of his foster parents, says that he never received the parental affection or family sympathy for which he longed. But according to his biographer, John H. Ingram, "Throughout life a morbid sensitiveness to affection was one of Poe's most distinguishing traits," and it is highly probable that any normal affection would have seemed insufficient to the neurotic boy.

The Allans sailed for England in June, 1815, taking with them their adopted son. Edgar was placed at school under Dr. Bransby in Stoke-Newington, then a suburb of London. This historic old place, with its shadowed walks and memories of great and ill-fated lords and ladies, became the home of the child of genius during the next five years; years in which the childish imagination was quickening into life, fed on the lore of the classics and the pervading atmosphere of antiquity; years in which the passionate love of beauty turned to the loveliness of the old English town for gratification; years, too, in which the first attempts at verse-making were begun. It goes without saying that had the sensitive boy spent those five impressionable years in a different atmosphere—had he then known a normal home life and formed the normal associations toward a father and mother—his story must have been vastly different. His absence from the Allans at this period definitely precluded the establishment of ties of affection which might in later years have changed both his attitude and theirs. In 1820, again in the summer, Edgar returned with the Allans to America. The importance to the dreamy child of these two long sea voyages must have been tremendous. Sea voyages predispose to introspection, and six weeks at sea on these two occasions provided a great stimulus to the boy's imagination and love of the beautiful. Many of his stories show clearly the effect of the sea upon him, and the close observation which he must at some time have given it.

Returning to Richmond, Edgar Allan entered a fashionable preparatory school. As he grew older he came to realize the anomalous position which he occupied in the Allan household and among the arrogant, aristocratic sons of Richmond. Albert

Mordell, in the introduction to *The Erotic Motive in Litera-ture*, writes: "His supremacy in intellectual training and his easy physical prowess made him the most illustrious schoolboy in Richmond, but he was not allowed to derive pleasure from this high eminence. His playmates, too well trained in genealogy and taught an extravagant pride of ancestry, did not let him forget that his mother was an actress and that the privileges he enjoyed and they envied were owed to the beneficence of a Scotch merchant. These reminders of his inheritance and environment forced him into an unnatural moodiness and deprived him in large part of that frank and friendly companionship based upon a sense of total equality." Such a situation, of course, increased Edgar's rebellious pride, made him feel the necessity for defending himself against the slightest suggestion of inferiority. Feeling or imagining himself either tolerated or scorned steadily intensified his desire for superiority. He became a daring swimmer, took great risks to show himself above others, and would endure no implication that anyone was his equal in his chosen sport. His early fondness for Byron possibly led him to make this identification with the British poet who was also noted for his prowess as a swimmer. His leadership in intellectual pursuits must have caused him to incur still further the enmity of his schoolmates. He appears to have made no effort to ingratiate himself with the young aristocrats; he would be sought rather than seek others. One of his schoolmates at this time says, "Poe, as I recall my impressions now, was self-willed, capricious, inclined to be imperious, and though of generous impulses, not steadily kind, or even amiable; and so what he would exact was refused to him." The result of such a strained situation was to be expected. The adolescent boy withdrew more and more within himself, seeking consolation in his own dreams and mental imagery, so that by the time he reached the University of Virginia, at the age of seventeen, he is spoken of as having many noble qualities and being endowed by nature with great genius and diversity of talent, but with a retiring disposition and possessing few intimate associates.

Poe was registered at the University of Virginia from February 14 to December 15, 1826. He was in good standing with the faculty and obtained distinction at the final examination in Latin and French, then the highest honors to be obtained. It had been the theory of Jefferson, whose creation the new university was, that there should be no restrictions on the students, other than the expectation that they would conduct themselves as gentlemen. The young bloods threw themselves with zest into the freedom of such a life; most of them wealthy and of high lineage, they set themselves to lead the life of reckless extravagance, of mingled bravado and chivalry, which they considered characteristic of a gentleman at that period. Gaming and drinking were indispensable to their ideas of what a gentleman should do. Poe fell readily into both these diversions, gambled recklessly, and left the university owing $2,000 as debts of honor. In his drinking he was noticed to drink a glass of punch at a gulp, apparently craving the stimulation rather than the flavor of the drink. One glass, too, was said to be all that he usually desired. This habit of drinking *en barbare*, as Baudelaire calls it, he kept up all through life. At the university, he was known for his ability in writing extravagant stories, as well as in verse-making.

The organic inferiority of both lungs and mind, if we follow the theories of Adler, demanded compensation, which the youth found in drawing and in writing stories and poems. His will to power, as we have seen above, would brook no superior, nor even equal, in either physical or mental pursuits, and it was this intolerance of the claims of mediocrity which brought upon him in later life the enmity of much of the literary world. He, himself, was known to both deny and affirm his great ambition, but his ideal goal of superiority as a *litterateur* must be considered the guiding fiction of his life. In his poems and in his stories he consistently narrowed his attempts to the one field in which he was preeminent, the depicting of beauty and horror. His insistence, as a critic, that beauty is the sole motive of poetry, may be regarded as an attempt to place the stamp of critical approval on that which he himself did best. His feeling of degradation and of inferiority fired him with the passionate determination to be on top. If his masculine protest could be satisfied in no other way he turned to the degrading of others, as witness his attacks on Longfellow and other poets as plagiarists. Poe himself believed that his absolutely unswerving devotion to truth was responsible for his scathing criticisms, but even when true, as they generally were, such criticisms represented not an abstract devotion to truth, for which he was willing to suffer deprivation and hardship, but were rather due to the pressure of his own guiding fiction, striving toward the maximation of his ego-consciousness. With women poets, Poe was seldom, almost never, critical. His desire for superiority seemed with women to take an entirely different form. He had the characteristic overvaluation of the opposite sex which, according to Adler, is invariably connected with the neurotic constitution.

The conclusions of Brill, based on studies of only or favorite children, are quite applicable to Edgar Poe. Brill found that the adult only child shows one prominent feature, namely, he is a very poor competitor in the struggle for existence. After leaving the university the young Poe entered Mr. Allan's office, where he found the work intolerable. Just as his father had done before him, he shirked facing the hard facts of prosaic, everyday life, to seek the freer atmosphere of the artistic world, where he could obtain greater gratification for his egoistic impulses. Going to Boston, the city his mother had loved and where she said she had found her "best and truest friends," he published a thin volume of youthful poems which attracted little attention. He was then nineteen and some of the poems had been written when he was twelve. Unable to support himself by literary endeavor in the city of his birth, he joined the army as a private, where he distinguished himself by his exemplary conduct and became a sergeant-major at the age of twenty. Lieutenant Howard testified later that "his habits are good, and entirely free from drinking"; Captain Griswold considered him "highly worthy of confidence"; Colonel Worth said that his deportment was "highly praiseworthy and deserving of confidence." His foster father then secured him an appointment to West Point, which he resigned in five months. A. B. Magruder, a contemporary, writes: "He was an accomplished French scholar, and had a wonderful aptitude for mathematics. . . . He was a devourer of books, but his great fault was his neglect of and apparent contempt for military duties. His wayward and capricious temper made him at times utterly oblivious or indifferent to the ordinary routine." His resignation not being accepted, and finding the life of the cadet so irksome, he deliberately infringed the rules and brought upon himself a court-martial and dishonorable dismissal. His conduct and his foster father's speedy remarriage after the death of Mrs. Allan in 1829 definitely severed his relations with Mr. Allan and removed any possibility of his securing the inheritance which he had been brought up to expect. From this time on his life is a weary record of struggles for the bare necessities of life. At the time when his first tale was accepted he was in such a deplorable state as to be too ashamed of his clothes to appear in decent society. In spite of his acknowledged genius and great industry, he was condemned to the life of a very poorly paid hack writer and magazine editor, was never able to make any headway toward securing anything approaching financial independence; his young wife died without even enough covering for her bed.

Brill further found that the only boy, constantly associating with grown-ups, "is usually precocious even in childhood, and as he grows older he finds it very hard to associate with persons of his own age." Bohannon by his extensive studies of only children confirms this judgment. He says, "134, out of a total of 269, get along badly with others, 54 only fairly well, while only 81 seem to be normal in their social relations. When they disagree with other children it is usually because of a desire to rule. If they fail in this desire they are likely to refuse to associate with the children who cause the failure, and in a measure succeed in the wish to have their way, either by choosing younger companions whom they can control, or older ones who are willing to grant indulgence." While Poe impressed many with his brilliance and charm, his erratic conduct constantly estranged from him even those friends he did make—and he seemed to make enemies far more easily than friends. He had the characteristic tendency of the neurotic of beginning life anew with each new friend and each change of circumstance, feeling a new enthusiasm and another opportunity, which he lost through the vagaries of his own conduct. In this connection his will to power manifested itself through his frequent reiteration that he had thousands of friends. Bohannon found precocity also to be the most prominent trait of only children, Poe's precocity has already been mentioned. It seems probable that no other English poet has written at so early an age such good poetry.

Likewise Brill found that the only child, through the coddling of his parents, is in adult life unable to bear the slightest depreciation. Poe showed this characteristic time after time in his undignified replies to criticisms which a more evenly balanced nature would have ignored. Also the only child develops into a confirmed egotist and is conceited, jealous, and envious. After precocity, Bohannon found as most prominent characteristics: selfishness, imaginativeness, affection, jealousy, mental defects, temper, self-will, vanity—all of which are more or less exemplified in the character of Edgar Allan Poe. His depreciation of so many of his literary brethren has already been noted. He himself declared, "My whole nature utterly *revolts* at the idea that there is any Being in the Universe superior to *myself!*" We see, then, the years of his life spent as the spoiled child of the Allans combining with his neurotic inheritance to effectively inhibit his making the necessary adjustments to the demands of reality. Bohannon's studies trace a further parallel. He found the only child has a less healthy and robust constitution, more commonly suffers from mental and physical defects; his social relations are characterized frequently by friction and his peculiarities more pronounced. Finally, Brill concluded from a study of 400 patients that the "majority of only children do not marry at all or they marry some near relative whom they unconsciously identify with their parent image." Edgar Poe also fits into the scheme; he married his first cousin, Virginia Clemm, although it seems doubtful if he married her for the above reason so much as because he was able to find security in the maternal love of her mother, as perhaps an unconscious manifestation and inhibition of the incest desire.

In considering the love life of Poe there were so many women whom he addressed in enraptured terms of adoration that it is difficult to know which, if any, had any lasting influence upon his development. His mother was to him an idealization of feminine charms, about as tangible as the vanished fragrance of unseen flowers. His boyish poet-soul, musing over the memory of a beautiful and unknown mother, whose tragic fate could not but win his sympathy, and clothing her image in all the matchless virtues of a fertile imagination, created around her name the first of those sadly lovely and unreal women who move softly through his stories and poems.

His foster mother provided his wants and even luxuries as well as some affection, but seems in no way to have satisfied his passionate desire for love and approval. It is significant that, as one of his schoolmates remarked, he was never known to take any boy into his home, always preferring to go to theirs. While in school in Richmond, at the age of fourteen, he met Mrs. Helen Stannard, the mother of a boy friend, and on her speaking kindly to him, became at once her humble adorer, offering to her the white flame of his adolescent worship. She became the confidante of all his boyish sorrows and the redeeming influence of his turbulent and passionate youth. On her death he felt himself intensely bereaved and could not endure the thought of her lying lonely in her tomb in the neighboring cemetery. So for months he is reputed to have gone nightly to the graveyard for solitary vigils by her tomb, keeping warm the memory of her who had been kind to him. His analytic mind showed always a peculiar fascination for the secrets of the tomb, a desire to probe into the last hidden process of life's disintegration. His feeling regarding his friend's loneliness was but one example of the idea by which he was haunted through life: that the dead are not wholly dead to consciousness. This theme is repeated many times in his writings; for instance, in the revival of his dead wife in the tale "Ligeia," or in the terrible return of the Lady Madeleine in "The Fall of the House of Usher." His broodings in the darkened cemetery by the tomb of the one person he felt had understood him must have laid a foundation for much that was weird and abnormal in his after life. The melodious poem, "To Helen," was inspired by the memory of this lady, whom he called "the one idolatrous and purely ideal love" of his boyhood. At another time he said, "The boyish poet-love is indisputably that one of the human sentiments which most nearly realizes our dreams of the chastened voluptuousness of heaven."

As a youth in Richmond he fell in love with S. Elmira Royster, who lived opposite the Allans. She remembers him as a beautiful boy whose general manner was sad, "warm and zealous in any cause he was interested in, being enthusiastic and impulsive." The two young people became engaged, but her father, thinking her too young, intercepted all the poet's letters from the University of Richmond, and not until a year or so later when she became Mrs. Shelton did he learn why his passionate appeals had met with no response. It was at this time that Poe left Richmond and the office of Mr. Allan to seek his fortune in Boston, and it is entirely possible that the hurt to his vanity, to his insistent guiding fiction that he must be supreme, drove him away that he might avoid seeing the girl he desired possessed by another. In his youth he appears to have loved two other young women, one a cousin, Elizabeth Herring, the other Mary Devereaux, both of Baltimore, where he went after leaving West Point. Mordell calls attention to the fact that by the age of twenty-three he had lost his mother, his foster mother, and Mrs. Stannard by death, and had parted from three sweethearts. These deaths and rejections Mordell held to be the cause of Poe's preoccupation with the subject of the death of beautiful women. It would seem, however, that such cause must be sought in the peculiar quality of the poet's own temperament rather than in external circumstances. The happenings of his early life undoubtedly must have conditioned his emotional reactions, but the close connection between love and death seems to have been the particular obsession on which his neurotic temperament fastened itself.

At the age of twenty-seven Poe married his fourteen-year-old cousin, Virginia Clemm. For some time previously he had made his home with his aunt, Mrs. Clemm, and from an early age Virginia had adored him. The attachment between him and his aunt was always very strong, she laboring and suffering for him as would a mother for an only son. Virginia's beauty and grace and sweetness, as well as her talent for singing, identified her with the image of the young and beautiful mother he had never known, while the maternal care and devotion of Mrs. Clemm offered him a refuge and safety from the troubles and disapproval of the outside world. His mother-image, being a creation of his own imagination, may be said to have split to take in the two personalities of his wife and mother-in-law— the one a radiant young creature, satisfying his aesthetic cravings, the other tender and untiring in maternal devotion satisfying the neurotic craving for protection. In later life Poe found many women friends, women of the highest attainment and character, who were his warmest defenders and for whom he expressed the deepest sentiments of affection. Among these were Mrs. Osgood, Mrs. Richmond, Mrs. Lewis, and Mrs. Helen Whitman. From the peculiar character of his will to power it is doubtful if individual women ever influenced him much. His nature demanded the adoration and approval of "woman," rather than sexual conquests, and he worshiped in his poems a feminine idealization to which he ascribed various names. These women are never human; they are not warm flesh and blood, loving, hating, or coming late to appointments —they are simply beautiful lay figures around which to hang wreaths of poetical sentiments. His emotional interest lay in himself, rather than in outer objects; he wished to be loved, rather than to love.

The poetry of Poe reveals two things: a very considerable degree of introversion (in the sense in which Jung uses the term) and a flight from reality. His poems are to an unusual degree "out of space—out of time." Where a Byron or a Shelley revolted against political injustice and became the ardent apostle of liberty, Poe passed serenely through the troublesome years of antislavery agitation apparently untouched by the passions of those around him, worshipping only the beauty whose expression is art, interested only in the inner conflict within his own soul. In his themes he is neither American, nor Virginian, nor of the nineteenth century. For him the world was depreciated till it scarcely existed; finding reality not to his satisfaction he fled to a world of his own creating. As he said in his story "Berenice": "The realities of the world affected me as visions, and as visions only, while the wild ideas of the land of dreams became, in turn—not the material of my everyday existence—but in very deed that existence utterly and solely in itself." Barbey d'Aurevilly speaks of what he calls Poe's *sècheresse*, the terrible dryness of his art, and says, "His intellect was real; everything else about him was exquisite feigning. His passion, his human sympathy, his love of nature, all the emotions that go into his fiction, have a counterfeit unreality." This view accords well with Jung's theory of the introvert who, interested in thinking rather than in feeling, assumes the conventionally correct emotions. Poe himself wrote: "In the strange anomaly of my existence, feelings with me *had never been* of the heart, and my passions *always were* of the mind." This last is in line with his general attitude toward women, which allowed him to love intellectually so many women, without craving the physical expression of that love. The Freudians would consider this the result of the damming of the libido, perhaps due to some early experience, and they would support their view by calling his stories of horror expressions of anxiety, which to them always has a sexual connotation. It is quite as plausible to accept his own explanation and to hold that his passions were largely of the mind, which, as noted above, is entirely consistent with the introverted type. Lowell, in his *Fable for Critics*, confirms this, saying that Poe "has written some things quite the best of their kind. But the heart somehow seems all squeezed out by the mind." Poe wrote to Lowell at the time when he was thinking he had found in the New England poet a congenial spirit: "I have been too deeply conscious of the mutability and evanescence of temporal things to give any continuous effort to anything—to be consistent in anything. My life has been *whim*—impulse—passion—a longing for solitude—a scorn of all things present, in an earnest desire for the future." Mrs. Whitman, in her introductory letter to Didier's *Life of Poe*, says that "his proud reserve, his profound melancholy, his *unworldliness*—of nature made his character one very difficult of comprehension to the casual observer."

The small volume of verse on which rest Poe's substantial claims to poetic genius represents the work of his life, which he was constantly refining. He composed with the care and effort of the introvert, revising his poems many times, usually to their improvement, intent on the perfection of quality rather than quantity. His themes are few, not from any paucity of imagination but from a complete absorption in a few dominant ideas. He sought, not the varied pleasures of the world, but the interpretation of beauty alone, the highest form of which he felt to be linked always with melancholy. In "The Assignation" he says "there still lurked (incomprehensible anomaly!) that fitful stain of melancholy which will ever be found inseparable from the perfection of the beautiful." He constantly moved in his poetic imaginings among

> ". . . the ideal,
> Dim, vanities of dreams by night—
> And dimmer nothings which were real—"(Tamerlane)

In struggling with the hard, unlovely realities of life, he cried out:

> Oh! that my young life were a lasting dream!
> My spirit not awakening, till the beam
> Of an Eternity should bring the morrow.
> Yes! tho' that long dream were of hopeless sorrow,
> 'T were better than the cold reality
> Of waking life, to him whose heart must be,
> And hath been still, upon the lovely earth,
> A chaos of deep passion, from his birth.

And later in the same poem, entitled "Dreams":

Dreams! in their vivid coloring of life
As in that fleeting, shadowy, misty strife
Of semblance with reality which brings
To the delirious eye, more lovely things
Of Paradise and Love—and all our own!
Than young Hope in his sunniest hour hath known.

In "A Dream Within a Dream" we find rebellion against the disappointments of life.

I stand amid the roar
Of a surf-tormented shore,
And I hold within my hand
Grains of the golden sand—
How few! yet how they creep
Through my fingers to the deep,
While I weep—while I weep!
O God! can I not grasp
Them with a tighter clasp?
O God! can I not save
One from the pitiless wave?
Is *all* that we see or seem
But a dream within a dream?

In still another poem called "A Dream" is seen the contrast between what he has and what he has wanted, between the real and the ideal world of fancy:

In visions of the dark night
I have dreamed of joy departed—
But a waking dream of life and light
Hath left me broken-hearted.

In his "Sonnet—To Science" he calls science the vulture which has

. . . torn the Naiad from her flood,
The Elfin from the green grass, and from me
The summer dream beneath the tamarind tree.

The shimmering irridescence of "Al Aaraaf," that mosaic of

407

sensuous beauty of sight and sound, the music and glowing images of which haunt our senses even while the mind does not comprehend it, opens with the description:

> O! nothing earthly save the ray
> (Thrown back from flowers) of Beauty's eye
> As in those gardens where the day
> Springs from the gems of Circassy—
> O! nothing earthly save the thrill
> Of melody in woodland rill—
> Or (music of the passion-hearted)
> Joy's voice so peacefully departed
> That like the murmur in the shell,
> Its echo dwelleth and will dwell—
> Oh, nothing of the dross of ours—
> Yet all the beauty—all the flowers
> That list our Love, and deck our bowers—
> Adorn yon world afar, afar—
> The wandering star.

Of his "Politian" he says:

> He is a dreamer and a man shut out
> From common passions.

He speaks to the singing Israfel:

> Yes, Heaven is thine; but this
>   Is a world of sweets and sours;
>   Our flowers are merely—flowers,
> And the shadow of thy perfect bliss
>   Is the sunshine of ours.

He is constantly manifesting in his poems the desire to flee the imperfections of this world. But even in his dream world he is sad; he loved melancholy and kept her ever close to his side. In his "Fairy-Land" are

> Dim vales—and shadowy floods—
> And cloudy-looking woods,
> Whose forms we can't discover
> For the tears that drip all over.

His "City in the Sea" is a picture of beauty desolated, of death reigning in the courts of life and love:

> There open fanes and gaping graves
> Yawn level with the luminous waves
> But not the riches there that lie
> In each idol's diamond eye—
> Not the gaily-jewelled dead
> Tempt the waters from their bed;
> For no ripples curl, alas!
> Along that wilderness of glass—
> No swellings tell what winds may be
> Upon some far-off happier sea—
> No heavings hint that winds have been
> On seas less hideously serene.

The poems of Poe are songs of sorrow: beauty is in them, most often dead beauty, love is there, most often the love of those who are dead to him, and madness is there, as if the expression of the prophetic powers of his unconscious. Often enough, in moments of extreme depression, under the influence of drugs or in the temporary insanity induced by the use of stimulants, must he himself have felt those "evil things, in robes of sorrow," which "assailed the monarch's high estate." The "Imp of the Perverse" came to him in actual life, and forced him to make appearances which he could neither have desired nor have calculated to benefit himself. His behavior in Washington which lost him the government appointment he desired, and his gratuitous insult to the Bostonians when, on being asked to lecture, he delivered a poem he had written as a child, must be considered as the perverse manifestation of the will to power which is gratified by putting a depreciation on others through one's own unbecoming conduct. This same striving for superiority is evidenced in "Israfel:"

> If I could dwell where Israfel
> Hath dwelt, and he where I
> He might not sing so wildly well

> A mortal melody;
> While a bolder note than his might rise
> From my lyre above the skies.

Poe's heroes are largely autobiographical; they are melancholy men, pursued by unrelenting fate; they are neurotic,
hypochondriac, monomaniac, victims of vain delusions; they are
the prey of melancholia, insane from sorrow or from the thirst
for revenge. In "Eleanora" he seeks to reassure himself, to take
the proudly characteristic attitude of defiance to the views of
the world. He writes: "Men have called me mad; but the question is not yet settled, whether madness is or is not the loftiest
intelligence: whether much that is glorious, whether all that
is profound, does not spring from disease of thought,—from
moods of mind exalted at the expense of the general intellect."
In the study of his own diseased thought he is distinctly psychological. He writes: ". . . what the world calls 'genius' is
the state of mental disease arising from the undue prominence
of some one of the faculties. The works of such genius are
never sound in themselves, and, in especial, always betray the
general mental insanity." This appears to be the artist's fore-
shadowing of some of the views of Lombroso and Adler, as
if Poe himself felt that only through his own defects was he
able to secure that superiority his soul demanded.

Poe's favorite poem, "The Sleeper," is occupied with his
dominant theme, the linking of sex and death. "All Beauty
sleeps!"

> The bodiless airs, a wizard rout,
> Flit through thy chamber in and out,
> And wave the curtain canopy
> So fitfully—so fearfully
> Above the closed and fringed lid
> 'Neath which thy slumb'ring soul lies hid.

This is only one of the many pictures he has given us of the
couch of beauty which is also a bier. "To One in Paradise,"

the "Sonnet to Zante," "Lenore," "Ulalume," "Annabel Lee," and the world-famous "Raven" are concerned with reflections over a beautiful woman who is loved and dead. "Annabel Lee," written after his wife's death, is reminiscent of his experiences as a boy when he kept his lonely vigils in the cemetery beside the tomb of his friend.

> And so, all the night-tide, I lie down by the side
> Of my darling—my darling—my life and my bride,
>   In the sepulchre there by the sea—
>   In her tomb by the sounding sea.

In the same poem his proud spirit defies even death, when he cries,

> And neither the angels in heaven above,
>   Nor the demons down under the sea,
> Can ever dissever my soul from the soul
>   Of the beautiful Annabel Lee.

The Philosophy of Composition claims to explain the conception and composition of "The Raven," and while it is very doubtful if he really wrote the poem in any such impersonal, intellectual, and rational manner, nevertheless his analysis contains some valuable hints, as when he writes: "Now, never losing sight of the object *supremeness* or perfection, at all points, I asked myself—'Of all melancholy topics, what according to the *universal* understanding of mankind, is the *most* melancholy?' Death—was the obvious reply. 'And when,' I said, 'is this most melancholy of topics most poetical?' From what I have already explained at some length, the answer here also is obvious—'When it most closely allies itself to *Beauty;* the death, then, of a beautiful woman is, unquestionably, the most poetical topic in the world—and equally is it beyond doubt that the lips best suited for such a topic are those of a bereaved lover.'" The psychoanalyst is prone to seek further into the poet's life to explain his preoccupation with death. It will be

411

recalled that his parents died early and under most unhappy circumstances; many an hour the sensitive, imaginative child must have brooded over the tragic end of his beautiful, gifted mother. Then at the impressionable adolescent period came the death of the woman he worshipped, Mrs. Helen Stannard. A few years later died the foster mother. Three sweethearts were lost to him. Then there were the six years of dread for Virginia's life. These he has described in a letter to a friend, dated January 4, 1846: "Six years ago, a wife, whom I loved as no man ever loved before, ruptured a blood vessel in singing. Her life was despaired of. I took leave of her forever, and underwent all the agonies of her death. She recovered partially, and I again hoped. At the end of a year, the vessel broke again. I went through precisely the same scene. . . . Then again—again—and even once again, at varying intervals. Each time I felt all the agonies of her death—and at each accession of the disorder I loved her more dearly and clung to her life with more desperate pertinacity. But I am constitutionally sensitive—nervous in an unusual degree. I became insane, with long intervals of horrible sanity. During these fits of absolute unconsciousness, I drank—God only knows how often or how much. As a matter of course, my enemies referred the insanity to the drink, rather than the drink to the insanity. I had, indeed, nearly abandoned all hope of a permanent cure, when I found one in the *death* of my wife. This I can and do endure as becomes a man. It was the horrible, never-ending oscillation between hope and despair which I could *not* longer have endured, without total loss of reason. In the death of what was my life, then, I received a new but—Oh God!—how melancholy an existence." Allowing all due discounting for the poetic picturing of himself in constant agony, there can be no doubt that "the horrible, never-ending oscillation between hope and despair" of those six years must have made an indelible impression upon the poet's brain. Little wonder, then, that he wrote of the death of beautiful women.

In his stories Poe continues this linking of death with sex. Another factor manifests itself, namely, the sadistic delight in torture. Let us recall a few of these stories. In "Berenice" the lover tears out the teeth of his beloved before her body is cold within the grave; in "The Black Cat," having cut out the eyes of the cat he abhors, and later killed it, he is tormented by another cat whom his wife protects; maddened by her attitude he seizes an ax and cuts through her brain, after which he walls up the body in his cellar and laughs with glee at the fumbling search of the police; there is the murder of Marie Roget, mutilation of the body and sinking of it in the river; in the "Murders in the Rue Morgue" he dwells over all the gruesome details of the masses of hair torn from the old woman's head, the throat cut with a razor, the daughter stifled in a chimney. The record was kept of seventeen stories of Poe as they appeared in an ordinary edition. Of these tales only three did not record violent or tragic deaths; these were "The Purloined Letter," which ends with a revenge; the "Man in the Crowd," a personification of crime; and the "Pit and the Pendulum," as terrible a delineation of torture as has ever been penned. Here is the death list from the other fourteen: Two dead in the "Gold Bug," two in "The Descent into the Maelstrom," the crews of two ships in the "Mss. Found in a Bottle," two in the "Murders in the Rue Morgue," two in the "Mystery of Marie Roget," two in the "Fall of the House of Usher," one in "William Wilson," one in "The Black Cat," one in "The Tell-Tale Heart," two in "The Assignation," the prince and his thousand attendants in "The Masque of the Red Death," one in "Berenice," two in "Morella," one in "Shadow." The list might be extended to cover the majority of the tales, but it seems unnecessary to pursue such inquiry further. Poe's

413

mind was preoccupied not only with death but with violent death, with murder and with pestilence.

The sadistic impulse is readily linked with sex. This is shown in a more subtle form in his favorite story "Ligeia." Here is the description of the bridal chamber prepared for a second wife:

"Some few ottomans and golden candelabra, of Eastern figure, were in various stations about—and there was the couch, too, the bridal couch—of an Indian model, and low, and sculptured of solid ebony, with a pall-like canopy above. In each of the angles of the chamber stood on end a gigantic sarcophagus of black granite, from the tombs of the kings over against Luxor, with their aged limbs full of immemorial sculpture. But in the draping of the apartment lay alas the chief fantasy of all. The lofty walls, gigantic in height —even unproportionably so—were hung from summit to foot, in vast folds, with a heavy and massive-looking tapestry—tapestry of a material which was found alike as a carpet on the floor, as a covering for the bed, and as the gorgeous volutes of the curtains which partially shaded the window, the material was the richest cloths of gold. It was spotted all over, at irregular intervals, with arabesque figures, about a foot in diameter, and wrought upon the cloth in patterns of the most jetty black. But these figures partook of the true character of the arabesque only when regarded from a single point of view . . . To one entering the room, they bore the appearance of simple monstrosities; but upon a farther advance this appearance gradually departed; and step by step, as the visitor moved his station in the chamber, he saw himself surrounded by an endless succession of the ghastly forms which belong to the superstition of the Norman, or arise in the guilty slumbers of the monk. The phantasmagoric effect was vastly heightened by the artificial introduction of a strong continual current of wind behind the draperies—giving a hideous and uneasy animation to the whole." Here again is the picture of the bed which is a coffin, and the heavy curtains move uneasily like the pall which covers the last resting place of the dead. In the center of the room swings the censer around which writhe serpent-like flames; the censer is of gold. In tending the sick lady Rowena, the husband offers her a cup of wine, into which he sees fall from an invisible hand a few ruby colored drops. Insensibly the reader feels that this is the revenge of the first wife,

Ligeia, on the one who has taken her place. Rowena dies, then revives, dies again, revives. Each time the husband does what he can to assist her, although he seems to desire that she shall die utterly and leave him in peace. When he thinks she is at last quiet in her final sleep she rises and reveals to him the wild eyes and streaming hair of his lost love, Ligeia.

In this tale are the three colors, gold and black and red, which Poe uses most; there is also beauty and death and sex. The bed and the entire room suggest a coffin in a tomb; the censer which is so frequently present in his descriptions is reminiscent of the church services which he attended twice each Sunday in England and which may very easily have become associated with funerals and death; the serpent-like flames represent the sex symbol. Here, too, is found another characteristic of much of his writing: the death wish, this time directed against the second wife. Then comes again the old feeling that the dead are not wholly dead and the dead woman is revealed as his first wife. Her expression is the projection of his own feelings of remorse both for taking another bride and for the death wish against Rowena.

The imagery of this story Poe uses over and over again. "The Assignation," another story of the love of a neurotic and the death of a beautiful woman, gives the picture of a strange room where "rich draperies in every part of the room trembled to the vibration of low, melancholy music." Here also are the swinging censers; the windows are of crimson tinted glass. In the "Pit and the Pendulum" the condemned wretch says, "I saw, too, for a few moments of delirious horror, the soft and nearly imperceptible waving of the sable draperies which enwrapped the walls of the apartment." In "The Raven" is heard the "silken, sad, uncertain rustling of each purple curtain." "Metzengerstein" has tapestry hangings which swing gloomily upon the walls. In "Shadow" are sable draperies. We read in "The Masque of the Red Death": "The seventh apartment was closely shrouded in black velvet tapestries that hung all over the ceiling and down the walls, falling in heavy folds upon a carpet of the same material and hue." It was not merely the thought of death which obsessed the poet, but death in all its details and in its visible symbol, the casket of the dead. From contemplation of the coffin the funeral pall or draperies came to have a peculiar significance, and when he wrote of rooms in which terrible deeds transpired he hung those rooms with the draperies of the dead. Not only that, but the curtains stir, to sad music, to strange winds, heightening the effect of horror, as the breezes which lift the pall over the face of the dead, increasing the agony of the spectator by giving the semblance of life where life has fled. In his poems are the same figures: a curtain is a funeral pall ("The Conqueror Worm"); "there passed, as a shroud, A fleecy cloud" ("Evening Star"); the eyes of the beloved "desolately fall on my funereal mind like star-light on a pall." ("To ———")

Then there are the colors: gold sometimes, but the principal contrast being the black and the red, symbols of death and of sex, the two ideas to which his thoughts ever returned. Black ships, black cats, clocks of ebony, sable condors, black marble flagstones, blackened goblets, black wings of pestilence, ebony tables, black silk-velvet palls, sable hearse plumes—these are a few of the symbolizations of death. For the sex motif are red lights, crimson-tinted glass, scarlet panes, the ruddy reflection from burning buildings, the fiery colored horse, fiery colored clouds, blood-red metal, intense light of rubies, the red of poppies, wine red as blood, rain that changed to blood, the fiery wall of the horizon, red clouds, the red eye of the sun, the crimson moon. No attempt has been made to cover all the uses Poe has made of the two colors, but it is very significant that these are the two which he used most often, and on which he rang so many changes. "The Masque of the Red Death" shows the effectively vivid combination of the two. The seventh chamber, completely covered with black draperies, has for windows scarlet panes, outside of which lamps are placed, so that the light falling on the black curtains must pass through the scarlet and so blend the two in a weird and unearthly aspect.

After the coffin, the poet's mind turned to the grave or tomb, and a vast number of allusions to this may be found in his writings. In "The Cask of Amontillado" he walls up his enemy in a living tomb; in "The Fall of the House of Usher" Madeleine is placed in a vault under the house; in "The Assignation" he rides in a "funereal gondola"; the "Gold Bug" is the story of treasure buried along with two men in a single grave; the Red Death masqueraded in grave clothes; he buries his victim under the floor in "The Tell-Tale Heart"; he thinks "what sweet rest there must be in the grave" ("The Pit and the Pendulum"), and in the same story "dreaded to move a step, lest I should be impeded by the walls of a *tomb*." He sings of the worm that never dies and prays that worms may creep softly around his sweetheart's body. In this connection also will be recalled his poem, "The Conqueror Worm."

The creeping of worms through dead bodies is considered a sexual symbol, and in this connection seems to show the presence of an erotic gratification at the thought of the dissolution of the bodies of beautiful women. The thought of the sweet rest within the grave is the desire to creep back into the mother's womb, which Jung and Silberer have considered so characteristic of the introvert.

The sadistic element is a compound of the sexual desire and the desire to give pain. These desires, repressed in Poe's life, are embodied in his poems and tales. With the child-wife, who was for years almost an invalid, he could never have enjoyed the satisfaction of a normal sex life, while his love for other women seems to have been of the mind rather than the body. Thwarted on this side of his nature, he turned to literary and artistic creation. In this he eked out the barest livelihood, and made enemies constantly by reason of his genius as well as of his intolerance of the claims of the mediocre many. Through the courts and by means of powerful invectives from his own brilliant, bitter pen he sought revenge on those who slandered or opposed him. But his victories were never wholly won; he never triumphed utterly over his enemies. His will to power, however, would be satisfied with nothing short of their annihilation, and, failing that in the actual physical world as well as in the literary and social world, he turned loose his sadistic impulses upon the creatures of his stories, some of whom must have represented very real figures to himself. In "The Cask of Amontillado" he says a wrong is never righted till the aggressor is punished and knows he is punished by the injured one. His imagination fairly gloats over the ingenious tortures it devises, many of which are equal to the most fiendish of the Inquisition.

Freud has written on the effect which whipping has on children in developing both sadism and masochism. On seeing other children whipped the child feels that he is then the favored one, and a sadistic element of joy at suffering is introduced. On being whipped himself the child may be animated either by a sadistic or a masochistic desire. Masochism can be explained as a turning back of sadism upon the ego and is not itself a primary sex urge. It is a sort of narcissistic or autoerotic sadism, or sadism focused on the person's own genital organs. Poe went to school in England at a time when fagging was in order and as a little fellow he must have come in for his due amount of punishment. In school at Richmond, under a schoolmaster who believed greatly in the efficacy of flogging, Poe was never known to be punished, this fact being remarked on as quite unusual by one of his classmates. His experience in England would allow for development of either masochistic or sadistic elements; that in Richmond would reinforce the sadistic. The son of his foster father's partner remarked on the mean delight which Edgar, then a boy, took in tormenting a sensitive girl by pointing an imitation serpent toward her. The serpent being the sexual symbol, the victim of the cruelty a girl, there seems an undoubted sadistic element here. The same gentleman tells of being thrown into some falls by Poe, who was then obliged to rescue the weaker boy, such an incident gratifying both the sadistic tendency and the will to power. The scene which he is reported to have made with the second Mrs. Allan when she was sick in bed indicates the same sadistic trend. All through his life the two things are found together: his will to power, thwarted, demanding sadistic revenge, his sadism gratifying and reinforcing his will to power.

There is an obvious death wish in many of the stories of Poe directed against a man. In "The Tell-Tale Heart" it is against an old man, whose murder he accomplishes; not satisfied with this he cuts off the limbs. He commences the story in an extenuating tone, but objects to being called mad. "True— nervous—very, very, dreadfully nervous I had been and am; but why *will* you say that I am mad?" Then telling of the murder, he continues: "It is impossible to say how first the idea entered my brain; but once conceived, it haunted me day and night. Object there was none. Passion there was none. I loved the old man. He had never wronged me. He had never given me insult. For his gold I had no desire. I think it was his eyes! yes, it was this!" This detailed setting forth of lack of reason for a murder indicates in the writer a defense mechanism against the unconscious wishes. There was one man for whose murder all such reasons would apply: the foster father, Mr. Allan. There had never been love or understanding between the two. He had brought up the gifted boy as his son, giving him his name, then had cast him off without a cent. He had insulted him and driven him from his house. He had refused to pay Edgar's gambling debts which the boy regarded as debts of honor, and so had placed him in a position of galling humiliation at the university. Had he died earlier Edgar would have inherited his gold. Had he not married again the fortune would probably have gone to the poet. In all the years of destitution, of pitiful struggle against a pitiless fate, never able to realize his cherished desire of founding a magazine because of lack of funds, seeing a young wife fade away lacking the money to buy her either the drugs or food her condition demanded—is it not reasonable to suppose that hatred should turn against the man who might have prevented all this, against the man who had taught him to expect and to desire luxuries and had disappointed him, against the man who had humiliated and insulted him? Object and passion were surely here sufficient for the unconscious, if not the conscious, death wish.

We come now to the masochistic tendency of Poe, which while not nearly so striking generally, is extremely well displayed in a few stories. It will be recalled that masochism is the regression of the sadistic impulse from the outer world onto one's own person. In "Loss of Breath" he describes his own tortures in tones of considerable enjoyment: his ears were cut off, incisions made into his stomach, the skull fractured, he was hanged and obligingly went through spasms for the benefit of the populace which encored. "A Predicament" tells the story of his being caught in a huge clock and the minute hand being imbedded in his neck till it cuts off the head:

> The ticking of the machinery amused me. *Amused me,* I say, for my sensations now bordered upon perfect happiness. . . . The eternal click-clack, click-clack, click-clack, of the clock was the most melodious of music in my ears. . . . The bar had buried itself two inches in my neck. I was aroused to a sense of exquisite pain. . . . My eyes, from the cruel pressure of the machine, were absolutely starting from their sockets . . . one actually tumbled out of my head. . . . I was presently relieved . . . by the dropping out of the other eye.
> The bar was now four inches and a half deep in my neck, and there was only a little bit of skin to cut through. My sensations were

those of entire happiness, for I felt that in a few minutes, at farthest, I should be relieved from my disagreeable situation. . . . At twenty-five minutes past five in the afternoon precisely, the huge minute-hand had proceeded sufficiently far on its terrible revolution to sever the remainder of my neck. I was not sorry to see the head which had occasioned me so much embarrassment at length make a final separation from my body. It first rolled down the side of the steeple, then lodged, for a few seconds, in the gutter, and then made its way, with a plunge, into the middle of the street.

The detail with which this is told and such expressions as "amused me," "a sense of exquisite pain," "entire happiness," are expressive of masochistic delight in suffering while the sardonic humor which laughs at his own dismemberment is a defense mechanism which the sensitive poet must have had to set up early in life, as protection against the ridicule of others.

"The Pit and the Pendulum" is the tale which best of all illustrates this masochistic tendency. It is told in the first person by a victim of the Inquisition. The man swoons on hearing his sentence and awakens to find himself in utter darkness in an underground cavern. There he narrowly escapes falling into a gruesome pool of nameless horrors. The invisible torturers plan for him one death after another, each more terrible than the last. In reality one feels that it is the author himself who takes delight in planning first one affliction, then another, and who enjoys the thought of his own body suffering such agonies. The story is like a dream in which we watch ourselves take part, feel with ourselves and yet are detached from ourselves. After a swoon the poor victim awakens to find himself bound flat upon the floor, utterly helpless save for one free arm with which he can reach the scanty food at his side, which is carefully calculated just to keep life in his body. He hears above him a strange ticking and perceives in the shadows what appears to be a large pendulum. As the hours pass he sees this pendulum slowly descend. It approaches his bound body, hour by hour coming nearer; after every swoon he awakens to find it closer; he sees the sharp steel of its point; it cuts the air in ever wider circles; fascinated, yet horrified, he watches for days the approach of death; in detail the author describes his body sensations. The rats have come out to snatch the last remnants of food; at length it occurs to him that by smearing the meat upon his bonds they will gnaw away his fetters. While the rats gnaw at his cords the steel pendulum sweeps nearer and nearer, its sharp blade cutting the air just above him. It touches his garments, it cuts the cloth above his breast, and just at the last second he is freed and crawls away. Immediately the pendulum is drawn up, showing how incessantly he is watched. Then there comes a light within the chamber, a strange light which shows up the horrible, fantastic figures of devils and ghosts upon the walls; these figures begin to glow with heat, the walls and floor are hot to the touch, he perceives that they are entirely of brass and capable of casting out an intense heat. Tortured by fear and by the increasing heat, he creeps to the edge of the pool, and gazes down, too horrified by what he sees to take the plunge. It is evident that the torturers design to drive him into the pool and he determines to resist at no matter how great suffering. The heat and his agony continue till at the limit of human endurance he is rescued by the armies of his sect who have taken the town. The meticulous detail of this story, the evident relish with which the author describes his sensations as, helpless on the floor he watches the nearing sweeps of the sharp blade of the pendulum, or as he recoils from the ever increasing heat, shows a masochistic delight in the thought of torture applied to his own body.

Mordell calls attention to the stories of ratiocination of Poe which he considers a further indication of masochism. "The Murders in the Rue Morgue," "The Mystery of Marie Roget," "The Purloined Letter," and "The Gold Bug" are masterly examples of the analytical genius of Poe. The careful study of the tedious details of the mysteries of the first three as well as the solving of the cipher in the last tale represent the delight of a mind which loved to torture itself.

This is clearly shown in the man's life as well. As editor of a Philadelphia journal he made the boast that man could invent no cipher which human ingenuity could not decipher, and set himself the task of solving the many cryptograms submitted. The busy editor yet found time to spend hours exercising his mental faculties, as if delighted by the irritating burdens he could place upon his mind. It is reputed that he never failed to make good his boast.

The analytical powers manifested by Poe in such stories as those mentioned above, and also strikingly evident in much of his critical writing, was a characteristic not commonly associated with his other gifts. He insisted, however, that there could be no genuine imagination without this capacity for analysis of the keenest sort. Certainly the verisimilitude of his most extravagant tales is greatly increased by the background of incisive thinking and detailed analysis which they evidence. Oliver Leigh has made an interesting study in the character of Poe as shown by his photographs. One side of the head, if duplicated, gives a picture of the bulging forehead and heavy brain of the hydrocephalic, the dwelling place of grotesque fancies and weird images of horror; the other side shows the square-headed, intellectual, analytical type, the brain which produced stories of ratiocination, critical essays of penetration and which distinguished itself in mathematics. These two types, confined within one brain, gave the world the dreamer, the neurotic, the poet, the analyst, and the thinker.

Poe's life after the death of Virginia in January, 1847, is sadder than any of his stories. The last two years before the end in 1849 are a miserable record of alternating hope and despair, of a body and mind on the downward grade of deterioration, checked now and again before its approaching dissolution to turn and attempt to struggle back to sanity and health, yet never quite succeeding. After his own illness at the time of his wife's death he never regained his former capacity of productivity, although his last years were marked by fitful gleams of that genius which has won for him in Europe the reputation of being America's one really great and original poet. The mad poem, "Ulalume," with its melody and weird effects of nameless horror; the beautiful death poem, "To Annie," in which he thanks Heaven that "the fever called living is over at last"; the onomatopoeism of "The Bells" and the prose poem, "Eureka," belong to this period. In these last years he also met and loved Mrs. Helen Whitman, formed an ardent friendship for "Annie," Mrs. Richmond, and became engaged to Mrs. Shelton who, as Miss Royster, had been his boyhood sweetheart. The last thing he wrote was the lyrical "Annabel Lee," which was not published until after his death.

"Eureka" represents a new departure into philosophical realms. Dedicated to Alexander Von Humboldt it is offered to "the dreamers and those who put faith in dreams as in the only realities" as a "Book of Truths, not in its character of Truth-Teller, but for the Beauty that abounds in its Truth; constituting it true." Through all its excursions into physics, astronomy, and higher mathematics it manifests the neurotic passion for unity—a seeking after a primal cause from which came all the universe and to which all must return. In this are passages suggestive of Ward's "primal homogeneity" and theory of filiation. The poet anticipates the time when the myriads of individual intelligences will become blended, as will the bright stars, into one. He closes with the triumphant thought: "Think that the sense of individual identity will be gradually merged in the general consciousness—that Man, for example, ceasing imperceptibly to feel himself Man, will at length attain that awfully triumphant epoch when he shall recognize his existence as that of Jehovah. In the meantime bear in mind that all is Life—Life—Life within Life—the less within the greater, and all within the Spirit Divine."

The rumors which still go the round of the clubs in Baltimore claim that Poe was definitely syphilitic. This has never been established, although the lesion on the brain and cerebral congestion from which he suffered in his last years increase the probability of the syphilitic infection. Whether this be true or not, he certainly displayed the same diathesis evidenced by many men of genius who are said to have been syphilitic—for instance, De Maupassant, Wilde, Nietzsche. In them, as in Poe, the phyletic tendencies died out and the egoistic ones came into dominance. This might be expected as a result of the disease which, depriving a man of the capacity for propagation, so cuts him off from the normal social interest in the future of the race, and turns the full force of the libido in the direction of personal ambition. Senescents and young people—those too young and too old to bear children—betray somewhat this same selfish absorption in the attainment of their own desires. These syphilitic geniuses, driven by the nature of their disease to concentration upon their own egoistic development as the sole means of satisfying their will to power, became to a great extent hyper-individualized, with an overexpansion of the ego which made them antisocial. Their sex interests, too, seem to make at least a partial transference from the normal object of the opposite sex. Oscar Wilde's glittering descriptions—of pomegranates bursting in the sun, of tall reeds of fluted ivory, of pale poppies, ostrich plumes like white foam, robes of tissued gold, ceiling of fretted silver, green bronzes, agates, lapis lazuli, bowls of amethyst, nightingales, and faint perfumes of jasmine —the manner in which he lingers lovingly over long pages of rare gems, rich embroideries and draperies, strange, heavy odors, and the sound of weird, barbaric music, betrays more than a mere aesthetic appreciation of beauty. There is a sensuous, sexual delight in these beautiful objects which far surpasses the normal enjoyment. Poe manifests this same attitude, although his range of enjoyment is more narrowed than that of Wilde, and even in his keenest appreciation of the loveliness of the inanimate world he is still haunted by the conceptions of horror and of death, which were to him inseparable from the realization of the highest beauty. This, too, would indicate a certain sexual displacement because of his constantly allying sex with death—the death of a beautiful woman being to him the most poetic of themes. Likewise his love of women, which was apparently of the mind so much more than of the senses, seems to signify an erethic sublimation which may have been, in the last analysis, based upon his physical condition.

It was in these last two years that Poe met and became engaged to Mrs. Helen Whitman. His love letters "To Helen" as well as his tenderly devoted letters "For Annie" at this time, form some of the finest products of his later writing. These letters "To Helen" have been extravagantly praised as showing the passion of a lover. This they do not. They show the passion of a poet, writing about love. He was writing literature under the form of love letters just as he had under the form of love poems, stories, or critiques. This passage has been often referred to as showing his deep devotion to Mrs. Whitman:

As you entered the room, pale, timid, hesitating, and evidently oppressed at heart; as your eyes rested appealingly, for one brief moment, upon mine, I felt, for the first time in my life, and tremblingly acknowledged, the existence of spiritual influences altogether out of the reach of my reason. I saw that you were Helen—*my* Helen—the Helen of a thousand dreams—she whose visionary lips had so often lingered upon my own in the divine trance of passion—she whom the great Giver of all Good preordained to be mine—mine only—if not now, alas, then at least hereafter and *forever* in the Heavens. You spoke falteringly and seemed scarcely conscious of what you said. I heard no words— only the soft voice, more familiar to me than my own, and more melodious than the songs of the angels. Your hand rested in mine, and my whole soul shook with a tremulous ecstasy. And then but for very shame, but for fear of grieving or oppressing you—I would have fallen at your feet in as pure—in as real a worship as was ever offered to idol or to God. And when, afterwards, on those two successive evenings of all—heavenly delights, you passed to and fro about the room—now sitting by my side, now far away, now standing with your hand resting on the back of my chair, while the preternatural thrill of your touch vibrated even through the senseless wood into my heart—while you moved thus restlessly about the room—as if a deep Sorrow or more profound Joy haunted your bosom—my brain reeled beneath the intoxicating spell of your presence (and it was with no human senses that I either saw or heard you. It was my soul only that distinguished you there.). I grew faint with the luxury of your voice and blind with the voluptuous lustre of your eyes.

Yet at the same time that he was writing to Mrs. Whitman in such a vein, he was writing to "Annie" in letters breathing a spirit of entire confidence and love. Mrs. Whitman was said to have been greatly hurt by the publication of these latter letters, but they in no sense diminish Poe's love for her, nor show any evidence of faithlessness. In all these letters he was simply being true to himself—true to his own needs, which required the loving approval of many women rather than the utter devotion of one, which could be satisfied as much by the sexless attachment to a married woman as by his engagement to Helen. After the breaking of the engagement with Mrs. Whitman, brought about by the efforts of friends of hers who objected to the match, Poe became engaged to Mrs. Shelton. His relations with women after Virginia's death represent a pitiful attempt to re-establish himself, to regain from the eyes of those who loved him his own self-respect. Mrs. Clemm was then too old and broken to afford him the solace and safety he so hopelessly craved. But from among all his women friends, from all who had relieved the dark hours of Virginia's death, all those who from their attachment to the poet ministered willingly to his mother-in-law after his death, no Gradiva appeared, not one was strong enough to rescue him from the perilous path his feet were straying on, not one was able to bring him peace, and faith, and a renewed interest in life.

But more than a woman's love he was needing the attention of a specialist and this he did not receive. The libido of the poet, thwarted in its former expression through his poems and his love for his wife, sought here and there for other outlets, in his attachments to other women, in his titanic dream of the universe wherein he sought to grasp the very essence and simplicity of unity itself, and in his obsessive desire to found a magazine of his own—sought, but did not find. The lesion on one side of his brain (diagnosed by the famous New York physician, Dr. Mott, and the nurse, Mrs. Shew, Poe's faithful friend for years) would not permit him to use stimulants or tonics without producing total insanity. N. P. Willis, the editor, in a tribute to Poe immediately after the unhappy end in Baltimore, alludes to this: "We heard, from one who knew him well, . . . that, with a single glass of wine, his whole nature was reversed, the demon became uppermost, and, though none of the usual signs of intoxication were visible, his *will* was palpably insane." Yet in times of deepest depression even insanity must have come to appear preferable to his own sad thoughts, and he sought feverishly "surcease from sorrow," whatever the means or the result. Before going to Richmond on the final journey he wrote to Annie: "No, my sadness is *unaccountable*, and this makes me the more sad. I am full of dark forebodings. *Nothing* cheers or comforts me. My life seems wasted—the future looks a dreary blank: but I will struggle on and 'hope against hope.'"

The attempted suicide from laudanum in Boston was only one evidence of the profound state of melancholia into which he had sunk. His physique deteriorated, and suffering from congestion of the brain, he should have been in a sanitarium instead of struggling about the country in the forlorn hope of founding his magazine. It was in quest of this "will o' the wisp" that in 1849 he set out for Richmond. He was at this time in the most wretched spirits; he expressed a presentiment to Mrs. Lewis that he would not return and arranged all his papers with Mrs. Clemm, telling her what to do in case he died. His delusion of persecution in Philadelphia is extremely suggestive of the beginnings of paresis. His state is described by Mr. Gill:

When he finally reached the residence of his kind friend, Poe was in a highly excited condition, almost distracted indeed. His mind seemed bewildered and oppressed with the dread of some fearful conspiracy against his life; nor could the arguments or entreaties of his friend convince him that some deadly foe was not, at that very moment, in pursuit of him. He begged for a razor for the purpose of removing the mustache from his lip, in order, as he suggested, that he might disguise his appearance, and thus baffle his pursuers. But, unwilling to place such an instrument in his hands, he was prevailed upon to allow his host to effect the desired change upon which he imagined his safety depended. The condition of Poe's mind was such that Mr. Sartain, after persuading him to lie down, remained watching with him through the night with anxious solicitude, unwilling to lose sight of the unfortunate sufferer for a moment. The following night, Poe insisted on going out. He turned his steps towards the River Schuylkill, accompanied, however, by his devoted friend, whose apprehension was strengthened by the vehemence with which, without cessation, he poured forth in the rich, musical tones for which he was distinguished, the fervid imageries of his brilliant but overexcited imagination. The all-absorbing theme which still retained possession of his mind, was the fearful conspiracy that threatened his destruction. Vainly his friend endeavored to reassure and persuade him. He rushed on with unwearied steps, threading different streets, his companion striving to lead him homeward, but still in vain.

Towards midnight, they reached Fairmount and ascended the

429

steps leading to the summit, Poe all the while giving free scope to the conversational powers for which he was always remarkable, insisting upon the imminence of his peril, and pleading with touching eloquence for protection. . . .

He didn't recover from this intense excitement until, subsequently, escaping from the house, he wandered out into the neighborhod of the city, and throwing himself down in the open air in a pleasant field, his shattered nerves found a comfortless but sorely needed repose. He woke refreshed. . . .

All that he could call to mind were the entreaties and persuasions of some "guardian angel" who had sought to dissuade him from a frightful purpose.

Such delusions would seem to have some correlation with the stories that he was unable to go to sleep after Virginia's death without the presence of Mrs. Clemm or some kind friend at his bedside. The fear of death, which he evidenced in his morbid prepossessions with the subject, may have grown in these "lonesome latter years" to be so portentous and awful a figure that he could never quite escape its shadowy horrors. Or again, the fear of life itself, of the futile mockery of life which he was leading, of himself as he had come to be in his weakness, might have been the ·cause of much of his terror. Either fear could easily, in his overwrought state, have led to the thought of suicide, which he had already once attempted, and this may have been the "frightful purpose" from which the "guardian angel" sought to dissuade him.

Temptation conquered for the time being, there came to him a momentary peace from his delusions and fears and a new enthusiasm for laying hold on the actual facts of reality. The possibility of a new life beckoned him smilingly, and he arrived in Richmond in unusually good spirits. There he was welcomed and made much of by old friends. He even took the temperance pledge with much earnestness, obtained a position in the city of his childhood, and planned to bring Mrs. Clemm down there. It was at this time that he is said to have renewed his addresses to Mrs. Shelton and she, a widow of independent means, to have accepted them. He lectured before a cultured audience, and left Richmond apparently more contented than he had been for some time, carrying with him, according to Bishop Fitzgerald, the proceeds of his lecture, which amounted to $1,500. Of the tragic, solitary end in Baltimore, little is known with any degree of accuracy. Poe arrived there at election time, at a period when it was customary for bands of men to seize helpless strangers, drug them, and carry them from poll to poll, registering their votes for whatever party they desired. It is believed generally that he fell in with such a gang. However that may be, he was found in a barroom, insensible, in the shabbiest of clothes. He was taken to a hospital where he lived about a week. He is reported as being part of the time in stupor, part of the time in delirium, during which he conversed vacantly with spectral or imaginary objects. His replies to questions were entirely unsatisfactory. Two of his doctors report that he made the statement that his best friend would be he who would blow out his brains. So, on October 7, 1849, was extinguished that flame of genius which had blazed, now so fitfully, now so brilliantly, for forty years. In the mystery of his last days, his life did indeed go out like a candle in the dark.

It is doubtful if the circumstances of his death matter so very much. If Baltimore rowdies came in to hasten the end, they were simply an incident in the inevitable close. The man had burned himself out. He had described his own condition when he wrote: "There are few men of that peculiar sensibility which is at the root of genius, who, in early youth, have not expended much of their mental energy in *living too fast;* and, in later years, comes the unconquerable desire to goad the imagination up to that point which it would have attained in an ordinary, normal, or well-regulated life. The earnest longing for artificial excitement, which, unhappily, has characterized too many eminent men, may thus be regarded as a psychal want, or necessity—an effort to regain the lost—a struggle of the soul to assume the position which, under other circumstances, would have been its due." He showed at the last very clearly that "psychal" want, the struggle of the soul to regain the lost, and in the nature of the case he was doomed to failure. That last brief lifting of the clouds in Richmond could have been only temporary; his weakened body and the congestion of the brain from which he was suffering made inevitable the return of his former condition of melancholia. That diseased brain which had supplied his writings with all its morbid, beautiful imagery and haunting melodies of death, came finally by its defects to render his further progress and development impossible. And when it failed him, and there was no longer possible a continuation of the superiority which he had won in his chosen field, his proud spirit, his guiding fiction, must have sought relief in some form of insanity or in death. Insanity had begun, under the depression of melancholia and the delusions of paresis; death he had sought before and would have sought again; the darkened close in Baltimore came as a release—a release not to be regretted by any who love Beauty as an end in itself and who crave for its expression a form no less perfect than that which Poe was able to give in the days of his greatest power.

1920

◘ LITERARY GENIUS AND

MANIC-DEPRESSIVE INSANITY

WITH SPECIAL REFERENCE TO

THE ALLEGED CASE OF DEAN SWIFT

Arthur C. Jacobson

There is a strong disposition among many writers to postulate the essential "insanity of genius." In the *Medical Record*, June 15, 1912, there occurs the statement that "apparently no writer can dare to aspire to literary distinction without running the risk of submitting to psychological dissection by the alienists. In many instances it is no longer a question as to whether a certain genius was insane or not. The modern query is 'From what form of insanity did he suffer?'" These remarks were prompted by an article which recently appeared in the *American Journal of Insanity*, under the title, "Manifestations of Manic-Depressive Insanity in Literary Genius," the author of which, Dr. Eva Charlotte Reid, one of the physicians at the Government Hospital for the Insane, at Washington, D. C., sets forth that the study of the life and works of the literary genius would indicate that the literature was incidental to the psychosis and simply formed an outlet for the abnormal feelings and passions of the writer. This mental disease, it will be remembered, is marked by alternations of elation and depression, of frenzy and despair, of mania and melancholia, and Dr. Reid discerns in the writings of many of our greatest authors much evidence that they experienced such emotional turmoil. She draws the conclusion that they were victims of manic-depressive insanity and that their infirmity was the motive force that drove them on to more or less glorious expression. "With an emotional instability which raises him (the literary genius) to the pinnacle of exaltation one day and plunges him into the depth of despair the next, his industry must be spasmodic." Unable to adapt himself to his surroundings, "in his literature he finds an outlet for all his abnormal feelings and passions. Here he pours forth, under various guises, his rapturous joys and fears, his dreams of bliss, and his dread of impending calamity. The manifestations of his abnormal mental condition, which are denied him in actual life, find an outlet in poetry and fiction, under the guise of literary and poetical inspiration."

The present writer finds it difficult to lend his intellectual sympathy to such a thesis, which practically amounts to claiming that geniuses are geniuses *because* they are insane. There is a vast amount of evidence showing a family history of insanity or degeneracy of some sort in the case of many, if not most, of the greatest geniuses, and such geniuses are unquestionably more likely to become insane than are less highly organized people—and do so become very frequently indeed—but the writer contends that these facts in no way justify such assumptions as those of Dr. Reid, and the great majority of writers who have occasion to touch upon the subject of genius. A watch is not built to withstand lawn mower usage. And it must not be forgotten that literary geniuses differ from most subjects of psychological or psychiatric study in that they have written themselves down, so to say. Their hopes and fears, in some

cases—like Rousseau—all their inner lives, are recorded. Who shall say that the emotional reactions portrayed are so vastly different in kind or in degree from those of other noble but less expressive minds under special stress? Then we ought to consider the adequacy of the factors entering into elation, depression, etc. If Swift was downhearted after his virtual banishment from England, if he was depressed after the death of his dearest friends, if he became choleric under the grievously hard political knocks he received from bitter enemies, if he was a sufferer from arteriosclerosis after the age of twenty-three, why must we read into such facts manic-depressive insanity, any more than the response to adequate factors that might be expected to occur in such a mighty mind, or even in any first-rate mind? Why is failure to react strongly to adequate intellectual stimuli made the criterion of sanity?

It seems an odd thing to the writer that a great literature is not emanating from the asylums of the land, if it be true that the relation of genius and insanity is so close. The answer is that the great genius must be eminently sane. He must possess in the highest possible degree the critical faculty directed toward his own literary productions. No great literary work can possibly be produced if this endowment be lacking. Such a lack is one of the most marked characteristics of the insane. The mind that produced Hamlet was super-sane. To the critic who insists upon intellectual mediocrity and slow emotional reaction as the criteria of sanity, such a mind seems essentially insane. The "normal" man, says Dr. Reid, rises above the common ills of life—poverty, sickness, and death, that is—[or] is not greatly or for very long affected by them. It was the presence of such things around him in Ireland, in superlative degree, that inspired the best efforts of the greatest of English satirists. The writer would say that Swift was the most "normal" man in the Ireland of his day because he did react so strongly to the terribly adequate factors that surrounded him, which reaction gave us the *Drapier*

Letters and awoke his compatriots from their moribund state. It is the abnormality of the social masses of today, and not their normality, that precludes an effective reduction of infant mortality. Those who realize the appalling conditions and are fighting them are not victims of manic-depressive insanity, either. No critic with only a partial sense of humor ought to examine the writings of literary geniuses with a view to their conviction on the score of manic-depressive insanity. To one in whom this sense is somewhat atrophied or absent De Quincey's *Murder as One of the Fine Arts* would certainly seem brimful of manic-depressive evidences. De Quincey, it is true, is cited by Dr. Reid as one of the group of insane geniuses. Probably a study of this masterpiece on murder helped to the fatal conclusion. To our mind, the writing of such a piece of literature is conclusive proof of what we have called super-sanity.

Dr. Reid confesses that Swift's brilliant satire, *A Modest Proposal for Preventing the Children of Poor People in Ireland from Being a Burden to Their Parents or Country*, convinced her of his insanity. How utterly lame such a conclusion really is the writer will endeavor to show in detail. The effort is worthwhile, for a strong light will be thrown on the hasty and superficial character of the conclusions drawn by those critics who are determined to make unconformable facts conform to their theories. Dr. Reid not only betrays a total lack of the ironic humor sense, but she is either unfair or grossly uninformed as to the circumstances in which the *Modest Proposal* was written. The piece in question was written in 1729, after Swift's final break with Walpole. It is a wonderful piece of sustained irony, suggesting with a ghastly vividness the horrible state of the Irish people, whose champion Swift was. In studying it we must take into consideration the frightful conditions that inspired it, the motive of the writer, and its political effect. When this is done it will be seen very clearly to have been justified. Read in ignorance of such considerations, the piece

437

might seem a diabolical fantasy. As a plain matter of fact it proved one of the most effective efforts of the great satirist. And it was only one of a long series of powerful attacks upon the indefensible English policy in Ireland against which Swift contended with all his tremendous intellectual power. The Irish "were a people to be crushed, ruined, persecuted, tormented, extirpated" (Sir William Wilde). England had done everything destructive to Ireland's interests that could well be conceived of by the ordinary mind, and it was merely left to Swift, the Irish patriot and man of unique political genius, to suggest ironically the suitability of Irish children for English food, "examining the conception in every aspect, following it out in all its consequences, and deriving from it, systematically and consistently, a train of the most grotesque incidents" (Lecky). Seeing that England had done almost every conceivable harm to the Irish, that she should eat them was at least metaphorically in order. Swift burned with a hatred of tyranny, injustice, and oppression, and while he had no special love for Ireland, if we may believe his own declarations, "his humanity and charity were equal to his wit, and required as good and true a taste to be equally valued" (Pope). In what better cause could he have employed his great powers of sarcasm and irony, trenchant, original wit, and tremendous invective, than in that of Ireland of the eighteenth century? The intellectual qualities of this terrible partisan made him the natural leader of the exploited Irish, who fully recognized his patriotic services, despite his Protestant creed, his profession, and his personal intolerance of Roman Catholicism. Lecky credits him with being the first man to teach the Irish to rely upon themselves and to lead them to victory at a time when they were deprived of every hope. "He gave a voice to their mute sufferings and traced the line of their future progress. . . . An intense and terrible sincerity was one of the chief elements of his power." The poverty and desolation prevailing in Ireland at this time, due to English exploitation, could hardly be exaggerated, and resistance on constitutional grounds was out of the question. Only the peculiar literary genius of Swift met the indications adequately. His was the voice of the people, and it spoke with success. Its echoes "marked the transition from an age of semi-barbarism to an age of civilization—from the government of force to the government of opinion." England had systematically crushed Ireland by draining her of sound money and substituting a debased currency (Wood's copper coinage, the patent for which was awarded to the king's mistress, the Duchess of Kendal, who jobbed it out to Wood for £10,000); by forbidding, in 1666, the importation of cattle from Ireland into England, cattle being the principal article of Ireland's commerce, three-fourths of which commerce was with England; by enacting, in 1696, that no goods of any sort could be imported directly from the colonies into Ireland; by penal laws of atrocious severity; by preventing as far as possible the holding of public office by Irishmen, lucrative and influential posts being given to Englishmen; by passing in 1699 an act "of crushing and unprecedented severity," which forbade the export of the Irish woolen manufactures not only to England, but to all other countries, this industry having threatened England's supremacy in the same field; by shipping her supernumerary beggars to Ireland, augmenting the alarmingly large number already in that unhappy country; and by smothering the legislative powers of the Irish Parliament and the utterances of Irish champions like Molyneux, whose "Case of Ireland" was formally condemned by the English House of Commons. Thus a premium was put upon destitution, chronic famine, beggary, crime, and servility. We are, of course, not unmindful of those apologists who tell us about political exigencies and the expedients sometimes forced upon even humane conquerors where the conquered present special problems, but their dialectics are not especially convincing.

Lecky appraised the celebrated piece of humor the inspiration

439

of which we have discussed at its proper value, and Sir Walter Scott saw in it nothing worse than "inimitable gravity of irony," relating with keen amusement how a foreign author had seriously accepted Swift's proposal that the rich English feed upon the poor Irish. Scott represents Swift as concerned with the emancipation of the country of his birth and as wholly indifferent to personal aggrandizement. The *Modest Proposal* is assuredly shocking. It was intended to shock the England of Walpole's day, and that country certainly needed all the shocking that could be administered by the masterful Irish satirist or anybody else possessed, not by insanity, but by superb intellectual and literary power, for of constitutional remedies there were none. But Dr. Reid is quite blind to its political and sociological significance and can only say: "Many of his (Swift's) writings could only be the productions of an insane mind. For instance in a pamphlet entitled *A Modest Proposal for Preventing the Children of Poor People in Ireland from Being a Burden to Their Parents or Country*, he suggests that these children be fattened, sold to the wealthy, killed, their bodies used for food, and their skins for gloves and shoes. He dilates in the most horrible manner on the age at which they would be most palatable, the best manner of cooking, and the relative weights and values at different ages."

Sir William Wilde, after a study of the available data, declared that there was no proof that Swift had ever been insane, and that his peculiarities in later life were due to the ordinary decay of nature. The opinion of this eminent Irish physician is practically conclusive.

A recent writer on true neurasthenia recites as leading emotional symptoms ill-humor, unreasonableness, peevishness, irritability, impetuousness, and a tendency to fault-finding, trifling occasions leading to outbursts of temper; a prevailing mood of depression and despondency is characteristic of these sufferers; frigidity or sexual impotence is frequently observed. Swift had all of these traits and the diagnosis may well stop short in his case at neurasthenia. Dr. Reid's citation of such traits amounts practically to an attempt to show that Swift ought to have been insane, even if he were not, but nothing beyond the implication of neurasthenia can be tortured out of them. That he should have been a neurasthenic is quite understandable, when one considers the man's stormy political life, ill health, and inability to marry because of a sexual defect, as well as his misfortunes in general, and what might be called his involuntary failure as an ecclesiastic. He was not the first man, and will not be the last, to be suspected of insanity because he ferociously and effectively assailed political corruption. For a considerable period, before his exile to Ireland, land of his birth and education, he controlled English public opinion more than any other man, and was influential to that degree that he became the most powerful defender and counselor of the Tory party, leading the way to the dismissal of Marlborough and the Peace of Utrecht. In the case of Swift we are not dealing with a second rate character, nor with a lunatic of any kind or degree, but with one of the greatest men of all time, possessed of marked defects easily lending themselves to the grossest exaggeration, and of traits that made him feared or hated by the pygmies and knaves of his own day and the "tin horn" critics of posterity. He was "the most tragic figure in the literature of the eighteenth century—the only man of his age who could be conceived as affording a groundwork for the creations of Shakespeare." One smiles in his case when he reads Dr. Reid's dictum that the industry of the victim of manic-depressive insanity must be spasmodic. There was nothing spasmodic about the indefatigable and continuous labors of the author of *Gulliver's Travels*. One laughs in his case when he learns from Dr. Reid that the manic-depressive genius is unable to adapt himself to his surroundings and that it is this which leads to the selection of literature as an outlet for the thoughts that

441

he has spun in his own unreal world. Swift had "an eminently practical mind, seizing with a happy tact the common-sense view of every question he treated, and almost absolutely free from the usual defects of mere literary men" (Lecky).

The writer has spoken of Swift's arteriosclerosis. At the age of twenty-three he began to suffer from dizziness and ringing in the ears. As he grew older his querulousness, irritability, and other symptoms increased. We are well aware today of the relationship sustained between arteriosclerosis and neurasthenia. The autopsy that was made after Swift's death disclosed cerebral shrinkage and arteriosclerosis. Dr. Reid claims that the aural symptoms marked the beginning of the psychosis from which she alleges he suffered. The terminal breakdown at the age of seventy-three (death came five years later) Dr. Reid calls an "engrafted arteriosclerotic dementia." To the writer's mind, Swift's case typified arteriosclerosis as Osler and other observers have noted this condition in the very young, the symptoms of cerebral neurasthenia therefore resting upon an organic basis, a relationship which has been dwelt upon particularly by Stengel. Being a simple and sensible view, based upon known facts interpreted in a non-sensational way by one who is not a professional alienist obsessed by the bizarre doctrine that postulates the essential insanity of genius, it may not appeal to the lovers of the *outré*. Let us discourage all such doctrines of the crowd, lacking as they do any sound or even defensible psychiatric basis. They belong in the class of Lombroso's arguments touching upon the alleged insanity of Christ, whom he considered and tried to prove a paranoiac. The simple truths of science and of life are fascinating enough.

That the true genius is necessarily crazy is essentially a vulgar view, fostered, apparently, by every intellectual plebeian. It is high time that it be shattered. There is a failure to distinguish between the insane temperament and actual insanity. Too fine a distinction for the bourgeoisie of science, it nevertheless is a vital point. Still finer for them is the fact that the insane temperament itself, only less than actual insanity, is a handicap to the genius and not his "motor force." It is easier to conclude the essential insanity of genius and save a deal of sound, hard thinking. Why, say these short-cut philosophers to the writer, you yourself admit insane family history, insane temperament, and the frequent occurrence of insanity. What are you driving at?

Genius makes for insanity, but neither insanity nor the insane temperament makes for genius. The genius is usually, if not always, of insane temperament, but his best creative work reflects the man at his best, that is to say, sanest. To the degree that clinical insanity enters in, to that degree is his work vitiated. Insanity is the nemesis of the delicately balanced genius, never his good angel. He does his work not because of, but in spite of, the Damoclean sword. The genius differs from other men in that he presents a curious capacity for superlative sanity alongside a similar capacity for insanity. In all respects clinical insanity is antithetic to the faculties that actuate the creative mind, but nature implants the insane diathesis in accordance with her law of compensation. Psychopathological states, the result of the insane temperament or of the toxins of tuberculosis or colon bacteriemia undoubtedly at times excite and color the creative labors of true geniuses, but they are not geniuses because of the psychopathology. The fundamental quality of mind is *sui generis* and the thesis of Dr. Reid utterly fallacious. Genius is not a disease.

1912